Understanding
Fossils

Understanding Fossils

An Introduction to Invertebrate Palaeontology

PETER DOYLE

School of Earth Sciences,
University of Greenwich, UK

with contributions by
FLORENCE M.D. LOWRY

JOHN WILEY & SONS
Chichester · New York · Brisbane · Toronto · Singapore

National   01243 779777
International   (+44) 1243 779777

Reprinted April 1997 with corrections, September 1997

Other Wiley Editorial Offices

John Wiley & Sons, Inc., 605 Third Avenue,
New York, NY 10158-0012, USA

Jacaranda Wiley Ltd, 33 Park Road, Milton,
Queensland 4064, Australia

John Wiley & Sons (Canada) Ltd, 22 Worcester Road,
Rexdale, Ontario M9W 1L1, Canada

John Wiley & Sons (Asia) Pte Ltd, 2 Clementi Loop #02-01,
Jin Xing Distripark, Singapore 129809

Library of Congress Cataloging-in-Publication Data

Doyle, Peter.
    Understanding fossils : an introduction to invertebrate
  palaeontology / Peter Doyle ; with contributions by Florence M.D.
  Lowry.
        p.   cm.
    Includes bibliographical references (p.   –   ) and index.
    ISBN 0-471-96351-8
    1. Invertebrates, Fossil.   I. Lowry, Florence M. D.   II. Title.
  QE770.D69   1996
  562—dc20   95–49411
                                                           CIP

British Library Cataloguing in Publication Data

A catalogue record for this book is available from the British Library

ISBN 0-471-96351-8

Typeset in 10/12pt Palatino by Dorwyn Ltd, Rowlands Castle, Hants
Printed and bound in Great Britain by Bookcraft (Bath) Ltd

This book is printed on acid-free paper responsibly manufactured from sustainable forestation, for
which at least two trees are planted for each one used for paper production.

Contents

Preface   vii

Acknowledgements   ix

Illustrations   xi

  1. What is Palaeontology?   1

PART I. KEY CONCEPTS

  2. Fossils and Fossilisation   11

  3. Fossils as Living Organisms   43

  4. Fossils and Evolution   67

  5. Fossils and Stratigraphy   93

  6. Summary of Part I   110

PART II. THE MAIN FOSSIL GROUPS

  7. Introduction to the Fossil Record   115

  8. Molluscs: Bivalves and Gastropods   136

  9. Molluscs: Cephalopods   159

 10. Brachiopods   182

11. Echinoderms   201

12. Trilobites   220

13. Corals   238

14. Graptolites   253

15. Bryozoans   267

16. Microfossils: Foraminifera   278

17. Microfossils: Ostracods   290

18. Trace Fossils   302

19. Summary of Part II   318

PART III. FOSSILS AS INFORMATION

20. Data from the Fossil Record   327

21. Studies in Palaeobiology   338

22. Studies in Palaeoenvironmental Analysis   355

23. Studies in Stratigraphy   372

24. Summary of Part III   385

Subject Index   389

Systematic Index   403

Preface

Fossils are among the most highly prized natural objects in the world. They figure in our everyday lives as decorative objects in our homes, and as the dinosaur products which fill the toy and book shops and which periodically appear in the cereal packets at our breakfast tables. Collecting fossils is an absorbing pastime which grades into a passion for weekend geologists, and many students enter higher education through their interest, reading for degrees in the earth sciences which have a direct benefit for the national economy.

Despite this, palaeontology is often one of the most neglected, misunderstood and poorly promoted subjects on the geological curriculum. It suffers from two preconceived ideas: that it is a subject steeped in Latin names, and that learning lists of species and genera is at the core of any teaching strategy. The names are important, of course; they are part of a truly international scientific language, but learning them parrot-fashion should be a task undertaken by only the most dedicated specialist. Palaeontology is much more than this. The reality is that each fossil has a tale to tell, as each one is a fragment of an ancient ecosystem, a frozen frame in an evolutionary lineage or a chronometer of geological time. Putting aside the long names and the stupefying detail of their component parts, it is the value of fossils in applied studies which determines that they should be included within the text of any geology course.

This book is intended for first-level students. It is an overview and introduction, and is not the last word on the subject. It is meant to demonstrate the geological applications of fossils. Each of the main fossil groups is deliberately dealt with in brief so that the tedium of unnecessary detail is pared down. Undoubtedly this treatment may dissatisfy, even annoy, specialists, but this book is intended for undergraduates, from those who will go on in palaeontology to those who may never study palaeontology beyond the first level of their degree. It is a book written out of a love for a subject born when I was a young boy collecting fossils in North Wales and North Yorkshire. If it goes some small way in inspiring interest in one of the cornerstones of geology, I shall have succeeded in my aim.

Peter Doyle
London, 1995

Acknowledgements

This book is in part the product of several years of feedback from undergraduates on palaeontology. I am grateful for their interest. When asked to provide a title for this book, my students came up with various ideas, most of them unprintable. I particularly liked the suggestion 'Why are dead things so ugly?'. There are several other people whom I would like to thank. For supplying photographs and illustrations, often at short notice, I am grateful to Mike Barker, Denis Bates, Martin Brasier, Des Collins, Jane Francis, Neville Hollingworth, Dave Horne, Florence Lowry, Dave Martill, Clare Milsom, Dave Norman, Adrian Rushton, Tom Sharpe, Peter Sheldon, David Siveter and the editors of *The Stereo-Atlas of Ostracod Shells*, Paul Smith and Ian Slipper. Many friends and colleagues read and commented on drafts of all or parts of this book, or helped with advice and wise words. They are numerous: my students Adie Meredith, Jon Roberts, Clare Youdan and Steve Tracey; my postgraduates Kez Baggley and Jason Wood; and my colleagues Alistair Baxter and Andy Bussell. The manuscript has particularly benefited from critical readings by Matthew Bennett, Florence Lowry, Angela Holder, Tony Hallam, Duncan Pirrie, Alistair Crame, Bob Owens, Colin Prosser, Jonathan Larwood and Paul Bown. Martin Gay, Hillary Foxwell, Pat Brown and Nick Dobson provided technical and library support, and worked hard to meet my (at times) almost impossible demands. Amanda Hewes and Nicky Christopher at John Wiley helped guide me through this book from its early days.

Finally, this book owes a lot to four allies: my wife Julie for her support through the long hours needed to complete the text; my close friend Matthew Bennett for his constant guidance; my friend and colleague Florence Lowry who helped me in the planning of the book and who contributed materially to its text by writing Chapters 16 and 17 and cowriting Chapters 4 and 15 with me; and my research assistant Angela Holder who read, criticised and returned text almost as soon as it was produced, and who helped in its production in many other ways.

Illustrations

Many of the illustrations in this book were drawn by Hillary Foxwell and Angela Holder, for the most part from actual specimens held in the collections of the University of Greenwich. In other cases, illustrations have been substantially modified from published figures. These are denoted in the text by the words 'modified from . . .', together with the the full reference to the original source. Some diagrams have been reproduced in their entirety from published sources. Permission to reproduce these has been sought from the original publishers. I am grateful to the following organisations for permission to reproduce original figures or photographs: John Wiley and Sons, Chichester (Boxes 1.1, 3.7, 5.4; Figures 4.9, 4.10, 5.1, 5.3–5.6, 10.12, 13.6, 21.6, 22.2); The Palaeontological Association, London (Box 2.4; Figure 3.1); Cambridge University Press (Figure 11.10); Dudley Museum and Art Gallery (Box 1.2); Leicestershire Museums (Figure 2.10); Royal Ontario Museum, Toronto (Figure 2.9); and British Geological Survey (Figure 2.7), reproduced by permission of the Director: NERC copyright preserved.

1
What is Palaeontology?

1.1 PALAEONTOLOGY: THE STUDY OF ANCIENT LIFE

The Earth is 4600 million years old. Life has existed on Earth for at least 3550 million years, and since its first appearance it has adapted and changed the planet. The early atmosphere, almost devoid of oxygen, was adapted by the first organisms which produced this gas as a by-product of photosynthesis. The bodies of countless millions of organisms, microscopic and macroscopic, form whole rocks; the invaders of the land, plants and animals, have helped shape the landscape by both accelerating and reducing erosion. Life on Earth, in every form, has contributed to the story of our planet. The story of the development of life on Earth, of the biosphere, forms the subject of palaeontology: the study of ancient life.

Palaeontology has its roots in two subjects: geology and biology. Geology and palaeontology are intimately linked. The birth of both subjects can be arguably traced to the work of one man, the Danish physician Niels Stensen, often known as Steno (1638–1686). Stensen discovered that the fossil shark's teeth enclosed in the rocks of Tuscany were in fact identical with those of modern sharks, and from this he concluded that the layered rocks forming the land surface had themselves been formed in the sea. Significantly, he concluded that the fossils within them were not the result of mysterious vapours pervading the Earth, as many thought at the time, but that they were actually the remains of once living animals. Drawing both upon geology and the biology of living organisms, Stensen explained the origin and occurrence of fossils, and laid the foundations of palaeontology.

Since Stensen's day, palaeontology has provided important tools for geologists and biologists alike. In geology, fossils are important in piecing together rock successions from the same time interval across the globe, and in interpreting the nature of ancient sedimentary environments. In biology, fossils are a legacy of the diversity of life in the geological past, and the most direct evidence of evolution of life on Earth. This book is primarily concerned with understanding fossils so that they can be widely used in these subjects.

1.2 THE SCOPE OF PALAEONTOLOGY

Palaeontology is fundamental to geology. From the study of the environmental tolerances of their living relatives, fossils provide the clearest insight into the nature and development of ancient Earth environments. Fossils are also un- rivalled as stratigraphical tools. The process of evolution acts as an irreversible clock in which the appearance of successive species through time can be used to match and correlate rock successions. Every day, microfossils are used in industry as routine stratigraphical ciphers, unlocking the relative age of successions of oil- bearing rocks. Palaeontology also has a pivotal role in biology, in providing proof of the evolution and diversification of life on Earth. Despite this, palaeontology is not popular with students. Dinosaurs have universal appeal, but simple inverte- brate fossils appear insignificant and dull. In many undergraduate courses, pal- aeontology is seen by students as a necessary – or, even worse, unnecessary – hurdle which has to be negotiated in order to pass through the course. The most common accusation is the 'plethora of long names' pervading the subject. In reality, palaeontology is more than a catalogue of fusty-sounding names: it is a living subject of fundamental importance to both geology and evolutionary biology.

The basis for any science is the accumulation and ordering of data in order to develop and test hypotheses. The scientific approach demands a rigorous data set. In palaeontology, this data set is based on the fossils themselves, and in particular, their occurrence and diversity. It is encompassed in **taxonomy**, the scientific or- dering and naming of fossil groups. Taxonomy provides the solid foundation of the science of palaeontology, and geologists and biologists alike can apply the information it provides in three fields: **palaeobiology, palaeoenvironmental re- construction** and **stratigraphy** (Figure 1.1). It is in these fields that the value of palaeontology lies, and these three subject areas provide the broad themes of this book.

Examining these themes, Palaeobiology is the study of fossils as once living animals and plants. It involves the interpretation of the function or mode of life (the functional morphology) of fossil organisms, and the study of the pattern, process and timing of evolution. Palaeoenvironmental reconstruction is possible because fossils are an important part of sedimentary rocks, and, when living, were an integral component of their environment. Through the interpretation of their ancient ecologies, fossils serve as indicators of past climate, oxygen levels, salinity, and a range of other environmental factors. The determination of ancient geographies and the unravelling of complex tectonic terranes are possible using the ancient distribution patterns of fossil organisms. Finally, fossils are important in stratigraphy as indicators of specific time periods, and as tools by which rock successions can be correlated.

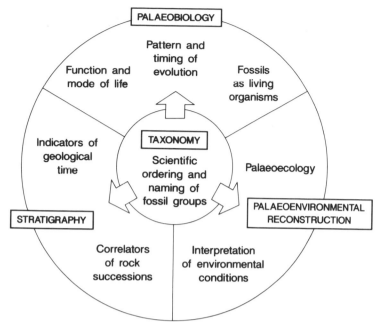

Figure 1.1 *Taxonomy as the basis for the three main fields of applied palaeontology: pal-aeobiology, palaeoenvironmental reconstruction and stratigraphy [Modified from: Clarkson (1993)* Invertebrate Palaeontology and Evolution *(Third edition), Chapman & Hall, Fig. 1.3, p. 6]*

1.3 THE AIM AND STRUCTURE OF THIS BOOK

This book is primarily intended for geologists, but will also be of interest to biologists. It assumes some basic knowledge of geology and biology. It is an attempt to illustrate the use of fossils in geological studies; in palaeobiology, stratigraphy and palaeoenvironmental analysis. It has three parts. In **Part I** the key concepts in palaeontology are examined: the processes of fossilisation, the principles of palaeoecology, the role of fossils in evolutionary studies, and the use of fossils in stratigraphy. In **Part II** are introduced the most important invertebrate fossil groups. These provide the basis for understanding the most useful fossil groups, and serve as an introduction to further study. In **Part III** specific case studies of the use of fossils in the three areas of applied palaeontology are discussed.

BOX 1.1: THE GEOLOGICAL TIME-SCALE

Palaeontologists are concerned with both great tracts of time, studying the large-scale changes in life on Earth over the past 3500 million years, and infinitely smaller intervals, examining with some precision the evolution of individual groups over thousands of years. The geological time scale is a standard frame of reference for geologists and evolutionary biologists. It has been developed over the last 150 years by the work of numerous scientists, and is seen as a crowning achievement in science. The time scale is based upon the dating of rock successions called **chronostratigraphical units**, calibrated by measuring the amounts of specific radioactive elements known to decay at a set rate. The boundaries of chronostratigraphical units are time-significant, as they are denoted by global events in the geological record. As an example, for much of the Phanerozoic (the Palaeozoic, Mesozoic and Cenozoic eras), the larger chronostratigraphical units have boundaries which are indicated by global mass extinctions or evolutionary radiations, such as the boundary between the Mesozoic and Cenozoic or Precambrian and Cambrian. The boundary of each unit is defined by international agreement at specific localities on the Earth's crust called **stratotypes**, providing a standard with which geologists from across the world can match in time or correlate their own rock successions. For much of the chronostratigraphical record it is the relative order of the evolutionary changes of the fossils which is of the greatest importance in correlating rock successions with the stratotype.

Sources: Berry, W.B.N. (1986) *Growth of the prehistoric timescale based on organic evolution*. Blackwell, Oxford; Doyle, P., Bennett, M.R. & Baxter, A.N. (1994) *The key to earth history*. Wiley, Chichester [Figure based on information in: Palmer (1983) *Geology*, **11**, p. 508]

BOX 1.1: (*cont.*)

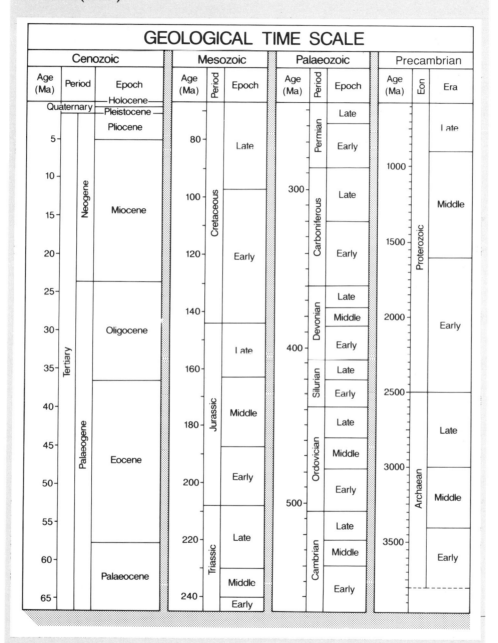

GEOLOGICAL TIME SCALE

Cenozoic			Mesozoic			Palaeozoic			Precambrian		
Age (Ma)	Period	Epoch	Age (Ma)	Period	Epoch	Age (Ma)	Period	Epoch	Age (Ma)	Eon	Era

BOX 1.2: FOSSILS IN SOCIETY

Fossils have figured in human culture since prehistory, and have a broader appeal than is widely appreciated. They figure as objects of the natural world in our everyday lives, in at least six areas:

- **As folklore objects**: many fossils have been part of folklore and mythology for centuries. Some fossils are known from early human burial sites; others, such as snakestones (ammonites) and devil's toenails (the oyster *Gryphaea*) are associated with specific myths; and some are considered to have healing powers ('thunderbolts', otherwise known as belemnites).
- **As objects of aesthetic beauty**: many fossils are prized as aesthetically pleasing, natural art objects, and in many cases utilised as part of interior design.
- **As objects of a recreational pursuit**: many people collect fossils either casually while visiting an appropriate locality, or as a hobby, grading into a semi-professional pursuit.
- **As objects of economic value**: a thriving fossil trade has existed in many parts of the world since at least the late eighteenth century. While some fossils are considered to be 'priceless' (e.g. the first bird, *Archaeopteryx*), others are offered at pocket-money prices. In some locations, such as Lyme Regis in Britain, the fossil trade is an important part of the local economy.
- **As objects worthy of scientific study**: stored in collections and museums, worthy of serious scientific attention, and subject to sensationalist journalism in the wake of exciting finds.
- **As an extension of dinomania**: the twentieth century has seen several dinosaur booms; each one, bigger and better than the last, focuses attention on the life of the geological past, and brings fossils to the public as toys, on cereal packets, and in the cinema.

BOX 1.2: *(cont.)*

[Poster reproduced with permission of the Dudley Museum and Art Gallery, West Midlands]

BOX 1.3: FOSSILS IN SCIENCE

Fossils are one of the most important sources of information from the geological record. At least ten broad categories of scientific information can be recognised:

- **Taxonomic**: fossils contain morphological information which allows them to be recognised and named, and their relationships to other taxa recognised.
- **Ethological**: fossils provide information which can lead to a direct understanding of the mode of life of once living, and now extinct, organisms.
- **Evolutionary**: fossils provide direct evidence of the evolution of life on Earth.
- **Ecological**: fossils and fossil assemblages provide insight into the nature and development of ecosystems, and of the interaction of plants and animals with each other and their ancient environment.
- **Environmental**: living organisms are limited in distribution and diversity by environmental factors. The nature of ancient environments, and the specifics of depth, temperature, salinity and oxygen levels, may be determined through the comparison of living and fossil assemblages.
- **Chemical**: fossil shells and other hard parts often contain vestiges of the biochemistry of the original organism, or have isotopic signatures which help in the determination of ancient temperatures or salinities, among others.
- **Sedimentological**: 'bones as stones'; fossils act as sedimentary particles and can provide important information on the nature of the hydraulic regime of flowing water, with some fossils commonly aligned parallel to current flow direction, for example, as well as determining the rate of sedimentary accumulation.
- **Diagenetic**: fossils provide information about the processes which occur in sedimentary sequences following death and burial through to their discovery.
- **Way up**: *in situ* fossils can prove valuable in the determination of the original 'right way up' of rock successions subjected to overturning in mountain building episodes.
- **Stratigraphical**: fossils are the most important guides in subdividing the stratigraphical column into units denoted by time boundaries.

Sources: Goldring, R. (1991) *Fossils in the field*. Longman, Harlow; Briggs, D.E.G. and Crowther, P.R. (eds) (1990) *Palaeobiology – a synthesis*. Blackwell, Oxford

Part I
KEY CONCEPTS

2
Fossils and Fossilisation

In this chapter the term 'fossil' is explained and the processes which lead to the preservation of fossils in the sedimentary rocks of the geological record are described.

2.1 WHAT ARE FOSSILS?

Fossils are the remains of once living plants and animals. Put simply, they are the visible evidence of life on Earth during the 3550 million years or so that geologists now know have sustained life. The name 'fossil' is derived from the Latin word, *fossilis*, which refers to any object which has been dug from the ground. The term was first applied in geology in the sixteenth century; at that time, and until the late eighteenth century, a fossil could also refer to any mineral object, archaeological artefact or curiosity dug from the ground. This is no longer the case. Since the birth of the science of **palaeontology** (the study of ancient life) in the late eighteenth century, the term 'fossil' refers to the remains of any ancient organism. Effectively, these remains are the physical evidence of past life found in rocks and sediments. There are two basic types: **body fossils** and **trace fossils**.

  Body fossils preserve elements of the original body of an organism, and have undergone the process of **fossilisation**. This usually means that the organism has died and been buried, and is therefore **preserved**, but does not imply great age, or even the process of 'turning to stone'. Effectively, therefore, a shell buried on a modern beach, a man or woman interred at a funeral, or an organism incorporated in sediments formed millions of years ago is encompassed within the definition. Other fossils include 'mummies' – organisms that have been preserved because of desiccation, without the necessity of burial. However, in practice, many scientists would exclude recently dead and buried organisms from the definition as a convenience, choosing as an arbitrary cut-off point the base of the

Holocene, the most recent geological time interval (Box 1.1). The nature of the preservation of body fossils is extremely important to palaeontologists: the better the preservation state, the greater the information available about the nature of ancient life and its changes through time. In essence, body fossils can be preserved intact or fragmented; they can be found complete with the most delicate soft body parts and their ancient biomolecules preserved, or as fragments, eroded and broken down.

Trace fossils are the physical evidence of the existence of plants and animals through their traces: tracks, burrows and borings which disturb the bedding surfaces and fabric of sedimentary rocks. Traces are defined on the interpretation of the action of the organisms that created them: feeding, moving, resting and so on. These traces are mostly ephemeral, created as disturbances in or on sediments. Hence, burial is important in the preservation of surface traces, but most traces are created *in situ* within the sediment. Both are effectively preserved through rapid sedimentation. A few other traces, notably **coprolites**, the fossil faeces of a variety of organisms, undergo a similar process of fossilisation to body fossils.

Together body and trace fossils furnish scientists with the information to interpret mode of life: the body fossil (e.g. a dinosaur bone) illustrates the form of the animal, the trace fossil (e.g. a dinosaur footprint) the way in which it interacted with its environment.

2.2 TAPHONOMY: THE PROCESS OF FOSSILISATION

The process of fossilisation through which fossils are created is complex, and the outcome is determined by a variety of interrelated physical, chemical and biological factors. As such the subject of fossilisation is almost a science in its own right, usually referred to as **taphonomy**. However, three broad stages can effectively be identified in the fossilisation of an organism. These are: **death**, **pre-burial**, and **post-burial** (Figure 2.1).

2.2.1 Death of the Organism

Death is the first process that has to occur before fossilisation can take place. Death and illness can be caused by old age, infection, parasitic infestation, predators, and through physical, chemical and biological conditions of the environment, such as changes in climate or exclusion of oxygen from the water column. However, few of these factors can ever be identified as the cause of death. It is often the case, when we find a fossil, that we are at the scene of the crime – the death of the organism in the geological past – but usually we have only circumstantial evidence of the cause of death, and very little idea of the motive. In some cases, we can identify illness, infection and parasites. Dinosaurs commonly give indications of medical conditions through their bone architecture; arthritis of joints, for instance, is fairly common. Parasites are also fairly common in invertebrate animals, and crinoids (Chapter 11) appear to be particularly prone to

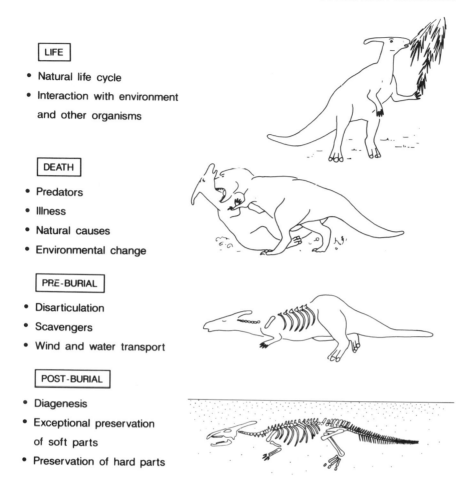

LIFE

- Natural life cycle
- Interaction with environment and other organisms

DEATH

- Predators
- Illness
- Natural causes
- Environmental change

PRE-BURIAL

- Disarticulation
- Scavengers
- Wind and water transport

POST-BURIAL

- Diagenesis
- Exceptional preservation of soft parts
- Preservation of hard parts

Figure 2.1 *The four phases of the fossilisation process, from life, through death and on to burial. Death can occur through a variety of factors, and the processes which act upon an organism before and after burial determine whether it is to be preserved as a fossil in the sedimentary record*

infestation by worm-like organisms, often with swellings and pits illustrating the parasitism. Other natural causes of death, such as old age, may be deduced from fossil remains. For example, mammoth 'graveyards' can be interpreted through the study of modern elephant bone sites in Africa caused by die-offs associated with drought or other environmental hardships, or just the sum of deaths from disease or old age over a long period of time. Accumulations of mammoth bones may be interpreted as a result of similar processes (Box 2.1). Mass death in communal organisms as a part of the natural life cycle, particularly after mating, has been recognised in other organisms, paralleling the behaviour of modern-day squid. However, the actual cause of death can be clearly determined in only very few instances. Predators are sometimes found with stomach contents containing the remains of other fossil organisms. In the Jurassic shales of Holzmaden in southern Germany, for example, a shark has been recovered with the remains of 250 belemnites in its stomach (Figure 2.2). This certainly illustrated the cause of death of the squid-like belemnites, but may also have lead to the death of the shark from some form of indigestion. Other instances of gluttony are also recognised and are clear indicators of the cause of death (Box 2.2). Similarly, fossils preserved within coprolites are also good pointers to mode of death – demonstrating the preferred diet of an ancient predator.

BOX 2.1: ACTUALISM AND ELEPHANTS

Much research has been carried out since the mid-1980s in the study of the remains and causes of death of elephants in Zimbabwe. This research was intended to establish the main causes of death and particularly mass death in elephant populations, in order that the same processes can be determined for mammoth and other fossil proboscidean remains. Seven causes of death were determined: bone fracture; accidental death through falls, becoming stuck in mud or drowning; injury, accidental or through fighting; disease; old age; drought-related stress; and human activity, particularly hunting. The main cause of catastrophic mass death in Zimbabwe was drought-related, from heat, dehydration and starvation. Similar studies in Zambia have recorded the death of 31 elephants around a water hole in a single drought event. Bones were characteristically fractured from scavengers, trampling or the effects of weathering.

Mammoth and other fossil proboscidean bones are commonly found in clustered assemblages in Eurasia and North America, and have often been interpreted in a context of human hunting. Many such sites lack the artefacts of human activity, such as stone tools. Bones displaying fractures have commonly been interpreted as the results of butchering by humans; yet similar fractures in modern elephant bone sites can be attributed to trampling or scavenging. Studies of late Pleistocene bone sites have shown that the ages of the animals that are found within them are similar to that of the non-mass kill sites in Africa. Here, hunting profiles show selective killing of males or young, while mass deaths from environmental causes affect all ages. Many of the end-Pleistocene bone assemblages previously thought to be the result of human activity have similar characteristics. Age profiles do not show selective mortality. It is probable that, like the modern elephants, these were mass die-offs associated with environmental stress, in this case probably rapid climatic change. 'Evidence' of butchering either reflects human or hyena scavenging, or trampling by mammoths and other large animals.

Source: Haynes, G. (1991) *Mammoths, Mastodonts and Elephants. Biology, Behaviour and the Fossil Record.* Cambridge University Press, Cambridge.

Figure 2.2 *A* Hybodus *shark from the Lower Jurassic of Holzmaden in southern Germany. The shark has eaten over 250 belemnites, the hard parts of which have accumulated in its stomach. The belemnites were obviously killed by the shark – but the build-up of belemnite skeletal remains may have ultimately lead to the death of the shark itself [Photograph: J.E. Pollard]*

Physical and chemical causes of death are, if substantiated, useful clues for the geologist in determining the nature of ancient environments. The clearest examples of physical death are organisms trapped in the sticky resin produced by trees as sap, or entombed in tar pits. Amber is fossil tree sap, and is common in some river deposits close to the site of ancient forests. Occasionally, amber contains the remains of fossil insects intact, preserved from the moment of entrapment by the tree resin. Tar pits enclosing the remains of larger animals trapped by upwelling asphalt represent another instance of entrapment and preservation. The pit at Rancho La Brea, in Los Angeles, California, USA, is a gruesome example. Here, during the Pleistocene, a variety of vertebrates came to drink from a water hole and were trapped, sucked in and drowned in the asphalt welling beneath its surface. In rare instances like this, geologists have an exceptionally clear illustration of the direct cause of death.

Changes in the physical or chemical environment can promote death on a large scale. Rapid **mass mortalities** are difficult to substantiate but may be represented by great accumulations of fossils under volcanic ash, as in the case of the human tragedy of the Roman cities of Pompeii and Herculaneum, in southern Italy, or associated with black shales in the sea indicating asphyxiation through low-oxygen conditions. Over a longer time scale, the death of coral reefs through drowning in deep water or exposure to the elements, or the inundation of forests by the sea, is recorded by the physical remains of the dead reef or forest surrounded by rocks indicating the environmental change. Even individual tragedy may be recorded. In the Jurassic limestones of southern Germany, *Eulimulus*, the king crab, is sometimes encountered at the end of a series of meandering trails, a record of the death throes of an organism in the harsh environment of the Solnhofen lagoon (Figure 2.3).

BOX 2.2: THE DEATH OF AN AMMONITE

Fossils rarely provide evidence of the nature of their death. In some exceptional cases, however, it is possible to determine the cause of death from the physical evidence presented by the fossil itself. Such evidence is useful as it provides an insight into a detailed aspect of the nature of the geological past.

One such example was documented by Kauffman and Kesling (1960). They described a large fossil ammonite shell (*Placenticeras*) in the Upper Cretaceous rocks of South Dakota which exhibited several sets of regularly spaced puncture marks. The puncture marks were of the same size as the teeth of the marine reptile *Prognathodon*. Could this ammonite have been the victim of an attack by a mosasaur? Ammonites are related to the present-day *Nautilus*; like them, they had buoyancy chambers maintained as a kind of pressure vessel. A bite from a mosasaur inflicting the punctures could have created a loss in buoyancy, disabling the ammonite and leading to its death. Comparison of the puncture marks with the jaws of coexisting marine reptiles demonstrated a clear relationship between the size and tooth spacing of the jaws and the tooth marks on the ammonite. Clearly, the mosasaur punctured the ammonite shell while attempting to eat it. The multiple bite marks show that this was a difficult task, although it is probable that the ammonite died in the attack. However, a similar *Placenticeras* with punctures, from the Upper Cretaceous of Canada, has been interpreted as an animal attacked *after* death, but while drifting before sinking to the sea bed (Hewitt and Westermann, 1989).

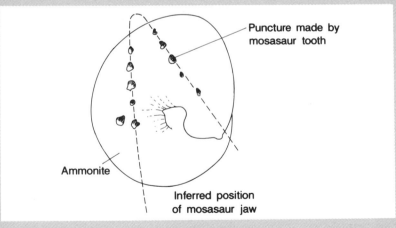

Sources: Kauffman, E.G. and Kesling, R.V. (1960) An Upper Cretaceous ammonite bitten by a mosasaur. *Contributions from the Museum of Paleontology, The University of Michigan*, **15**, 193–243. Hewitt, R.A. and Westermann, G.E.G. (1989) Mosasaur tooth marks on the ammonite *Placenticeras* from the Upper Cretaceous of Alberta, Canada. *Canadian Journal of Earth Sciences*, **27**, 469–472. [Figure modified from: Pollard (1990) *In* Briggs & Crowther (eds) *Palaeobiology – a synthesis*, Blackwell, Fig. 1A, p. 369]

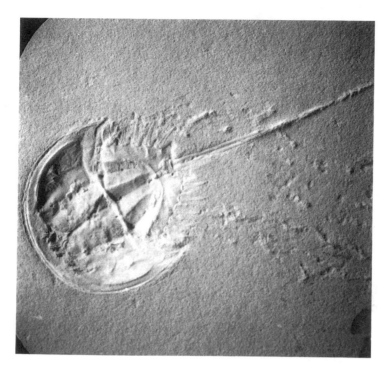

Figure 2.3 *Death of a king crab in the late Jurassic Solnhofen lagoon, southern Germany. The Eulimulus has died at the end of its meandering trails in the hostile environment of this lagoon [Photograph: T. Sharpe]*

Death is the first process in fossilisation because on death the organism is ready to be incorporated in the sedimentary record. The processes that follow death, however, govern the potential for the subsequent incorporation of the organism into the fossil record.

2.2.2 Effects on the Dead Organism before Burial

The death of the organism leads to an immediate commencement of the break-down and decay of the body parts. This break-down is arrested through the process of **rapid burial**, or through otherwise **excluding the supply of oxygen**. Rate of burial is the biggest single factor in determining the preservation of a fossil organism. Rapid burial, instantaneous with the time of death, effectively ensures that normal processes of attack by scavengers, physical degradation by transport through currents and wind action, and biochemical break-down into constituent molecules are arrested, thereby achieving almost perfect preservation (Figure 2.4). Death of an organism in an environment low in oxygen will also ensure that the processes of decay will be arrested. In most cases, though, this is rare, and most fossils have been subject to some decay and degradation processes before burial.

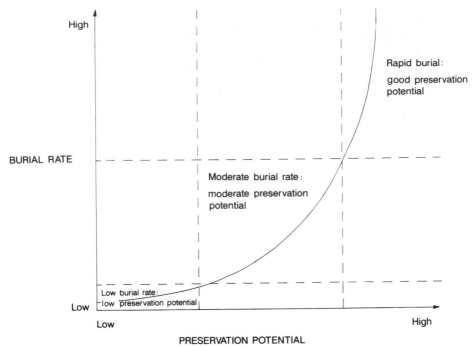

Figure 2.4 *Schematic graph demonstrating the relationship between burial rate and preservation potential. In general, with a high burial rate there is a correspondingly greater chance of preservation*

This part of taphonomy is sometimes referred to as **biostratinomy**, and it is this which mostly governs the relative richness of the fossil record, effectively a game of chance.

In most cases, it is the soft parts which are the first to be attacked before burial, usually through the actions of scavengers and the biochemical processes of decay. Scavengers can quickly promote break-down of soft-bodied organisms through the action of feeding on the body, and through physical tearing and scattering of flesh and skeletal remains. In general terms, scavengers are more likely in the marine environment, in well-oxygenated waters of normal marine salinity. Most soft parts are, however, destroyed through biochemical reactions. In normally oxygenated conditions, they are quickly reduced to water and carbon dioxide. In low-oxygen conditions this process may be slowed but not arrested, and decay leads to the production of more complex hydrocarbon molecules. Preservation of soft parts is therefore unusual prior to burial, although early mineralisation of soft tissue has been recorded (Box 2.3). However, in hot and arid or cold environments unburied soft parts can become dried leaving mummified remains, such as the recently discovered Neolithic man from the Alps (Box 2.4). Dinosaur skin impressions from Montana and the mummified remains of seals in Antarctica are also representative of this process (Figure 2.5). Despite this, in most cases preservation of soft parts is through the growth of minerals early after the burial of an organism.

Figure 2.5 *Mummified seal remains from the Antarctic Peninsula. The seal has been desiccated by the dry Antarctic air and preserved. It is 60 km away from open water and may be at least 10 000 years old [Photograph: P. Doyle]*

During and after the decay of the soft parts, hard parts may be subject to attack from both biological and physical processes (Figure 2.6). On death the organic tissue which keeps the skeletal parts articulated and in contact decays, leading to the eventual disintegration of the skeleton. This is particularly important to those animals with complex, articulated skeletons, such as arthropods, vertebrates, and echinoderms such as crinoids. Scavengers intent on eating the dead organism will inevitably disturb and scatter constituent parts of the skeleton. Finally, physical effects of current and wind activity, for instance, will lead to the disaggregation and transport of these components far from their point of life (Figure 2.6). In all these cases, rapid burial will arrest the disintegration process.

In a great many cases, physical transport also leads to the displacement of fossil shells and other skeletal parts far from their point of life and death. Swimming or floating organisms, for example, may drift a great distance after their death, before they finally sink and become incorporated into the sedimentary record. Even bottom-dwelling organisms such as gastropods may float from their point of death due to the build-up of gases during the decay process. Such displaced fossils are said to be **allochthonous**, and this has a great bearing on the interpretation of assemblages of fossils as once living communities of animals and plants. In some cases, allochthonous fossils may be identified by the physical damage left by the action of transport, or by the accumulation or particular orientation of skeletal remains according to prevailing current or wind direction. As physical transport is common before burial, recognition of in-place, or **autochthonous,** fossils is certain only in cases where the fossil is found in life position, such as within

BOX 2.3: EXCEPTIONAL PRESERVATION OF FISH FROM BRAZIL

The Santana Formation of northern Brazil is a series of Cretaceous limestones and shales which have long been famed for the beautiful preservation of their fossil fish. Most of the fish are contained within carbonate nodules or concretions which formed around each fish and helped preserve it in three-dimensional form. The fish and other fossils, including insects, of the Santana Formation are usually collected by the local farmers, and sold to tourists or exported, often illegally.

Martill (1988) made a study of the death and preservation of the fossil fish from Brazil. He concluded that many were killed through changes in salinity of the water mass, and that they represented a mass mortality event. Other swimming organisms are rare, and there are no bottom-dwelling organisms or potential predators. Through detailed examination of the fossils and sediments, Martill concluded that the normal marine waters were stratified, with highly saline bottom waters and normal marine salinity surface waters. Periodic influxes of hypersaline waters into the surface zone led to mass death of the fish population, which then sank to the sea bottom. Many thousands of fish were probably killed in this way. On reaching the sea floor, fish became entangled in an algal mat which prevented them from rising to the surface as the decomposition gases built up within each fish. Preservation of soft parts was through the early precipitation of phosphate minerals (francolite) which are found replacing muscle fibres, gills and so on. The photographs below illustrate the level of detail, comparing recent (A) and fossil (B) gill filaments. Phosphate is relatively rare in sea water, but each trapped fish helped alter the chemical environment surrounding it, leading to the build-up of carbon dioxide gas and lowering the pH, both of which help promote the precipitation of francolite.

 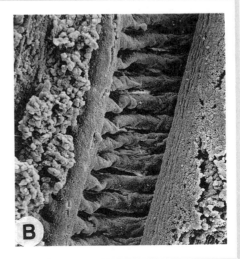

BOX 2.3: (*cont.*)

Additional phosphate was available from bacteria feeding on phosphorus-rich biomolecules within the carcass itself, and together these sources led to replacement of the muscle fibres by francolite. In this way, phosphatisation of the soft parts probably took place within hours of the death of the fish. Later, burial and precipitation of carbonates led to the creation of concretions which formed around the outline of each fish and helped preserve its three-dimensional form.

Source: Martill, D.M. (1988) Preservation of fish in the Cretaceous Santana Formation of Brazil. *Palaeontology*, **31**, 1–18. [Photographs: D. Martill]

BOX 2.4: THE MAN IN THE ICE

In 1991, one of the most important archaeological finds of the twentieth century was made. The complete body of a Neolithic man, some 5300 years old, was found encased in glacier ice high in the Alps which separate Austria from Italy. Never before had a body this old been recovered from an alpine glacier. Bodies are regularly recovered from the ice, but most of them are mountaineers, such as the Englishman lost in the 1930s and recovered together with his horn-rimmed glasses and pipe, or soldiers killed in the two world wars. In most cases the bodies are imperfectly preserved, and they are often deformed by the motion of the glacier. Commonly, they are preserved as 'grave-wax' which is created through the transformation of the fats of the body into a stable lipid in the damp, low oxygen conditions of glaciers. Drowned bodies display a similar state. The 'ice man' was unique in that he was a true mummy, preserved through almost complete desiccation of his soft parts, and was found together with his Neolithic clothing and equipment – a truly important discovery.

The preservation of this Recent fossil was through a combination of exceptional circumstances. Firstly, the ice man died alone high in the Alps from injuries and from exposure, his body freezing in a prone position as he rested. Secondly, his body was quickly covered by snow dry enough to allow free flow of air between the ice crystals, and dense enough to prevent attack by insects and other scavengers. Thirdly, the ice man's body was almost completely dehydrated and mummified through the action of the cold, dry, alpine air. Snow turns to ice over a period of about 20 years, during which time incorporation of the mummy and his artefacts into the glacier assured continued preservation. Miraculously, the body was not greatly deformed by the glacier during its 5300 years of interment. Perhaps even more incredible is that the conditions under which the ice man was released – mass melting of the glacier ice – probably only lasted for six days, during which time he was discovered.

Source: Spindler, K. (1995) *The Man in the Ice*. Phoenix, London

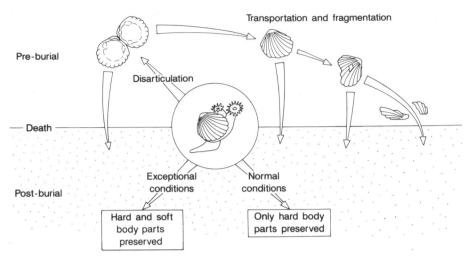

Figure 2.6 *The physical effects of taphonomy. After death, and before burial, the bivalve will become disarticulated, and, with transport, will become increasingly fragmented. Such fragments may become incorporated into the sediment at any time. After burial it is mostly the hard parts which are fossilised, although in exceptional circumstances soft parts may also be preserved*

burrows, or growing in life attitude, as with corals and tree stumps (Figure 2.7). This is relatively rare, and in most cases, fossils can be described only as **semi-autochthonous**, that is, having undergone at least some transport, often exhibiting a stable position relative to the surrounding sediment. Figure 2.8 illustrates the hypothetical case. To the left of the diagram, the organism progresses from life through death and burial, leaving the fossil (A) close to life position. This is truly autochthonous. Fossil B has been transported after death but before burial; fossil C represents an organism that died away from its normal habitat but was not transported after death. Both fossils B and C are semi-autochthonous in position. Fossil D represents an organism which died away from its normal habitat and was transported after death. This fossil is truly allochthonous. Fossils A–D can all be eroded from their sediments and reworked as allochthonous fossils.

2.2.3 Effects on the Dead Organism after Burial

After burial, the dead organism can be affected by a variety of chemical and physical factors. Rapid burial ensures that the organism is not under physical attack from scavengers, and/or mechanical transport by currents and wind action. Soft parts may be preserved in this way, and delicate, articulated skeletons may be held in place.

Most records of actual soft-part preservation are associated with low-oxygen (**anaerobic** and **dysaerobic**) conditions and rapid burial associated with a high sedimentation rate. In such environments, the decay process is slowed, but bacteria which can survive in such environments (anaerobic bacteria) assist in breaking

Figure 2.7   *Fossil lycopod tree stumps (*Stigmaria*) preserved in life position in Carboniferous rocks near Glasgow [Photograph: British Geological Survey]*

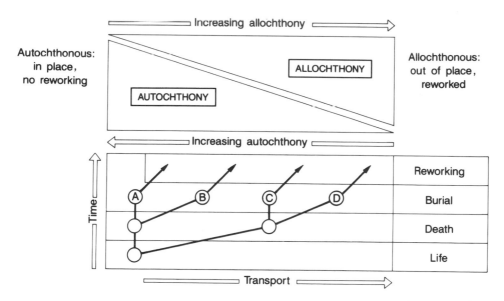

Figure 2.8   *The potential for transport and reworking of fossil organisms. Truly in place, or autochthonous, fossils lived, died and were buried with minimal transport (**A**). Completely reworked or allochthonous fossils have been transported after death and before burial (**D**). Intermediate states exist (**B** and **C**). All fossils may be exhumed, reworked and transported [Modified from: Brouwer (1967)* General Palaeontology, *Oliver and Boyd, Fig. 8, p. 14]*

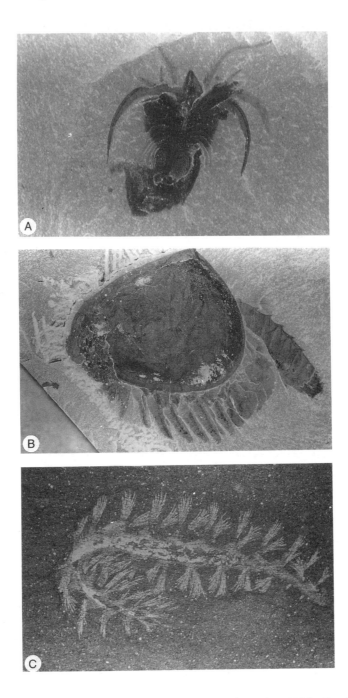

Figure 2.9 *Typical fossils preserved with their soft parts from the Middle Cambrian Burgess Shale of British Columbia. These fossils were all preserved through rapid smothering which excluded the oxygen. Subsequent mineral growth preserved the soft parts in great detail.* ***A:*** Marrella. ***B:*** Canadaspis. ***C:*** Burgessochaeta *[Photographs: D.H. Collins]*

down the soft parts into hydrocarbons. Usually it is not the actual soft parts which are preserved, but a replica or outline created by the growth of minerals soon after the death of the organism. The type of mineral (pyrite, carbonates, phosphates and silicates) replacing the soft parts is determined by the nature of the chemical environment, with, for example, pyrite growth being favoured in anaerobic conditions. The commonest type of preservation is mineral coating, where mineral growth occurs on the surface of the decaying soft body, leaving behind an outline of the original soft body. In the Cambrian Burgess Shale of British Columbia, Canada, large numbers of soft-bodied organisms are preserved in this way, the soft parts indicated by a carbon film with a mineral coating formed in anaerobic conditions (Figure 2.9). Here, the diversity of those organisms without hard body parts outnumber those with hard body parts.

In other cases, the physical impressions of the soft parts may be preserved in some sediments, particularly in fine-grained ones. These preserve no mineralised trace of the soft parts, but rather the physical presence and surface features. An important example of such preservation is the record of the late Proterozoic Ediacaran Biota, a series of ancient soft-bodied organisms preserved as impressions in a variety of locations across the world (Figure 2.10). In general, burial increases the chances of soft-part preservation, as it helps prevent biochemical break-down though the exclusion of oxygen. However, once buried, the organism

Figure 2.10 Charnia masoni, a late Precambrian fossil belonging to the Ediacaran Biota which is preserved as a simple impression of its soft body parts. The depth of the impression suggests that this organism may have had a quilted structure [Photograph: Leicestershire Museums, reproduced by permission]

comes under chemical attack from pore fluids contained in the sediments, and from physical disturbance as the sedimentary pile is compacted, or distorted by later tectonic activity. These changes are collectively referred to as the process of **diagenesis.**

There are six processes associated with diagenesis: **preservation of original material, recrystallisation, impregnation, encrustation, solution** and **compaction**. Preservation of the **original skeletal material** indicates that the flow of pore fluids is restricted (Figure 2.11). For example, in shells the original chemistry may remain unaltered and, in some instances, colour patterns or mother-of-pearl coatings may be preserved intact (Figure 2.12). Original skeletal material is more commonly preserved in younger rocks, as with increasing age the likelihood of alteration increases. **Recrystallisation** is one of the commonest effects of diagenesis. In some cases, recrystallisation is achieved without change in the chemical composition. The unstable mineralogical phase of calcium carbonate ($CaCO_3$), aragonite, is common in many invertebrate shells, and is quickly recrystallised to its more stable, calcite phase. In other cases, recrystallisation involves the replacement of the original skeletal material by a new mineral. Common replacement minerals are silica (SiO_2) and pyrite (FeS_2). Replacement can be through the growth of large mineral crystals at specific points, at the expense of the original

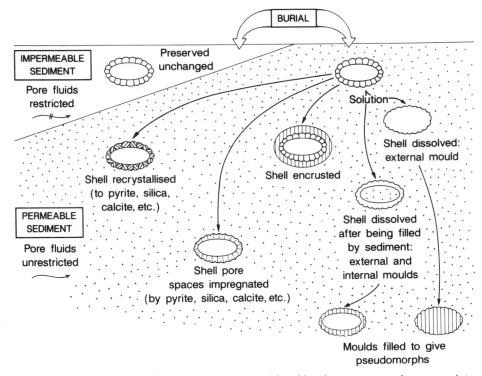

Figure 2.11   *The process of diagenesis. After burial fossil hard parts may undergo a variety of effects. Impermeable sediments provide a greater chance that fossils are preserved intact with their original shell chemistry and colour patterns, for example. Permeable sediments have a freer flow of pore fluids, and shells are subject to a greater range of processes*

structure (**grain growth**) or through progressive replacement of the original material through chemical change (**metasomatism**). **Impregnation** is common where skeletal or plant material is notably porous. Here, mineralised pore fluids lead to precipitation of minerals inside the pore spaces of bones, shells and plant stems, for instance. Impregnation is also often referred to as **petrification** (literally meaning 'turning to stone'), and is associated with the Triassic silica-impregnated fossil forests of Arizona, USA (Figure 2.13). **Encrustation** takes place where the skeletal or plant material is surrounded by a crust of new material. This is common in areas of hot springs where mineral salts supersaturate the warm waters and are quickly precipitated on to shell and plant materials.

The commonest diagenetic process is that of **solution**. Here the original skeletal material is dissolved leaving a natural cavity (Figure 2.14). Several preservation states result (Figure 2.11). Firstly, in some sediments it is possible for the cavity left behind after dissolution of the shell or other skeletal material not to be filled. In the case of a shell, this results in a cavity which bears the external features of the shell, known as an **external mould**. In many cases, the original shell cavity left after the decay of the soft parts will be filled before the shell itself is dissolved, and this leads to replication of the internal features of the shell, an **internal mould** (Figures 2.14 and 2.15). Often the cavity is later filled by sediment or minerals precipitated after dissolution of the original shell, to produce a **pseudomorph**, otherwise known as a **cast**. As this simply fills the space vacated by the original shell material, it preserves none of its original shell structure, although it faithfully replicates the external and internal features preserved by the mould (Figure 2.11). In some cases, the shell may have remained empty prior to dissolution of the shell. Here, the pseudomorph replicates only the external features.

After incorporation of the fossil into the sedimentary record, it may be **deformed**. In some cases this is due to **compaction** of the sediment due to loading. During lithification the sediment may lose its pore water, with a corresponding increase in pressure. In both cases, fossils may be crushed, usually displaying characteristic cracks associated with this process. Fossils may also be deformed as part of the sedimentary rock during tectonic processes. Here, distortion of the fossil is common, and is associated with the tectonic fabric induced by the regional stress of the tectonic forces (Figure 2.16). In such cases, the fossils themselves become valuable as indicators of the very forces that deformed them. Some fossil species, such as the trilobite *Angelina sedgwickii*, are known only from metamorphosed sediments, and have to be reconstructed in order to interpret the range in morphology of the species (Box 2.5).

Finally, it is possible for buried fossils to be exhumed or **reworked** during any part of the diagenetic process (Figure 2.8). This can cause confusion to geologists as it may result in fossils from a more ancient interval being weathered out of a sedimentary rock body and incorporated into much younger sediments. Potentially, any body fossils could have been reworked, and the common signs are erosion and weathering, but in some cases this is extremely difficult to recognise, and care must be taken to examine all body fossils for signs of reworking in any palaeoenvironmental analysis.

Figure 2.12   *Fossil gastropod shells preserved with their colour patterns from the Palaeogene of the Isle of Wight [Photograph: M.J. Barker]*

Figure 2.13   *Fossil tree trunks from the Arizona fossil forest of Triassic age.* **A:** *Fossil log with branch, lens cap 50 mm.* **B:** *Section through the trunk showing concentric growth lines, tree rings, which have been impregnated by silica [Photographs: J.E. Francis]*

Figure 2.14   *Fossils preserved as moulds caused by the original shell material being dissolved in a permeable sediment, from the Miocene of southern Spain. **A:** External and internal moulds of bivalve shells. **B:** External moulds of bivalve shells [Photographs: P. Doyle]*

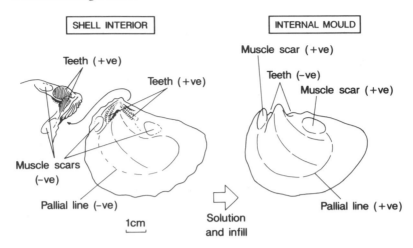

Figure 2.15   *The relationship of internal shell morphology to its commonly found internal mould in the Jurassic bivalve* Trigonia. *Positive and negative elements of the shell interior are preserved as negative and positive features of the mould*

Figure 2.16   *Ordovician fossil brachiopods from South Wales showing distortion from tectonic activity [Photograph: D. Bates]*

2.2.4 The Preservation of Trace Fossils

Trace fossils are the tracks, trails, burrows, borings and faeces of fossil organisms, and their preservation is important to the interpretation of the mode of life of a great many organisms. Trace fossils are particularly important because it is rare for them to be reworked, and therefore they are reliable *in situ* sources of information about the nature of the ancient environment.

Coprolites undergo the same processes of fossilisation as body fossils. Most other traces are by nature ephemeral and their incorporation into the fossil record is largely a function of sedimentation rate. Traces can be divided on the basis of whether they were formed within the sediment itself (**endogenic**), such as burrows, or on the surface of accumulating sediment (**exogenic**), such as trackways, footprints, and so on (Figure 2.17). Endogenic traces are effectively already buried, and have a greater preservation potential than exogenic traces. However, many are destroyed by other organisms burrowing through the same sediments, creating new traces which cross-cut the earlier ones. Although this gives a useful indication of the diversity of life within the sedimentary record at any one time, intense activity (**bioturbation**) by many trace makers effectively homogenises the sediment and makes identification of traces difficult.

Endogenic traces are subject to diagenesis. In particular, some burrows can act as conduits for mineralising pore fluids, and in some cases may become a repository for the precipitation of certain minerals, such as the iron oxides, hematite and goethite. Exogenic traces are more vulnerable to erosion because they are created as depressions from organisms moving or resting on the sediment surface. The actions of wind or currents may completely remove such trackways, unless they are buried rapidly. On burial, exogenic traces are subject to the same constraints of bioturbation, compaction and tectonic processes as endogenic traces.

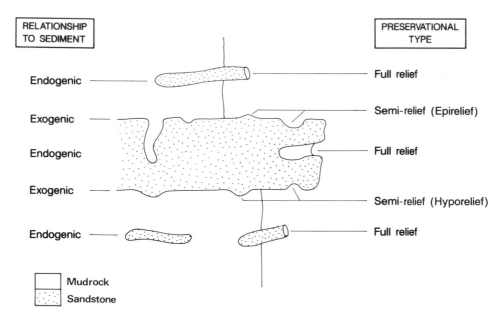

Figure 2.17 *The preservation of trace fossils. Trace fossils can be classified on the basis of their relationship with their containing sediment [Modified from: Bromley (1990),* Trace fossils, *Unwin Hyman, Fig. 10.1, p. 165]*

BOX 2.5: RESTORING DEFORMED FOSSILS

Fossils in ancient rocks are very often deformed through the stresses created when rocks are folded during major episodes of tectonic movement, usually associated with continental collisions in the geological past. Such fossils are very useful to geologists interested in the structure of the Earth, as the nature of the deformation of the fossil gives an indication of the level of stress during tectonic activity.

One such example is the trilobite *Angelina sedgwickii* Salter, 1859. This trilobite is common in Ordovician rocks in North Wales, but is only known from distorted specimens, often stretched or squashed along their long axes (Figure A). Although specimens of *Angelina* give a good indication of the levels of stress applied during the Ordovician mountain building episode known as the

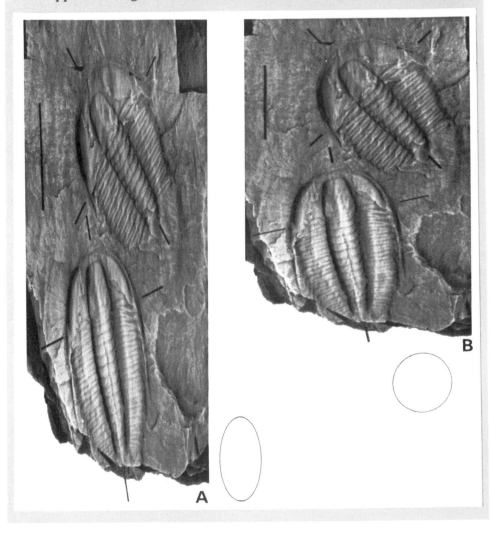

BOX 2.5: (*cont.*)

Caledonian Orogeny, palaeontologists have long puzzled over the true shape of this animal's body.

Most techniques use complex statistical formulae and computer software to restore deformed fossils. Others use comparison with undistorted specimens; Fortey and Owens (1992) compared specimens of *Angelina* from Wales with a single, undistorted, specimen from Shropshire. Recent attempts have unveiled what may be the true shape of *Angelina* – using a photocopier (Figure B). Many photocopiers can 'squash' and 'stretch' illustrations along two orthogonal axes; Rushton and Smith (1993) have shown that the secret of the true shape of *Angelina* can now be revealed by this method.

Sources: Fortey, R.A. and Owens, R.A. (1992) The trilobite *Angelina* unstretched. *Geology Today*, 8, 219–222. Rushton, R.A. and Smith, M. (1993) Retrodeformation of fossils – a simple technique. *Palaeontology*, 36, 927–930. [Figure reproduced from Rushton and Smith (1993), *Palaeontology* 36, Fig. 1, p. 928]

2.3 IS THE FOSSIL RECORD COMPLETE?

The **fossil record** is the theoretical framework within which we can examine the nature of life in the geological past. It encompasses both the documented records of fossils and their occurrence, and the yet to be discovered and described fossils contained within sedimentary rocks. The fossil record is the foundation of our interpretation of the evolution of life through geological time and the nature of the biosphere at any given interval. However, organisms are incorporated into sedimentary rocks largely by chance. It is the time interval between death and burial which governs the likelihood of preservation, and it is in this interval that most potential fossils are destroyed. Rapid burial, excluding oxygen and potential scavengers, is the key to preservation, but even after burial loss is still to be expected from the processes of diagenesis.

The fossil record is therefore incomplete. Not all organisms will be preserved. There are at least two areas of difficulty. Firstly, land-based organisms are less likely to be preserved than aquatic organisms. The nature of the terrestrial environment is one of erosion and net sediment loss, and this contrasts sharply with the mostly depositional aquatic environments, particularly marine ones. Secondly, soft-bodied or fragile organisms are less likely to be preserved than organisms possessing hard parts or a robust structure. Figure 2.18 illustrates the problem. The fossil record of shelly organisms living in an aquatic environment is extremely good, comparing favourably with the diversity of present-day species. This is particularly true of the Brachiopoda, a major group of shelly organisms more abundant in the geological past than the present day. The most diverse

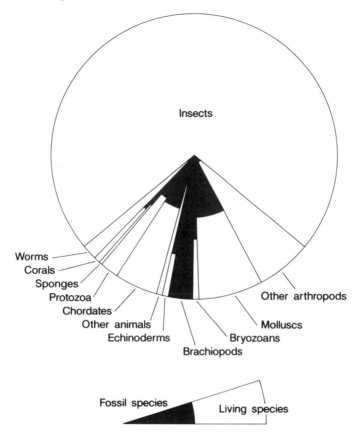

Worms
Corals
Sponges
Protozoa
Chordates
Other animals
Echinoderms

Insects

Other arthropods

Molluscs
Bryozoans
Brachiopods

Fossil species   Living species

Figure 2.18   *The proportion of living and fossil animal species. Note that insects and worms have a poor fossil record, while brachiopods and other shelly fossils have a good one*

animals living today are the insects. Insects can be found in almost every environment on Earth, and yet their fossil record is poor because of their mostly terrestrial mode of life and the nature of their fragile jointed limbs and appendages. In another case, the worms, the record is poorer still. Both examples are illustrative of organisms that first appeared early in the diversification of life on Earth, but which are under-represented in the fossil record.

Given these problems, just how incomplete is the fossil record, and is it adequate as a scientific database? Charles Darwin (1809–1882), like his contemporary, the famous geologist Charles Lyell (1797–1875), was of the opinion that the fossil record represented just a fraction of the total life on Earth. Darwin reached this conclusion because of the then unconvincing evidence for evolving species and intermediates in the record, and he used a whole chapter in his *Origin of Species* to discuss the perceived imperfection of the fossil record: 'Why . . . is not every geological formation and every stratum full of . . . intermediate links? . . . The explanation lies, as I believe, in the extreme imperfection of the fossil record'. The debate continues today, with arguments both for and against relative completeness. The so-called **Lazarus taxa**, for example, are species or other taxa which appear to become extinct at one interval, but reappear at a much later date and clearly demonstrate gaps in our knowledge from imperfections in the fossil record (Figure 2.19). However, despite the vagaries of preservation of both sedimentary environments and fossil organisms, the fossil record does represent an extremely important source of information, comparable with the data sources of most sciences (Box 2.6). Several observations support this. Firstly, the major patterns of evolution and extinction are clearly displayed and corroborated at many sites across the world. Examples are the identification of mass extinction events, rapid colonisation events such as the evolution of the Cambrian marine fauna, and the rapid spread of the flowering plants in the Cretaceous (Chapter 7). Secondly, details of the evolution of individual species can be documented in many sections with a resolution of thousands or even hundreds of years as calculated from absolute dating techniques. Thirdly, the subdivision of geological time

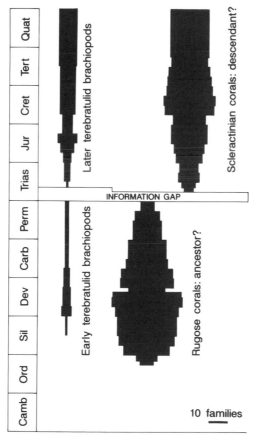

Figure 2.19   *The concept of Lazarus taxa. An important information gap exists in the record of many taxa. In these examples, there is no current record for the terebratulid brachiopods for much of the early Triassic, although they appear again later in this interval. For the corals, there is an important gap between potential ancestor (the rugose corals) and descendant (the scleractinian corals) at the same interval*

BOX 2.6: THE ADEQUACY OF THE FOSSIL RECORD

The fossil record is usually considered to be incomplete, often inadequate to demonstrate the diversity and evolution of life on Earth. This has been frequently overstated and is often used as an excuse in order to explain away difficult or puzzling patterns. However, it is clear that the fossil record, though incomplete, provides an extremely important source of data on the nature and evolution of life on Earth. Paul (1985) set out to determine if the fossil record was flawed as a source of scientific data. His work led to the following conclusions:

1. Evidence from the fossil record is as reliable as any other line of evidence in Earth science.
2. Irrespective of its completeness, in about 95% of cases, the sequence of fossil species as found in the fossil record reflects the order in which they actually evolved.
3. The sequence of fossils provides evidence of the pattern of evolution but not the mechanisms.
4. The sequence of fossils provides the most rigorous test of evolutionary hypotheses derived from comparisons of morphology.
5. In all cases, detailed fossil evidence should be plotted against detailed, accurately measured stratigraphical sections, rather than with reference to established biostratigraphical units. This provides a greater element of objectivity, necessary for comparative work. The fossil record is a rigorous test of evolutionary hypotheses.

Source: Paul, C.R.C. (1985) The adequacy of the fossil record reconsidered. *Special Papers in Palaeontology*, 33, 7–15.

intervals using fossils is possible in some cases with pin-point precision, corroborated by non-palaeontological indicators such as event horizons. This clearly illustrates the true nature of the fossil record: that it is surprisingly complete despite the chance nature of the process of fossilisation.

2.4 LAGERSTÄTTEN: WINDOWS ON AN ANCIENT WORLD

Lagerstätten are defined as deposits in which fossils are either **exceptionally preserved** or **exceptionally concentrated**. The name is derived from a German mining term referring to exceptional mineral concentrations or 'bonanzas'. Lagerstätten therefore represent palaeontological bonanzas which are of extreme importance to the interpretation of ancient life and environments.

Concentration Lagerstätten are formed in many ways (Figure 2.20). Firstly, fossils may become concentrated through sedimentary processes. In such cases, fossils are gathered together before burial through the action of winds, waves or currents, or are accumulated over a long time interval during which the rate of sedimentation is low. Such accumulations, such as the Ludlow Bone Bed at the base of the Silurian Přídolí Series in England, consist mainly of allochthonous fossils, and contains great accumulations of skeletal remains (Figure 2.20). Secondly, organisms may be gathered together in traps which acted upon the organisms before death, and in most cases caused the death of the organism. These are effectively autochthonous fossils. The commonest trap deposits are those containing larger vertebrate fossils. Examples include the Rancho La Brea tar pit in Los Angeles, already mentioned, and the Bernissart Mine in Belgium, a cavern into which fell a great many *Iguanodon* dinosaurs. Concentration Lagerstätten are important on two counts. Firstly, those accumulated by sedimentary processes are illustrative of the nature of those processes. Secondly, trap concentrations are of extreme importance because they are composed of autochthonous organisms which may be pieced together to reconstruct the morphologies of the contained animals. This is particularly true of the Bernissart dinosaurs, which dramatically influenced our understanding of dinosaurs away from their reconstruction as quadrupeds towards a bipedal stance (Figure 2.21).

   Conservation Lagerstätten are justly the most famous. They include deposits in which soft-part preservation is the norm, and where spectacular preservation is

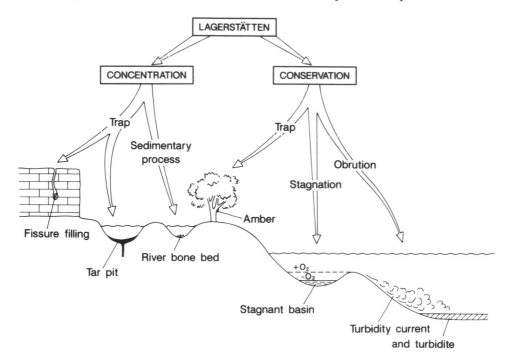

Figure 2.20   *Types of Lagerstätte. Concentration Lagerstätten are important accumulations of fossils, usually their hard parts. Conservation Lagerstätten are records of exceptional preservation of hard and soft parts [Modified from: Seilacher* et al., *(1985),* Philosophical Transactions of the Royal Society of London, ***B331**, Fig. 1, p. 6]

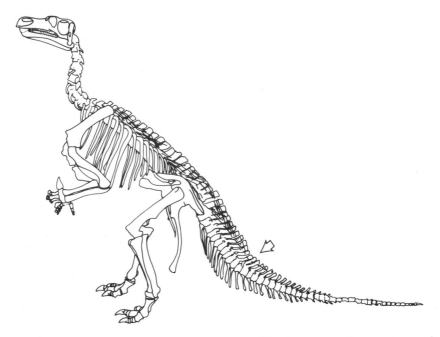

Figure 2.21   *A traditional bipedal reconstruction of the Cretaceous dinosaur* Iguanodon ber-nissartensis *based upon bones recovered from Bernissart in Belgium, a concentration Lagerstätte. The great accumulation of bones allowed intense study in the late nineteenth century which demonstrated that they were not true quadrupeds. In fact, recent study of the same skeletons by David Norman has suggested that the adult* Iguanodon *may have been both bipedal and quadrupedal. This is demonstrated by the artificial compaction of some of the vertebrae in the traditional reconstruction, indicated by an arrow [Drawing: D.B. Norman]*

common. Conservation Lagerstätten can be divided into three basic types related to the process of preservation: low oxygen (**stagnation**); rapid burial (**obrution**) and conservation traps (Figure 2.20). In some cases the cause of exceptional pre-servation may be a function of all three processes. The most studied examples are stagnation deposits. Here, the nature of the environment is such that oxygen is excluded, and the preservation of the soft parts is therefore made possible. Ex-amples of this type of deposit are found in the Jurassic and Eocene rocks of southern Germany. The Posidonienschiefer is a Lower Jurassic black mudrock which preserves the soft body parts of vertebrates and invertebrates (Figure 2.22). It is known for its ichthyosaurs, marine reptiles with the outlines of their soft bodies preserved, some in the process of giving birth to young. The Solnhofen Limestone is an Upper Jurassic deposit formed in a stagnant lagoon. It is well known for its diverse organisms, with invertebrates and vertebrates alike pre-served without disarticulation. It is most famous for containing the only known specimens of the first bird, *Archaeopteryx*, preserved with its feathers intact, but contains a range of almost perfectly preserved soft-bodied organisms (Figure 2.23). The most spectacular stagnation deposit of all is that preserved at Messel, Germany. This Eocene oil shale preserves vertebrates intact: mammals with hair, bats with their wing membranes, and so on (Figure 2.24). All these deposits yield precise information on the nature and mode of life of their preserved fauna.

Obrution deposits preserve their soft-bodied fauna through exclusion of oxygen and scavengers because of rapid burial. A famous example of this is the Carboniferous Mazon Creek fauna, of Illinois, USA, with a diverse range of soft-bodied organisms preserved at the front of a rapidly growing delta. The Burgess

Figure 2.22   *Exceptional preservation of the fragile giant crinoid* Seirocrinus *from the Lower Jurassic Posidonienschiefer of Holzmaden in southern Germany. The crinoid may have been either floating attached to the central log, or growing from the sea bed with the same attachment. Either way, the delicate articulated stem of this echinoderm has been preserved in the low-oxygen environment of this conservation Lagerstätte [Photograph: T. Sharpe]*

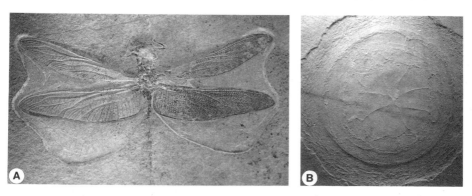

Figure 2.23   *Exceptional preservation in the Upper Jurassic Solnhofen Limestone of southern Germany. These delicate organisms, a dragon-fly (**A**) and jellyfish (**B**), were preserved in the low-oxygen conditions of the Solnhofen lagoon, a conservation Lagerstätte [Photographs: T. Sharpe]*

Figure 2.24 *Exceptional preservation of articulated skeletons and soft body parts of a bat* (***A***) *and frog* (***B***) *in the Eocene oil shale of Messel in southern Germany, a conservation Lagerstätte [Photograph: T. Sharpe]*

Shale, of British Columbia, Canada, is the best known of all Lagerstätten. It is a conservation deposit formed through both obrution and stagnation. Here, the Cambrian marine fauna was swept up in a turbidity flow of fine sediments which carried the animals to a stagnant part of the sea floor. It preserves a diversity of organisms truly difficult to interpret (Figure 2.4). Finally, conservation traps also exist. They are comparable to concentration traps, except that here soft and delicate body parts are also preserved. Insects in amber are most readily recognisable as conservation traps – the insects trapped by the amber which excluded oxygen and scavengers to preserve the organisms intact.

The importance of conservation Lagerstätten should not be underestimated. The Burgess Shale and Mazon Creek faunas, for instance, preserve the hard body fossils normally associated with rocks of Cambrian and Carboniferous age, but in association with a diverse assemblage of soft-bodied organisms. Under normal conditions the soft-bodied fauna is not preserved, and the fossil assemblage of hard-bodied organisms is unrepresentative of the fauna actually living in the sea or on land during the time interval studied. As discussed above, the fossil record is incomplete; the strands of our understanding are perilously thin at times. However, distributed through the geological record are Lagerstätten which allow us a rare glimpse of the true diversity, a kind of window which opens on something approaching the true diversity of life from the ancient geological past.

2.5 SUMMARY OF KEY POINTS

- **Fossils** are the remains of once living plants or animals. Effectively, these remains are the physical evidence of past life found in rocks and sediments. There are two basic types: **body fossils** and **trace fossils**.
- Body fossils preserve elements of the original body of an organism that have undergone the process of **fossilisation**. Trace fossils are the physical evidence of the existence of plants and animals through their traces, tracks and burrows preserved in sedimentary rocks.
- The process of fossilisation is referred to as **taphonomy**. This process has three elements: death; the processes which act on a body before burial; and the processes which act on a body after burial. After death, rapid burial ensures the best chances of preservation. If burial is not rapid, physical degradation through transport and scavengers acts to destroy the organism before it is buried. After burial, the organism may be subject to several processes created by the physical and chemical environment of the sediment. These processes of **diagenesis** may preserve the organism intact or transform it through **recrystallisation**, through the **impregnation** of pore spaces, through **encrustation**, or, where the sediments are particularly permeable, through **solution**. Dissolution of the skeletal component (shell or bone, for example) leads to the creation of internal and external **moulds**; these may later be filled to create **casts** or **pseudomorphs** which resemble the original form but preserve nothing of their internal structure. **Compaction** may lead to fossils being distorted from their original shape and form.
- The fossil record is incomplete, as organisms that live on land or that do not possess hard parts are less likely to be preserved than those organisms that live in the sea and that have some elements of a hard skeleton. However, in many cases the fossil record is an extraordinary resource illustrative of the evolution of life.

- **Lagerstätten** are exceptional fossil bonanzas which tell us much about ancient environments and the organisms which inhabited them. There are two broad types. **Concentration Lagerstätten** are exceptional concentrations of fossils. **Conservation Lagerstätten** are fossil assemblages which show exceptional preservation, particularly of soft parts. Both types illustrate the nature and diversity of the ancient world.

2.6 SUGGESTED READING

Ziegler (1983) provides a well-illustrated account of taphonomy. Allison (1988) gives a detailed analysis of the formation of conservation Lagerstätten, while Whittington and Conway Morris (1985) is a compilation of papers on the nature and formation of these palaeontological bonanzas. Clarkson (1993) devotes a chapter to reviewing several exceptional faunas, while Barthel *et al.* (1990) provide an interesting review of the geology and palaeontology of one of the most famous Lagerstätten. Briggs and Crowther (1990) is an extremely important multi-authored text with many chapters on preservation, taphonomy and the fossil record. Dodd and Stanton (1990) has chapters on biogeochemistry and taphonomy. Donovan (1991) is an accessible overview of the subject of taphonomy.

Allison, P. 1988. Konservat-Lagerstätten: cause and classification. *Paleobiology,* **14,** 331–344.

Barthel, K.W., Swinburne, N.H.M. & Conway Morris, S. 1990. *Solnhofen. A Study in Mesozoic Palaeontology.* Cambridge University Press, Cambridge.

Briggs, D.E.G. & Crowther, P.R. (eds) 1990. *Palaeobiology – A Synthesis.* Blackwell Scientific Publications, Oxford.

Clarkson, E.N.K. 1993. *Invertebrate Palaeontology and Evolution.* Third edition. Chapman & Hall, London.

Dodd, J.R. & Stanton, R.J. 1990. *Paleoecology. Concepts and Applications.* Second edition. John Wiley, New York.

Donovan, S.K. (ed.) 1991. *The Processes of Fossilisation.* Belhaven Press, London.

Whittington, H.B. & Conway Morris, S. (eds) 1985. Extraordinary fossil biotas: their ecological and evolutionary significance. *Philosophical Transactions of the Royal Society of London,* **B311,** 1–192.

Ziegler, B. 1983. *Introduction to Palaeobiology. General Palaeontology.* Ellis Horwood, Chichester.

3
Fossils as Living Organisms

This chapter introduces the concept of fossils as once living organisms, and explains how we can interpret their life, and the nature of their environment, from the fossil record.

3.1 EARLY CONCEPTS OF FOSSILS

Fossils have long been been collected and prized by human beings, but they have not always been considered as once living organisms. Fossils have passed into folklore as objects which have been used to help cure sick people or animals, to keep away evil spirits, or to improve success with the opposite sex. These mystical associations date from at least the Middle Ages, a time when the origin of fossils was unknown. As a best guess, the early natural philosophers thought that fossils resembled living organisms, but that they were some kind of failed attempt at life, mimics planted on the Earth by pervasive vapours which passed through it. As to their purpose, most early observers envisaged that they were placed in the solid rocks of the Earth to test the faith of human beings in God. In effect, early scientists had recognised the resemblance of fossils to living organisms, but were not ready to make the conceptual leap to explain their origin through natural processes.

This leap was made in the sixteenth and seventeenth centuries. Scientists of the day cast aside the mystical association of fossil objects and were unwilling to accept that the resemblance of fossil objects to living organisms was nothing more than a divine test or coincidence. Instead, scientists such as Conrad Gesner (1516–1565) and Niels Stensen built the scientific credentials of palaeontology and the interpretation of fossils as living organisms. Gesner instituted the systematic study of fossils; in his book *De Rerum Fossilium Lapidum et Gemmarum* (1565) he used illustrations with descriptions and referred to a collection of appropriate specimens. He also sponsored steps towards a proper interchange of ideas with scientists across the known world. Stensen was the first person to really appreciate the organic origin of fossils through the application of **comparative anatomy**, a science perfected much later, but entailing the comparison of the form and function of one natural object with another. Stensen compared fossils known as Glossopetrae (tongue stones) with the teeth of a recent shark and came to the conclusion that the two were of the same origin. The birth of palaeontology as a science can arguably be traced to these two men.

Acceptance of fossils as once living animals or plants followed on quickly from Stensen's discovery, and the seventeenth and eighteenth centuries saw a struggle to reconcile the biological origin of fossils with biblical events. Observers suggested that most fossils were the product of Noah's Flood which drowned the landscape and brought with it the living creatures of the sea. One, Johann Scheuchzer (1672–1733), even went as far as recognising the body of a human 'sinner' in the rocks of Germany which he called *Homo diluvii testis* – a witness to the flood – now in fact known to be the fossil remains of a large amphibian. However, the final acceptance that there had been a succession of organisms through time which were unrelated to a single flood was primarily the result of the labours of one man, Georges Cuvier (1769–1832). Cuvier perfected the technique of comparative anatomy, through which he was able to pronounce that the Siberian mammoth was actually a separate species of elephant which was now extinct. This was the first time that species extinction had been proved to exist in the geological past. With further study, Cuvier and others confirmed that fossils were mostly the remains of biological species which had become extinct, and that it was possible to recognise a succession of extinct animal and plant species through geological time. As a result of these labours, by the end of the eighteenth and beginning of the nineteenth centuries, scientists were confident in naming biological species on the basis of fossil remains and assigning them to living families, orders and so on.

3.2 THE CONCEPT OF THE SPECIES IN PALAEONTOLOGY

Early scientists had long struggled with a satisfactory classification of fossils. The first attempts defined groups on the basis of colour or texture, for example, mostly with reference to their mineral structure. However, later observers considered that closer comparison with living organisms was possible, and characters such as shape, and the form and function of body parts, became more important. At this point, scientists began to describe fossils in much the same way as living organisms, and to consider them as ancient biological species.

In biology, the term **species** is used to illustrate morphological (e.g. shape and size), behavioural (e.g. birdsong and hibernation) and genetic differences between organisms, and as such is generally accepted as the natural taxonomic unit. A modern definition of a biological species would be 'a group of individuals that look alike and that are able successfully to interbreed to produce fertile young'. In palaeontology, the interpretation of fossils as biological species is important to the interpretation of ancient environments. However, without the aid of a time machine, it is impossible to determine whether groups of fossils were able successfully to interbreed, although individual sexes have been recognised for some fossil groups (Figure 3.1). The determination of true species, tricky enough in living organisms, is especially difficult in fossils. Palaeontologists have to rely heavily upon the first part of the definition of species, and recognise groups which look like each other. Therefore the morphology of a fossil group has the greatest importance in palaeontology, and the accurate recognition of new species is reliant on stringent methods to identify accurately both differences and similarities in shape and form.

Three methods can be used to determine species in palaeontology: **morphological resemblance**, **biometry** and **shape analysis**. All three are effectively different components of the same process: the analysis of morphology. Morphological resemblance is the traditional method, reliant upon the visual observation of similarities and simple measurement. The human eye is a powerful tool in distinguishing small shape differences, but this method has been often criticised because of the in-built subjectivity of the observer. Biometry employs a set of detailed measurements of shape and skeletal characters in order to determine

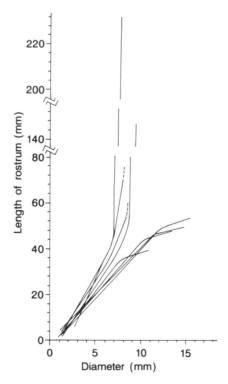

Figure 3.1   *Growth curves showing sexual dimorphism in the belemnite genus* Youngibelus *from the Lower Jurassic of Yorkshire. At the onset of sexual maturity the two belemnites diverge in shape [Reproduced with permission from: Doyle (1985)* Palaeontology, *28, Fig. 3, p. 142]*

similarities and differences. Measured characters are then compared against one (bivariate) or more (multivariate) other characters and a numerical signature for an individual group can be determined. Bivariate analysis generally involves comparison of simple measurable parameters such as height and width to characterise shape. For some shapes this is appropriate (Figure 3.2), but for most others more detailed comparison of a range of characters is necessary. Critics of this method suggest that some characters cannot be adequately measured and therefore some of the most important characteristics of a species may be left out of the

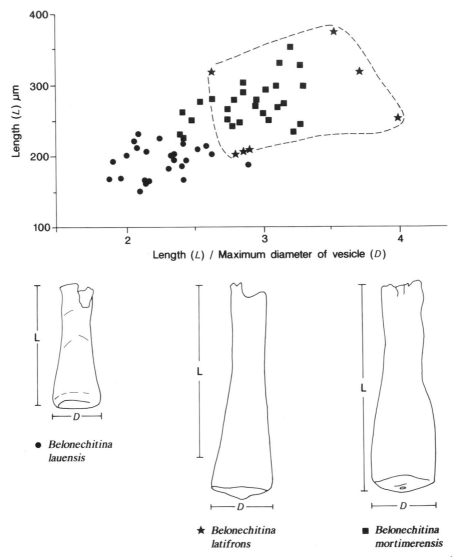

Figure 3.2   *Bivariate plot showing the morphology of three species of chitinozoan (probable algal cysts) from the Lower Palaeozoic of England [Modified from: Sutherland (1994), Monographs of the Palaeontographical Society, **591**, Fig. 25, p. 43]*

analysis. Shape analysis is a development of the other two methods. It utilises detailed measurements but relies upon computer programs to compare the detailed three-dimensional shape of the organism studied. This method is relatively new, and has had its greatest application so far in the comparison of microfossil species.

In all methods of determining species, palaeontologists strive to be rigorous. This is especially important since individuals within a species can vary dramatically in their shape and form, and in some cases the individuals at each end of a range of **intraspecific variation** may not closely resemble each other. For example, think of the variation created by selective breeding within the dog *Canis familiaris*. From a single ancestral stock, and within a biological species, the variation is dramatic: from the smallest Chihuahua to the largest St Bernard. Both belong to the same species, and could, theoretically at least, interbreed. A visitor to the Earth may yet be tempted to treat these morphological types as separate species. Although slightly artificial, this example is representative of a fundamental problem in palaeontology: where does one draw the boundary between morphological types when there is no hope of observing an interbreeding population? The only answer is to examine as many specimens as possible from a single sedimentary horizon – a bedding plane, effectively the ancient sea bed. The bedding plane assemblage represents the closest approximation to a population, and therefore to the morphological range of individuals living at the same time, that can be achieved in palaeontology. In fact, such an assemblage will include at least several generations, and if the rate of sedimentation has been exceedingly slow, then it may actually represent the accumulated bodies of several million years. However, the study of such assemblages is necessary in order to be aware of the potential morphological variation in any palaeontological species.

3.3 TAXONOMIC HIERARCHY: THE SYSTEM OF NATURE

The species is the standard unit of **taxonomy**, the subject which defines the natural morphological and behavioural boundaries between organisms and provides a system for comparing them. Taxonomy is also called **systematics** because of this. The formal basis for taxonomy is discussed in Box 3.1.

Through taxonomy scientists can gain a true understanding of the form and diversity of life on Earth, both in the geological past and in the present. The taxonomic system is a hierarchical one, with similar species grouped into genera, genera into families and so on. Effectively the hierarchical system is a way of illustrating **similarity** and **ancestry**. This may be most rigorously carried out through the application of **cladistics**, sometimes called **phylogenetic systematics**. This technique, described in Box 3.2, involves the determination of the evolutionary relationship of organisms through an objective analysis of shared characters. Cladistics therefore allows the recognition of taxonomic groups with a common ancestor, which should form the basis for a properly founded classification.

The largest subdivisions of the taxonomic system are the **kingdoms** (animal, plant, and so on) and the **phyla** (molluscs, arthropods, etc.). These were the first

BOX 3.1: TAXONOMY

Modern taxonomy can be traced to the genius of one man, Carolus Linnaeus (1707–1778). Linnaeus devised a system for classifying organisms which could be used and understood across the world, a true scientific language which transcended all other language barriers. The Linnaean system is very straight-forward, and is based on a hierarchical approach. Although modified and extended, and subject to an international bureaucracy, Linnaeus's scheme is fundamental to both biology and palaeontology.

The scheme has several important rules. Firstly, the species is identified by not one name, but two, denoted by *italic* script. The actual species is the second of the two names, the first of the two being the **genus**, the first of many hierarchical terms denoting similarities between species and other groupings. Secondly, the definition of a new species has to be widely accepted by the international community. Therefore, it has to be made widely available through **publication** in books or journals. This usually has to contain a *diagnosis*, defining the main characters of the species, a fuller *description*, and an *illustration* of the species itself. On publication, the author's name and the date of publication are usually appended to the species name, in order to assist future researchers. Finally, the species has to be tied to a permanent point of reference, a **type specimen**, which should be clearly identified in the original publication and preserved for posterity in a museum, to allow comparison with other specimens and to assist in further study.

Unfortunately, many species are described in this way more than once. This results in more than one name for the same group of organisms, and the **principle of priority** is used to determine which name should be used, the first name having the priority, and any younger name being a junior **synonym**. In some cases, usually very confusing, the *same name* may be given to two completely different species. In this case, the principle of priority determines that the first to be given the name retains it, and the second has then to be renamed. Where disputes arise, the **International Commissions for Zoological and Botanical Nomenclature** can be called upon to give a ruling.

Source: International Commission for Zoological Nomenclature (1985) *The International Code for Zoological Nomenclature*. British Museum (Natural History), London.

groupings of organisms to appear on Earth, and their diversification through time is illustrated by the number of smaller subdivisions which appeared as evolution proceeded. Therefore, the hierarchical system represents the evolution of life on Earth, and, as such, it may be represented as a branching tree, from the stem of the kingdoms and phyla to the branches of genera and species (Figure 3.3). Both fossil and living organisms may be represented by this tree.

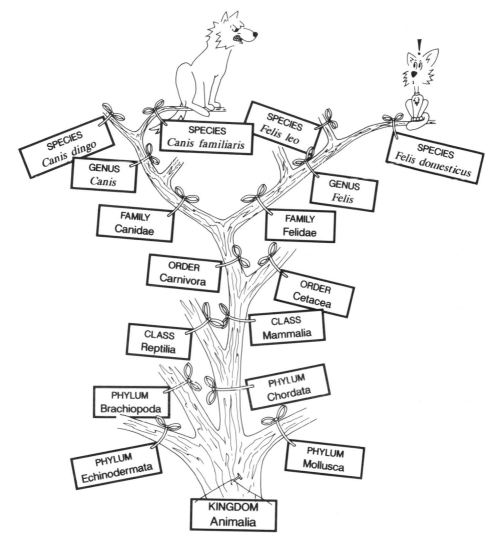

Figure 3.3 *Cartoon demonstrating the concept of taxonomic hierarchy*

3.4 TAXONOMIC UNIFORMITARIANISM: THE BASIS FOR RECONSTRUCTION OF FOSSIL ORGANISMS

Fossils may be classified using their morphological characteristics as species, and placed within a hierarchical classification, but what tools enable us to interpret fossils as once living organisms? **Uniformitarianism** is a fundamental geological principle that is also the basis for all reconstructions of the mode of life and habitat of fossils. It can be summarised using the phrase 'the present is the key to the past'. In geology, uniformitarianism, or **actualism** as it is sometimes called,

BOX 3.2: CLADISTICS

Cladistics is a method of grouping organisms through determining their common ancestry. The basis for cladistics is that only strictly **monophyletic groups** (comprising all the descendants of a common ancestor) represent valid biological entities. These groups (called **clades** – clusters of branching lineages) are diagnosed and identified by new evolutionary features (derived characters or **synapomorphies**) which evolved in the ancestor and passed to the descendants. By contrast, **paraphyletic groups** do not include all the descendants, while **polyphyletic groups** cluster organisms which do not possess a common ancestor, and neither are valid biological entities. The end result of a cladistic

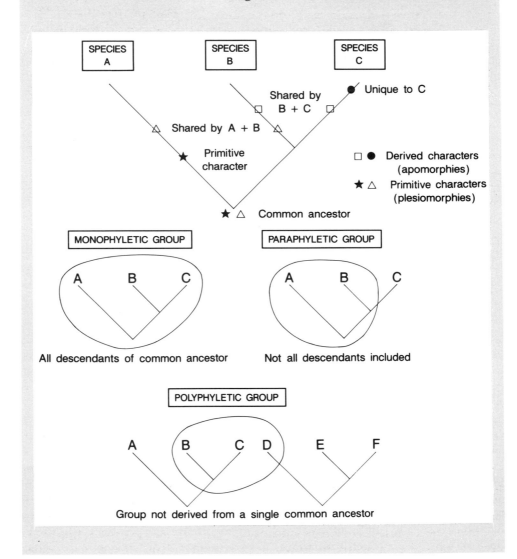

BOX 3.2: (*cont.*)

analysis is a branching diagram known as a **cladogram**. The cladogram shows the closeness of relationship by the arrangement of the groups – the shorter the links on the diagram, the closer is the relationship.

A cladistic analysis of a group of taxa is begun by selecting characters which can be analysed for their **polarity**, that is, the direction of evolution from a primitive to a derived state. Characters which are anatomically and functionally equivalent (**homologous**) are compared in a number of groups in order that the recency of their common ancestry can be established. In simple terms, this means ordering the groups on the cladogram so that the taxa on immediately adjacent branches have the most derived characters in common. The cladogram does not strictly represent an evolutionary tree (a **phylogeny**) as an analysis can be carried out without reference to the stratigraphy, and living representatives of organisms with primitive character states can be compared with fossil representatives with a greater number of derived characteristics, for example. Transformation of a cladogram into a tree involves the application of the stratigraphical relationships.

Cladistics is an extremely important technique with a great range of possible applications. Most importantly, it can predict the evolutionary history of living forms with a limited fossil record, or be used to determine the geographical relationship of fossil groups through the application of similar clustering techniques. Above all, cladistics provides a rigorous approach to the classification of organisms on the basis of their phylogenetic relationships.

Sources: Padian, K., Lindberg, D.R. and Polly, P.D. (1994). Cladistics and the fossil record: the uses of history. *Annual Reviews of Earth and Planetary Science*, **22**, 63–91. Smith, A.B. (1994). *Systematics and the Fossil Record*. Blackwell Scientific Publications, Oxford.

allows scientists to interpret rock bodies as the product of an ancient environment. This process entails the comparison of the products of present-day environments with those of the geological past, the rock bodies. For example, a present-day desert environment contains dunes and desert lakes; the rock record contains sandstones with the internal structures of sand dunes and fine-grained lake sediments with desiccation cracks. From this comparison geologists can make the assumption that the environmental conditions operating in the present-day environment are those which created the rock record.

Taxonomic uniformitarianism utilises the same basic principle, but applied to the biological components of an environment. It assumes that the study of present-day organisms holds the key to interpreting the shape, form and life history of the organisms in the geological past. Taxonomic uniformitarianism assumes that the fossil remains of animals and plants which resemble organisms alive today also functioned in a similar manner and lived in similar

Figure 3.4   *Mid-Victorian reconstructions of the dinosaur* Iguanodon *in Crystal Palace Park in southeast London. As reconstructed, these are scaled-up versions of the living* Iguana *[Photograph: P. Doyle]*

environments. At its most detailed level this entails the use of **comparative anatomy**, the comparison of individual components or body parts of both fossil and living organisms. A classic illustration of the use of comparative anatomy was the comparison of the fossil teeth of the first dinosaur to be discovered, *Iguanodon*, with those of the modern lizard, *Iguana*, by Gideon Mantell in 1825. Although the teeth are very different in size, they have broadly the same shape and form, adapted to slicing coarse vegetation. The comparison of these teeth therefore led to the consideration that *Iguanodon* (literally '*Iguana*-tooth') was really a scaled-up, extinct, version of *Iguana* (Figure 3.4).

Taxonomic uniformitarianism has three important functions. Firstly, it provides a mechanism for the interpretation of **functional morphology**. This is the consideration of the function of individual body parts of fossils through comparison with similar or comparable (**homologous**) body parts in living organisms. Secondly, it provides the tool for the interpretation of fossil assemblages as ancient ecologies. It is therefore the basis for **palaeoecology**. Thirdly, taxonomic uniformitarianism is the basis for broad-scale interpretation of ancient environments, **palaeoenvironmental analysis**.

The accuracy of the uniformitarian approach is constrained by geological time and evolution. Effectively, the more recent the fossil, the greater the chance that there is an organism which closely resembles it living in the present day. With increasing age, comparisons become more difficult, and in many cases, especially with the most ancient rocks, interpretation is more a matter of inspired guesswork

(Box 3.3). More subtle is the possibility that certain organisms have evolved and changed their environmental preferences through geological time, and live today in very different environments than they did in the geological past without significant morphological change.

The uniformitarian approach is also directly applicable to the interpretation of trace fossils. Trace fossils may be classified according to **ethology**, that is, the study of the behaviour of organisms. This is interpreted directly from the traces preserved in the fossil record (Figure 3.5). Some are obvious, such as the footprints of dinosaurs, but others are less so, and require the examination of modern equivalents. In many cases the problems encountered with the changes in the ecological tolerances of body fossils through geological time are not encountered with trace fossils, as the morphology and environment of trace fossils appear to have remained conservative. In general, broadly similar groups of organisms, producing broadly similar sets of tracks and trails, can be encountered throughout the geological record of life on Earth.

3.5 INTRODUCTION TO PALAEOECOLOGY

Ecology can be defined as the study of the interaction of organisms with each other and with their environment. **Palaeoecology** can be defined as the study of the interaction of fossil organisms with each other and with the environment in which they lived *in the geological past*. Like ecology, palaeoecology is extremely

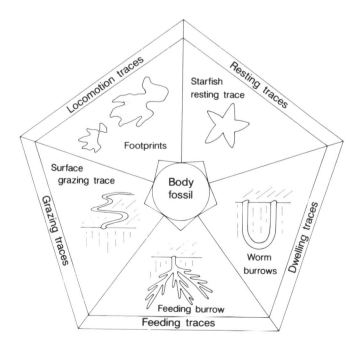

Figure 3.5   *The ethological classification of trace fossils*

BOX 3.3: THE TALE OF *HALLUCIGENIA*

Hallucigenia is a peculiar, soft-bodied animal preserved as one of the assemblage of organisms within the Cambrian Burgess Shale of British Columbia, Canada. It was named by Simon Conway Morris (1977), the name indicating that it seemed to belong in a nightmare. The organism was preserved flattened, its body outline given by a pyrite coating. There appeared to be a blob at one end, a tentacle at the other. Along one side there was a single row of what appeared to be sinuous tentacles, along the other a double row of spike-like appendages. No organism exists like this in the present day. Conway Morris was forced to consider the functional morphology of each of the parts. The blob was interpreted as a head, the tentacle as the organism's anal region. The spike-like appendages were paired and are therefore likely to represent the limbs, the row of tentacles some sort of protective or feeding mechanism.

Recently, a discovery in rocks of the same age in China has lead to the reinvestigation of the functional morphology of this strange animal (Bengtson 1991). Here, a similar fossil was discovered which indicated that *Hallucigenia* actually possessed two rows of tentacle-like appendages. With the benefit of

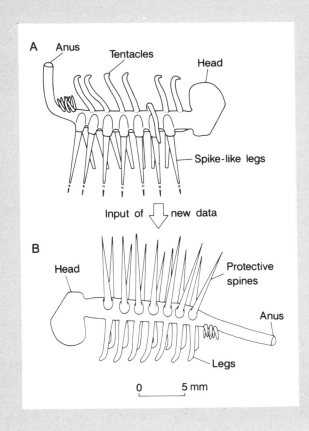

BOX 3.3: (*cont.*)

this discovery the reconstruction could be turned upside-down; the spike-like limbs were probably defensive spines, the double row of tentacles probably walking limbs. This example shows how functional morphology may be used to reconstruct the life of an ancient unknown organism, and how new discoveries can change our perspective.

Source: Conway Morris, S. (1977). A new metazoan from the Cambrian Burgess Shale of British Columbia. *Palaeontology*, **20**, 623–640; Bengston, S. (1991). Oddballs from the Cambrian start to get even. *Nature*, **351**, 184–185.

important in determining the nature of the biosphere and in recording changes in environment. Palaeoecology is therefore one of the most important tools in determining the nature and evolution of the ancient world.

The basis for interpreting ancient ecologies is taxonomic uniformitarianism, the interpretation of ancient fossil assemblages in the light of modern-day communities. There are two branches to palaeoecology, the relationship of groups of organisms to each other and to their environment (**palaeosynecology**), and the relationship of individual or small groups of organisms to their environment (**palaeoautecology**). Trace fossils have a special role to play in palaeoecology, as they represent the interaction of organisms with the sedimentary environment. Together the study of the ecological relationships of body fossils and trace fossils are of paramount importance in **palaeoenvironmental analysis**.

3.5.1 Palaeosynecology

Palaeosynecology is concerned with the relationship of groups of organisms with each other and their environment. In biology, this forms much of the detailed subject matter of ecology. In particular, it is concerned with the study of **communities**. A community is defined as a group of organisms from one or more species that occupy the same habitat in life. The identification of living communities is relatively straightforward, as it is possible to examine in detail a particular habitat (e.g. freshwater lake, lagoon and reef) and observe directly the interaction of its constituent organisms. In palaeoecology, however, identification of communities is much more difficult. Relatively few fossils are found in their life position. Most have been transported, and some may be derived from a completely different habitat. It is preferable to use the term **assemblage** to describe a grouping of fossils preserved in a given rock unit, as it may not necessarily reflect the nature of the original community. Recurring assemblages suggest a greater ecological significance, and these are referred to as **associations**.

Most importantly, it must always be remembered that all fossil assemblages are **death assemblages**, as only in exceptional circumstances do they come anywhere near the nature of the living community, the **life assemblage**. As Derek Ager put it in his book, *Principles of Palaeoecology* (1963):

> The palaeoecologist must never forget that he or she is studying not the living inhabitants of the village but only the bodies in the churchyard, and then only after many visits by grave robbers. Usually the fossil assemblage bears very little re-semblance to the living community which it represents.

For example, in most fossil assemblages, there will not only be allochthonous fossils present that were not native to the original community, but in most cases the soft-bodied organisms will be absent. Only Lagerstätten can come close to representing the living assemblage as it originally existed, but even then al-lochthonous fossils may be present, and other organisms absent.

Individual relationships between species may be recognised more confidently in the fossil record. Four common species relationships may be recognised: **com-mensalism**, **mutualism**, **parasitism** and **epibiosis** (Figure 3.6). All four are repres-entative of **symbiosis**, a situation where two different species live in close association with each other, with either beneficial or harmful consequences for at least one of the partners, although epibiosis does not necessarily involve two living species. **Commensalism** is when two species coexist without harm to each other. One of the partners may gain from the relationship, but the other suffers no disadvantage. **Mutualism** is a relationship where both partners gain without disadvantage to each other, an important example being the presence of algae (zooxanthellae) within the bodies of reef-building corals. In the simplest terms, the algae benefit from carbon dioxide given off from the corals; the corals benefit from the oxygen given off from the zooxanthellae. Another example of mutualism

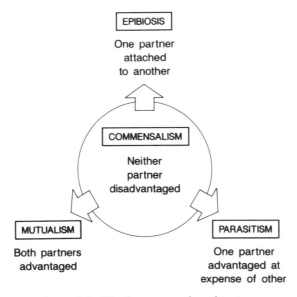

Figure 3.6   *The four types of symbiosis*

is discussed in Box 3.4. **Parasitism** is where one partner benefits at the expense of another. Parasites can live both on the surface of the host, or within its body. As already mentioned, cysts illustrating the infestation of crinoid shells by parasites are relatively common in the fossil record. **Epibiosis** is where one organism (the epibiont) lives attached to another. The epibiont is effectively attaching itself to a firm substrate, and it is unimportant whether that substrate is living or dead. Common examples are the encrustation of living mollusc shells (oysters, for example) by worms. Where growth of an epibiont interferes with the life cycle of the host, epibiosis grades into parasitism. In addition to symbiosis, it is possible to recognise **predation**, the consumption of one organism by another, and it is possible to recognise the effects of predation on both fossil plants and animals (Box 2.2).

3.5.2 Palaeoautecology

Palaeoautecology is concerned with the relationship of individual or small groups of organisms to their environment, and particularly their response to a series of external factors which limit their **diversity** and **distribution**. These factors are known as **limiting factors**, and they are extremely valuable in the interpretation of the nature of ancient ecologies and in palaeoenvironmental analysis. The basis for this interpretation is in taxonomic uniformitarianism, as the response of living organisms to limiting factors may be directly compared to close relatives in the geological past. As before, the time factor is of paramount importance, and with increasing age, the confidence levels for the interpretation of response to limiting factors decrease.

Some of the most significant limiting factors are: **light, climate, oxygen, salinity, water depth, substrate, water turbulence** and **food supply**. In most cases these factors are closely interrelated, and the diversity and distribution of organisms may be controlled by several such factors. **Light** promotes photosynthesis and is therefore important to the success of plants and the food chains that they support. Light is more intense at the Equator, and the angle of incidence of the sunlight reaching the Earth decreases towards the poles. This has great bearing on the success of photosynthesising plants, for example, and the densest vegetation is situated at the equator. Light is directly related to **climate**, and in particular temperature. There is an appreciable temperature gradient, decreasing from the Equator to the poles, at the present time, and this has the effect of limiting the distribution of both terrestrial and aquatic organisms. **Oxygen** is an important limiter, as in environments with reduced oxygen, e.g. stagnant, anaerobic water bodies, faunal diversity is often dramatically reduced. **Salinity** is of great significance to aquatic organisms. Although some organisms can survive in freshwater and marine water conditions, and others can manage in brackish conditions, normal salinity is essential to most marine organisms. Aquatic organisms are also limited by **water depth**, largely because the deepest waters have the least amount of light penetration, although free-swimming organisms such as ammonites may also be limited by increasing water pressure. Of particular importance to bottom-

BOX 3.4: HYDRACTINIANS AND HERMIT CRABS: SYMBIOSIS IN THE FOSSIL RECORD

Some ecological relationships between organisms are easy to deduce in the fossil record. Serpulid worm tubes are commonly found cemented to a host oyster or gastropod, and examples of such epibiosis are easily identified. Parasitic cysts are common enough in crinoid stems. Such physical relationships are easy to recognise and interpret; deducing commensalism or mutualism is another matter. In both cases, taxonomic uniformitarianism holds the key to interpreting the record.

Olivero and Aguirre-Uretta (1994) described a symbiotic relationship between a hydractinian, a type of coral characteristically forming an encrusting colony made of globular chambers, and a hermit crab. Hermit crabs usually inhabit empty gastropod shells, but as they grow they have to leave the safety of their shelter in order to find a bigger shell to live in. Hydractinians have to attach themselves to a hard substrate, and are often attached to gastropods. Olivero and Aguirre-Urreta discovered an unusual hydractinian in the Upper Cretaceous rocks of Antarctica. This animal was seen to construct a special spiral chamber during its growth, and the Antarctic fossils were seen to contain the claws and other remains of hermit crabs. In the present day, hermit crabs are known to live in symbiosis with a range of organisms, particularly sea anemones. Here, the sea anemone lives attached to the gastropod shell within which lives the hermit crab. Both parties benefit: the hermit crab is protected by the stinging tentacles of the anemone, while the anemone gains waste food from the crab. When the crab has to move, it takes the sea anemone with it,

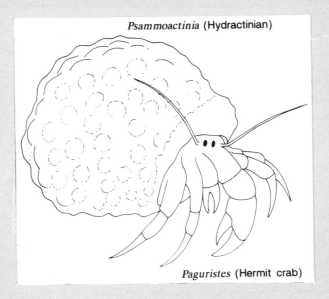

Psammoactinia (Hydractinian)

Paguristes (Hermit crab)

BOX 3.4: (*cont.*)

re-establishing the relationship once a suitable shell is found. Using such recent examples, Olivero and Aguirre-Urreta interpreted the hydractinian–crab symbiotic relationship as mutualism. The growth of the hydractinian colony and the creation of its spiral chamber were seen as a positive advantage to the crab; it would no longer have to move as its growth was matched by that of the hydractinian. The hydractinian, similar to the sea anemone, gains a firm substrate and food from the crab.

Source: Olivero, E.B. and Aguirre-Urreta, M.B. (1994) A new tube-builder hydractinian, symbiotic with hermit crabs, from the Cretaceous of Antarctica. *Journal of Paleontology*, **68**, 1169–1182. [Illustration modified from: Olivero and Aguirre-Urreta (1994) *Journal of Paleontology*, **68**, Fig. 1, p. 1170]

dwelling organisms is the nature of the **substrate**, which, for example, determines whether they are able to construct burrows, or live on a firm surface without sinking. Substrate is important for bottom-dwelling aquatic organisms; if a substrate is too soft or too hard the organism may not be able to burrow or graze. In most cases, substrate is interlinked with **turbulence**, which is important to some suspension feeders which require continuous agitation of suspended food particles. Finally, **food supply** is of great importance to living organisms, as it determines their success or failure in a given environment. The greatest diversity of marine organisms may be found on the continental shelf, within the zone known as the **photic zone** (Box 3.5). This is the depth of maximum light penetration, approximately 200 m, and the Photic Zone is the area of greatest food resources for many marine organisms.

Limiting factors directly influence the distribution and diversity of living organisms. **Biotic factors**, the interaction between organisms, particularly in the competition for habitat space, and in the distribution of prey and predators, for example, may also limit organisms. However, their influence is often difficult to detect in the geological record. On a small scale, both sets of factors may affect individuals or communities, while on a much larger scale they have a direct influence on the distribution of plants and animals across the globe, the subject of **biogeography** and its geological counterpart, **palaeobiogeography** (Box 3.6). The distribution of organisms is of particular relevance to palaeobiogeography. Here it is recognised that some fossil groups, like many living species, are restricted in distribution. For example, the Southern Beech, *Nothofagus*, was restricted to the high latitudes of the Southern Hemisphere continents of the Cretaceous, the remnants of the supercontinent of Gondwana, and is found in similar regions today (Figure 3.7).

Diversity is a valuable indicator of the nature and hostility of an environment, and, together with the density or abundance of individuals of a particular species, is an important palaeoecological tool (Figure 3.8). Generally, environments of a

BOX 3.5: CLASSIFICATION OF MARINE ENVIRONMENTS

The majority of fossils are found in marine sediments that have been deposited in water in depths of up to 200 m, upon the submerged continental shelf which surrounds the continental masses of the Earth. The total area of continental shelf available has fluctuated through geological time. For example, during the Cretaceous, a time of ice-free 'greenhouse' climate, sea levels were at an all-time high, with a much greater amount of epicontinental sea. Continental shelves are therefore the most important elements of the marine environment, but others exist.

Marine environments can be classified on the basis of **topography** and **water depth**. In topographical terms, the marine environment can be divided into five components: coastal zone; continental shelf; continental slope; abyssal plain; and trench. Water depth is related to topography: littoral (between low and high tide marks in the coastal zone); sublittoral (equivalent to the continental shelf, descending 200 m); bathyal (continental slope, 200–4000 m deep); abyssal (abyssal plain, 4000–5000 m deep); and hadal (trench, descending deeper than 5000 m). The boundary between the continental shelf and the continental slope is especially important as this marks the effective limit of light penetration, the boundary between the photic and aphotic zones.

Marine organisms can be classified on the basis of their relationship with the **substrate**. There are three types: benthonic, restricted to the sea floor; planktonic, which are free-floating; and nektonic, which are free-swimming. These may be further grouped into: neritic organisms restricted to the continental shelf, including benthonic, planktonic and nektonic organisms; and pelagic organisms, which include planktonic and nektonic organisms restricted to the surface waters of the open ocean.

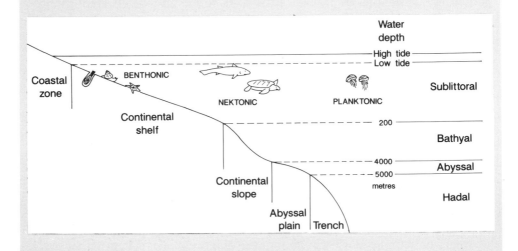

BOX 3.6: PALAEOBIOGEOGRAPHY

Palaeobiogeography is the study of the distribution of plants and organisms across the world in the ancient past. It has as its goal the determination of these distribution patterns, and the interpretation of the factors which limited the geographical range of ancient organisms. In some cases, particularly in the ancient past, such distribution patterns are powerful tools in their own right in determining the configuration of ancient continental areas, for example. As an example, it is now well known that an ocean, **Iapetus**, existed during the early Palaeozoic which separated the continent of Laurasia (North America plus Scotland) from Baltica (Scandinavia) and Avalonia (including England).

The existence of this ocean was first determined by J.T. Wilson in 1966 on the basis of the distribution patterns of trilobites. Wilson noticed that the trilobites of Scotland were wholly different from those of England, and that the Scottish trilobites closely resembled those of the same age in North America, rather than Europe. If England and Scotland had been joined in the Palaeozoic, then the two groups would surely have been mixed. Wilson therefore concluded that a deep ocean separated these trilobites, which they could not cross, and that England and Scotland only became united in the later Palaeozoic. In this case, the distribution of the trilobites was recorded, the factors limiting their distribution interpreted (the presence of an ocean), and this led to an important geological discovery.

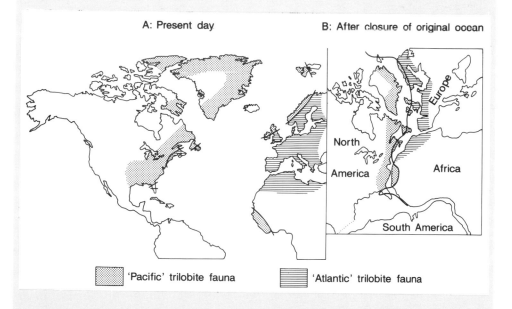

A: Present day   B: After closure of original ocean

North America Africa

South America

'Pacific' trilobite fauna   'Atlantic' trilobite fauna

Source: Wilson, J.T. (1966). Did the Atlantic close and then re-open? *Nature*, **211**, 676–681. Newton, C.R. (1990). Palaeobiogeography. *In* Briggs, D.E.G. and Crowther, P.R. (eds) *Palaeobiology – A Synthesis*, Blackwell, Oxford, 452–460. [Figure modified from: Wilson (1966) *Nature*, **211**, Fig. 1, p. 676]

Figure 3.7   *The Southern Beech,* Nothofagus. *This genus was restricted to southern high latitudes in the Cretaceous and lives in similar environments today in Patagonia [Photograph: N.F. Glasser]*

relatively hostile nature, such as those with high or low salinities or low oxygen, are characterised by an assemblage which is low in diversity, often being monospecific. Conversely, abundance of individuals may be high. In these stressed environments, most taxa are excluded, including most predators, so that the available resources are used by a limited number of successful species. This leads to the development of the low diversity but high density of the assemblage. Often, the colonisation of such habitats may be rapid, the species concerned being **opportunists**.

In less limited environments, such as normal marine salinities and fully oxygenated conditions, the diversity of species may be high, but the abundance of individuals may be correspondingly lower. This reflects the partitioning of the same resources available to the low-diversity assemblage between a greater number of species, with a corresponding increase in predators. In such environments, although there are many species producing young, density is kept low through the competition for resources, and by the action of the predators. Species in these environments are known as **equilibrium species**, maintained in equilibrium by the quantity of the resource.

3.5.3 The Role of Trace Fossils in Palaeoecology

The study of trace fossils (**ichnology**) is extremely important to palaeoecology for three reasons. Firstly, trace fossils are conservative; the same types of traces are

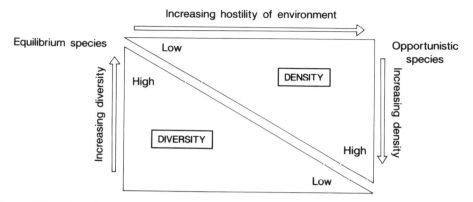

Figure 3.8 *The relationship of density and diversity. In the most hostile environments, communities commonly display a low diversity, composed of opportunistic species which reproduce rapidly. Under normal conditions, communities may be more stable and diverse, composed of equilibrium species with less need to reproduce rapidly and in great numbers*

intimately associated with certain sedimentary environments throughout geological time. Secondly, trace fossils are usually found *in situ*, and are therefore more reliable indicators of the actual living communities than body fossils, which are often reworked or transported. Thirdly, trace fossils can be illustrative of the presence of soft-bodied organisms in an environment, and in some cases may be the only fossil record within a given sedimentary environment. Clearly, trace fossils are consistent in demonstrating the activity of organisms in direct relationship with their sedimentary environments. The results of the trace producers in disturbing the sedimentary fabric through burrowing are usually referred to as **bioturbation**.

Trace producers were subject to the same range of limiting factors as any other organisms, and these have determined the abundance and diversity of trace fossils. Specific trace fossil assemblages, called **ichnofacies**, can often be associated with certain sedimentary facies suggestive of overall control by particular limiting factors, such as salinity or oxygenation. For example, at least four assemblages of marine trace fossils appear to have a relationship with depth and substrate throughout geological history, and consequently a series of depth-related ichnofacies have been determined (Box 3.7). In these and other cases, the study of the abundance and diversity of the trace fossil assemblage can be used as a kind of yardstick with which to measure the intensity of operation of a given limiting factor. Working examples of this process are discussed in Part III of this book.

3.5.4 Palaeoenvironmental Analysis

Palaeoenvironmental analysis is the determination of the nature of the ancient environment using the sediments and their palaeoecology. Effectively it entails piecing together, fragment by fragment, the nature of ancient environments from all the available evidence. The sedimentary rocks themselves provide the most

BOX 3.7: PALAEOBATHYMETRY FROM TRACE FOSSILS

It is now commonly accepted that trace fossil assemblages in marine sedimentary rocks are related to the relative depth of the depositional environment. This follows the work of Adolf Seilacher, who recognised that there were a relatively small number of communities of trace fossils which appear limited to different sedimentary facies. Seilacher recognised five distinct assemblages. In coarse, shallow marine sediments the traces were largely simple dwelling burrows of worms (e.g. *Skolithos*). Within shelf marine sediments the traces were indicative of a range of crawling (e.g. *Cruziana*), feeding and more complex dwelling traces. Turbidite sequences commonly contained the complex sediment-mining trace *Zoophycos*, while submarine fan sediments were characterised by complex winding, surface-grazing traces (e.g. *Nereites*). Although it is now accepted that the *Skolithos*-type traces are capable of developing in coarse sediments offshore, the *Skolithos, Cruziana, Zoophycos* and *Nereites* trace fossil biofacies (ichnofacies) are broadly accepted as representative of progressively more offshore environments, as illustrated. These ichnofacies are therefore powerful tools in palaeoenvironmental analysis.

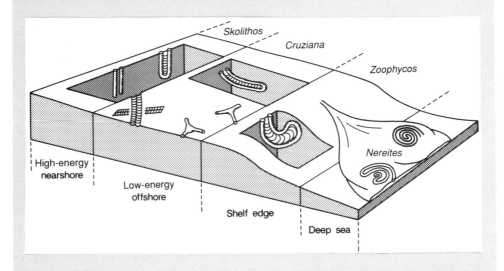

Source: Seilacher, A. (1967) Bathymetry of trace fossils. *Marine Geology* **5**, 413–428. [Diagram reproduced from: Doyle *et al.* (1994), *The Key to Earth History*, Wiley, Box 5.7, p. 97]

important environmental evidence in determining the nature of an ancient environment. The original environment of deposition of each sedimentary rock body may be deduced through the concept of **sedimentary facies**: the sum total of all the characteristics of a rock unit. Sedimentary facies are identified on the basis of **rock type, sedimentary structure** (ripple marks and dune bedding, for example), **rock-body geometry** and **fossil content**.

Uniformitarianism is the theoretical basis for the interpretation of sedimentary facies. It is possible to observe both processes and products of sedimentary environments today, but in the rock record we have only the product. Comparison of the characteristics of ancient and modern sediments is therefore an extremely important tool in environmental interpretation. Lithology can give direct evidence of environment. For example, we know that coral limestones form in fully marine conditions, while red, oxidised sandstones form mostly on land. Equally, comparison of ancient and modern sedimentary structures provides information as diverse as palaeowind or flow directions; while geometry determines whether the environment was spatially limited, a river channel for example.

Fossils are an integral part of sedimentary facies and palaeoecology is one of the most important components of palaeoenvironmental analysis. This is simply because palaeoecology involves the identification of fossil assemblages as once living communities of organisms bounded in space by limiting factors. Interpretation of fossil assemblages hinges on the identification of autochthonous assemblages, and on the determination of the limiting factors which control the diversity and abundance of each fossil group, through comparison with living relatives, the principle of taxonomic uniformitarianism. The process is discussed in detail in Part III of this book, and the main limiting factors for each of the main fossil groups are listed in Part II. At a more fundamental level, fossils can provide direct evidence of whether sediments were formed in marine or non-marine conditions back to the Cambrian. This is difficult using sediments alone. Together, sedimentary facies and palaeoecology provide as accurate a picture as is possible of the operation of ancient environments.

3.6 SUMMARY OF KEY POINTS

- **Species** are biological entities defined on the basis of morphological resemblance, genetics and behaviour, and on the ability to reproduce successfully. Fossil species are necessarily based solely on morphological characters.
- The system of **taxonomic hierarchy** is a method of demonstrating similarity and ancestry between groups of organisms. The largest subdivisions are the kingdoms and phyla, which in turn are composed of classes, orders, families, genera and species.
- The basis for reconstructing fossils as living organisms is **taxonomic uniformitarianism**, which assumes that the study of present-day organisms holds the key to interpreting the shape, form and life history of organisms in the geological past.
- Ecology is the study of the interaction of organisms with each other and with their environment; **palaeoecology** is the study of the interaction of fossil organisms with each other and their environment in the geological past.

Palaeosynecology is the study of the relationship of groups of organisms to each other and their environment; **palaeoautecology** is the study of the relationship of individual or small groups of organisms with their environment.

- **Palaeoenvironmental analysis** is the determination of the nature of ancient environments using sedimentary rocks and the palaeoecology of their contained fossils.

3.7 SUGGESTED READING

General introductions to the reconstruction of fossils as living animals are given by Raup and Stanley (1978), Ziegler (1983) and Goldring (1991). Ager (1963) provides a very readable, if outdated, introduction to palaeoecology; a much more up-to-date approach is taken by Dodd and Stanton (1991). Bosence and Allison (1995) and Briggs and Crowther (1990) are extremely important multi-authored texts which deal with palaeoenvironmental interpretation. Bromley (1990) is a well-written text on trace fossils, while Selley (1985) represents a good introduction to the nature of sedimentary environments. Finally, Rudwick (1972) provides a fascinating insight into the early concepts of fossils and the birth of palaeontology.

Ager, D.J. 1963. *Principles of Paleoecology*. McGraw-Hill, New York.
Bosence, D.W.J. & Allison, P.A. (eds) 1995. *Marine Palaeoenvironmental Analysis from Fossils*. Geological Society Special Publication No. 83, London.
Briggs, D.E.G. & Crowther, P.R. (eds) 1990. *Palaeobiology – A Synthesis*. Blackwell Scientific Publications, Oxford.
Bromley, R.G. 1990. *Trace Fossils*. Unwin Hyman, London.
Dodd, J.R. & Stanton, R.J. 1991. *Paleoecology. Concepts and Applications*. Second edition. John Wiley, New York.
Goldring, R. 1991. *Fossils in the Field. Information Potential and Analysis*. Longman, Harlow.
Raup, D.M. & Stanley, S.M. 1978. *Principles of Paleontology*. Second edition. Freeman, San Francisco.
Rudwick, M.J.S. 1972. *The Meaning of Fossils: Episodes from the History of Palaeontology*. Macdonald, London.
Selley, R.C. 1985. *Ancient Sedimentary Environments*. Chapman & Hall, London.
Ziegler, B. 1983. *Introduction to Palaeobiology. General Palaeontology*. Ellis Horwood, Chichester.

4
Fossils and Evolution

This chapter outlines in brief the most important aspects of biological evolution and discusses the role of fossils in the interpretation of the evolution of life on Earth. Evolution is a familiar word to us which effectively specifies change through time. As applied to living organisms, **organic evolution** involves change at several scales: from one population to the next, from one species to another, or in the pattern of the development through geological time of the most important groups of organisms in the fossil record. As such, the study of organic evolution involves two components: biology and palaeontology. Biology provides an understanding of the mechanism of evolution through the examination of living organisms. Palaeontology is most important in providing a temporal framework for evolution, and in illustrating the evolutionary patterns of the development of life on Earth. Together biology and palaeontology explain the huge variability of life, its origin and its development.

4.1 THE PROCESS OF ORGANIC EVOLUTION

4.1.1 Darwinian Theory

Organic or biological evolution is the cumulative change in characteristics from ancestral populations of organisms to descendant populations. Put simply, this definition illustrates that evolution occurs where perceptible differences arise within successive populations of organisms. The fossil record represents the most powerful testimony that life has evolved in this way through time. As an illustration, a popular conception is that human beings have been seen to evolve, with the loss of ape-like characteristics such as a protruding jaw and a stooped stance (in *Australopithecus*), and with the gain of characteristics such as a flatter face, a bigger brain and a fully bipedal stance (in *Homo*). These data are almost exclusively gained through the detailed examination of the fossil record of humans by scientists, and the popular conception is therefore drawn directly from palaeontological evidence. This simplistic example demonstrates the pivotal nature of palaeontology in proving the existence of evolution, but it is clear that palaeontology cannot provide all the answers.

The early authors of evolutionary theories drew their facts from an examination of the natural world in conjunction with the fossil record. Such early evolutionists as Jean Baptiste Lamarck (1744–1829) and Robert Chambers (1801–1871) strove to explain the diversity of life and the record of change through time as illustrated by fossils. Charles Darwin (1809–1882) was the first scientist to outline a viable theory of evolution as a result of natural phenomena, based on his intimate knowledge of both the natural world and the fossil record. His book, *On the origin of species by means of natural selection, or the preservation of favoured races in the struggle for life,* first published in 1859, had an immediate impact on biology and palaeontology alike, and it remains central to the study of evolution today.

Darwin's theory was based upon the twin concepts of **heredity**, the inheritance of characteristics from one population to the next, and what he termed **natural selection**. Darwin himself summarised his theory in his introduction to *Origin of Species*:

> As many more individuals of each species are born than can possibly survive; and as, consequently, there is a frequently recurring struggle for existence, it follows that any being, if it vary however slightly in any manner profitably to itself, under the complex and sometimes varying conditions of life, will have a better chance of surviving, and thus be *naturally selected*. From the strong principle of inheritance, any selected variety will tend to propagate its new and modified form.

At the root of Darwin's theory are four observed truths about the natural world: that animals reproduce more young than can actually survive; that, because of the overproduction of young, there must be competition (for food, living space, mates, etc.) within a species – Darwin's concept of the 'struggle for existence'; that within a species all organisms vary, as no two individuals are exactly the same; and that it is those individuals who possess characteristics that enable them to thrive in a particular environment who are successful. This process Darwin called **natural selection**. The successful individuals will therefore successfully reproduce young which resemble themselves, and this is the process of **inheritance**.

The twin principles of natural selection and inheritance form the basis for the Darwinian theory of evolution. Their operation would effectively lead to an increase in the frequency of those individuals suited or *selected* to their environment within a population through time, the definition of evolution introduced above. Darwin considered that the origin of new species came about through the gradual accumulation of different favourable characteristics within successive populations, leading eventually to the separation of new species which are adapted to a particular environment. However, he was unable successfully to explain how inheritance worked, how the favourable characters were accumulated, for instance, and how new characters arise. For example, Darwin believed that the characteristics of offspring were a result of equal mixing of the characteristics of the two parents. If this were true, the ultimate result of this simplistic model would actually be the *reduction* of variability in successive generations. Therefore, not only must characteristics be inherited, but also some must be inherited unaltered, while others undergo change or **mutation** in order to allow for the appearance of new characteristics. Successful mutations – that is, those which bestow an advantage upon the host – must then be subsequently inherited.

The process of inheritance was first outlined over a century ago by Gregor Mendel (1822–1884), and this still forms a central part of modern evolutionary theory. Mendel was able to demonstrate through a series of controlled experiments the process by which characters are inherited. Mendel recognised that the process required the existence of some sort of carrier of hereditary characters which would be present in both parents. This carrier is known as the **gene**, which carries a **genetic code** which includes all of the information needed to define an individual organism. The discovery and development of **genetics** coupled with Darwinian theory provides the basis for evolution. This coupling is often referred to as the **neo-Darwinian synthesis**, and it has a symbolic starting point in the gathering together of modern developments in the famous book *Evolution, the Modern Synthesis*, written by the biologist Julian Huxley in 1942.

4.1.2 Heredity and Genetics

The development of molecular biology in the 1950s led to the determination of the nature of genes and of how the genetic code is carried and transferred. Although palaeontology can do little to advance the study of genetics, (Box 4.1), it is important to understand the process of inheritance in order to appreciate fully the mechanism of evolution.

All **eukaryotic cells** (present in all organisms except bacteria and viruses) have two components: an outer zone called the **cytoplasm**, which contains all the minute organs concerned with the life processes of the cell; and an inner zone, the **nucleus**, which is concerned with reproduction. Cells are reproduced by the process of cell division which takes place all the time during growth and repair of an organism. Detailed examination of the nucleus at the moment of division shows that its contents become organised into a number of threads known as **chromosomes**. Each chromosome is composed of two parallel threads, and during the process of division (**mitosis**), the number of chromosomes remains constant for each species. For example, humans (*Homo sapiens*) have 46 chromosomes in each cell, while the various species of the fruit fly *Drosophila* have between six and 12. This constancy of chromosome numbers in a species suggested to earlier observers that they may be the carrier of hereditary material, and this was confirmed by the study of the formation of sperm and egg cells, the **gametes**.

In the reproductive organs of plants and animals the gametes undergo a different process of cell division from other cells, called **meiosis**. During meiosis it is the paired chromosomes, each containing two strands, that are divided. After this first division two nuclei are created, and each one contains half the number of chromosomes present in the parent nucleus. In the case of humans this would be

BOX 4.1: DNA FROM FOSSILS

Recent advances have illustrated that fossils may contain more information about the living organism than could previously have been thought possible. In recent years biochemical analyses have been developed which can reliably separate and analyse extremely small samples (<1 μm), and this has meant that original organic molecules of the once living organism can be studied. Although care is needed in associating the molecules extracted from the fossil with those from the actual living organism, rather than as the result of a later contaminant, organic compounds have been isolated and characterised from a wide range of fossil organisms, mostly in the more recent fossil record (Mesozoic–Recent). Although free amino acids are the most commonly encountered fossil molecules, in many cases exhibiting remarkable preservation, it is the potential for fossil DNA that has captured the popular imagination. DNA has been recovered from very recent fossils, Egyptian mummies just 2000 years old; but more ancient examples have yet to be reliably confirmed. Present knowledge suggests that the DNA molecule is prone to biochemical break-down, and is therefore likely to be rare in the fossil record. More common, however, are the residues created by this break-down, such as proteins, and these may provide at least a partial understanding of ancient biochemical systems.

Source: Curry, G.B. (1987) Molecular palaeontology: new life for old molecules. *Trends in Ecology and Evolution*, **2**, 161–165.

23, and for the various species of *Drosophila* between three and six. In males these nuclei become the sperm, in females the unfertilised egg. During sexual reproduction, the sperm penetrates the egg and the nuclei of the two gametes fuse so that the fertilised egg or **zygote** has the full complement of chromosomes typical of the species. The discovery of this process led to the acceptance that it was the chromosomes which carry the hereditary material, the genes first identified by Mendel in his experiments. However, it was not until the modern study of molecular biology that we had a clearer understanding of what a gene was, and of how the genetic code is carried and transferred.

Early in the twentieth century it was established that chromosomes were composed of two chemical constituents: **proteins** and **nucleic acid**. Proteins are chemical compounds produced only by living organisms and consist of large chain-like molecules built up of small sub-units known as **amino acids**. Proteins are the major component of living tissue, including, for example, collagen (the major component of hair, skin and bones) and the haemoglobin in blood which carries oxygen; each cell in the human body contains around 10 000 different types of protein. Because of this complexity, it was originally thought that proteins were the carriers of genetic messages, but experimental work in the 1950s demonstrated that it was actually the other component of the chromosome, the nucleic acid, which was the carrier.

There are two types of nucleic acid: **deoxyribonucleic acid** (DNA), contained within the chromosomes in the cell nucleus; and **ribonucleic acid** (RNA), which is found outside the cell nucleus, in the cytoplasm. The chemical composition of the nucleic acid molecules was well known, but it was not until the the discovery of the structure of the DNA molecule that there was any indication that it could have contained coded messages in the form of genes. The discovery that DNA formed a complex double helix by James Watson (b. 1928) and Francis Crick (b. 1916) was a major step forward in the understanding of the nature of genes. Watson and Crick found that the DNA molecule resembles a kind of free-standing spiral staircase, in which the sides are formed from chains of alternate sugars (dioxyribose in DNA) and phosphates, and that each step is composed of one of two pairs of chemicals called **bases**: adenine and thymine or guanine and cytosine (Figure 4.1). These base pairs form each 'step' and may occur in any sequence between the sides of the 'staircase'; in addition, each base may be found to the left or right of a 'step'. The structure of the DNA molecule therefore provides a method of carrying coded messages through its coded sequence of bases. For example, along a given side chain of alternating sugars and phosphates there may be any one of the four bases attached to each sugar, so that the sequence of bases can be given in a coded message, denoted by the initial letter of each base (A, adenine; C, cytosine; G, guanine; and T, thymine). The genes are arranged along the strands of the DNA and the 'genetic code' is a limited language based upon the combination of these four letters, with its function to specify the amino acids which are needed to create proteins. The purpose of the genetic code appears to be solely to assemble proteins, and the extraordinary variety of life appears to be a function of little more than

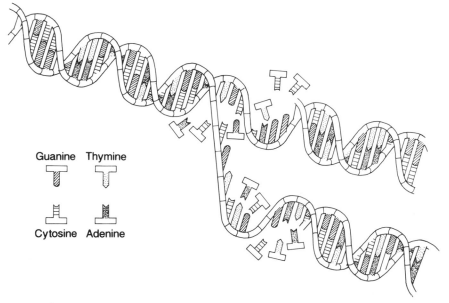

Guanine   Thymine

Cytosine   Adenine

Figure 4.1   *The structure of the DNA molecule, showing the base pairs as interlocking steps on a spiral staircase [Modified from: Patterson (1978),* Evolution, *British Museum (Natural History), Fig. 10, p. 28]*

differences in the sequences of amino acids. Within the DNA molecule, the two strands of the double helix have two separate purposes. One is to provide the genetic code of bases; the other, a complementary series of bases which carry a different message. This provides the mechanism for replicating the DNA molecule. During replication, the two strands separate along the junctions between the base pairs, and it is the complementary strand which acts as a kind of template in replicating both the molecule and the message carried on the other strand (Figure 4.1).

Clearly then, the principal purpose of the DNA is to code for the production of proteins; however, protein synthesis is not carried out in the nucleus, but in other elements of the cell contained within the cytoplasm, called **ribosomes**. If the DNA is to control this process, it must pass messages to the ribosomes. It does this by producing a single-stranded near-replica of itself, RNA, which passes to the ribosomes. Messenger RNA is actually a family of molecules, each adapted to recognise a separate portion of the genetic code and to add an appropriate amino acid in the creation of a protein. There are many thousands of genes to code the production of the many thousands of proteins which make up a living organism.

Mendel's original experiments demonstrated that within a species there were what were termed **dominant** and **recessive** genes. During sexual reproduction, gametes from different parents fuse to form the fertilised egg. The resulting matched genes on the new chromosome pairs may either be the same as those of the parent (**homozygous**), or different (**heterozygous**), and the feature controlled by a particular gene may be intermediate between that of the two parents. Commonly, however, one gene is dominant over the other and in such cases the dominant gene is always the homozygous one. The proportion (the Mendelian Ratio) of these genes remains constant for given species, and is known as its **genotype**. This is distinct from its physical appearance or **phenotype**; for example, the caterpillar, chrysalis and butterfly all possess the same genotype, but plainly represent different phenotypes of the same species. Other phenotypes include genetically identical organisms raised in different environments, but which differ in morphology because they are subject to different environmental influences, such as poor soil or different climatic conditions acting upon plants. Such phenotypes are called **ecophenotypes**.

The theory of Mendelian genetics has two major strengths. One is that it not only permits but also predicts variability in genotype and phenotype. The other is that it provides a mechanism whereby parental genes are preserved for future generations even if the exact genotype and phenotype change. This is a direct contrast with the old view of a simple 'blending' of parental attributes in offspring, which would reduce the possibility of variability and specify the loss of parental genes. However, Mendelian genetics does not fully explain evolutionary theory. For this, it must be considered with **natural selection**, the mainstay of Darwinian theory. Together, these provide the basis of modern evolutionary thought, neo-Darwinism.

4.1.3 Natural Selection

Natural selection is clearly displayed in most groups of organisms, although it is rare to be actually able to record changes within a short time span (Box 4.2). As

BOX 4.2: THE BEAK OF THE FINCH

The Galapagos finches have a special place in evolutionary theory. These finches are descendants of land birds blown out into the Pacific which found refuge in the small group of islands off the Ecuadorian coast known as the Galapagos Islands. Charles Darwin visited the islands in 1835 during the voyage of HMS *Beagle*, and was impressed at the variety of beak forms possessed by the finches, adapted to a variety of food types (fruit, insects, etc.). In many ways, these finches were instrumental in providing Darwin with the physical evidence of natural selection at work – successive generations of birds developing adaptations which were successful in their chosen environment. But Darwin was unable to record the process of natural selection at work on an actual population. An English family of scientists, the Grants, have spent much of their lives studying the Galapagos finches. Through detailed observation and measurement, they have been able to record the process of natural selection at work on successive populations of finches.

The Grants concentrated on studying the beaks of several Galapagos finch species, with each beak a testimony to the variety of food resources present upon each island. Through detailed measurement of beaks and body size, they have been able to observe variation in an extremely short period of time: a matter of months. For example, the medium ground finch *Geospiza fortis* was observed over several years in its endeavours to crack the seeds of a particularly tough indigenous plant, *Tribulus*. Only the biggest birds with the deepest beaks could crack such seeds. The Galapagos Islands are subject to drought, and the Grants observed that it was only the largest, *G. fortis* which survived the drought, as the only food sources avaliable were the *Tribulus* seeds. After one such drought, the surviving population was an average of 5–6% larger than the dead, and had an average beak depth (important for cracking the seeds) of 9.96 mm, an increase of over 0.5 mm; just enough to make a difference. Clearly, natural selection was taking place, with those finches of more powerful body size and deeper beaks surviving. The observations of the Grants are almost unique in demonstrating the actual process of evolution in 'real time'.

Source: Weiner, J. (1994) *The Beak of the Finch: Evolution in Real Time*. Jonathan Cape, London.

outlined above, observation of any population reveals that more offspring are generally produced than survive to adulthood. The natural drive for any individual is to survive and reproduce so that the future viability of the species is guaranteed. This endeavour may be overcome by external factors such as changes to the environment or supply of resources necessary for life. It may also be influenced by the fitness of the individuals. An over-abundance of offspring ensures that sufficient 'fit' individuals mature to adulthood. Through mutation and Mendelian heredity patterns, offspring of different genotypes can and will be produced by any single set of parents. Any advantage the resulting slight changes in genotype may bestow on an individual may improve the chances of survival of that individual.

Natural selection can operate in a number of ways. It can give direction to evolutionary changes. For example, if greater size is an advantage to a species, successive generations will be selected on that factor. It can also stabilise a population if the preferred characteristics are intermediate in nature. If extremes are less fit they will be less successful in reproduction and therefore they will constantly be selected out of the population, allowing it to continue unaltered. Finally, natural selection can lead to speciation by disrupting the evolutionary pattern. This can occur if extreme forms are selected at the expense of intermediate forms, so that the extreme genotypes will gradually become reproductively isolated and **speciation**, the formation of a new species, will take place.

Without natural selection, how could evolution proceed? **Mutations**, or changes in the genetic configuration, do happen, and are sometimes a function of changes in the rate of growth, known as **heterochrony**, within individual evolving populations (Box 4.3). It is impossible to demonstrate a pattern in the way they happen, but the rate of mutation can be predicted based on data from controlled experiments on populations. The route by which genetic information is passed from one generation to the next is sufficiently complex to allow a number of points where errors can develop. For example, the duplication process by which RNA is derived from DNA is complex and often imperfect. The recombination of chromosomes is also frequently inaccurate. The important point to remember is that mutations are without direction. In that sense they are random, even if certain patterns can be recognised at a molecular level.

4.2 PALAEONTOLOGY AND EVOLUTION

Biological study is of paramount importance in determining the pattern of inheritance and variation, and in some instances it is possible to recognise the development of new characters within a population on the human time scale (Box 4.2). This is rare, however, and in general it is only palaeontology which provides the ability to observe evolutionary changes over any appreciable amount of time. Therefore, the fossil record, although imperfect, is the only real evidence of the time scale (**tempo**) and pattern (**mode**) of evolution. The fossil record actually reveals two scales of evolutionary pattern: evolution of populations up to and including the development of new species (**microevolution**) and the evolution of the higher taxonomic levels, such as families or classes (**macroevolution**). In both cases, palaeontology has made significant contributions to our understanding of evolution.

4.2.1 Microevolution: the Small-scale Changes

Microevolution is defined as the small-scale changes in populations with time, up to and including the development of new species. In this definition, most of the

Figure 4.2   *The dodo,* Didus ineptus, *from the island of Mauritius. The dodo was extinguished by humans in the seventeenth century [From: Hutchinson (1894)* Creatures of Other Days, *Chapman & Hall, Plate 15, p. 165]*

evolutionary studies of living populations are concerned with microevolution. However, it is relatively rare to recognise the actual appearance of new species within the human time scale. For example, some recent studies in the Galapagos Islands, set in the Pacific Ocean off the coast of Ecuador, suggest that speciation is active in the very finches that Darwin studied as a young man, but this discovery has taken a lifetime of detailed study (Box 4.2). It is much more commonplace to be able to observe species extinctions, especially those induced by human actions (Figure 4.2).

In reality, the recognition of **lineages** – that is, lines of descent of evolving species linked by their basic morphologies – is much more common in the fossil record. As discussed in Chapter 2, Darwin himself was unable to show that evolution has proceeded through a succession of species in a lineage, and he therefore doubted the completeness of the record. However, detailed studies after the publication of Darwin's theory illustrated that lineages could be determined (Box 4.4). We now recognise that although it is rare for the fossil record to be so complete that successive generations of an evolving population are preserved, the inadequacy of the fossil record is frequently overstated. In fact, the fossil record offers an enormous fund of data, and detailed analyses of populations of organisms can provide a wealth of information on what morphological changes occur and how they take place (Box 2.6). The first of these points, what changes occur, is relatively easily answered through detailed observation, measurement and recording. The second, how the changes take place, is more difficult and is therefore the subject of much debate.

BOX 4.3: HETEROCHRONY

Within a species, each individual grows during its lifetime according to a series of events (its **ontogeny**) , the nature and timing of which are genetically controlled. The eventual size and shape of an organism is generally associated with the timing of development, and if the rate of change from fertilised egg to adult is speeded up or slowed down, this will result in size or shape changes. **Heterochrony** is a branch of evolutionary studies which is concerned with the pattern of growth within an evolving species. It is defined as changes through time in the appearance or rate of development of ancestral characters, and it may be the basis of many of the evolutionary innovations which appear within an evolving lineage.

There are two basic results of heterochrony: differences in **size** and **shape**. Size changes may be created by changing the rate of development so that growth in a descendant speeds up and goes beyond that of the ancestor, or slows down to produce the opposite effect. Shape changes are created by two basic processes: **peramorphosis** and **paedomorphosis**. In peramorphosis, the descendant adult passes morphologically beyond that of the ancestor, so that, in effect, an extra developmental stage is added to the life history. In paedomorphosis, the reverse is true, so that the descendant adult passes

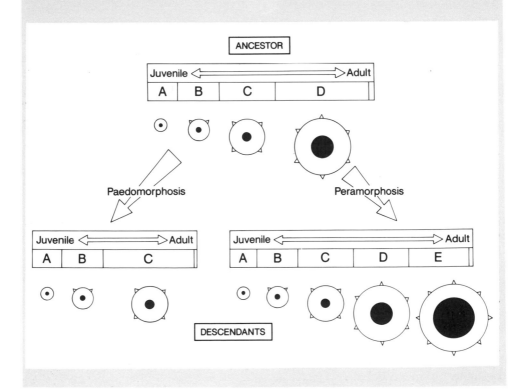

BOX 4.3: (*cont.*)

through fewer growth stages and therefore resembles the juvenile of the descendant. In effect, these changes are created through a mutation in the genetic code controlling growth. If such mutations and resulting shape changes confer selective advantage upon the descendant population, then it has the chance to be spread through the population, leading to the development of a new species through eventual reproductive isolation. An example of paedomorphosis is the relationship of the various species of the oyster *Gryphaea* from the Lower Jurassic. Here, the ancestral juvenile (of *G. arcuata*) closely resembles the descendant adult (of *G. gigantea*), and therefore the evolutionary process may have occurred through paedomorphosis. Heterochrony provides a basis for rapid evolutionary change, and may be of great importance in both micro- and macroevolutionary patterns.

Sources: McNamara, K.J. (1990). Heterochrony. *In* Briggs, D.E.G. and Crowther, P.R. (eds): *Palaeobiology – a Synthesis*, Blackwell Scientific Publications, Oxford, 111–119. Hallam, A. (1982). Patterns of speciation in Jurassic *Gryphaea*. *Paleobiology*, **8**, 354–366. [Figure modified from McNamara (1990) *In* Briggs and Crowther (Eds) *Palaeobiology – a Synthesis*, Blackwells, Figs 1&2, p. 112 & 113]

The traditional Darwinian view of evolution favoured slow, gradual change consisting of the accumulation of small variations from one generation to the next. New species are created by this mechanism in two ways, through **anagenesis** and **cladogenesis** (Figure 4.3). In anagenesis new species are created by the gradual change of a lineage through numerous intermediate stages in an otherwise stable environment. Favourable mutations are spread throughout the whole gene pool by the operation of natural selection, and new species are created when the shift in morphology of the end members of the lineage is so great that they are reproductively isolated. This type of speciation, specifically associated with anagenesis, is known as **sympatric speciation**. In cladogenesis, a branch is created in the lineage (Figure 4.3). Cladogenesis proceeds through speciation in small, isolated communities on the periphery of the geographical range of a species, known as **allopatric speciation**. Allopatric speciation operates because such small communities are isolated from the main gene pool of the population. Advantageous mutations are therefore rapidly communicated through the population which would therefore have a greater chance of becoming reproductively isolated and form new species. After branching, anagenesis resumes. Together, these types of speciation are representative of a model which has been termed **phyletic gradualism** (Figure 4.3). Phyletic gradualism can be considered as the modern representation of Darwinian evolution, and both types of speciation require as proof the existence of a full range of intermediate forms between successive species. The search for such intermediates, sometimes referred to as 'missing links', has taxed

BOX 4.4: THE EVOLUTION OF THE HORSE

The evolution of the horse was seen as one of the first triumphant proofs of the process of evolution as demonstrated by the fossil record. Abundant fossils in the Cenozoic sedimentary rocks of Europe and North America led in the nineteenth century to the development of a complex story of horse evolution based on a progressive size increase, a successive change in the upper and lower molars, and, famously, a decrease in the number of digits in the limbs, creating hooves. This 'proof of evolution' was first developed by A. Gaudry in 1867, demonstrating, just eight years after the publication of Darwin's *Origin of Species*, an evolutionary lineage of horses from the Eocene–Pliocene (Palaeogene–Neogene) sediments of Europe. This example was further developed by O.C. Marsh (1831–1899), who recognised a fuller sequence of horses evolving in North America. This became a classic example of 'straight-line' evolution which was a powerful testimony of Darwin's theory. T.H. Huxley (1825–1895), an ardent supporter of Darwin, was so taken with Marsh's evolutionary history of the horses that he believed that the specimens housed at Yale University 'demonstrated the evolution of the horse beyond question, and for the first time indicated the direct line of descent of an existing animal'. Unfortunately, the classic evolutionary lineage of the horse is now seen to be a dangerous oversimplification of what is actually a very complex story. Marsh's story was constructed using several different branches of what is now known to be a highly complex evolutionary tree. However, the evolution of individual genera of horses still provides important evidence of microevolutionary processes, and as such will continue to be studied as a classic of evolutionary theory.

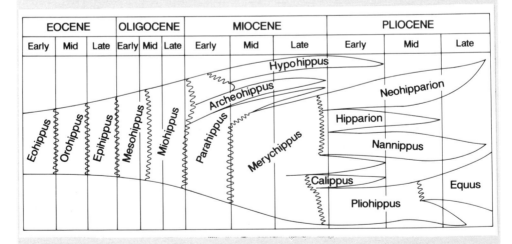

Source: MacFadden, B.J. (1992) *Fossil Horses: Systematics, Paleobiology and Evolution of the Family Equidae.* Cambridge University Press, Cambridge. [Figure modified from MacFadden (1992) *Fossil Horses: Systematics, Paleobiology and Evolution of the Family Equidae.* Cambridge University Press, Fig. 10, p. 32]

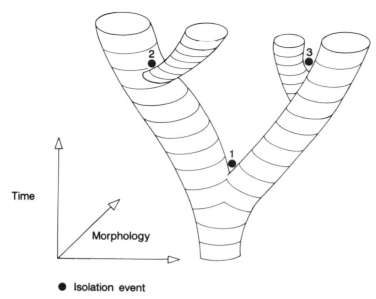

Figure 4.3 *Phyletic gradualism. Evolution proceeds through either gradual morphological change (anagenesis) or lineage splitting through the isolation of peripheral populations (cladogenesis) [Modified from: Skelton (1993),* Evolution: a Biological and Palaeontological Approach, *Addison Wesley, Fig. 10.20A, p. 487]*

many evolutionary biologists, and ultimately phyletic gradualists could claim that their theory is infinitely defensible as all missing intermediates can be explained as gaps in the fossil record, just as Darwin did before them.

Up to the early 1970s evolution was thought to have proceeded solely through the processes of phyletic gradualism. However, in 1972 Niles Eldredge and Stephen Gould caused a minor revolution in palaeontology when they suggested an alternative mode of microevolution, which they called **punctuated equilibrium**. Eldredge and Gould were convinced that true phyletic gradualism – that is, gradual change through time of the investigated species – was acually very rare, and that it was more common for species to remain *unchanged* over great intervals of geological time. Eldredge and Gould considered that there was an observational bias of scientists looking for *change* rather than equilibrium, and that as a result periods of little or no change had been ignored or overlooked. They suggested instead that the fossil record supported the hypothesis that most groups evolve in short, rapid spurts (**punctuations**) followed by longer periods with little or no change (**stasis**) (Figure 4.4). Fossil evidence would appear to support this model in many cases, as apparently sudden appearances of new species are common phenomena. Eldredge and Gould suggested that the mechanism for punctuational change was through allopatric speciation in small, geographically or ecologically isolated communities on the periphery of the geographical range of a species. However, there would be little chance of preservation of such isolated populations, and therefore only when the new forms became more widespread would they be recorded in the fossil record. In this way their appearance would seem instantaneous, punctuating an

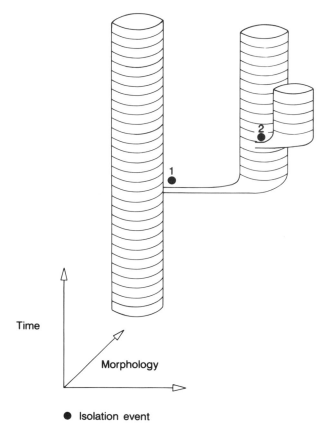

Figure 4.4   *Punctuated equilibrium. Evolution proceeds through rapid morphological change after isolation of peripheral populations. No gradual changes occur in between these events [Modified from: Skelton (1993),* Evolution: a Biological and Palaeontological Approach, *Addison Wesley, Fig. 10.20C, p. 487]*

otherwise static record (Figure 4.4). The punctuational model does not support any morphological change until the speciation event (Box 4.5). The known fossil record actually appears to support such a theory to a much greater extent than that of phyletic gradualism, and particularly anagenesis, although this may be partially an artefact of observer bias (Box 4.6).

Since Eldredge and Gould's paper, there has been a rash of case histories claiming to prove or disprove one or other of what have been considered by some as competing processes of microevolution. In many cases, new evidence has led to the re-evaluation of old ideas. The evolution of the Jurassic oyster *Gryphaea* is one such case (Figure 4.5). *Gryphaea* has been the subject of evolutionary attention since the 1920s, when it was thought to be representative of anagenesis, with gradual change in shell characters such as coiling, shell thickness and size. Careful reappraisal of this example illustrates that increase in shell size is gradual, but that change in other morphological features, for example coiling of the shell, proceeds in steps and is therefore representative of punctuated equilibrium. The

BOX 4.5: STASIS IN BIVALVES

In an extremely detailed study, Stanley and Yang (1987) observed the nature of the evolutionary changes in 19 separate evolutionary lineages of Neogene bivalves. These lineages were studied using a combination of detailed measurements of 24 variables, involving a total of 43 000 separate measurements. As the sequences studied were only 4 million years old, Stanley and Yang were able, on the basis of their measurements, to compare their 19 Pliocene bivalve species with their closest living relatives. They found that 12 out of the 19 could be directly assigned to living species. In order to gain an idea of the variability within the morphology of the living bivalve species, Stanley and Yang carried out a similar set of measurements and comparisons within geographically separated living populations for eight of the species studied. They were able to show through a variety of statistical techniques that, with minor exceptions, the differences between ancient and living representatives of bivalve species were no greater than the differences observed between the individual populations of the living species. This convincingly demonstrates that over an interval of 4 million years, at least 12 out of 19 bivalve species have remained in morphological stasis, with no gradually accumulating net change in shape or form.

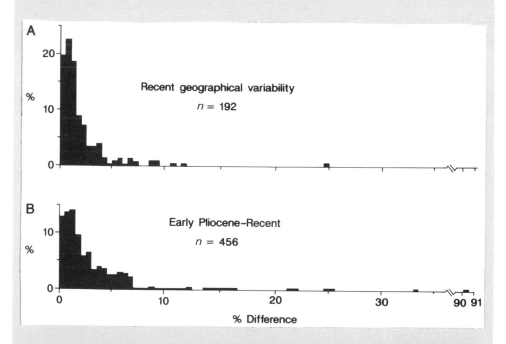

Source: Stanley, S.M. and Yang, X. (1987) Approximate evolutionary stasis for bivalve morphology over millions of years: a multivariate, multilineage study. *Paleobiology*, **13**, 113–139. [Figure modified from Stanley and Yang (1987), *Paleobiology*, **13**, Fig. 7, p. 123]

BOX 4.6: OBSERVERS' PUNCTUATED EQUILIBRIUM

The search for punctuated equilibrium or phyletic gradualism in fossil lineages is fraught with difficulties and may be almost impossible to prove one way or another. In many ways, phyletic gradualism may be the most difficult to illustrate, as in any lineage evolutionary change can be depicted as a series of steps composed of stasis and punctuational jumps. In this way, gradualism may always be demonstrated as a succession of an infinite number of punctuational jumps. Therefore, in some cases, the perceived differences between punctuated equilibrium and phyletic gradualism could be simply an artefact of observer bias, based upon a desire to observe one or other of the two processes, or through collector bias, based upon an inadequate sampling strategy. In both cases, observers need to be rigorous in their approach to drawing conclusions about the nature of the microevolutionary patterns they are recording.

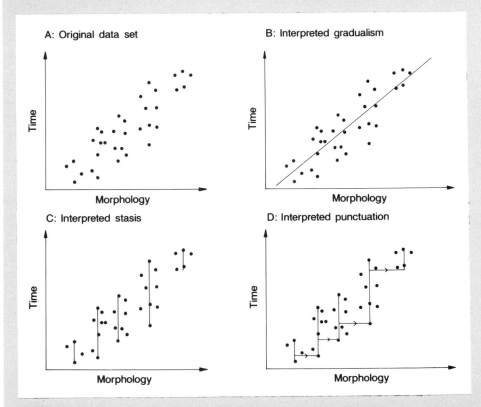

Source: Fortey, R.A. (1985) Gradualism and punctuated equilibria as competing and complementary theories. *In* Cope, J.C.W. and Skelton, P.R. (eds) Evolutionary case histories from the fossil record, *Special Papers in Palaeontology*, **33**, London.

Cretaceous echinoid, *Micraster*, was also the subject of detailed early studies which demonstrated gradual change with intermediates, particularly in the shape of the shell in the detail of its architecture (Figure 4.6). However, this example has been reappraised in the light of punctuated equilibrium, and appears to demonstrate clear steps in the development of a number of morphological features leading to improved feeding. Further studies have failed to reveal intermediaries, and this remains an example of punctuated equilibrium.

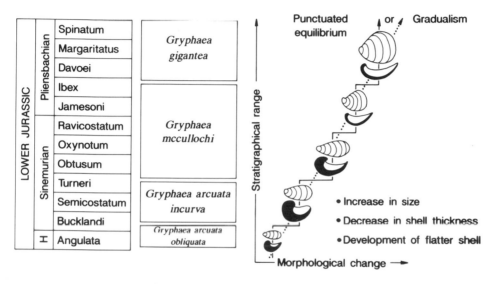

Figure 4.5   *Patterns of evolution in the Lower Jurassic oyster,* Gryphaea

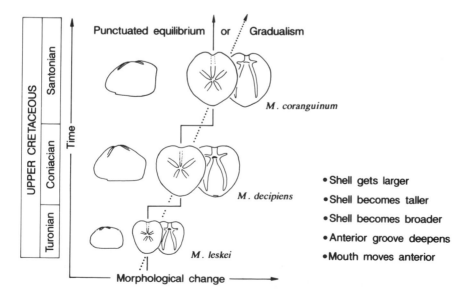

Figure 4.6   *Patterns of evolution in the Upper Cretaceous echinoid,* Micraster

Does this suggest that all evolution is punctuated? Gradualism can be credibly defended where the record is complete and sufficient representatives of the group under study are available for study. Marine plankton, such as planktonic forms of the foraminifera (Chapter 16), are particularly useful in this regard. Their small size, abundance and widespread distribution make them useful subjects in evolutionary studies. The evolution of the genus *Orbulina* in the Miocene is an example of rapid change over a relatively short time span of 0.5 million years, in which all intermediate forms are known in an exceptionally complete stratigraphical sequence (Figure 4.7). Following this short, rapid burst, *Orbulina* remained unchanged to the present day, a span of 16 million years of stasis. Should the fossil record have been less complete, this event may have been represented by a sudden speciation event followed by a period of stasis.

Clearly the case histories of both *Orbulina* and *Gryphaea* indicate that anagenesis and punctuated equilibrium are not necessarily competing theories. In fact, in these and other examples, evolution may proceed as **punctuated anagenesis** (sometimes called **punctuated gradualism**), with gradual change, rather than stasis, occuring between rapid bursts of punctuational change (Figure 4.8). In the case of *Gryphaea*, this is manifest in the fact that coiling changes in rapid bursts between intervals of stasis, while size increases gradually through time. In other cases, the patterns of punctuated equilibrium or phyletic gradualism may be a function of the relative stress in the environment. Some benthonic organisms may be susceptible to punctuational change, evolving in a more unstable environment unable to support successive change in new populations; while planktonic

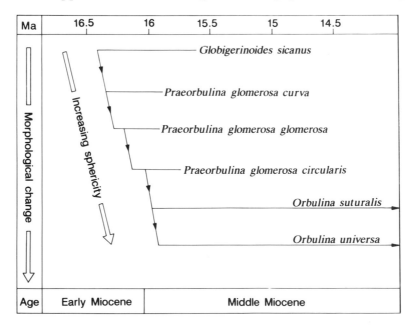

Figure 4.7 *Evolution in the Neogene foraminifer* Orbulina, *exhibiting both gradual change and stasis [Modified from: Banner and Lowry (1985), Special Papers in Palaeontology **33**, Fig. 5, p. 126]*

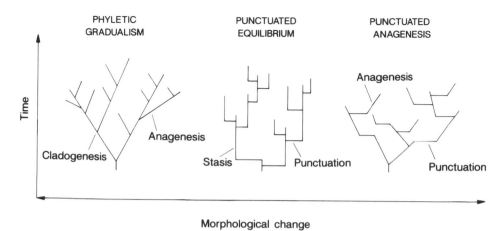

Figure 4.8 *Contrasting modes of microevolution: phyletic gradualism, punctuated equilibrium and punctuated anagenesis*

organisms, living in a more stable environment, may promote anagenesis. Either way, enough case histories have been documented to illustrate that both punctuational and gradual evolution are present in the fossil record (Box 4.7).

4.2.2 Macroevolution: The Broad Patterns

Species transitions of the sort described above are the domain of microevolution, but how do major new groups of animals and plants form? Macroevolution is concerned with the origin and evolution of the higher taxonomic groupings, and reflects the major cumulative changes in the fossil record through time. Whereas the study of microevolution is limited by the incomplete fossil record, this is less of a problem in the case of macroevolution. Indeed, palaeontology probably has most to offer in the study of large-scale changes and broad patterns of evolution.

Macroevolution as illustrated by the fossil record includes the appearance and disappearance of the higher taxonomic groups. The origin of such major groups and the direct relationship of micro- and macroevolutionary processes is still an area of active research, but it is clear that the summation of microevolutionary processes must lead to large-scale changes in the biosphere. It is also probable that macroevolutionary processes reflect large-scale environmental changes: changes that result in the operation of natural selection processes that lead to changes in a large number of organisms at the same time. Two macroevolutionary processes that appear to be of extreme importance in the development of the biosphere are **adaptive radiations** and **mass extinctions**.

The basis of taxonomy has been discussed in Chapter 3. In it, the definition of higher taxonomic groups appears to be superficially simple. In their definition, morphological similarities are significant, but the primary basis for classification is phylogenetic. For example, taxa sharing the same ancestral stock are grouped

BOX 4.7: GRADUALISM AND PUNCTUATION IN FORAMINIFERA

Planktonic foraminifera have formed an important test for the development of ideas in microevolution, as they are readily preserved in the relatively complete deep-ocean sediments, and are found in extreme abundance. During the late Miocene (between 7 and 5 million years ago) populations of *Globorotalia conomiozea* showed a spread of geographical variation from temperate to warm tropical sites in the southwest Pacific. These populations were in contact with each other, and although there was considerable variation from one end of the geographical distribution to the other there was a definite evolutionary trend in all populations towards having a flatter cone with fewer chambers through time. However, detailed observations of the morphology of closely spaced *G. conomiozea* in stratigraphical sections demonstrated to Wei and Kennett (1988) that this relationship was severed at the Miocene–Pliocene boundary. The main, temperate, populations display a gradual transformation of *G. conomiozea* into a new species, *G. sphericomiozea* during an interval of 0.2 million years,

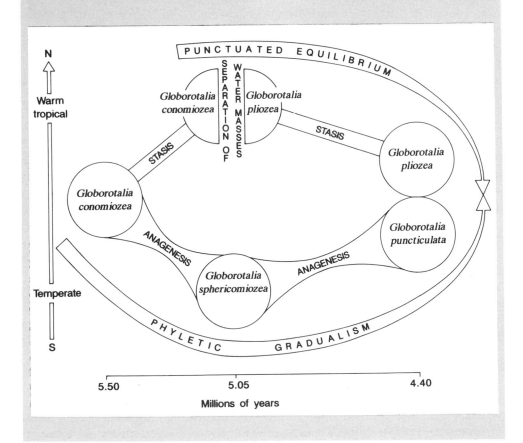

BOX 4.7: *(cont.)*

with all measured variables during the interval showing continuous and steady changes. This contrasts with populations in the peripheral, warm tropical sections which showed rapid transition to a new species, *G. pliozea*, within an interval of 0.01 million years. After speciation, *G. pliozea* exhibited morphological stasis for a further 0.6 million years. This suggests that at the Miocene–Pliocene boundary, the peripheral tropical populations of *G. conomiozea* became isolated from the main temperate populations, possibly by the separation of water masses, and that from this point the two main population groups adopted different modes of microevolution. Wei and Kennett's sudy convincingly demonstrates that the two 'alternative' models of microevolution actually complement each other, and are not mutually exclusive.

Source: Wei, K.-Y. and Kennett, J.P. (1988) Phyletic gradualism and punctuated equilibrium in the late Neogene planktonic foraminiferal clade *Globoconella*. *Paleobiology*, **14**, 345–363. [Figure modified from Wei and Kennett (1988), *Paleobiology*, **14**, Fig. 7, p. 359]

together in **monophyletic groups**. Such groupings have formed the basis of many taxonomic revisions using cladistics, a technique based on the recognition of monophyletic groups (Box 3.2). Rates of evolution vary widely through time, and this phenomenon can be recognised at all taxonomic levels. Although the pattern varies in detail in different groups, there is one mode which is common. In most cases, the initial appearance of a new taxon is followed by a period of rapid evolution. This early burst takes place as the new form spreads into new areas and adapts to new environmental pressures. This is termed '**adaptive radiation**'. Such events are generally triggered by the introduction of a new morphological innovation or the opening of new ecospace. This may allow the taxon to colonise new areas or to compete successfully with existing taxa. A rise in sea level, resulting in a relative transgression of land areas by the sea, is frequently associated with adaptive radiations in marine groups due to the increased habitat. Once the new form has become widespread, the rate of adaptation slows down.

Just as the rate of appearance of new taxa is variable, so the rate of disappearance or extinction of taxa is also variable. Extinction at a scale much beyond what could be normally expected is termed a '**mass extinction**'. Mass extinctions take place when the standing diversity of higher taxa falls dramatically over a short period of time. At least five major mass extinction events have been recognised from the geological record, as well as many minor events (Figure 4.9). The most famous is the end-Cretaceous event which saw the end of the dinosaurs, although many other groups were also affected, both on land and in the sea. This was not the most dramatic mass extinction, however, as this honour goes to the end-Permian extinction event which affected over 50% of all marine invertebrate

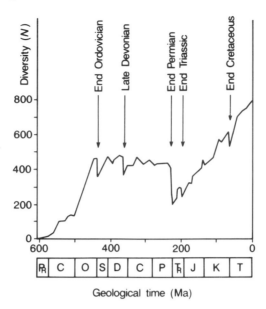

Figure 4.9   *The five major mass extinctions of the Phanerozoic [Modified from: Sepkoski (1982) Geological Society of America Special Paper **190**]*

families. Events of lesser magnitude have been recorded in the late Ordovician, the late Devonian, and the late Triassic (Figure 4.9).

The cause of mass extinctions is uncertain and there are four main hypotheses currently available to explain them. One is **sea-level variations**. Sea level is known to have fluctuated through geological time. The effects of sea-level change are known to have had a profound effect on the abundance and diversity of the marine fossil record. For example, the sea-level rise at the beginning of the Cambrian is thought to have influenced the radiation of marine organisms by increasing the size and availability of suitable habitats (**ecospace**), in particular that of shallow marine shelf areas. Conversely, a fall in sea level may increase the competition for ecospace among marine organisms, and therefore lead to species extinction.

Another hypothesis is **climatic change**. The Earth's climate has fluctuated between 'ice-house' and 'greenhouse' states through geological time. Climate, especially temperature, is an important limiting factor on organisms today. It is possible to identify extinctions that are probably climate controlled, such as the extinction of large mammals in the Pleistocene through the onset of the Quaternary 'ice age'. However, it is difficult to relate the mass extinction of both land and marine organisms directly to climate.

A third hypothesis is **vulcanicity**. A major volcanic episode may have caused the end-Cretaceous mass extinction. The catastrophic eruption of volcanoes can lead to the input of large quantities of volcanic gases and ash into the upper atmosphere. This could produce a 'volcanic winter', a phenomenon which is caused when ash particles and aerosols are injected into the upper atmosphere. This reduces the amount of solar radiation received by the Earth's surface which in turn causes intense climatic cooling for a period of years. The end-Cretaceous extinction can be correlated with the eruption of large amounts of basaltic lava, and it has been argued that these eruptions may have caused a short-term deterioration in the world's climate and thereby caused a failure of the global ecosystem.

The final hypothesis is **extra-terrestrial impact**. The mass extinction at the Cretaceous–Palaeogene boundary (usually referred to as the Cretaceous–Tertiary or K–T boundary) is associated with a layer of clay rich in iridium. Iridium is common only in meteorites and other extra-terrestrial bodies, and this has led to the suggestion that the mass extinction at the end of the Cretaceous may have been caused by the impact of an extra-terrestrial body. The impact of a meteorite would create what is known as an 'impact winter' similar to a 'volcanic winter' but induced by dust introduced into the atmosphere by the impact of a meteorite. It has also been argued that if the impact had taken place in an ocean, vaporisation of the water during collision would have increased the global cloud cover leading to an accelerated greenhouse effect. Some authors have suggested that meteorite impacts occur at regular intervals as our solar system moves through the galaxy. These authors point to the apparent 26 million year cyclicity of extinctions identified within the geological record as evidence of this. This view has, however, received considerable criticism and is as yet unproven; it is discussed further in Part III of this book.

In summary, all four of these mechanisms may clearly be interrelated and it is unlikely that there is a single mechanism for all mass extinctions. As an example, it is conceivable that climatic change (cooling) would lead to sea-level change (fall) through the growth of ice sheets. Any resulting mass extinction could therefore be caused by a combination of both processes. Although the mechanism of mass extinction is still hotly debated, and is an area of popular interest, it is clear that mass extinctions have occurred and have had a profound effect on the evolution of the biosphere.

Periods of mass extinction are often followed, and thereby balanced, by periods of adaptive radiation which effectively 'restock' the depleted biosphere. The success of these organisms is usually associated with the development of a new adaptation which gives them an advantage in repopulating the environmental space vacated by the organisms killed off during the mass extinction. Together, mass extinctions and adaptive radiations effectively control the stocking and restocking of the biosphere through time. This pattern of extinction and radiation is illustrated in Figure 4.10, which shows the **clades** or clusters of evolving groups of animals and plants. These clusters represent the diversity of life on Earth at any given time, and they reflect the painstaking work of many specialists. Extinctions are indicated by rapid reductions in diversity (i.e. the width) while radiations are shown by similar rapid increases in the faunal diversity over a short interval of time (Fig. 4.10).

4.3 SUMMARY OF KEY POINTS

- **Evolution** can be defined as the cumulative change in characteristics from an ancestral population of organisms to a descendant. It demonstrates that

90

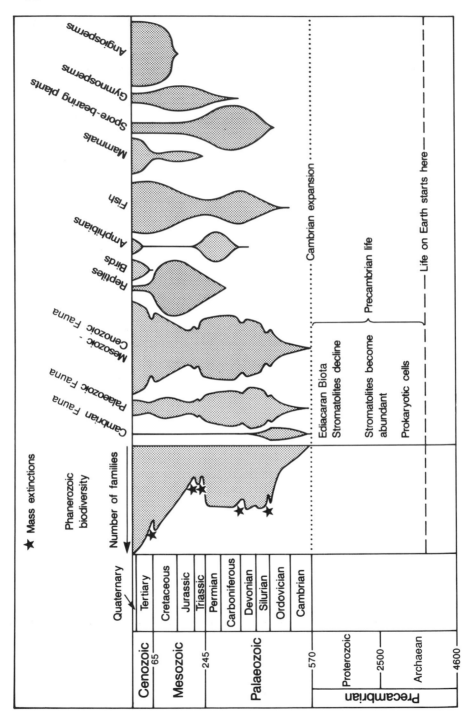

Figure 4.10 Changes in the biosphere through geological time [Reproduced with permission from: Doyle et al. (1994) Key to Earth History, Wiley, Fig. 10.8B, p. 169]

evolution occurs where perceptible differences arise with time in successive populations.

- **Darwinian theory** (now called the **neo-Darwinian synthesis**) remains at the core of our understanding of biological evolution, and involves the twin concepts of heredity, the inheritance of characteristics from one population to the next; and natural selection, the selection of the fittest individuals to reproduce.
- The process of inheritance is understood through the study of genetics and molecular biology. The genetic code is carried on the DNA molecule within the nucleus of eukaryotic cells. Its function is to code for the production of the proteins which together make up an organism. Mutations provide a mechanism whereby alterations are made in the genetic code. If mutations are favourable, then individuals possessing the new characteristics have a greater chance of reproducing.
- The fossil record provides a powerful testimony of the process of evolution. It is able to demonstrate both evolutionary rate and evolutionary pattern. Two scales of evolution may be recognised from the fossil record: microevolution and macroevolution.
- **Microevolution** is represented by the small-scale changes from generation to generation which result in a new species. The fossil record appears to support two modes of microevolution: **phyletic gradualism**, with a steady rate of gradual change; and **punctuated equilibrium**, characterised by stasis punctuated by rapid changes.
- **Macroevolution** is represented by large-scale changes, particularly in the appearance, diversification and extinction of major groups.

4.4 SUGGESTED READING

Patterson (1978) is a well-written, simple and jargon-free account of biological evolution, while Skelton (1993) provides a most comprehensive coverage of evolution from both palaeontological and biological perspectives. Clarkson (1993) has a chapter which introduces the biological basis for evolution. Briggs and Crowther (1990) contains many important papers on the nature of evolution as recorded by the fossil record. Patterns of evolution as demonstrated by the fossils are described in the volumes edited by Hallam (1977), Cope and Skelton (1985), Allen and Briggs (1989) and McNamara (1990). Eldredge and Gould (1972) is a classic paper which first introduced punctuated equilibrium. Stanley's (1979) textbook reviews the nature of macroevolution, while Donovan (1989) is a good review of mass extinctions in the fossil record.

Allen, K.C. & Briggs, D.E.G. (eds) 1989. *Evolution and the Fossil Record*. Belhaven Press, London.

Briggs, D.E.G. & Crowther, P.R. (eds) 1990. *Palaeobiology – A Synthesis*. Blackwell Scientific Publications, Oxford.

Clarkson, E.N.K. 1993. *Invertebrate Palaeontology and Evolution*. Chapman & Hall, London.

Cope, J.C.W. & Skelton, P.R. (eds) 1985. *Evolutionary Case Histories from the Fossil Record*. Special Papers in Palaeontology, 33, London.

Donovan, S.K. (ed.) 1989. *Mass Extinctions. Processes and Evidence*. Belhaven Press, London.
Eldredge, N. & Gould, S.J. 1972. Punctuated equilibria, an alternative to phyletic gradualism. *In* Schopf, T.J.M. (ed.), *Models in Paleobiology*. Freeman, Cooper & Co., San Francisco, 82–115.
Hallam, A. (ed.) 1977. *Patterns of Evolution as Illustrated by the Fossil Record*. Elsevier, Amsterdam.
McNamara, K.J. (ed.) 1990. *Evolutionary Trends*. Belhaven Press, London.
Patterson, C. 1978. *Evolution*. British Museum (Natural History), London.
Skelton, P.R. (ed.) 1993. *Evolution. A Biological and Palaeontological Approach*. Addison-Wesley, Wokingham; and Open University, Milton Keynes.
Stanley, S.M. 1979. *Macroevolution – Pattern and Process*. Freeman, San Francisco.

5
Fossils and Stratigraphy

Fossils are of paramount importance in interpreting much of the Earth's history, both in indicating the nature of past environments, and in providing a framework of time through the evolution of organisms on Earth. This chapter examines the application of fossils in providing this time framework for geologists. It does so by first introducing the principles of stratigraphy before discussing the application of fossils in biostratigraphy and chronostratigraphy.

5.1 PRINCIPLES OF STRATIGRAPHY

Stratigraphy is the study of the Earth's history and its development through time. In effect, it allows the interpretation of the Earth's geological record as a sequence of events through time. In order to achieve this, stratigraphy involves the processes of **observation, description** and **interpretation** of the rock units present.

Lithostratigraphy is the observation and description of rock units on the basis of their lithology. Each rock unit so defined is bounded solely by changes in rock type. The fundamental unit of lithostratigraphy is the **formation**, which is defined as a unit of rock which is thick enough to be recorded on a 1:10 000 map, and which has a distinct enough lithology to be easily distinguishable from those units immediately adjacent to it. It is a task of every geologist to determine the nature and extent of lithological units, and to record them on geological maps, which plot out the distribution and lateral extent of formations. This type of information is extremely valuable as a record of the materials and structure of the Earth's crust for a given area. However, it is limited; strictly speaking, the process of lithostratigraphy makes no assumption of either the nature of the lithological units present, or their geological age. Other information needs to be gathered to build up an accurate picture of the sequence of events, in interpreting both **facies** and **relative chronology**.

Each rock unit and formation contains clues to the environments in which it was created. The term **facies** is used to express the sum total of these characteristics, enabling a given rock unit to be interpreted as the product of a particular set of processes. The basis for this interpretation is the principle of uniformitarianism, the same principle as applied to the reconstruction of fossil organisms from their living relatives. Here present-day environments give clues to the formation of ancient rocks. For sedimentary rocks, the facies may be related to particular marine or non-marine environments (Box 5.1), which vary in position and

---

BOX 5.1: ANCIENT SEDIMENTARY ENVIRONMENTS

Sedimentary rocks contain many clues that allow geologists to deduce the nature of the ancient environment in which they were formed. There are many types of sedimentary rock, and all of them can contain fossils. The most important are **clastic** and **carbonate** rocks. Geologists deduce the nature of the environment in which rocks formed by studying a range of factors: rock type, structures such as bedding, the physical extent and geometry of the body of sedimentary rock, and fossil content.

Clastic sedimentary rocks are composed of particles which have been eroded from the landscape of older rocks. These particles can be as large as boulders, or as microscopic as clay. Typical clastic rocks are conglomerates, sandstones and clay. Clastic rocks are associated with the erosion and deposition of such particles by wind, water and ice, and are extremely important in the geological record. Typical environments in which clastic rocks are formed include deltas, deserts, and the deep, open sea. Desert sediments exhibit bedding and geometry illustrative of sand dunes; sedimentary structures showing desiccation; sand particles frosted by continuous wind action; and few fossils. Deep-sea sediments typically exhibit continuous finely laminated beds of fine-grained sediment, and the tracks, trails and body fossils of numerous organisms.

Carbonate sedimentary rocks, or limestones, are composed predominantly of calcium carbonate particles. They are formed by either organic or inorganic means. Organic carbonate rocks are composed of accumulations of whole or fragmentary calcareous organisms. Chalk, for example, is largely composed of nanofossils, extremely small (10^{-9} m) organisms which accumulated in deep water. Bioclastic limestone, as its name suggests, is a limestone made of the fragments of shells and other fossils. Inorganic limestones are less common, and are produced by chemical precipitation of calcium carbonate, e.g. in cavities and by hot springs. Typical environments for organic limestones include reefs, shallow seas and deeper-water settings. Reefs exhibit massive limestones packed with corals and other reef-dwelling organisms, and a geometry illustrative of the reef and its front, under constant wave attack.

Source: Selley, R.C. (1985) *Ancient Sedimentary Environments*. Chapman and Hall, London.

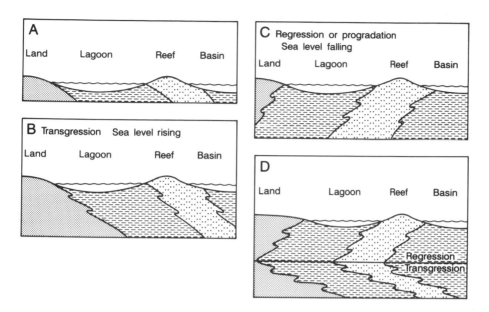

Figure 5.1 *Facies patterns caused by transgressions and regressions of the sea. **A:** Distribution of facies in a hypothetical marine environment. **B:** With rising sea level, the facies gradually transgress onshore. **C:** With falling sea level, the facies gradually regress offshore. **D:** The pattern produced in the stratigraphical record [Reproduced with permission from: Doyle et al. (1994), Key to Earth History, Wiley, Fig. 5.4, p. 71]*

geographical extent through geological time. In most cases there is a complex interaction of processes which leads to the production of several facies types in close relationship. For example, a barrier reef commonly consists of several interconnected environments: the lagoon behind the reef with fine-grained sediments; the reef itself with a mass of reef-building organisms such as corals and algae; the reef front, comprising a talus slope of reef debris broken by the crashing waves; and the outer-reef environment characterised by fine-grained sediments (Figure 5.1). The sedimentary processes acting in each one of these environments creates a facies with its own character and even rock type.

Clearly the distribution of facies, and therefore of lithostratigraphical units, in time and space is determined by the nature of the depositional environment. Although the relationship of one environment to another is often one of equilibrium – such as the relationship between lagoon, reef, reef front and basinal mud – the relative positions of these environments may change through time. The deposits produced, for example during a sea-level rise or fall (Figures 5.1 and 5.2), will result in a lithostratigraphical unit which is internally homogeneous, but which has been formed at different times over its lateral range. In these cases, the lithological boundaries of lagoonal and basinal muds and of reef and reef talus limestones transgress time boundaries and are said to be **diachronous** (Figure 5.2). Recognition of diachronism requires an independent means of determining relative chronology in order to determine time boundaries.

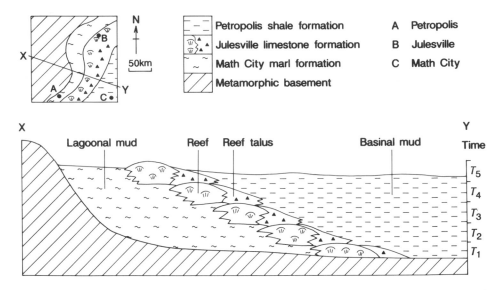

Figure 5.2 *The concept of diachronism. With rising sea level, the facies shift landwards through the time interval from T_1 to T_5. This process leads to the creation of rock units of uniform lithology. These may be mapped and named as formations, although each may have been formed at different times through the extent of the outcrop. Biostratigraphy provides one of the most efficient tests of diachronism*

From the early days of geology, it was possible to determine a **relative chronology**, or time scale of events. The **principle of superposition**, in which for any given stack of sedimentary strata the oldest and first formed rocks will be those at the bottom of the pile, is fundamental to stratigraphy. However, as we have seen, diachronism of the boundaries between some lithological units means that no assumption can be made that certain rock types formed in certain time periods. Therefore, in order to build up an accurate picture of the distribution of sedimentary environments for a given time interval, and plot any changes through time, an independent means of comparing rocks of the same age is needed. The basis for this comparison is the evolution of life, the fossil record illustrating the progressive evolution and extinction of organisms. Effectively, the irreversibility of the evolutionary process provides a method of relative ordering or chronology of fossil-bearing rocks, through the successive replacement of organisms by more advanced forms, the **principle of faunal and floral succession**. This principle, the subject matter of both biostratigraphy and chronostratigraphy, is discussed below.

5.2 FAUNAL AND FLORAL SUCCESSION

Life has existed on the Earth for at least 3550 million years, during which time it has evolved and developed. Different species of animals (fauna) and plants (flora) have appeared, evolved and become extinct through time. The evidence for this succession of species is recorded in the fossils within the rock record. This princi-ple is known as **faunal and floral succession** and can be used to provide relative dates for geological units, since evolution is time-dependent and irreversible.

This principle was first developed by the English canal engineer, William Smith (1769–1839). Smith was the first person to construct a detailed geological map of England and Wales, published in 1815. The geological units chosen by Smith for his map were based on distinctive lithologies which contained unique as-semblages of fossils. This was significant as, for the first time, *strata were identified by their distinctive fossils* and used as a tool in tracing Smith's geological units over great distances. As discussed in Chapter 3, a contemporary of Smith's, Georges Cuvier, was the first to demonstrate the concept that species were not constant, but that they eventually became extinct. Cuvier favoured catastrophic causes for the extinctions that he recognised, but it was not until the publication of Charles Darwin's *Origin of Species* in 1859 that evolution was presented as the all-encompassing theoretical basis for the successions of different fossils recognised by Smith, Cuvier and others.

Smith's discovery that strata could be identified by the fossils contained within them, together with Cuvier's discovery of species extinction, paved the way for the realisation that fossils could be used as indicators of relative age irrespective of sedimentary rock type. In this way the foundations for the use of fossils as an independent means of correlation, and of biostratigraphy, were laid.

5.3 BIOSTRATIGRAPHY

Biostratigraphy is the subdivision of rock units on the basis of fossil content. Unlike lithostratigraphy, this subdivision is time-significant, as the boundaries between the rock units are coincident with evolutionary changes in the organisms used to characterise them. Biostratigraphy is the basis for the correlation, or comparison in time, of lithological units. It provides the time framework for interpreting sedimentary rock units as the product of a network of interfingering environments. In this context, fossils act as geological tools enabling the com-parison in time of a range of geological units. However, not all fossils are useful or reliable in this task. Those that are suitable are known as **guide fossils**.

5.3.1 Guide Fossils: the Tools of Biostratigraphy

The most useful guide fossils (also called **index** or **zone fossils**) are those which, when living, were widely distributed both geographically and environmentally and which therefore allow a variety of rocks formed in widely spaced localities and in different environments to be correlated. As few fossil species fulfil all these ideal requirements, it follows that not all fossils are of equal value in biostratigraphy.

It is possible to draw up a set of criteria that can be used as a 'check-list' of the suitability of fossils as correlation tools. Guide fossils should ideally be: relatively independent of their environment (i.e. substrate); fast-evolving; geographically widespread; abundant; readily preserved; and easily recognisable. Few fossils qualify for honours in all of the criteria, but it follows that the more they possess the better they are as guide fossils (Figure 5.3).

Fossils should be relatively independent of their environment to be of value in interregional correlation. Bottom-dwelling marine animals, for example, may be dependent on the nature of the sea bottom sediment (substrate) or water depth. Fossils which are strongly dependent on a narrow range of environmental parameters are of limited use as guide fossils, because they only occur in specific

Criteria / Fossil	Independent of environment	Fast to evolve	Geographically widespread	Abundant	Readily preserved	Easily recognised	Status as guide fossils
 Graptolites	✔ (Plankton)	✔	✔ (Plankton)	✔	✔	✔ (Simple form)	Good (Ordovician to Silurian)
 Ammonites	✔ (Free swimming)	✔	✔ (Free swimming)	✔	✔	✔ (Great diversity)	Good (Devonian to Cretaceous)
 Corals	X (Need warm shallow sea)	X	X	✔	✔	✔	Poor (Carboniferous)
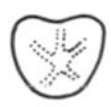 Echinoids	X (Bottom dwelling)	X	X	✔	✔	✔	Poor (Cretaceous)
 Barnacles	X (Need rocky shore)	X	X	X	X	✔	Bad (not used)
Foraminifera	✔ (Plankton)	✔	✔ (Plankton)	✔	✔	✔	Good (Particularly Mesozoic to Recent)
Pollen	✔ (Wind blown)	✔	✔ (Wind blown)	✔	✔	✔	Good (Cretaceous to Recent)
 Coccoliths	✔ (Plankton)	✔	✔ (Plankton)	✔	✔	✔	Good (Mesozoic to Recent)
Birds 	✔ (Flying)	X	✔ (Flying)	X	X (Fragile bones)	✔	Bad (not used)

Figure 5.3   *Examples of good and bad guide fossils judged against the ideal criteria [Reproduced with permission from: Doyle* et al. *(1994),* Key to Earth History, *Wiley, Fig. 4.1, p. 38]*

environments. For example, most barnacles are restricted to rocky foreshores, while corals are strongly restricted by light, salinity and temperature (Figure 5.3).

Fossils with restricted environmental tolerances are known as **facies fossils**. Despite their inadequacy, some facies fossils have been pressed into service as guide fossils. Corals, in particular, have been used where a uniform environment is achieved over a wide area, such as in the Lower Carboniferous rocks of England (Box 5.2). In contrast, organisms that are independent of substrate, such as those adapted to a free-swimming or floating mode of life, are well suited for correlation because they may float or swim above, and therefore drop into, a

BOX 5.2: BIOZONES IN THE LOWER CARBONIFEROUS

The Lower Carboniferous rocks of Britain are predominantly limestones and subordinate shales, which contain a rich fauna of brachiopods, corals and other reef-forming fossils. Deposition occurred in basins between structural highs over the area we now know as Britain, and the formation of limestones and reef faunas was in part due to Britain's equatorial position at this time.

In the early part of the twentieth century, the first real attempt to subdivide the Lower Carboniferous limestones of Britain into biozones was made, based on a thick sequence exposed in the Avon Gorge, near Bristol in southwest England. Here, Vaughan (1905) erected a scheme of biozones based on the available rugose coral and brachiopod species. These zones were based upon the ranges of the following taxa (in order of appearance): *Cleistopora* (K), a coral; *Zaphrentis* (Z), a coral; *Caninia* (C), a coral; *Seminula* (S), a brachiopod; and *Dibunophylum* (D), a coral. Prior to Vaughan's study, only limited correlations could be made on the basis of the two biozones which had been previously recognised. Vaughan was aware of the disadvantages of his biozonation, as in using just one section in the Avon Gorge the scheme was in need of testing at other sections. However, later work in other parts of Britain showed that the Avon Gorge had significant gaps, but that in general Vaughan's scheme was workable. Vaughan's biozones were based on coral and brachiopod facies fossils, but this is appropriate for the marine areas of Britain and Ireland which were predominantly warm, clear carbonate seas with rich reef-forming faunas. Correlation is possible because broadly the same facies are present across the area to be correlated. Vaughan's scheme continues to influence Lower Carboniferous stratigraphy, but for wider-scale correlation, matching of the coral–brachiopod zonation with those for ammonoids, microfossils and other non-facies fossils is necessary. This is the subject of ongoing research.

Sources: Riley, N.J. (1993). Dinantian (Lower Carboniferous) biostratigraphy and chronostratigraphy in the British Isles. *Journal of the Geological Society*, **150**, 427–446. Vaughan, A. (1905). The palaeontological sequence in the Carboniferous limestone of the Bristol area. *Quarterly Journal of the Geological Society of London*, **61**, 181–307.

variety of different depositional environments. Such organisms make the best guide fossils, and examples of their application in biostratigraphy are given in detail in Chapter 23. The geographical extent of fossils obviously controls the area over which correlations can be made. Thus if an organism is world-wide in its distribution, then there is the potential for world-wide correlation of stratigraphical sequences.

Rates of evolution are known to vary through geological time. Some fossils evolved quickly with the development of new species (species turnover) at regular intervals of less than 1 million years. High rates of species turnover, that is of evolutionary change, mean that a given fossil will exist within a smaller proportion of the stratigraphical record. For example, if a species survived for a long time then it could be found in rocks of widely different ages, but if it survived for only a short span of time its presence in a rock ties that rock to a more specific period of time. Consequently a fossil with a rapid species turnover allows the geological record to be subdivided more finely than one in which new species only appeared after long intervals. The so-called living fossils – such as *Nautilus* (the pearly nautilus), *Lingula* (an intertidal brachiopod) and *Limulus* (the king crab) – have remained unchanged in overall morphology for vast periods of time and are therefore of very limited value in biostratigraphy.

The last three criteria are important because they control whether a fossil can be easily employed as a guide fossil, irrespective of whether it is naturally suited to the task. Fossils should be abundant: they will be of little use if they satisfy the first three criteria, but are impossible to find. The first bird, *Archaeopteryx*, for instance, is otherwise well suited as a Jurassic guide fossil, but only eight specimens are known to exist. Similarly, if fossils are too delicate, or their morphology too bland, or too complex, then practising stratigraphers will be unable to use them effectively. In general, birds have hollow bones which are easily broken; although otherwise well suited as guide fossils, they are limited by their poor fossil record. Graptolites preserve a simple morphology which can be recognised in even deformed rock sequences, and are excellent guide fossils. Fossils must therefore be readily preservable and recognisable to be of value.

Among the best fossils which can be employed in biostratigraphical correlation are ammonites, a group of molluscs that became extinct at the end of the Mesozoic (Chapter 9); and graptolites, an extinct group of colonial organisms common in the Palaeozoic (Chapter 14). Ammonites were free-swimming organisms which had a widespread distribution and were not tied to a particular substrate. Importantly, ammonites evolved rapidly with the production of new species and the extinction of old ones each within an estimated time span of 0.5–1 million years. The practical result of this for biostratigraphy is that refined, high-resolution correlation can be achieved which allows fine subdivision of the Mesozoic stratigraphical record. Graptolites were free-floating organisms which have been used for intercontinental correlation of Palaeozoic sequences. Graptolites evolved quickly and, like ammonites, were not restricted to a substrate or particular type of marine environment. Both groups were abundant, readily preserved and are easily recognisable with the aid of standard reference works. Examples of their application are given in Chapter 23.

Microfossils are also particularly important in biostratigraphy, particularly as they are small enough to be extracted from the cuttings and small-diameter rock cores produced from boreholes. This is obviously an advantage in the interpretation of underground sequences drilled in the quest for oil or other natural resources. Particularly important guide microfossils include foraminifera (Chapter 16), spores and pollen.

5.3.2 The Basic Unit of Biostratigraphy: The Biozone

The basic unit of biostratigraphy is the **biozone**, often just referred to as the zone in older literature. Biozones are strata organised into stratigraphical units on the basis of their content of guide fossils. Biozones may be recognised on local or regional scales.

The concept of the biozone was developed by Albert Oppel (1831–1865) in the 1850s. Oppel recognised that the vertical (stratigraphical) range of fossils was time-significant and that it was independent of the lithology containing the fossils. He subdivided the Jurassic System into units defined on the vertical ranges of a number of fossil assemblages. In many ways this has parallels with Smith's original work, but Oppel differed in not tying the fossil assemblages to lithology. Each of Oppel's zones was formally defined and named, usually after one distinctive fossil in an assemblage, and each zone could be traced across continental Europe (Box 5.3).

Oppel's concept of the zone, now rechristened the biozone to avoid confusion with other uses of the term in geology, remains valid today, and some types of assemblage biozone are given the name **Oppel biozones**. In an **assemblage biozone**, the biozone is defined on the basis of the vertical ranges of a number of fossils (Figure 5.4). Often assemblage biozones are utilised where there are few good guide fossils available, as is often found where most of the fossils have a benthonic (bottom-dwelling) rather than planktonic (free-floating) or nektonic (free-swimming) mode of life. An assemblage biozone is often limited in use because it relies on the recognition of a number of fossils. Other types of biozone have also been recognised. **Total range biozones** are based on the total vertical range of a single fossil, usually a suitably qualified guide fossil, such as an ammonite or graptolite. **Partial range biozones** utilise part of the total vertical range of a fossil, particularly of organisms which were relatively slow to evolve. The partial range is usually defined as being between the first and last appearances of other fossils (Figure 5.4). Other biozones, such as the **acme biozone**, which is based on an abundance of a fossil group, are more difficult to recognise in practice because of the overall imperfection of the fossil record.

The lower boundary of a biozone is usually drawn at the first appearance of the next one. These boundaries are sometimes related to an evolutionary lineage or line where the replacement of species is directly related to the evolution of the group from one species to another. Such biozones are called **consecutive range biozones** (Figure 5.4). In practice they are hard to prove and rely upon detailed stratigraphical study. In other cases the boundaries of biozones may be denoted

BOX 5.3: ALBERT OPPEL AND HIS CONCEPT OF ZONES

Between 1856 and 1858, a young German, Albert Oppel, published a monumental work which was to alter stratigraphical practice altogether, and to increase the precision by which correlations could be effected. The book, *Die Juraformation Englands, Frankreichs und des südwestlichen Deutschlands*, was a landmark simply because in it Oppel defined his concept of **zones**. Oppel divided the Jurassic System of eight separate regions of Europe into 33 zones which could be correlated on the basis of their fossil content. In developing his system, Oppel believed that correlation

necessarily involves exploring the vertical range of each separate species in the most diverse localities, while ignoring the lithological development of the beds; by this means will be brought into prominence those zones which, through the constant and exclusive occurrence of certain species, mark themselves off from their neighbours as distinct horizons (translated by Arkell, 1933, p. 16).

Clearly, Oppel had identified the need to define units of strata on the basis of the recorded stratigraphical ranges of fossils. For the most part, Oppel used assemblages of fossils, commonly with 10–30 species, but he was aware that with greater accuracy in defining species and recording their ranges, there would be a corresponding increase in accuracy in subdivision and correlation. Although Oppel died young, at the age of 34, his monumental work led to the acceptance of the principle of biostratigraphical correlation through the erection of a series of standard biozones, based on accurate recording of range data.

Sources: Arkell, W.J. (1933). *The Jurassic System in Great Britain*. Clarendon Press, Oxford. Hancock, J.M. (1977). The historic development of concepts of biostratigraphic correlation. *In* Kauffman, E.G. and Hazel, J.E. (eds), *Concepts and Methods of Biostratigraphy*, Dowden, Hutchinson and Ross, Stroudsberg, 3–22.

by migrations, which mark the migration of a species from one geographical area to another and may be unrelated to the organisms of the preceding biozone. In practice, this is relatively common. The theoretical basis of any biozonation scheme is that the biological changes recorded in the scheme should be synchronous across the world. A new species will not evolve and appear everywhere in an instant but will migrate progressively from a centre across a region or continent. Consequently the appearance of a new species may not be synchronous across an area. However, this is not a problem given the sheer scale of geological time and that the process of species migrations will not be detectable within the resolving power of the geological record. They can, therefore, be considered for most purposes to be instantaneous. Other not strictly biozonal schemes using the first and last appearances of fossils have proven to be of great value in the correlation of rock sequences (Box 5.4).

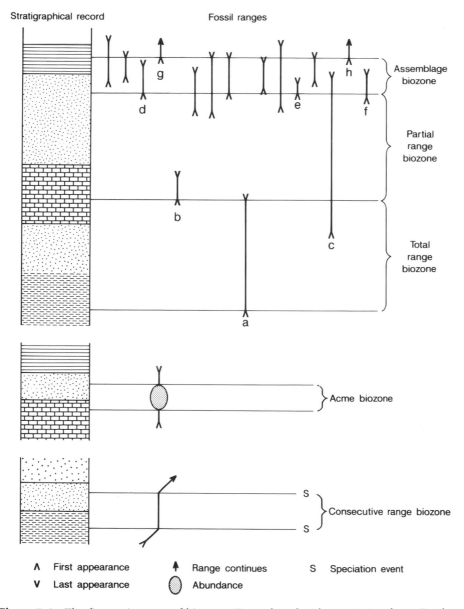

Figure 5.4 The five main types of biozone [Reproduced with permission from: Doyle et al. (1994), Key to Earth History, Wiley, Fig. 4.3, p. 42]

In terms of evolution, the concept of punctuated equilibrium, whereby species undergo periods of rapid change between long periods of stasis, has been recognised from the stratigraphical record. Many zonal schemes may in fact be a reflection of such dramatic evolutionary change and may give greater relevance to the biozonal schemes based upon it, although very detailed stratigraphical study is required to prove it.

BOX 5.4: BIOSTRATIGRAPHICAL CORRELATION WITHOUT BIOZONES

Biozones are largely based upon the total ranges of species as defined from their first appearance to their last appearance in the rock record. However, in general terms it is mostly the lower of these two, the first appearance, which is taken as the most significant boundary, as the base of one biozone (drawn on the first appearance of one fossil) can be used to define the upper boundary of another biozone (based on the range of another fossil). Correlation of rock successions is usually made through reference to standard biozones and, in practice, to a standard stratigraphy from which the biozonal boundaries are recorded. However, in some cases, the stratigraphical section may be incomplete or the zonal fossils may not be present, and therefore correlation between sections is difficult. Correlation may be achieved, however, through the application of graphic correlation, a technique first introduced by Shaw (1964). In graphic correlation, the thickest section is selected as a standard, and

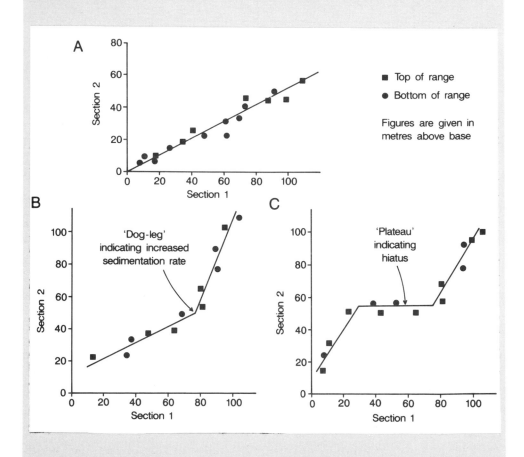

BOX 5.4: (*cont.*)

from this the ranges of all fossil species present, using both their first and last appearances, are constructed. Other sections and their fossil ranges are also measured and compared with the standard section by means of plotting a graph. On this graph the first and last appearances of fossil taxa are plotted, and a **line of correlation** is drawn to connect the first and last appearances of each fossil group which have similar ranges in both sequences. Where such a line can be drawn, then the two sections can be correlated. In many cases the slope of the line changes, illustrating variation in the sedimentation rate, but in others correlation using the fossils collected cannot be carried out. The graphic correlation method is advantageous as it makes no assumption about the validity of using one guide fossil over another in the erection of biozones. It simply utilises all available data to construct a correlation, usually with a high degree of precision.

Sources: Shaw, A.B. (1964) *Time in Stratigraphy*. McGraw-Hill, New York. Miller, F.X. (1977) The graphic correlation method in biostratigraphy. *In* Kauffman, E.G. and Hazel, J.E. (eds) *Concepts and Methods of Biostratigraphy*. Dowden, Hutchinson and Ross, Stroudsberg, 165–186. [Figure reproduced with permission from: Doyle *et al.* (1994) *The key to Earth History*, Wiley, Box 4.2, p.44]

5.4 CHRONOSTRATIGRAPHY

Chronostratigraphy is the study of rock units bounded by time planes. The recognition of chronostratigraphical units allows comparison of the environments and past life of specific time intervals across the Earth. Effectively, chronostratigraphy encompasses one of the most important goals in stratigraphy – the establishment of a global standard or chronology of geological units, the Chronostratigraphical Scale. The Chronostratigraphical Scale, or Geological Time Scale is a summation of all stratigraphical knowledge and as such there is no single section on the surface of the Earth at which all its units are exposed (Box 1.1). Biostratigraphy is the most important tool used for the recognition of time-equivalent units in chronostratigraphy (Box 5.5).

Chronostratigraphical units are bodies of strata that were formed during specific periods of geological time. The boundaries of chronostratigraphical units are time-significant as they are of the same age across the Earth (i.e. they are isochronous). Chronstratigraphical units are sometimes referred to as time-stratigraphical units to distinguish them from rock-stratigraphical units (lithostratigraphical units). The Chronostratigraphical Scale provides the global standard with which local sequences may be correlated. A simplified version of the currently accepted scale is given in Box 1.1. This scale is a standard with which geologists can correlate their individual rock sequences. It comprises a set of

BOX 5.5: BIOSTRATIGRAPHY AND CHRONOSTRATIGRAPHY COMPARED

The primary goal of biostratigraphy is to enable correlation of local rock sequences. Biostratigraphy provides a method for determining the relative chronology of a given set of rock units and therefore a given set of evolving environments. Chronostratigraphy is more far-reaching; its aim is to create units, bounded by time planes, which act as repositories for geological knowledge for a given interval of Earth history. In this way, each chronostratigraphical unit contains all the rocks, and therefore environments, formed during given intervals of geological time. The international Chronostratigraphical Scale is the global standard for comparison of rocks of the same age.

Biostratigraphy and chronostratigraphy are closely related through their reliance on fossils as indicators of relative time. Fossils are by far the most important tool in recognising the time boundaries which constrain chronostratigraphical units. Therefore, in most cases, the boundaries of chronostratigraphical units, from the smallest to the largest scale, are coincident with biostratigraphical boundaries. A case in point is provided by the boundary stratotype, or international reference section, for the base of the Silurian System at Dobs Linn in the Southern Uplands of Scotland. Here, the time plane forming the lower boundary of the Silurian system is coincident with the base of the *acuminatus* graptolite biozone, useful in the correlation of rocks of this age in Scotland and elsewhere. The stratotype was ratified by international agreement in May 1985, selected from a choice of several sites across the world, and the final choice was influenced by the occurrence of rich graptolite faunas which can be correlated across the world.

Source: Cocks, L.R.M. and Rickards, R.B. (eds) (1988) *The Ordovician–Silurian Boundary: A Global Synthesis.* Bulletin of the British Museum (Natural History), Geology, **43**, London.

major units known as **systems** (e.g. the Carboniferous System or Triassic System). Each system consists of rocks deposited during the same time interval.

Most of the boundaries of chronostratigraphical units are determined using biostratigraphy, although other techniques are used. Generally, the boundaries between chronostratigraphical units are therefore coincident with changes in the fauna. Since there is no locality at which all the chronostratigraphical units which make up the global scale are exposed, individual boundaries are identified through stratotype sections located across the world. In other words, the best exposed example of the boundary between each unit is selected as typical, and designated as a stratotype section, usually through international agreement (Box 5.5). This allows geologists to correlate their individual sections with a known, protected, locality which they can visit. The systems were originally defined largely in geological and geographical terms and as a consequence the boundaries

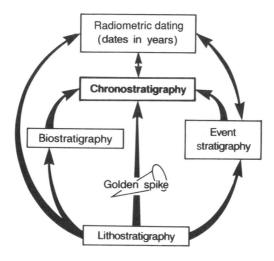

Figure 5.5 *The mechanism of chronostratigraphy. Chronostratigraphical units are bodies of rock whose boundaries are time-significant. International agreement is needed to determine where the boundaries of standard chronostratigraphical units, such as systems, should lie and at that point a symbolic golden spike is 'driven in'. Correlation of rock sequences with this standard is undertaken on the basis of methods such as biostratigraphy or event stratigraphy. Absolute dates may be obtained for the duration of chronostratigraphical units through radiometric dating [Reproduced with permission from: Doyle et al. (1994),* Key to Earth History, *Wiley, Box 4.5, p. 53]*

were not always fixed, often causing confusion. More recently the boundaries have been decided by international agreement and in each case a symbolic spike, known as a golden spike, has been driven into the chosen stratotype section to mark the agreed position of the time-significant boundary (Figure 5.5).

The systems may be grouped into larger units, known as **erathems**. These, too, are defined by faunal changes. John Phillips (1800–1874), the nephew of William Smith, broke down the part of the geological record which contained shelly fossils into three main subdivisions based on major changes in the fauna (Figure 5.6). The boundaries of these erathems are marked by mass extinction events. Phillips named them with respect to the nature of their fauna: Palaeozoic (old life), Mesozoic (middle life) and Cainozoic (new life: now commonly called the Cenozoic), reflecting increasingly familiar fossil organisms through time to the present. The Palaeozoic–Mesozoic boundary is denoted by the Permian–Triassic mass extinction and the Mesozoic–Cenozoic by the Cretaceous–Tertiary mass extinction. The boundary between the older primary or Precambrian rocks and the Palaeozoic was taken at the first appearance of shelly fossils, also now interpreted as a biological event horizon associated with the diversification of life on the planet. In this way, the major subdivisions of the Chronostratigraphical Scale are bounded by biological event horizons.

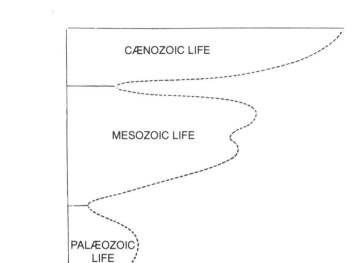

Figure 5.6 *Phillips's erathems, based on faunal diversity. The boundaries of the erathems were drawn at intervals of major diversity decline [From: Phillips (1860)* Life on the Earth: Its Origin and Succession, *Fig. 4, p. 56]*

5.5 SUMMARY OF KEY POINTS

- Stratigraphy is the interpretation of the Earth's geological record as a sequence of events through time. It has several components. **Lithostratigraphy** is the observation and description of rock units on the basis of their lithology. **Biostratigraphy** is the subdivision of the rock record into units based upon the vertical ranges of fossil species. **Chronostratigraphy** is the organisation of the rock record into rock units with time-significant boundaries.
- The fundamental object of biostratigraphy is to aid in the correlation of rock sequences using fossils. Some fossil groups are more important in this respect than others. These are known as **guide fossils**. Ideal guide fossils need to be: independent of their environment; fast-evolving; geographically widespread; abundant; readily preservable; and easily recognisable.

- **Biozones** are the primary unit of biostratigraphy. They are defined on the basis of the vertical ranges of one or more guide fossils, and are the means by which correlation is achieved.

5.6 FURTHER READING

Doyle *et al.* (1994) provides an up-to-date introduction to the principles of stratigraphy. Eicher (1976), although dated, is a well-written and accessible book on the principles of stratigraphy. Raup and Stanley (1978) devote a chapter to the use of fossils in stratigraphy, and Kauffman and Hazel (1977) is an edited volume of over 25 papers on the application of fossils in biostratigraphy.

Doyle, P., Bennett, M.R. & Baxter, A.N. 1994. *The Key to Earth History*. John Wiley, Chichester.
Eicher, D.L. 1976. *Geologic Time*. Second edition. Prentice Hall, Englewood Cliffs, NJ.
Kauffman, E.G. & Hazel, J.E. (eds) 1977. *Concepts and Methods of Biostratigraphy*. Dowden, Hutchinson & Ross, Stroudsberg, PA.
Raup, D.M. & Stanley, S.M. 1978. *Principles of Paleontology*. Second edition. Freeman, San Francisco.

6
Summary of Part I

The first part of this book examined the key concepts necessary to understand the breadth of the subject of palaeontology, the study of ancient life. This chapter provides a recap of these concepts and forms an introduction to the interpretation of the main fossil groups that follows in Part II.

The basis for palaeontology is the science of **taxonomy**, the scientific ordering and naming of fossil groups. All geological and biological applications of fossils have their roots in taxonomy. The taxonomic system is a scientific language which can be applied the world over and which provides the solid foundation which ensures that scientists are working with the same groups of animals or plants across the world, and that they are directly comparable. From taxonomy springs the basis for the three main applications that fossils provide: **palaeobiology**, **palaeoenvironmental analysis** and **stratigraphy**. Examples of the applications of the major fossil groups are given in Part II, and are discussed in detail in Part III.

Fossils are defined as the remains of once living organisms which are now preserved in the rock record. They are the visible expression of the existence of life on Earth over the last 3550 million years of Earth history. There are two basic types: **body fossils** and **trace fossils**. Body fossils are the physical remains of animals and plants that have undergone a process of preservation known as **fossilisation**. The processes of fossilisation are diverse and complex, but they effectively revolve around two basic principles: if organisms are to be preserved they should be rapidly buried or otherwise entombed, in order to prevent physical breakdown by currents activity and scavengers; furthermore, if they are to be exceptionally preserved, oxygen needs to be excluded, or the decay process slowed in an antiseptic environment, for example frozen in ice. In general terms, most fossils are a direct result of chance preservation through burial, and the greatest opportunity for this to happen is in the continuous sedimentation of the marine environment. Because of this, the commonest fossils are marine organisms.

Fossils have not always been considered to have been once living organisms. Early concepts considered them to be relicts of mysterious vapours which pervaded the Earth's crust. The discovery of **comparative anatomy**, the comparison of the form and function of living and fossil organisms, paved the way for the acceptance of fossils as extinct animals and plants. This process is still very much used today in the interpretation of fossil organisms. In considering fossils as living organisms it is possible to consider their interaction with each other and with their environment. This branch of palaeontology is known as **palaeoecology**, and its fundamental basis is **taxonomic uniformitarianism**, the consideration that living relatives of extinct species can be used to determine the nature of the ecological tolerances and relationships of the past. Taxonomic uniformitarianism is also the basis for **palaeoenvironmental analysis**, as it follows that the factors such as temperature, salinity and oxygen levels which limit the diversity and abundance of living organisms also limited their fossil ancestors. Levels of these parameters can therefore be interpreted for the ancient environment where fossil assemblages can be confidently identified as once living communities.

Fossils provide the most convincing testimony to the pattern and process of evolution. It is argued that the fossil record is incomplete, but in fact the rate (timing) and pattern of evolution in groups from individual species to phyla can be reliably determined from fossils preserved in the rock record. The most important role of palaeontology in evolution is to provide the dimension of time lacking from the study of modern faunas and floras. Through this dimension of time, it is clear that evolution proceeds at two scales: **microevolution**, a generation to generation transition to new species; and **macroevolution**, the origins, diversification and extinction of the major groups. Palaeontology is the key to documenting and understanding these patterns.

From a geological perspective, the most valuable role for fossils is as stratigraphical ciphers which enable geologists to subdivide and correlate rock sequences independently of lithology and over great distances. Many fossils are suited to this task, and the succession of their remains provides a chronometer to the formation of the rock record.

Part II
THE MAIN FOSSIL GROUPS

7
Introduction to the Fossil Record

In this chapter the major features of the fossil record are introduced before going on to discuss individual groups in greater detail. Each chapter which follows contains a discussion of the general features, main aspects of morphology and evolution of the major fossil groups, together with examples of their application in palaeobiology, palaeoenvironmental analysis and stratigraphy.

7.1 MAJOR FEATURES OF THE FOSSIL RECORD

The history of the development of life on Earth is illuminated by the fossil record. Although undoubtedly incomplete – a function of the poor preservation potential of some organisms, and the loss through erosion of the rock record (Chapter 2) – the fossil record provides a remarkable account of the major features and patterns of evolution. Since the early days of the science, palaeontologists have been able to piece together its exceptional story. The Precambrian, the greatest interval of geological time, was always a mystery to the early palaeontologists, appearing to be entirely barren of life. Discovery of life in the Precambrian came in the later twentieth century, and slowly a pattern of the early development of life, from anaerobic prokaryotic cells to multicellular eukaryotes, has been teased from the imperfect record of the Precambrian.

The Phanerozoic, the interval of 'visible life', records the rapid evolutionary development of the multicellular metazoans. The pattern of mass extinction and adaptive radiation which has shaped this record has been well known since the mid-nineteenth century. Darwin himself commented upon the sudden appearance of the Cambrian Fauna and the evolutionary expansion of the flowering plants; while the division of the Phanerozoic into Palaeozoic, Mesozoic and

Cenozoic eras was determined on the basis of mass extinctions by John Phillips in 1866 (Fig. 5.6). The Phanerozoic records the development of the invertebrate metazoans in three evolutionary faunas which are characteristic of marine life at specific intervals of its 560 million years of Earth history. It also records the development of the land plants, an important aspect for the ecosystems of terrestrial environments, and the rise of the vertebrates. This section examines the nature of the fossil record in these two major intervals of geological time, the Precambrian and the Phanerozoic.

7.1.1 Life in the Precambrian

The Precambrian comprises most of Earth history. It commences from the origin of the planet some 4600 million years ago, and ends with the diversification of multicellular life around 560 million years ago. The first life appeared in the early Precambrian, and two major phases can be identified in the development of life during this interval: the first records of life and its evolution in the earliest or Archaean rocks (4600–2500 million years old); and the appearance and diversification of more complex organisms in the Proterozoic rocks (2500–560 million years ago). These are discussed below.

Archaean Life

The origin of life has been debated for many decades. Indirect evidence of the presence of early life is provided by carbon (graphite) deposits in some of the most ancient rocks, but the first real fossil organisms are recorded from rocks which have been dated at some 3550 million years old. These fossils were discovered in Western Australia, where they occur in the Warrawoona Group, a series of volcanic and sedimentary rocks which formed in a shallow marine environment. Two types of fossil structure have been found: **stromatolites** and individual **cell filaments.**

Stromatolites are sedimentary structures associated today with **cyanobacteria** (Box 7.1). Today, stromatolites are still forming, and the best known are those from Shark Bay in Western Australia. These present-day stromatolites serve as important uniformitarian interpreters of Precambrian life. At Shark Bay, carbonate domes are developed in lagoons with up to twice the salinity of normal sea water. The domes are constructed by filaments of cyanobacteria which grow across the surface of the dome (Figure 7.1). Sedimentary particles are trapped by the cyanobacteria, and build up into a series of concentric layers, through which the filaments penetrate and continue their role as sediment traps (Figure 7.1). Similar stromatolites are known through much of the Precambrian and were probably formed in much the same way (Figure 4.10). The oldest known stromatolites so far discovered come from the Warrawoona Group, although they are uncommon. Cyanobacterial filaments have never been discovered within them, but isolated cell filaments have been recovered from associated cherts. These filaments, first discovered in 1980, represent the oldest known *direct* evidence of early life. Detailed examination of them indicates their close relationship with living cyanobacteria which possess a simple **prokaryotic** cell (Box 7.1). Prokaryotic cells are small, have no nucleus, and the DNA, the building block of life, is not contained within chromosomes (Figure 7.2).

BOX 7.1: PRINCIPAL GROUPS OF ORGANISMS IN THE BIOSPHERE

The biosphere represents the total number of organisms present upon the planet at a given time. Organisms are known to inhabit almost every known environment, from the smallest cavity to the largest open space. There are currently five kingdoms recognised, organised into two superkingdoms on the basis of their cell structure. The superkingdom Prokaryota has simple single-celled organisms belonging to the kingdom Monera. These include the first life to appear on Earth some 3550 million years ago. The prokaryotic cell is simple, without a nucleus. The superkingdom Eukaryota is characterised by the possession of the eukaryotic cell, which has a nucleus allowing greater genetic variability. This superkingdom combines simple single-celled microscopic organisms (protists) with multicellular fungi, plants and animals. Each kingdom is composed of a number of major groups, the phyla, which characterise the range and diversity of the organisms present.

Superkingdom Prokaryota

Kingdom Monera	(Bacteria, Cyanobacteria)	Archaean–Recent

Superkingdom Eukaryota

Kingdom Protista	(Algae, Foraminifera)	Proterozoic–Recent
Kingdom Fungi	(Fungi)	Silurian–Recent
Kingdom Plantae	(Plants)	Ordovician–Recent
Kingdom Animalia	(multi-celled Animals)	Proterozoic–Recent

Source: Whittaker, R.H. (1969) New concepts of kingdoms of organisms. *Science*, **163**, 150–160.

Other direct evidence of prokaryotic cells in the Archaean are rare, but are well known from suitable sedimentary rocks, particularly cherts. The Fig Tree Group of southern Africa, for example, dated at 3400 million years old, contains convincing stromatolites and cell filaments, and other occurrences are known. It is probable that these early prokaryotic cells were able to survive in an anaerobic or oxygen-poor environment, since it is thought that the Precambrian atmosphere was composed of methane, carbon dioxide, and hydrogen sulphide produced by volcanic degassing as the Earth's crust cooled. The presence of stromatolites is illustrative of the first development of photosynthesis, which had a profound influence on the planet's atmosphere. The development of photosynthesis, which uses light as an energy source, is one of the most significant events in the history

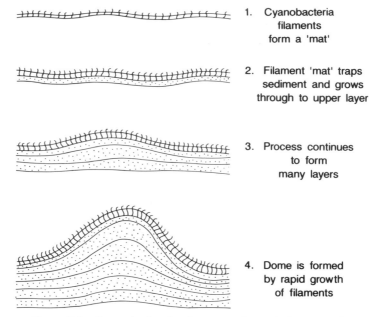

1. Cyanobacteria
   filaments
   form a 'mat'

2. Filament 'mat' traps
   sediment and grows
   through to upper layer

3. Process continues
   to form
   many layers

4. Dome is formed
   by rapid growth
   of filaments

Figure 7.1   *Stages in the development of a typical stromatolite*

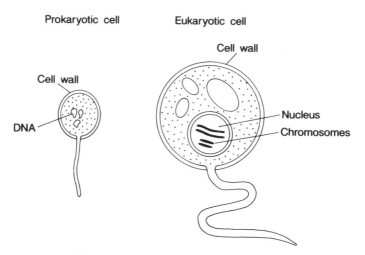

Figure 7.2   *Prokaryotic and eukaryotic cells*

of the biosphere. In photosynthesis solar energy is transformed to chemical energy when carbon dioxide is reduced by hydrogen, donated either by hydrogen sulphide in the case of certain anaerobic bacteria, or by water in the case of cyanobacteria and of virtually all other photosynthetic organisms. Sulphur is released when hydrogen sulphide is used, while oxygen is released when water is the hydrogen donor. The first photosynthetic organisms lived in the early anaerobic atmosphere of the Earth. The development of a photosynthetic pathway which utilised water as the source of hydrogen and released oxygen as a by-product led to a gradual, but radical, change in the Earth's atmosphere. By the end of the Archaean, the Earth's atmosphere was enriched in oxygen by the activities of such photosynthetic organisms.

Proterozoic Life

By the beginning of the Proterozoic, some 2500 million years ago, the Earth's atmosphere had become increasingly oxygen-rich as a product of the cumulative effect of photosynthesis. This is recorded in the presence of oxidised red sandstones for the first time in the Proterozoic, direct evidence of free oxygen in the atmosphere. In many ways the subdivision of the Precambrian into the Archaean and the Proterozoic approximates to the change from an anaerobic (oxygen-poor) to an aerobic (oxygen-rich) atmosphere. The early Proterozoic is denoted by a dramatic increase in the abundance and diversity of stromatolites, and a coincident increase in the oxygen content of the developing atmosphere (Figure 7.3). Prokaryotic cell assemblages are common in appropriate rock types such as the Gunflint Chert of southern Ontario in Canada (2000 million years old), from which the first Precambrian cell fossils were extracted in the early 1950s.

Probably the most important evolutionary step during the Proterozoic was the appearance of the first **eukaryotic** cell (Figure 7.2). This type of cell has not only a nucleus and complex of chromosomes, but also a means of sexual reproduction and therefore a method of genetic variation and of natural selection leading to rapid evolutionary change. Most organisms living today possess a eukaryotic cell type (Box 7.1). It is not known exactly when this event occurred, but it could not have taken place in the anaerobic environment of the Archaean as eukaryotes require oxygen. It is possible that eukaryotic cells developed through an association of several prokaryotes. The oldest reported evidence of eukaryotes are **acritarchs**, reproductive stages and cysts of planktonic algae, common in rocks 750 million years old, and traceable back to 1400 million years ago. In addition, *Glenobotrydion* is a disputed eukaryotic cell from the late Proterozoic rocks (850 million years old) of Bitter Springs, Australia.

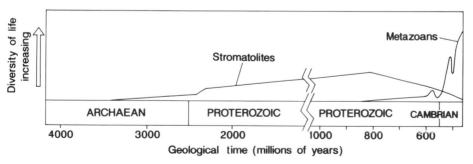

Figure 7.3 *Life in the Precambrian. Stromatolites reached a diversity maximum in the Proterozoic, and declined with the appearance of the metazoans [Modified from: Conway Morris (1992) In Brown et al. (Eds) Understanding the Earth, Cambridge University Press, Fig. 22.10, p. 455]*

Multicellular organisms (metazoans) developed from these early eukaryotes. The first evidence of multicellular organisms is found in rocks 900 million years old and consists of simple trace fossils, suggesting the beginning of burrowing activity (Figure 7.3). The most spectacular evidence of Proterozoic metazoans is given by a distinct assemblage of body fossils preserved as impressions, and known as the **Ediacaran Biota**. This biota was discovered in 1947 in the Ediacara Hills of Australia, and has been dated at 600 million years. The members of this biota have since been discovered in England and Wales (the Charnian Biota), Africa, Russia and North America. Over 1400 specimens have been collected, and they appear to fall into four distinct types: jellyfishes (medusoids); soft corals (pennatulaceans); worms (annelids); and uncertain fossils (Figures 2.10 and 7.4). Although they can in some cases be compared with living examples, it has been suggested that the Ediacaran organisms are totally distinct from living organisms, as most appear to have a peculiar quilted structure which is unknown in animals today. They are interpreted as **autotrophic**, that is, taking nutrients directly from their surroundings into their body, and not reliant on the ingestion of other organisms (**heterotrophy**) for their nourishment. This interpretation is supported by their quilted structure which may indicate the utilisation of a large surface area for this process. This biota was extinguished at the end of the Proterozoic, apparently leaving no direct descendants, and was replaced by an early fauna of shelly fossils, precursors to the abundant shelly life of the Phanerozoic (Figure 7.3).

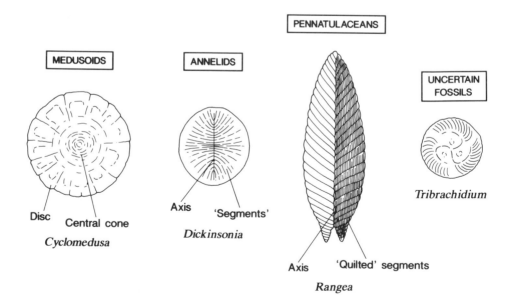

Figure 7.4   *Typical representatives of the Ediacaran Biota. Four main groups may be identified: medusoids (jellyfish); annelids (worms); pennatulaceans (soft corals); and an uncertain group. The affinities of this biota are still open to debate*

7.1.2 Life in the Phanerozoic

The Phanerozoic is that interval of geological time which encompasses the development of the abundant life we know today, from 560 million years ago to the present day. The evolutionary development of life in the Phanerozoic follows a consistent pattern of adaptive radiations punctuated by mass extinctions, which together stocked and restocked the developing biosphere with successive animal and plant groups (Figure 4.10). Three main macroevolutionary themes can be recognised: the development of the marine invertebrate fauna; the evolution of the terrestrial flora; and the evolution of the vertebrates. These are dealt with below.

The Development of the Phanerozoic Invertebrate Fauna

The development of the Phanerozoic invertebrates can be considered with reference to three main evolutionary faunas: the **Cambrian Fauna**, the **Palaeozoic Fauna** and the **Modern** or **Mesozoic–Cenozoic Fauna** (Figure 7.5). These evolutionary faunas are sets of higher taxa, representing groups of organisms which have similar histories of diversification and evolution, and which dominated the marine biota for a great interval of geological time. Their development is associated with adaptive radiations, and the reduction in their importance with major mass extinctions (Figure 4.10).

The **Cambrian Fauna** is characterised by the first appearance of animals with hard body parts, such as shells or other skeletal elements. Shelly fossils are found in the late Proterozoic, almost contemporary with the Ediacaran Biota, but by the end of the Proterozoic the Ediacaran organisms had become extinct, and shelly organisms had increased dramatically in diversity (Figure 7.3). The beginning of the Phanerozoic is marked by what is perhaps the most striking of all adaptive radiations. This radiation is commonly referred to as the Cambrian explosion or expansion and it refers to the rapid diversification of animals with hard parts (i.e. shells and skeletons) which took place at the start of the Phanerozoic (Figure 7.6). This diversification may have been assisted by the effects of the widespread late Proterozoic glaciation, which had two effects. First, it increased the mixing of water masses and therefore the supply of nutrients. Second, sea level increased significantly after the end of this 'ice age' and flooded large areas of continental margin, creating shallow seas. The uptake of phosphate and then carbonate nutrients by Cambrian organisms in these shallow seas allowed them to form skeletal material for the first time. The explosion of animals with hard parts may reflect a need for protection from scavengers and predators, a result of the development for the first time of heterotrophs.

The Cambrian Fauna is exclusively marine and dominated by trilobites (Chapter 12). Archaeocyathans, extinct sponge-like organisms, also form part of this fauna. The trilobites are found together with early representatives of the Palaeozoic fauna: molluscs, brachiopods and echinoderms (Chapters 8, 10 and 11). The Cambrian Fauna is archaic and did not dominate the marine environment for long (Figures 4.10 and 7.5). The evolutionary history of this fauna is short, and

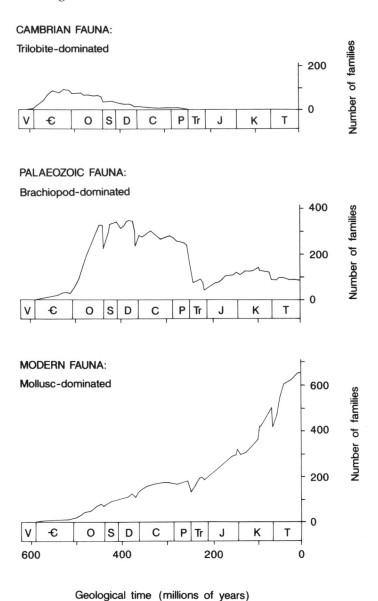

CAMBRIAN FAUNA:

Trilobite-dominated

PALAEOZOIC FAUNA:

Brachiopod-dominated

MODERN FAUNA:

Mollusc-dominated

Geological time (millions of years)

Figure 7.5 *The evolutionary faunas of the Phanerozoic. Each fauna is composed of higher taxa with a similar evolutionary history [Modified from: Sepkoski (1990) In Briggs & Crowther (Eds)* Palaeobiology, A Synthesis, *Blackwells, Fig. 2, p. 39]*

major extinctions at the end of the Cambrian, and particularly at the termination of the Ordovician, associated with sea-level or climatic changes, helped reduce its importance. The final remnants of this trilobite-dominated fauna were extinguished along with many other marine organisms in the end-Permian mass extinction event (Figure 7.5).

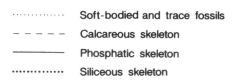

LATE PROTEROZOIC	EARLY CAMBRIAN	
		Cnidaria
		Annelida
		Brachiopoda
		Mollusca
		Arthropoda
		Echinodermata
		Archaeocyatha and related taxa

············· Soft-bodied and trace fossils

− − − − − Calcareous skeleton

────── Phosphatic skeleton

·············· Siliceous skeleton

Figure 7.6 *Diversification of soft-bodied and skeleton-bearing metazoans in the late Proterozoic and early Cambrian*

The **Palaeozoic Fauna** developed from the Cambrian expansion, but reached pre-eminence after the end-Cambrian extinction (Figure 7.5). It is typified by brachiopods (Chapter 10), a phylum of shellfish unrelated to molluscs but which are characterised by a two-halved (bivalve) shell. Brachiopods are relatively uncommon in modern marine environments, but inhabited a range of shallow marine environments for much of the Palaeozoic. Other members of the Palaeozoic Fauna are the rugose and tabulate corals (Chapter 13), which, together with brachiopods, calcareous algae, bryozoans (Chapter 15) and crinoids (Chapter 11) created the first real reefs. In the open sea, graptolites, a group of complex colonial organisms, were a common component of the plankton (Chapter 14). This fauna diversified throughout the Palaeozoic, surviving the Ordovician and Devonian (Frasnian–Fammenian) extinction events, but was severely curtailed by the end-Permian event when many of its most important components were extinguished (Figure 7.5). Following this extinction event, the Palaeozoic Fauna never recovered its dominance, although brachiopods, cephalopods, corals and bryozoans continued as a subordinate to the Modern Fauna up to the present day, surviving extinctions at the end of the Triassic and Cretaceous periods (Figure 7.5).

The **Modern** or **Mesozoic–Cenozoic Fauna** replaced the Palaeozoic Fauna in the aftermath of the Permian extinction (Figure 7.5). Like the Palaeozoic Fauna, the Modern Fauna has its roots in the Cambrian expansion, but unlike it, the molluscan (Chapter 8), microfossil (Chapters 16 and 17) and other components of the Modern Fauna gradually increased in diversity throughout the Phanerozoic. Following the end-Permian extinction event (Figure 7.5) the nature of the shallow marine fauna changed: the Palaeozoic Fauna, dominated by brachiopods, was replaced by a fauna dominated by molluscs, particularly bivalves and gastropods. Although the end-Cretaceous (K-T) extinction event had a noticeable effect, the results of the subsequent recovery and radiation remain characteristic of the shallow marine environment today.

The Evolution of the Terrestrial Flora

The development of a terrestrial ecosystem, dominated by plants, is an extremely important evolutionary story of the Phanerozoic. The development of this flora can be considered with reference to four major adaptive radiations, associated firstly with the initial colonisation of the land, and then with successive stages in the evolution of the plant reproductive cycle. These four events are: the first colonisation of the land in the Ordovician–Silurian; the development of the lycopod/sphenopsid coal forests in the later Palaeozoic; the Mesozoic gymnosperm ('naked seed') flora; and the angiosperms ('enclosed seed') of the later Mesozoic (Figure 4.10). These are discussed briefly below.

The first land plants developed in the Ordovician–Silurian interval. This became possible through the diversification of plants which acquired the adaptive advantage of a rigid stem and, later, tissue which was capable of carrying nutrients throughout the plant (vascular tissue) and allowed plants to leave the aquatic environment for the first time. A famous conservation Lagerstätte, the Scottish Rhynie Chert, gives insight into the form of these early plants and the early terrestrial ecosystem which they supported during the Devonian. Continued evolution of the woody and root tissue of plants allowed the development of the coal swamps composed of lycopod and sphenopsid trees, and ferns in humid locations. Their adaptive advantage was an improvement of the vascular tissue coupled with the increase in supportive woody tissue, leading to the development of the first trees and forests. However, like the earliest plants, the later Palaeozoic forests were tied to damp environments, as in both cases their reproductive system required fertilisation through an aquatic medium (Figure 7.7). Both groups of plants were seedless, and reproduction is through the creation of an intermediate stage, the **gametophyte**. This is a small plant in its own right, and is developed from **spores** produced on the leaves or special stalks of the mature plant, the **sporophyte**. The spores do not need fertilisation, and are usually scattered by the wind. When they fall on damp ground, the gametophyte stage is developed. The male gametophyte produces sperm which is mobile and needs the damp, aquatic medium to swim to the female gametophyte which develops the eggs. The sporophyte, the adult plant, is developed from this fertilised egg, and the process is then repeated (Figure 7.7).

The Carboniferous lycopod/sphenopsid seedless trees were replaced by the Mesozoic flora of gymnosperm plants which radiated widely, through the

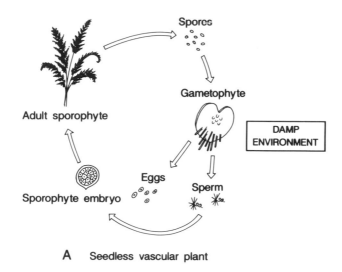

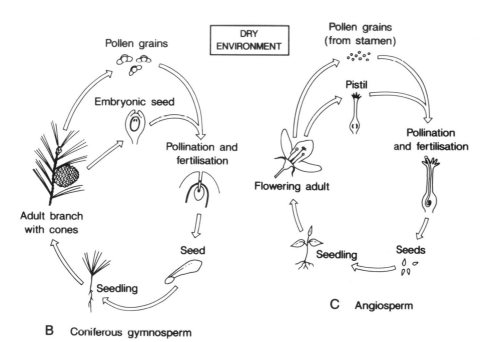

Figure 7.7 *The reproductive processes of plants. Early plants were tied to a damp environment to reproduce (**A**), but later gymnosperm (**B**) and angiosperm (**C**) plants could colonise a dry environment through the possession of seeds [Modified from: McAlester (1968) The History of Life, Prentice Hall, Figs 5.3, 5.9 and 5.14, pp. 87, 93 and 98]*

development of a reproductive system which was not dependent on water (Figure 4.10). In these plants, reproduction is through the seed, which is fertilised on the plant, without the need for an intermediate stage (Figure 7.7). Gymnosperms, such as the familiar conifers of today, have male and female cones. The female cone contains the unfertilised embryonic seed; the male cone pollen grains. The pollen protects the sperm from drying out and removes the need for the damp medium. Pollen are carried by the wind or on the backs of animals to other plants and the unfertilised embryonic seed of the female cone. The pollen lands in a drop of water secreted by the female cone and the sperm then swims to fertilise the seeds. The fertilised seed is then carried by wind, water or animals and develops into a seedling, nourished by the starchy nutrients which make up the seed itself (Figure 7.7). This process, independent of a damp environment, was a major adaptive advantage for the gymnosperms, which led to the colonisation of dry, and particularly upland, areas for the first time. Typical gymnosperms from the later Palaeozoic and Mesozoic include cycads, ginkgos and conifers, all of which have living relatives today.

The dominance of the gymnosperms was reduced with the appearance of the flowering, or angiosperm plants in the Cretaceous (Figure 4.10). Today, they dominate the land, with around 96% of the present-day flora represented by the angiosperms. The success of the angiosperms is associated with their improvement of the seed-bearing reproductive system (Figure 7.7), and their ability to invade habitats unavailable to other plants. Angiosperms have flowers which are reproductive structures bearing both seed and pollen, often surrounded by coloured petals designed to attract animals and insects. In this way, the angiosperms do not have to wait for the pollen grains carried by the wind to fertilise their embryonic seed. As a consequence, the angiosperms coevolved with certain insects, which provided the means of fertilising the seed, and the development of the angiosperms is matched by the diversification of insect life. In angiosperms the seed is dispersed by a range of mechanisms, through enclosure in a fleshy, edible fruit attractive to animals, through the development of sticky burs which adhere to animals, or through special wind dispersal mechanisms. In all cases this has contributed to the success and rise of the angiosperms such that flowering plants can be found in the greatest range of envionments possible, from the frozen tundra to the equatorial rainforests.

The Development of the Vertebrates

Animals with backbones (vertebrates) belonging to the phylum Chordata (possessing a nerve chord) first appeared in the late Cambrian in the form of primitive fishes, which continued to diversify throughout the later part of the Palaeozoic (Figure 4.10). The earliest fishes were jawless (agnathans), and with the development of jaws and an increasing complexity of skeletal parts the fishes became important elements of the marine ecosystem in the later Palaeozoic (Figure 4.10). Fish first diversified in the Silurian and Devonian, with an important adaptive radiation of groups with external armoured plates. The first jaw-bearing fishes, the placoderms, developed in the Devonian and included the arthrodires, giant carnivores up to 10 m long. These early fishes had external armour but their internal skeleton was largely unmineralised. Sharks and bony fishes, mostly without external armour but possessing a complex internal skeleton, replaced the placoderms and agnathans in the Carboniferous, and have continued to develop in importance until the present day, when they outnumber terrestrial vertebrates in diversity and numbers of individuals (Figure 4.10).

In addition to the fishes, conodonts are common chordate fossils in the Palaeozoic (Figure 7.8). Conodonts are microscopic tooth-like phosphatic fossils which form multi-element apparatuses. They flourished during the Palaeozoic and are common fossils up to their probable extinction at the end of the Triassic. Prior to 1983, the assignment of these microfossils to any one animal, phylum was a difficult task. That year, a fossil soft-bodied animal complete with conodont apparatuses, was discovered in specimens collected from the Carboniferous rocks of Edinburgh. This animal has an elongate body with simple fin-rays on both sides of the tail, suggesting an affinity with the living myxinoids – primitive fish-like chordates.

The first terrestrial vertebrates developed from the bony fishes in the late Devonian. The transition to land is associated with one group of bony fishes, the lobe-fins. These fishes have two important characteristics which allowed them to make the transition to land: a bone and muscle structure which extended into the fins from the body, and the development of an auxillary 'lung' which allowed them to survive in times of desiccation. Similar 'lungfish' live in ephemeral water

Figure 7.8 *Typical conodont apparatuses from the Upper Carboniferous of Illinois, × 50 [Photograph: P. Smith]*

bodies in Africa, Australia and South America and are able to survive through air breathing when the lakes and streams periodically dry up. These adaptions provide the basis for land-dwelling; a means of locomotion through modification of the lobe-fins into true limbs, and a lung for air breathing. The first land-dwelling vertebrates, the amphibians, probably developed from one group of such lobe-finned fishes, the crossopterygians, in the late Devonian (Figure 4.10). Up to 1938, the crossopterygians had been considered extinct since the Cretaceous, but a living specimen was captured by South African fishermen, and this 'living fossil', *Latimeria*, has helped clarify the crossopterygian ancestry of the early amphibians.

The amphibians expanded and diversified in the Carboniferous (Figure 4.10). Like their descendants, the early amphibians were tied to water in order to reproduce. These early amphibians, the labyrinthodonts, were common in the Carboniferous and are associated with aquatic or marshy environments, and are commonly encountered in the Carboniferous coal swamp deposits. The amphibians were replaced as the dominant land-dwelling vertebrates by the reptiles in the Permian, although the earliest example known is from the Carboniferous. This reptile, which was discovered in the Carboniferous sediments of Bathgate, near Edinburgh, in the 1980s, captured media attention as 'Lizzie the lizard', and was subsequently given a more sedate name, *Westlothiana lizziae*.

Reptiles overcame the need to be close to water bodies for reproduction through the development of the egg. They colonised a variety of land environments. The early reptiles, the cotylosaurs, gave rise to the dominant mammal-like reptiles, such as *Lystrosaurus* and *Dicynodon*, in the Permian and Triassic. Thecodonts – a diverse group of reptiles which included some bipedal (i.e. able to walk on the hind limbs) species – as well as marine reptiles (ichthyosaurs and plesiosaurs), turtles, lizards and snakes all arose from cotylosaur ancestry in the Triassic, and by its close had replaced the mammal-like reptiles as dominant land-dwelling vertebrates. Thecodonts are extremely important as it is from their ancestry that the dinosaurs and pterosaurs (flying reptiles) developed. The thecodonts, like the mammal-like reptiles, were greatly affected by a mass extinction in the Triassic. Following this extinction, the dinosaurs became dominant, but the reptilian assemblage was diverse, including pterosaurs, marine reptiles, crocodiles, lizards and so on (Figure 4.10).

The great diversity of reptiles which developed in the Jurassic and Cretaceous was effectively devastated by the end-Cretaceous extinction (Figure 4.10). This event has captured popular imagination, mainly because it extinguished the dinosaurs, pterosaurs and marine reptiles, leaving the crocodiles, turtles, lizards and snakes as remnants of this diverse fauna. The dinosaurs were diverse and lived in a matching diversity of terrestrial environments. Their extinction opened these niches which were filled by the mammals and birds which consequently underwent a radiation in the Palaeogene (Figure 4.10). Birds are descendants of the dinosaurs; the earliest bird, *Archaeopteryx*, known only from the Upper Jurassic of Solnhofen, Germany, is close to the coexisting small dinosaur *Compsognathus*, but differs in its possession of feathers and other bird characteristics, such as an opposed claw for perching. Mammals can be derived from the mammal-like reptiles and developed early in the Mesozoic (Figure 4.10). Their oldest known fossil remains are dated as late Triassic, and comprise a few fragmentary bones, which demonstrate the shrew-like form of these early mammals. Following the extinction of the dinosaurs, the birds and mammals (including humans) radiated to their position of dominance in the present day.

7.2 THE MAIN FOSSIL GROUPS

Fossils may be found of even the most fragile or rare organisms, and new discoveries add each year to our understanding of the fossil record, and hence of the diversification of life through time. However, fossils not only provide an insight into the diversity of life in the geologically distant past, but also provide tools important in unravelling the secrets of past environments, and in the determination of relative time in stratigraphy.

The main subject matter of this book is the invertebrates. Invertebrate fossils are abundant, relatively simple to understand, and have the greatest application in geology and palaeobiology. This is primarily a function of their size and preservation potential. Invertebrate fossils are commonly encountered components of most sedimentary rocks, and in some cases form the fabric of the rock itself, particularly in limestones composed of their calcareous skeletal remains. Some fossils are extremely small, microscopic in scale, and these microfossils are particularly abundant; one small sample of sedimentary rock may contain many thousands of invertebrate fossils, each one a potential tool in determining ancient biologies, environments or ages.

The fossil groups selected for this book are those which are the most commonly encountered, and which have the greatest application in the three components of applied palaeontology: palaeobiology, palaeoenvironmental analysis and stratigraphy. In palaeobiology, this may mean that the fossil group is important in defining rates and patterns of evolution, or in the determination of the functional adaption of skeletal components, for example. In palaeoenvironmental analysis, fossils play an important part in determining such parameters as salinity, oxygenation, water depth, turbulence levels, and so on. In stratigraphy, those fossil groups which are widely distributed, fast-evolving and not substrate-dependent have the most application. The fossil groups selected here are those which have an important role in at least one of these applied fields. Those selected are: molluscs (bivalves, gastropods, cephalopods), brachiopods, echinoderms (echinoids and crinoids), trilobites, corals, graptolites, bryozoans, foraminifera and ostracods. Other invertebrate groups of limited utility have been omitted: sponges, worms, insects and other non-trilobite arthropods, for example. Trace fossils are also discussed, and have an important role in all three fields of applied palaeontology.

Fossil vertebrates and plants are not discussed. Vertebrates are of value in palaeobiological studies but are often large and prone to disarticulation and therefore are relatively rare as fossils. Because of this, vertebrates have in some cases limited application in stratigraphy and palaeoenvironmental analysis, although

BOX 7.2: FOSSIL VERTEBRATES IN STRATIGRAPHY

In the Permo-Triassic Beaufort Group of the Karroo Basin in South Africa, vertebrates are plentiful and well preserved. The sediments of the Beaufort Group were formed in meandering rivers with a wide flood-plain upon which a great diversity of vertebrates lived. Fossil reptiles were first discovered in the Karroo Sequence in 1838, and since then the Beaufort Group in particular has become a focus for studies of the evolution of Permian and Triassic mammal-like reptiles, as it represents one of the most completely preserved ecological assemblages of pre-mammalian terrestrial vertebrates. The fossils are relatively small (skull lengths of 0.1–0.5 m are common), diverse, and are unusually complete, with whole skulls common. Seeley (1892) was the first scientist to recognise that reptiles could be used as guide fossils in the Karroo, proposing

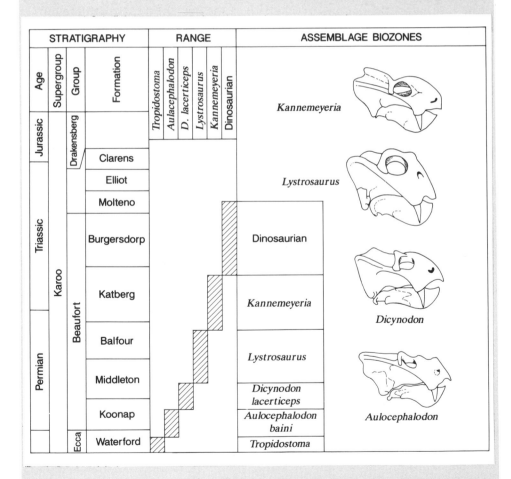

BOX 7.2: (*cont.*)

five biozones defined on the vertical range of five genus groups. Detailed collecting and taxonomic work by the Geological Survey of South Africa has refined the original biozones. Based on a collection of over 2500 skulls, Keyser and Smith (1979) erected five assemblage biozones which were similar to Seeley's originals, but tied for the first time to a proper lithostratigraphical framework. Each assemblage zone is constructed around the total or partial vertical ranges of a number of reptile taxa, but is named after the commonest occurring species which can be recognised in an unprepared or incomplete state.

This example is perhaps unique, but is illustrative of the fact that where vertebrates are common and well preserved they have considerable potential as guide fossils, particularly in terrestrial environments.

Sources: Seeley, H.G. (1892) Researches on the structure, organization and classification of the fossil Reptilia. *Philosophical Transactions of the Royal Society,* **182**, 311–370. Keyser, A.W. and Smith, R.M.H. (1979) Vertebrate biozonation of the Beaufort Group with special reference to the western Karroo Basin. *Annals of the Geological Survey, Republic of South Africa,* **12** (for 1977–78), 1–35. [Figure modified from: Keyser and Smith (1979), *Annals of the Geological Survey, Republic of South Africa,* **12** (for 1977–78), Fig. 5, p. 29]

there are notable exceptions, such as microvertebrates in the Palaeozoic, rodent teeth in the Cenozoic, and isolated examples of large vertebrate body fossils where they are abundant (Box 7.2). In addition, conodonts have a greater range of applications in almost all fields of applied palaeontology than other chordates. Plant fossils are of great utilitarian value in all fields of applied palaeontology (Box 7.3), but are complex biological entities which in many cases require a greater depth of anatomical knowledge than can be supplied here.

The discussions of the main fossil groups which follow are laid out in order to give the following information: taxonomy (characteristic features and classification); morphology; evolution and application in palaeobiology, palaeoenvironmental analysis and stratigraphy. The classification given for each group is based on the current understanding and is restricted to the higher taxonomic levels, usually class or subclass level, although in some cases, such as the foraminifera and ostracods, suborder and order levels are used. The morphological characteristics discussed are those which facilitate an understanding of the group as a whole, and their application in general. Suggestions for follow-up reading are provided at the end of each chapter.

7.3 SUMMARY OF KEY POINTS

• The oldest known fossil evidence of life is dated at 3550 million years old, and consists of **cell filaments**. These, together with **stromatolites**, illustrate the

BOX 7.3: PLANT FOSSILS IN GEOLOGY

Plant fossils are important sources of information for geologist and biologist alike. In industry, for example, the most commonly used fossil plants are microfossils: spores, pollen, acritarchs and dinoflagellate cysts. For the most part, however, plant macrofossils remain a closed book to many geologists. This may be a function of the relative complexity of their structure, of the convention of different taxonomic names for different parts of the plant, or simply because palaeobotany is not routinely taught in geology degrees. Notwithstanding these difficulties, fossil plants are abundant and represent an extremely important storehouse of geological information.

The vast majority of plant fossils represent parts of a plant organ whose relationship to the parent plant can be unknown. The best plant fossils for applied studies are microfossils and those macrofossils which represent organs that were produced abundantly by commonly occurring plants, and which are relatively easy to recognise, even when in a fragmentary state. The main applications for fossil plants in geology are in palaeobiogeography, biostratigraphy, and palaeoenvironmental interpretation.

Plants are extremely important palaeobiogeographical tools. They have limited geographical ranges, as migration is dependent upon the dissemination of seeds, spores and pollen, many of which can not cross open sea water. Plants have been used in the reconstruction of continental areas, such as Alfred Wegener's construction of Gondwana on the basis of the leaf *Glossopteris*, and

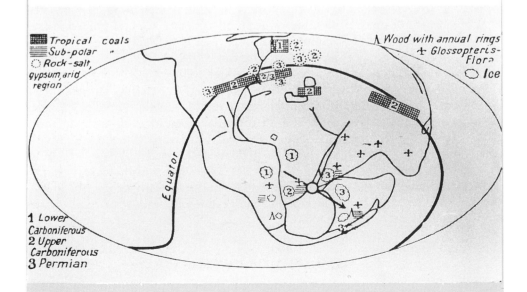

BOX 7.3: (*cont.*)

in the determination of floral zones with their attendant implications for ancient climates. Analysis of tree rings in gymnosperm and angiosperm wood, for example, is an extremely important indicator of climatic conditions. In biostratigraphy, the greatest potential is with terrestrial successions rich in plant remains and microfossils. Correlation of Upper Carboniferous successions, in both northern Europe and North America, has been based largely upon floral assemblage biozones, for example. Surprisingly, the least satisfactory area is with palaeoenvironmental analysis, in Palaeozoic successions at least. This may be a function of the difficulties in applying the taxonomic uniformitarian approach to plants with no direct living descendants. In addition, it is relatively rare to find plants other than roots in their life position, and this reduces the viability of the contribution of plants to the determination of palaeoenvironments. Despite this, plants are an extremely important component of the terrestrial ecosystem, and their fossils and microfossils have much potential for palaeoenvironmental work, particularly in Mesozoic and Cenozoic successions.

Sources: Cleal, C.J. (ed.) (1991) *Plant Fossils in Geological Investigation. The Palaeozoic.* Ellis Horwood, Chichester. Traverse, A. (1988) *Palynology.* Unwin Hyman, New York. [Figure reproduced from Wegener (1924), *The Origin of Continents and Oceans*, Methuen, Fig. 17, p. 100]

development of simple **prokaryotic** cells. Cyanobacteria, creating the stromatolites, live through photosynthesis, and the cumulative effect of photosynthesis was to oxygenate the initial anaerobic atmosphere.

- The Proterozoic commenced 2500 million years ago, and rocks of this age contain both prokaryotes and, for the first time, **eukaryote** cells. These probably developed from the amalgamation of several prokaryotes and have a nucleus with chromosomes and a mechanism of sexual reproduction, and therefore rapid evolutionary change. The latter part of the Proterozoic saw the development of metazoans, the **Ediacaran Biota**.
- The Phanerozoic commenced 560 million years ago and is the interval of abundant life as we know it today. The development of most of the diverse invertebrate and vertebrate faunas, and of terrestrial flora, took place in this interval.
- The development of the marine invertebrate fauna can be tracked through three main **evolutionary faunas** which group together major sets of higher taxa with similar histories of diversification and evolution, and which dominate the marine biota for a great period of geological time. There are three such faunas: the **Cambrian Fauna** (dominated by trilobites); the **Palaeozoic Fauna** (dominated by brachiopods); and the **Modern** or **Mesozoic–Cenozoic Fauna** (dominated by molluscs).
- The evolution of the terrestrial flora is linked to four major adaptive radiations associated with a particular adaptive advantage: the first colonisation of the

land in the Ordovician, with the development of the cuticle and vascular tissue; the growth of the lycopod/sphenopsid coal forests of the later Palaeozoic, with the development of improved woody tissue; the spread of the gymnosperms in the Mesozoic through the development of the seed; and the rapid spread of the angiosperms in the later Mesozoic, with their improved reproductive and dispersal system.

- The vertebrates first appeared in the Cambrian. The early vertebrates were fishes, and the first terrestrial vertebrates, the amphibians, evolved from the lobe-finned bony fishes in the Devonian. The first reptiles, no longer tied to water, developed in the Carboniferous, and these early reptiles gave rise to the mammal-like reptiles in the Permian and Triassic. The dinosaurs arose from another group of early reptiles, the thecodonts, in the Mesozoic. By the end of the Mesozoic most of the land, sea and flying reptiles had been killed off in the end-Cretaceous extinction event, and they were replaced by a radiation of mammals, derived from the mammal-like reptiles, and the birds, derived from the dinosaurs.

7.4 SUGGESTIONS FOR FURTHER READING

Cowen (1994) gives a well-written basic account of the development of life on Earth. McAlester (1968) is now dated but provides a good overview of the nature of the fossil record. Stanley's (1989) text is comprehensive and well written, and treats the development of life in the broader context of Earth history. Bradbury's (1991) book documents the development of the biosphere with a geological perspective. The paper by Sepkoski (1981) explains the concept of evolutionary faunas in the Phanerozoic. Briggs and Crowther (1990) is an extremely important text of edited papers, and the first part of the book in particular gives an account of the major features of the fossil record. Papers in Allen and Briggs (1989), particularly those by Strother, McMenamin, and Selden and Edwards, provide an account of key phases in the development of the Earth's biosphere. Bengtson (1994) is an accessible volume of collected papers on early life. Glaessner (1984) is an interesting book on the Ediacaran Biota, which is supplemented by Seilacher's (1989; 1992) assertions of a completely different mode of life for these organisms. Gould's (1989) book gives an interesting insight into the diversity of life in the Cambrian as preserved in the Burgess Shale. Conodonts and their applications are more fully discussed in the volumes edited by Aldridge (1987) and Austin (1987). Briggs *et al.* (1983), is the paper which first identified the conodont animal. Finally, the edited volume by Benton (1994) is a scholarly, factual compilation of all families represented in the fossil record.

Aldridge, R.J. (ed.) 1987. *Palaeobiology of Conodonts*. Ellis Horwood, Chichester.
Allen, K.C. & Briggs, D.E.G. 1989. *Evolution and the Fossil Record*. Belhaven Press, London.
Austin, R.L. (ed.) 1987. *Conodonts. Investigative techniques and applications*. Ellis Horwood, Chichester.
Bengtson, S. (ed.) *Early Life on Earth*. Columbia University Press, New York.

Benton, M.J. 1994. *The Fossil Record 2*. Chapman & Hall, London.

Bradbury, I.K. 1991. *The Biosphere*. Belhaven Press, London.

Briggs, D.E.G. & Crowther, P.R. 1990. *Palaeobiology – A Synthesis*. Blackwell Scientific Publications, Oxford.

Briggs, D.E.G., Clarkson, E.N.K. & Aldridge, R.J. 1983. The conodont animal. *Lethaia*, **16**, 1–14.

Cowen, R. 1994. *History of Life*. Second edition. Blackwell Scientific Publications, Oxford.

Glaessner, M. 1984. *The Dawn of Animal Life. A Biohistorical Study*. Cambridge University Press, Cambridge.

Gould, S.J. 1989. *Wonderful Life. The Burgess Shale and the Nature of History*. Hutchinson Radius, London.

McAlester, A.L. 1968. *The History of Life*. Prentice Hall, Englewood Cliffs, NJ.

Sepkoski, J.J. 1981. A factor analytic description of the Phanerozoic marine fossil record. *Paleobiology*, **7**, 36–53.

Seilacher, A. 1989. Vendozoa: organismic construction in the Proterozoic biosphere. *Lethaia*, **22**, 229–239.

Seilacher, A. 1992. Vendobiota and Psammocorallia: lost constructions of Precambrian evolution. *Journal of the Geological Society of London*, **149**, 607–613.

Stanley, S.M. 1989. *Earth and Life Through Time*. Second edition. Freeman, New York.

8
Molluscs: Bivalves and Gastropods

8.1 BIVALVE AND GASTROPOD TAXONOMY

The molluscs are a diverse group of organisms which evolved and diverged from a simple common ancestor to become one of the most successful animal phyla. Today, molluscs are found in fresh, brackish and marine waters and terrestrial environments. They are mostly active hunters, scavengers, passive filter feeders and deposit feeders attached to the substrate or living in burrows. This chapter and the next outline the characteristics of the most common molluscan groups, the bivalves, gastropods and cephalopods.

Molluscs, particularly bivalves and gastropods, are common members of present-day shallow marine environments. Bivalves are familiar to us as the sea shells commonly washed up on beaches (Figure 8.1). They are wholly aquatic and are found in a range of habitats in marine, and to a lesser extent fresh, waters. Gastropods, or snails, are successful organisms, and are the only molluscan group to have colonised both aquatic (marine and freshwater) and terrestrial environments. Both groups typically have a hard, calcareous shell, and as such have an extensive fossil record, but are commonest as the dominant members of the Modern or Mesozoic–Cenozoic evolutionary fauna. Both bivalves and gastropods are particularly important in palaeobiology and palaeoenvironmental analysis.

8.1.1 General Characteristics of Bivalves

Bivalves are characterised by their two-halved, usually aragonitic calcareous shell which protects the soft parts, and which is hinged by an elastic ligament to allow the functions of burrowing, respiration and feeding. Other groups, belonging to

Figure 8.1 *Bivalve shells on a rocky beach in southern Spain [Photograph: P. Doyle]*

different phyla, also have two-part shells – in particular, the brachiopods (Chapter 10) and the ostracods (Chapter 17) (Figure 8.2). However, bivalves are readily distinguished from brachiopods (phylum Brachiopoda) by shell symmetry, as brachiopods have valves which are symmetrical about a central axis; and from ostracods (phylum Crustacea), which are mostly microscopic in size, with valves which do not display incremental growth lines, having been formed by moulting.

Bivalves have only limited capability for movement, most living a **sedentary** life in burrows or attached to the substrate. The majority of bivalves live in burrows which are constructed by the muscular contractions of the mantle muscle or **foot** (Figure 8.3). The foot protrudes from the front or anterior margin of the shell to dig its burrow in soft sediment. In shallow-burrowing bivalves, which are commonly washed out and exhumed from their burrows, the foot is retracted into the shell on closure; in some deeper-burrowing forms, a **gape** allows the foot permanent access to the sediment for burrow renewal. Some burrowing bivalves are able to construct their burrows in hard substrates, such as a rocky foreshore, using a combination of a rasping shell and chemical attack of the substrate to form a symmetrical cavity. The remainder of bivalves live directly on the sediment itself. Surface-dwelling bivalves may live as free-living **recliners**, or directly attached to a hard substrate by cementing one of their valves to it as **cementers**, or through attachment by organic threads, known as the **byssus**. Most often these are more irregular in shape than the burrowing bivalves.

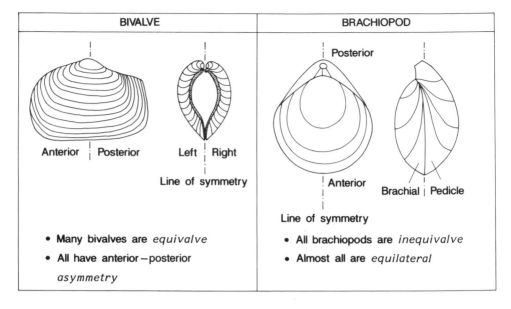

Figure 8.2   *Distinguishing bivalve and brachiopod shells on the basis of shell symmetry*

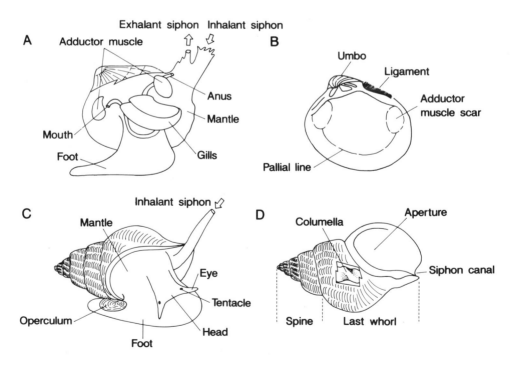

Figure 8.3   *General characteristics of the soft parts (**A**) and shell (**B**) of a living bivalve, and the soft parts (**C**) and shell (**D**) of a living gastropod*

Bivalves mostly feed from food particles suspended in the water column, although some burrowing bivalves feed directly from the sediment surrounding their burrows. Suspension-feeding bivalves feed by filtering food particles suspended in the water column through their modified gills, which are composed of a series of filaments (Figure 8.3). These filaments are arranged like teeth in a comb, and feeding is effected when the filaments are made to beat in a regular fashion, drawing a stream of water and suspended food particles into the shell through the **inhalant siphon** (Figure 8.3). Spent water is expelled through the **exhalant siphon**. The siphons are modified parts of the soft body or mantle cavity which may or may not extrude from the posterior of the shell. In general terms, shallow-burrowing and surface-dwelling bivalves have siphons which are relatively short, and like the foot, which may be withdrawn completely within the shell. Similarly, in deep-burrowing bivalves the siphons may be long in order to reach the sediment surface. Although some may be retracted within the shell, in others an equivalent gape to that for the foot is provided to allow the siphons permanent access to the water column.

8.1.2 General Characteristics of Gastropods

Gastropods, familiar to us as the common snail, are mostly characterised by their coiled, mostly aragonitic calcareous shell (Figure 8.3). Coiling can be in many planes. Usually it is vertical, such that the cone is constructed into one of three basic shapes; a high spire, shallow cone or bulb, each of which develops around a central column or cavity. In other cases, coiling may be in the horizontal plane, producing a flattened (planispiral) form like that of a coiled snake. Other gastropods, such as the limpet shells characteristic of rocky shores today, are not obviously coiled and are cap-like. Gastropod shells have a single chamber and no internal dividing walls, and are therefore readily distinguished from the other coiled molluscs, the cephalopods, which have chambers designed to aid in flotation (Chapter 9). All snails are capable of movement upon their muscular foot through muscular contractions. Together with their well-developed heads, the foot can be completely retracted within the shell, and the opening or **aperture** can be closed off by an organic or calcareous lid called the **operculum** (Figure 8.3). Some gastropods feed as scavengers, scraping algae and other detritus from hard substrates using a rasping tongue known as the **radula**. Other snails are predators, however, and may strip the flesh from other organisms using the radula, or even, as with the genus *Natica*, drill holes in bivalves to attack and destroy the muscles which keep the shell closed, in order to get to the flesh beyond. Most terrestrial taxa are vegetation browsers.

The mostly spiral gastropod shell contains all the vital organs, with the body or mantle cavity containing the gills positioned in the last spiral (**whorl**) of the shell (Figure 8.3). The gills are bathed in oxygenated water either by a **siphon**, or by water taken directly into the shell through the aperture. In land and freshwater snails, gills are absent and the mantle cavity is modified as a lung. The position of the mantle cavity in relation to the head differs in some gastropod groups, having undergone the process referred to as **torsion**. This involves the rotation of the mantle cavity and anus laterally in an anticlockwise direction so that they effectively lie above the head. Most primitive gastropods have undergone this process, but later snails have undergone a partial or complete reversal of the trend, **detorsion.** The significance of this process has been heavily debated, and may or may not have a direct relationship with the development of a coiled shell from an ancestral mollusc with a simple cap-like shell. It may also be important that in rotating the soft parts from a posterior to an anterior position, the animal was able to sample fresh water for its gills in the direction of its movement, rather than from areas that it has since passed over.

8.1.3 Classification of Bivalves and Gastropods

Bivalves and gastropods form classes of the phylum Mollusca. A breakdown of their classification is given below. Classification of bivalves is dependent upon features of the hinge margin and other internal features of the shell, as well as the gill structure. In gastropods, coiling and functional adaptations for siphons are important, but for the most part classification is based on the soft body parts of living gastropods, particularly the gill structure. An alternative classification of gastropods emphasises torsion in the gastropods. This is more complex and is not followed here.

Phylum Mollusca Linnaeus, 1758
Class Bivalvia Linnaeus, 1758 (Cambrian–Recent)
(also known as Lamellibranchia or Pelecypoda)
Bivalved molluscs adapted to a burrowing (infaunal) or surface-dwelling (epifaunal) aquatic habitat. Bivalves feed through filtering food particles suspended in water (suspension feeders), or from the sediment itself (deposit feeders). The class is divided into four subclasses.

Subclass Palaeotaxodonta Korobkov, 1954 (Cambrian–Recent)
Infaunal deposit feeders with aragonitic shells and regular (taxodont) hinge teeth arrangement. Small leaf-like gills (protobranch).

Subclass Isofilibranchia Iredale, 1939 (Cambrian–Recent)
Variable, mostly epifaunal suspension feeders with aragonitic or calcitic shells which are attached to the substrate by organic fibres (byssal threads). Gills in the form of sheets of filaments (filibranch). Includes the oysters and mussels.

Subclass Heteroconchia Hertwig, 1895 (Ordovician–Recent)
Aragonitic shelled bivalves with variable hinge teeth arrangement and a varied mode of life. Gills filibranch or eulamellibranch – similar to filibranch with sheets of filaments, but this time with cross-bar supports creating cavities between the sheets. Includes the epifaunal hippuritids ('rudists') and *Trigonia*, an infaunal, thick-shelled bivalve with complex hinge teeth.

Subclass Anomalodesmata Dall, 1889 (Ordovician–Recent)
Specialised infaunal suspension feeders with aragonitic shells and lacking hinge teeth but having an internal ligament platform. Gills mostly eulamellibranch. Includes mostly deep infaunal bivalves.

Class Gastropoda Cuvier, 1797 (Cambrian–Recent)
Molluscs with mostly coiled calcareous shell, adapted to a mobile life as scavengers or predators and equipped with a muscular 'foot' for movement and a head with sensory organs. Currently divided into three subclasses.

Subclass Prosobranchia Milne-Edwards, 1848 (Cambrian–Recent)
Marine, mostly with helical spiral shells with simple gill structure. Body has undergone full torsion to rotate the mantle cavity and anus anteriorly so that they overlie the head.

Subclass Opisthobranchiata Milne-Edwards, 1848 (?Carboniferous–Recent)
Marine, mostly with much reduced or absent shell and complex gill structure. Body undergone detorsion and straightened out.

Subclass Pulmonata Cuvier, 1817 (Mesozoic–Recent)
Land-dwelling gastropods with or without (e.g. the common slug) coiled shell with the mantle cavity modified as a lung, no gills. Some have become secondarily adapted to freshwater habitats.

8.2 BIVALVE SHELL MORPHOLOGY

Bivalve shell morphology is relatively simple and is an important indicator of mode of life. The shell serves as a hinged calcareous cover for the soft body which is variously shaped to suit the function of the bivalve. There are two basic modes of life, burrow-dwelling (**infaunal**) or surface-dwelling (**epifaunal**). Most infaunal bivalves can be distinguished by the fact that their shells have two halves with mirror-image symmetry, while many, but not all, epifaunal bivalves do not. These features are discussed in detail below.

Bivalves all possess two shells known as **valves** which are permanently joined at the **hinge**, and which open and close in order to carry out the function of feeding and respiration (Figure 8.3). Each valve contains a record of the life history of the individual bivalve shell, as the growth lines on its exterior illustrate the incremental growth of the shell, created by the soft body or **mantle**. The first formed part of the shell is locked into the **umbones** (singular: **umbo**) which overlap the hinge margin; the last growth increment is represented by the join or **commissure**. Bivalve shells are all calcareous, aragonitic or calcitic, but are covered externally in life by an organic outer layer known as the **periostracum** or **epithelium**. Valves are described as left or right valves, determined by the relative position of the umbones. Convention dictates that in equally paired or **equivalve** shells, valve orientation may, with some exceptions, generally be determined by holding the shell with the umbones pointing away from the observer, the left or right valves relating to the left or right hand of the observer. In unequally paired or **inequivalve** shells, the determination of the valve orientation is difficult, but convention has it that the larger shell is equivalent to the left valve. Bivalves are distinguished from the somewhat similar two-part brachiopod shells on the basis of shell symmetry (Figure 8.2). Almost without exception, individual valves of a bivalve shell are asymmetrical about an axis which runs from the umbo to the commissure. Brachiopods are almost always inequivalve, and almost always **equilateral**, an equivalent axis dividing each valve equally (Figure 8.2).

The shell articulation mechanism in bivalves is relatively simple and has three components: the **ligament**, designed to open the shell automatically, acting rather like an organic 'spring'; the **adductor muscles**, which work against the opening action of the ligament to force the valves shut; and the **hinge teeth**, which act as an interlocking hinge mechanism to prevent misalignment of the valves when opening and shutting (Figure 8.3).

The interior of a typical bivalve displays the following information: the **hinge** contains the ligament either set in a pit outside the shell or set into the hinge margin itself, together with the hinge teeth if present. The hinge teeth are used as an important character in the classification of the bivalves (Figure 8.4). Commonly, the teeth radiate in a small cluster of **cardinal teeth** from the umbo. Cardinal teeth are commonly found in two configurations: spread out along the entire length of the hinge margin (**taxodont dentition**), or limited to a small cluster beneath the umbo but joined by simple **lateral teeth** which are parallel to the hinge margin (**heterodont dentition**) (Figure 8.4). Most shallow-burrowing bivalves have heterodont dentition. In some bivalves, particularly epifaunal ones, the hinge teeth are reduced (as in the mussel *Mytilus*) or absent (as in the oyster *Ostrea*), and the task of opening and closing the shell is taken by a greatly modified ligament and adductor muscle arrangement (Figure 8.4). The position of the adductor muscle attachments can be seen as **muscle scars** on the interior of the shell. These scars are paired either side of the hinge margin in equivalve (usually infaunal) bivalves, or consist of a single large and subcentral muscle scar where the bivalves are inequivalve (epifaunal). Finally, the position of the mantle inside the valves is denoted by the **pallial line**, a distinct line parallel to the outer margin of the shell forming an arc which either connects the two adductor muscle scars or joins the hinge line (Figure 8.3). In some cases, there is a distinct embayment within the pallial line, known as the **pallial sinus**. This is common in infaunal bivalves and represents the position when retracted inside the shell of the siphons used for suspension feeding.

For convenience, the bivalves can be divided into three main groups on the basis of their mode of life in relation to the substrate: **shallow infaunal**; **deep infaunal**; and **epifaunal**. This represents a simplification but includes the majority of bivalves commonly encountered. Their characteristics are discussed below:

1. *Shallow infaunal bivalves* (Figure 8.5). Shallow infaunal bivalves have the following generalised characteristics:
- an equivalve shell form, often, but not always, heavily ribbed
- a subcircular shell shape
- strong hinge teeth
- two subequal muscle scars
- an entire pallial line or small pallial sinus.

These characteristics are reflective of the need for shallow-burrowing bivalves to protect themselves if washed out or otherwise exhumed from their burrows. The equivalve shell form is suited to burrowing. The subcircular shape and ribs give strength to the shell, appropriate when it is periodically washed from its burrow. Equally, the strong teeth and equal muscles are designed to allow the shell to have

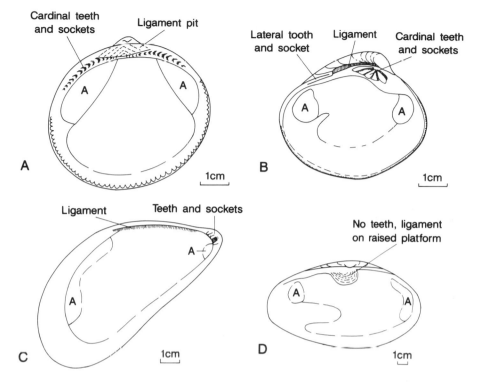

Figure 8.4 *Detail of the hinge area of four typical bivalves. Adductor muscle scars denoted by the letter A.* **A:** Glycimeris, *showing taxodont dentition with numerous cardinal teeth.* **B:** Venus, *showing heterodont dentition, with a small group of cardinal teeth and two lateral teeth.* **C:** Mytilus, *showing dysodont dentition, with a small group of teeth and sockets near the umbo.* **D:** Mya, *showing desmodont dentition, composed of an internal ligament platform*

a strong, protective hinge mechanism. The entire pallial line is indicative of the shortness of the siphons, which along with the foot can be withdrawn into the shell when clasped shut to prevent drying out.

2. *Deep infaunal bivalves* (Figure 8.6). Deep infaunal bivalves possess the following generalised characteristics:
- an equivalve shell form, usually unornamented with ribs
- an elongate shell shape
- a shell gape in many cases
- reduced or absent hinge teeth
- two unequal muscle scars
- a large pallial sinus.

The equivalve shell and elongate shape promote efficiency in deeper burrowing. This is enhanced by a smoother shell than is found in the shallow-burrowing bivalves, although rock-boring bivalves may have a coarse surface texture. A shell gape, at both anterior and posterior for permanent extrusion of foot and siphons, is a common feature of deep-burrowing bivalves, a function of the need for extended periods within the burrow. Because of this, the hinge is less critical, and

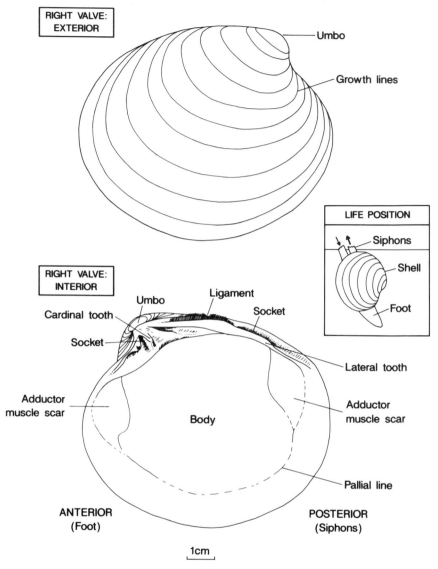

Figure 8.5   *Shell characteristics of a typical shallow-burrowing bivalve,* Arctica

teeth may be reduced, and this is associated with possession of muscles of different sizes, reflecting less of a need for a strongly closed shell. The large pallial sinus is a function of the elongate siphons needed to reach the sediment surface.

3. *Epifaunal bivalves* (Figures 8.7 and 8.8). Epifaunal bivalves are difficult to group together, but most (e.g. oysters, pectinids) are inequivalve. Relatively few (e.g. the mussels) are equivalve. Inequivalve epifaunal bivalves possess:

- a weak or strongly inequivalve shell
- a rounded or irregular shell shape

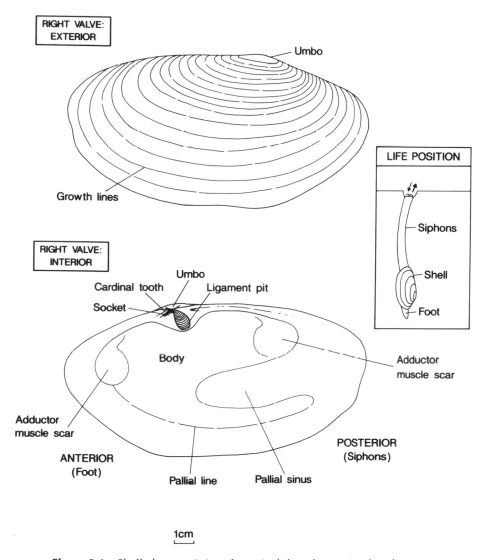

Figure 8.6 *Shell characteristics of a typical deep-burrowing bivalve,* Lutraria

- no hinge teeth, ligament enlarged
- a single, large, subcentral muscle scar
- an entire pallial line.

Inequivalve bivalves reflect a reclining or cemented mode of life, with the valves of unequal shape and size because of this. The shell shape is generally irregular. Oysters, for example, are cemented to their substrate to withstand the high energy of this environment, and shape is often a function of this plus the nature of competition for living space (Figure 8.7). Living in the intertidal zone, such bivalves may be exposed to the atmosphere for long periods, for instance when the tide falls. In these cases, the greatest leverage is required to shut the shells

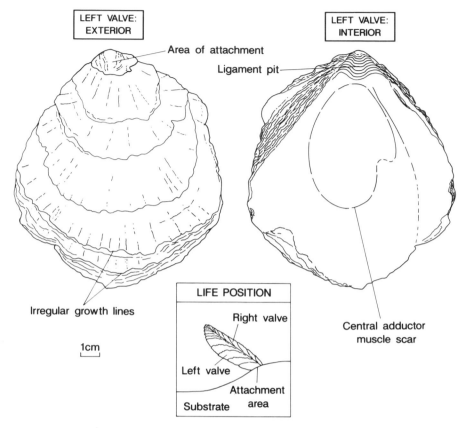

Figure 8.7   *Shell characteristics of an inequivalve epifaunal bivalve,* Ostrea

tightly to prevent desiccation. In such bivalves, the teeth are reduced, and as a consequence, the ligament becomes a strong component of the hinge structure, which is reacted against by the action of a single, centralised muscle. Some bivalves, such as the scallop *Pecten*, have utilised this strong spring-like mechanism to enable them to swim short distances. The pallial line is entire as the siphons are much reduced in size in accordance with the surface-dwelling mode of life.

Equivalve epifaunal bivalves (such as the mussels *Mytilus* and *Modiolus*) possess:
- a lozenge-shaped equivalve shell
- greatly reduced hinge teeth
- paired, unequal muscle scars – posterior scar usually larger
- an entire pallial line.

They are adapted to a byssally attached mode of life in which the byssus is extruded from a gape in the lower surface of the shell (Figure 8.8). The lozenge shape is a function of this sedentary habit and reflects the need for strength in attachment to a hard substrate. Hinge teeth are reduced to the apex of the lozenge and the posterior of the shell has the largest muscle, as this does most of the work in maintaining the shell in a tightly closed position, acting in an opposite position to the teeth. The entire pallial line reflects the need only for small siphons as a surface-dwelling bivalve.

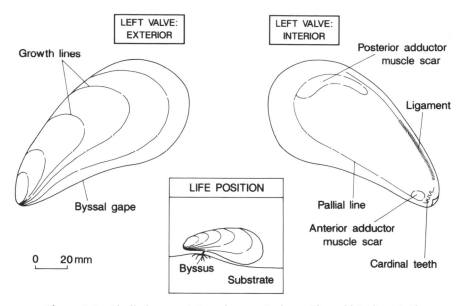

Figure 8.8 *Shell characteristics of an equivalve epifaunal bivalve,* Mytilus

8.3 GASTROPOD SHELL MORPHOLOGY

Gastropods have relatively simple shells. Most consist of a coiled cone, which generally has a right-handed (**dextral**) coil, with the aperture to the right of the spire, but in some cases may have a left-handed (**sinistral**) coil, with the aperture to the left of the spire (Figure 8.9). Others may be **planispiral**. The individual coils (**whorls**) are usually in close contact with each other. These coils are mostly developed vertically around a central column, the **columella**, but in others the central parts of the whorls do not meet and no columella is created, leaving instead a central cavity or **umbilicus** (Figure 8.9). Coiling may also be developed in a horizontal plane, creating a **planispiral** shape. In some gastropods with siphons, a slit may be set into the opening or **aperture** of the shell to house the exhalant siphon. This is a particular feature of the first gastropods to appear in the fossil record.

8.4 BIVALVE AND GASTROPOD EVOLUTION

8.4.1 The Molluscan Archetype

The phylum Mollusca is one of the most diverse of all animal phyla. It contains many groups which do not otherwise resemble each other, such as the free-swimming cephalopods, (Chapter 9), as well as the bivalves and gastropods and a range of other minor groups. However, despite their differences, the majority of molluscs possess some basic features in common: a **shell**, a **muscular foot**, a **mantle cavity** in which are housed the **gills**, and a feeding system consisting of a rasping

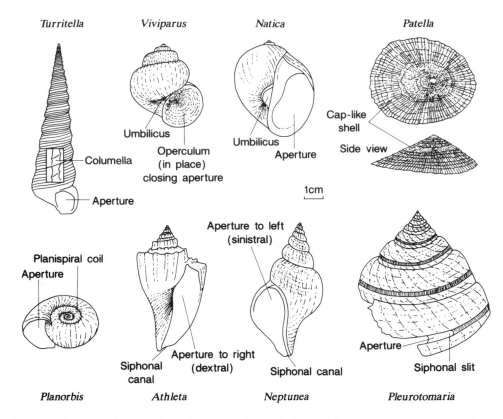

Figure 8.9 *Typical examples of gastropod morphology. All taxa are Recent, apart from* Pleurotomaria *(Jurassic),* Athleta *and* Turritella *(Eocene), and* Neptunea *(Pleistocene)*

tongue or **radula**. It is clear that molluscs must have diverged from a common ancestor which possessed these characteristics, but so far no clear candidate for such an ancestor has been identified. A hypothetical **archetype** or 'blueprint' has been developed in order to determine how and why the molluscs diversified.

The archetype possesses all the characteristics of the soft body, housed under a simple conical shell. Feeding was through scavenging, using its radula to scrape up food particles, and it had a simple respiratory system which bathed the gills in oxygenated water. From consideration of this 'blueprint' of an early mollusc, it is possible to determine that the evolution of the various molluscan groups was associated with the development of different feeding patterns. For example, the gastropods are broadly comparable to the primitive ancestor, feeding using its radula and moving on its muscular foot, but they have developed a greater sensory awareness so as to be able to feed as scavengers or predators. The bivalves have adapted to a sessile life, have dispensed with their radula, and have modified their gills in order to feed mostly through filtering out suspended particles. Finally, the cephalopods (Chapter 9) have adapted their shell for buoyancy, and have a well-developed brain and sensory apparatus in order to be able to live as active hunters, adding a set of jaws to their radula.

8.4.2 Bivalve Evolution

The bivalves have an evolutionary history which extends back to the Cambrian, with two important genera: *Pojetaia* found in Australia; and *Fordilla*, known from North America, Scandinavia and Siberia. The origins of the palaeotaxodont and isofilibranch bivalves can be traced respectively to these two genera, and it is probable that both had a common ancestor sometime in the early Cambrian. From an imperfect record in the Cambrian, the bivalves radiated in the Ordovician, when all the major bivalve groups appeared (Figure 8.10). It is likely that the isofilibranch bivalves gave rise to the rest of the groups at this time. The

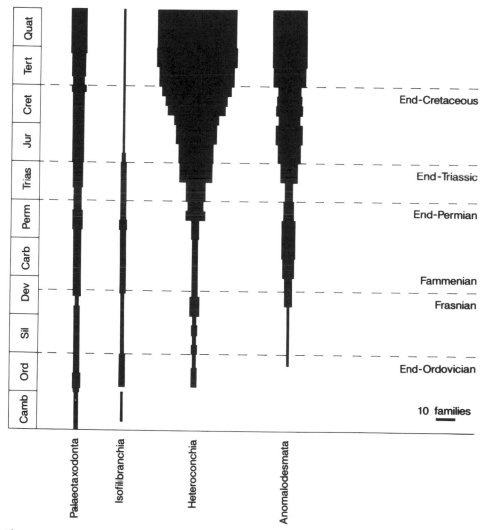

Figure 8.10 *The diversity of bivalve families through geological time. The main extinction events are indicated [Compiled by A.L. Holder from: Benton (1993) The Fossil Record 2, Chapman & Hall]*

Ordovician bivalves filled much the same range of environments as bivalves today, with epi- and infaunal bivalve species. A second adaptive radiation took place at the close of the Palaeozoic, when the bivalves displaced the brachiopods as dominant suspension feeders in the shelf environment (Figures 7.5 and 8.10). At this time the bivalves perfected their siphons to allow deeper burrowing, and the exploitation of a greater range of shallow marine environments. Since the early Mesozoic the bivalves have been common members of the shallow-sea biota, from the intertidal zone through to the outer shelf (Figure 8.10).

8.4.3 Gastropod Evolution

In many ways the gastropod remains relatively true to the 'blueprint' original common ancestor for the Mollusca discussed above. The early ancestral form of all molluscan groups may have had a simple conical shell which protected the vital organs, and which fed through the process of scavenging, while moving by means of muscular contractions of its mantle muscle. Gastropods reflect this, but their evolution to a position of dominance in the shallow marine and terrestrial environments of today is testimony to their adaptability (Figure 8.11). All three of the major gastropod groups occur in the present day, and although they have undergone periods of extinction, they reradiated in the Mesozoic and Cenozoic to fill a wide range of niches, on land and in the sea.

8.5 BIVALVE AND GASTROPOD APPLICATIONS

8.5.1 Palaeobiology

Functional Morphology

Individual bivalve and gastropod groups have played an important part in detailed functional morphological studies. Both groups have the advantage that they are relatively stable and that they have an abundance of living representatives in the present day to provide a uniformitarian base to compare with the fossil representatives. This is particularly important in palaeoenvironmental interpretation, which is discussed more fully below.

Functional morphology studies of fossil bivalves are for the most part relatively straightforward, and are usually directly comparable with the abundant living representatives. However, some groups are more bizarre and need a greater amount of interpretation and extrapolation from distant living relatives to unravel their story, and this is particularly true of the extinct rudist bivalves, common in the Mesozoic Tethys Ocean. The rudists, their name derived from the Latin *rudis*, meaning rough, are a bizarre group of extinct epifaunal bivalves which belong to the family Hippuritidae. Rudists take many unusual forms which can be summarised into three types: **elevators**, tall, barrel-shaped bivalves with a lid-like right valve; **clingers** (encrusters), bun-like forms with a broad encrusting lower

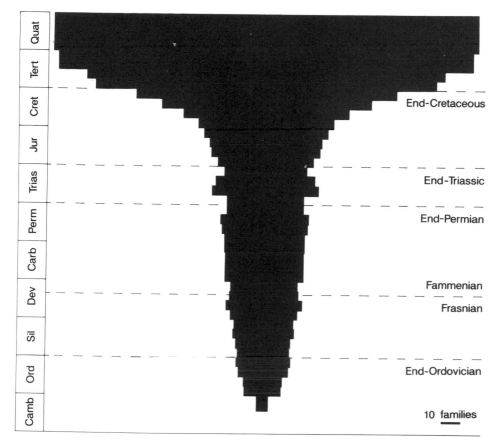

Quat
Tert
Cret
Jur
Trias
Perm
Carb
Dev
Sil
Ord
Camb

End-Cretaceous

End-Triassic

End-Permian

Fammenian

Frasnian

End-Ordovician

10 families

Figure 8.11 *The diversity of gastropod families through geological time. The main extinction events are indicated [Compiled by A.L. Holder from: Benton (1993) The Fossil Record, 2, Chapman & Hall]*

surface; and **recumbents**, which were large and free-living (Figure 8.12). The interpretation of the mode of life of the rudist bivalves has involved detailed study of their associations and comparison with living, large epifaunal bivalves. It has long been thought that the rudists were reef-forming, with elevators providing the core to the reef and recumbents and clingers forming the reef slope and periphery. This association of forms has been questioned, but probably represents a broad approximation of the truth (Figure 8.12).

A well-documented example of gastropod functional morphology is that of the inferred use of frills developed on the margin of each whorl in the Palaeozoic gastropod *Euomphalopteris* (Figure 8.13). Most gastropods are mobile, but it would appear that the presence of a frill or apron of shell extending from the whorls would have hindered such motion. Comparison with the living gastropod *Xenophora* has lead to a functional interpretation for these frills. *Xenophora* incorporates foreign, empty shells into its own in order to act as props. These prop the gastropod above the sediment surface, so that the animal can feed on

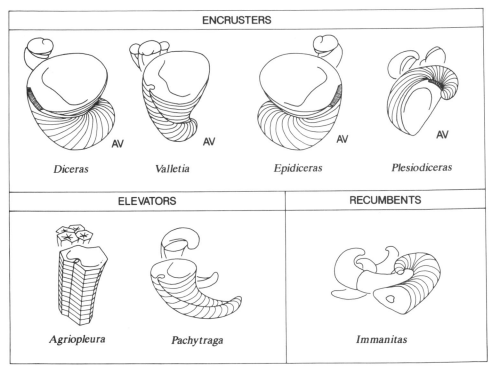

Figure 8.12   *The main morphological type of rudist bivalve shells. AV is the attached valve [Modified from: Skelton (1985)* Special Papers in Palaeontology **33***, Fig. 1, p. 161]*

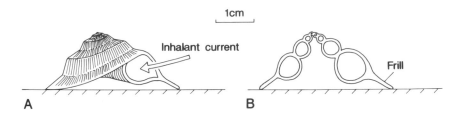

Figure 8.13   *Interpreted mode of life of a Palaeozoic gastropod,* Euomphalopterus. *This gastropod has a frill which may have acted as a prop to support it on the sedimentary surface [Modified from: Linsley* et al. *(1978)* Lethaia **11***, Fig. 3, p. 110]*

accumulated detritus by hanging down from its aperture. The frills in *Euomphalopteris* probably acted in much the same way, both gastropods adopting a semi-sessile mode of life (Figure 8.13). This is a classic example of the use of living analogues in the interpretation of the function of extinct species.

Evolution

Both bivalves and gastropods have been important in the determination of evolutionary processes in the geological record. Bivalves are readily preserved, in some cases in life position, and are abundant. Although the rate of evolution of some bivalve species is relatively slow, their preservation potential allows the detailed examination of populations of largely *in situ* bivalves which can provide an extremely valuable data set (Box 4.5). For example, examination of Jurassic sediments rich in the early Jurassic oyster *Gryphaea* has fuelled a debate on its evolution since the 1920s.

Early studies concentrated on the origin of coiling in *Gryphaea*, while the recent debate, discussed in Chapter 4, has centred around whether *Gryphaea* displays a punctuated or gradual mode of evolution. *Gryphaea* was originally thought to have developed through progressive coiling and reduction in the attachment area of the left valve from the 'flat', cemented oyster *Liostrea liassica* to the tightly coiled, free-living oyster *Gryphaea arcuata*. A protracted debate raged in the late 1950s on the accuracy of this observation, and a direct link between these two species is no longer considered likely. However, it is clear that from *Gryphaea arcuata* there developed a lineage in which there was an overall *decrease* in coiling accompanied by an overall increase in size, in the lineage *Gryphaea arcuata – G. mccullochi – G. gigantea*. Since the development of the punctuated equilibrium hypothesis this lineage has been reappraised, and it is now throught that the morphological changes in coiling displayed by the three species appeared rapidly, punctuating stasis in coiling and gradual change in size (Figure 4.5). *Gryphaea* continues to be a test bed for evolutionary theory because of the abundance of its fossil remains in Jurassic rocks.

Gastropods have had a pivotal role in the development of the punctuated equilibrium model, as they were one of the groups originally used to demonstrate the plausibility of the hypothesis. Particularly important are the abundant Quaternary land snails (*Poecilizonites*) in Bermuda, where the examination of ancient populations of land snails has demonstrated the presence of rapid morphological changes which punctuate an otherwise unremarkable period of stasis. Here, the isolation of *Poecilizonites* populations through temporary sea-level highs led to the development of new characteristics. These were passed quickly through the small gene pool of the isolated population, and led to allopatric speciation through reproductive isolation. Three successive subspecies arose in this way on the periphery of the main population, each one replacing the other on its extinction, subsequently spreading and colonising the empty niches. The geological record of these snails is therefore representative of stasis in each of the *Poecilizonites* species which is interrupted by the appearance of new forms. These were developed by rapid morphological changes as the peripheral populations migrated and recolonised the area previously inhabited by the main population. This is a classic demonstration of allopatric speciation, the driving mechanism of punctuated equilibrium.

8.5.2 Palaeoenvironmental Analysis

Bivalves and gastropods are of great value in palaeoenvironmental analysis because of their association with particular substrates. Bivalves and gastropods are almost all benthonic (although there are some planktonic gastropods), and mostly neritic, and are most commonly limited by water depth, substrate, salinity and oxygenation (Table 8.1). The close study of present-day environments demonstrates that bivalves and gastropods may be clustered on the basis of **substrate preference** and **feeding strategy**. Typical substrate preferences are infaunal, epifaunal and vagile (freely moving). Infaunal bivalves include rock-borers, burrowers, and nestlers – 'squatters' inhabiting pre-constructed burrows or cavities (Figure 8.13). Epifaunal bivalves include free-living recliners, strongly attached cementers and byssally attached shells. Vagile bivalves are rare but include the partially free-swimming genera *Pecten* and *Lima*. Infaunal gastropods burrow through the sediment in search of food, and most are vagile (crawlers, active burrowers or, rarely, planktonic) or epifaunal (attached or cemented) (Figure 8.14). Typical feeding strategies for bivalves and gastropods are as infaunal or epifaunal suspension feeders (both mostly bivalves) and as detritus feeders and predators (including some bivalves but mostly gastropods).

Study of shallow-water environments today demonstrates that, typically, certain substrate preferences and feeding strategies are associated with certain environments. For example, epifaunal suspension feeders are commonly associated with hostile, low-salinity or low-oxygen environments, while a greater diversity of infaunal suspension-feeding groups may occur in more open marine conditions. Although this example is simplistic, the patterns of association of benthic (bottom-dwelling) bivalves and gastropods can give an extremely important insight into the nature of the factors limiting them. This has proven to be of particular value in salinity and oxygenation studies, explored more fully in Chapter 22. On an individual basis, certain groups are indicative of particular environments,

Table 8.1 *Bivalve and gastropod limiting factors*

Temperature	Bivalves and gastropods have broad temperature ranges. In general, shell size and thickness are related to temperature; with decreasing temperature, size and thickness decrease because $CaCO_3$ is undersaturated in cold waters.
Oxygenation	Bivalves and gastropods are commonest in fully oxygenated waters, although individual opportunist species may be found at low levels.
Salinity	Bivalves and gastropods have broad salinity ranges, but are most diverse in fully marine conditions. Individual taxa may occur in fully marine to brackish-water conditions. Some bivalves are found in fresh waters, and some gastropods are found in fresh waters or on land.
Depth	Bivalves and gastropods inhabit a wide range of water depths. In general, deep-burrowing bivalves are known from shallow waters, while shallow-burrowing bivalves range from shallow to deep waters. Deposit feeding bivalves are more common offshore.
Substrate	The morphology of bivalves and gastropods is commonly related to substrate, reflecting the range from hard substrates (rock-borers and clingers) to soft substrates (burrowers).
Turbulence	Bivalves and gastropods can live in a range of water turbulence levels, though most live in moderate turbulence levels, with cementing, nestling, rock-boring and rapid-burrowing forms in highly turbulent conditions.

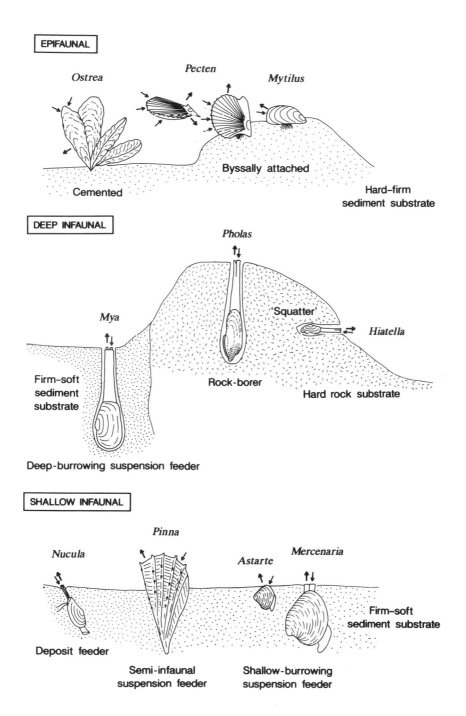

EPIFAUNAL

Ostrea   *Pecten*   *Mytilus*

Byssally attached

Cemented

Hard–firm
sediment substrate

DEEP INFAUNAL

Pholas

Mya

'Squatter'

Hiatella

Firm–soft
sediment
substrate

Rock-borer

Hard rock substrate

Deep-burrowing suspension feeder

SHALLOW INFAUNAL

Pinna

Nucula   *Astarte*   *Mercenaria*

Firm–soft
sediment substrate

Deposit feeder

Semi-infaunal
suspension feeder

Shallow-burrowing
suspension feeder

Figure 8.14 *Modes of life of typical bivalve shells*

such as the Cenozoic freshwater gastropod *Paludina* or the Carboniferous non-marine bivalve *Carbonicola*. Other taxa, such as the hippuritid (rudist) bivalves, probably had a climatic limitation on their distribution as they are most commonly found located within a narrow latitudinal belt either side of the tropics, and associated with the Mesozoic Tethys Ocean. Their occurrence is therefore suggestive of tropical or warm-water environments, which makes them valuable in biogeographical studies.

8.5.3 Stratigraphy

Bivalves and gastropods have, in general, very little application in stratigraphy. They are strongly facies-limited, associated with certain substrates, and are mostly neither free-swimming, nor fast-evolving. However, bivalves are used in some instances, where other suitable guide fossils are absent or lacking. For example, in the Carboniferous, non-marine mussels such as *Carbonicola* and *Anthracomya* have been traditionally employed in the correlation of local coal-bearing rocks in Britain (Figure 8.15). Here a series of six total range biozones based upon these freshwater bivalves have been shown to have considerable value in the correlation of coal sequences in Britain and the rest of Europe. Bivalves have also been employed as guide fossils in the Cretaceous, *Buchia* assemblage biozones being employed in Russia and the Western Cordillera of North America. Planktonic gastropods (pteropods) also have potential for correlation because of the nature of their passive dispersal seas and oceans.

8.6 SUGGESTED READING

Detailed taxonomic studies of bivalves and gastropods can be found in the relevant parts of the *Treatise on Invertebrate Paleontology* (Moore, 1969a; 1969b), while Clarkson (1993) and Pojeta *et al.* (1987) provide a more accessible, but none the less comprehensive discussion of them. Peel (1985) and Skelton (1985) provide illustrations of the most commonly occurring taxa of gastropods and bivalves, respectively. The fossil record of the family groups of bivalves and gastropods is given by Skelton and Benton (1993) and Tracey *et al.* (1993). Functional morphology studies worthy of examination are: Skelton (1976), Linsley *et al.* (1978), Kelly (1980) and Allmon *et al.* (1990). The papers by Hallam (1959; 1982), Johnson and Lennon (1990) and Johnson (1994) give an insight into the use of *Gryphaea* in microevolution, while Gould (1969) explores the microevolution of the Bermudan land snails. Examples of the principles and practices of bivalve palaeoecology and palaeoenvironmental analysis are provided by Hudson (1963), Stanley (1970), Liljedahl (1984) and Wignall (1990). The use of bivalves and gastropods in stratigraphy is demonstrated by the classic paper by Davies and Trueman (1927), and by Sohl (1977), Blackwelder (1981) and Janssen (1990). Donovan (1992) reviews these applications in the light of a single group, the Hippuritidae.

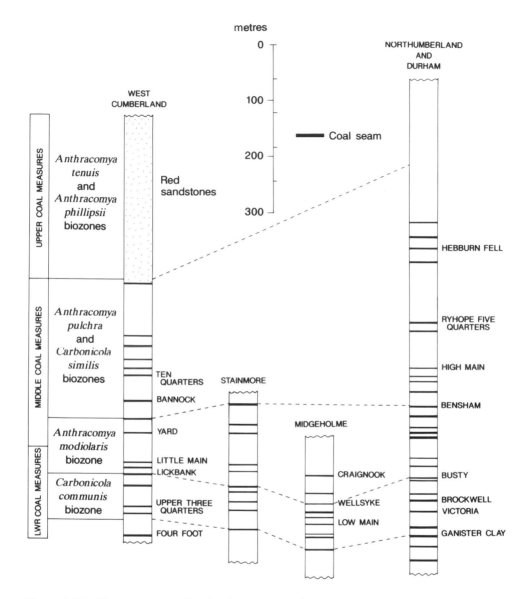

Figure 8.15 *The non-marine bivalve biozones in the Coal Measures of northern England* [Modified from: Taylor et al. *(1971)* British Regional Geology: Northern England, *HMSO, Fig. 23, p. 66]*

Allmon, W.D., Nieh, J.C & Norris, R.D. 1990. Drilling and peeling of turritelline gastropods since the late Cretaceous. *Palaeontology*, **33**, 595–612.

Blackwelder, B.W. 1981. Late Cenozoic stages and molluscan zones of the U.S. Middle Atlantic Coastal Plain. *Paleontological Society Memoir*, **12**.

Clarkson, E.N.K. 1993. *Invertebrate Palaeontology and Evolution.* Third edition. Chapman & Hall, London.

Davies, J.H. & Trueman, A.E. 1927. A revision of the non-marine lamellibranchs of the Coal Measures, and a discussion of their zonal sequence. *Quarterly Journal of the Geological Society of London*, **83**, 210–259.

Donovan S.K. 1992. A plain man's guide to rudist bivalves. *Journal of Geological Education*, **40**, 313–320.

Gould, S.J. 1969. An evolutionary microcosm: Pleistocene and Recent history of the land snail P. (*Poecilozonites*) in Bermuda. *Bulletin of the Museum of Comparative Zoology, Harvard University*, **138**, 407–532.

Hallam, A. 1959. On the supposed evolution of *Gryphaea* in the Lias. *Geological Magazine*, **96**, 99–108.

Hallam, A. 1982. Patterns of speciation in Jurassic *Gryphaea*. *Paleobiology*, **8**, 354–366.

Hudson, J.D. 1963. The recognition of salinity-controlled assemblages in the Great Estuarine Series (Middle Jurassic) of the Inner Hebrides. *Palaeontology*, **11**, 163–182.

Janssen, A.W. 1990. Long distance correlation of Cainozoic deposits by means of planktonic gastropods ('pteropods'); some examples of future possibilities. *Tertiary Research*, **11**, 65–72.

Johnson, A.L.A. 1994. Evolution of European Lower Jurassic *Gryphaea* (*Gryphaea*) and contemporaneous bivalves. *Historical Biology*, **7**, 167–186.

Johnson, A.L.A. & Lennon, C.D. 1990. Evolution of gryphaeate oysters in the mid-Jurassic of western Europe. *Palaeontology*, **33**, 453–486.

Kelly, S.R.A. 1980. *Hiatella* – a Jurassic bivalve squatter? *Palaeontology*, **23**, 769–781.

Liljedahl, L. 1984. Ecological aspects of a silicified bivalve fauna from the Silurian of Gotland. *Lethaia*, **18**, 53–66.

Linsley, R.M., Yochelson, E.L. & Rohr, D.M. 1978. A reinterpretation of the mode of life of some Palaeozoic frilled gastropods. *Lethaia*, **11**, 105–112.

Moore, R.C. (ed.) 1969a. *Treatise on invertebrate paleontology, Part I, Mollusca 1*. Geological Society of America and University of Kansas Press, Lawrence, KS.

Moore, R.C. (ed.) 1969b. *Treatise on Invertebrate Paleontology, Part N, Mollusca 6*. Geological Society of America and University of Kansas Press, Lawrence, KS.

Peel, J.S. 1985. Gastropoda. *In* Murray, J.W. (ed.), *Atlas of Invertebrate Macrofossils*. Longman, London, 102–114.

Pojeta, J., Runnegar, B., Peel, J.S. & Gordon, M. 1987. Phylum Mollusca. *In* Boardman, R.S., Cheetham, A.H. & Rowell, A.J. (eds), *Fossil Invertebrates*. Blackwell Scientific Publications, Palo Alto, CA, 270–435.

Skelton, P.W. 1976. Functional morphology of the Hippuritidae. *Lethaia*, **9**, 83–100.

Skelton, P.W. 1985. Bivalvia. *In* Murray, J.W. (ed.), *Atlas of Invertebrate Macrofossils*. Longman, London, 81–100.

Skelton, P.W. & Benton, M.J. 1993. Mollusca: Rostroconcha, Scaphopoda and Bivalvia. *In* Benton, M.J. (ed.), *The Fossil Record 2*. Chapman & Hall, London, 237–264.

Sohl, N.F. 1977. Utility of gastropods in biostratigraphy. *In* Kauffman, E.G. & Hazel, J.E. (eds), *Concepts and Methods of Biostratigraphy*. Dowden, Hutchinson & Ross, Stroudsberg, PA, 519–540.

Stanley, S.M. 1970. *Relations of Shell Form to Life Habits in the Bivalvia (Mollusca)*. Geological Society of America Memoir 125, Lawrence, KS.

Tracey, S., Todd, J.A. & Erwin, D.H. 1993. Mollusca: Gastropoda. *In* Benton, M.J. (ed.), *The Fossil Record 2*. Chapman & Hall, London, 131–168.

Wignall, P.B. 1990. Benthic palaeoecology of the Late Jurassic Kimmeridge Clay of England. *Special Papers in Palaeontology*, **43**.

9
Molluscs: Cephalopods

9.1 CEPHALOPOD TAXONOMY

Cephalopods are familiar to us today as the octopus and squid, both of which are fished for food. Cephalopods are actively mobile molluscs, and possess a well-developed nervous system, complex eyes which are in many ways comparable to those of the vertebrates, and a large brain. These animals are difficult to equate with their relatives, the substrate-dwelling snails and bivalves, but the living *Nautilus*, found today in the Indo-Pacific oceans, provides a clue to their common ancestry. Like gastropods in particular, *Nautilus* possesses a calcareous shell, mantle muscle, rasping 'tongue' or radula and gills, all of which are found in the most primitive of molluscs.

Cephalopods are exclusively marine and were one of the most important predators in the Palaeozoic and Mesozoic oceans. They have an extensive fossil record, and are among the commonest components of the Palaeozoic and Modern evolutionary faunas. Cephalopods, particularly the ammonites, have an important role in correlation and in the determination of relative ages in stratigraphy.

9.1.1 General Characteristics of Cephalopods

Cephalopods are the only molluscs able to swim for a sustained period, and they do so by two specific adaptions of their body plan. Firstly, in most cases cephalopod shells have buoyancy chambers, a shell architecture unique to the group (Figure 9.1). In other cases, however, the shell is reduced and buoyancy is achieved by other means. Secondly, cephalopods are able to propel themselves through the water column using 'jet propulsion'.

The first cephalopod to evolve may have developed its buoyancy chambers by chance, through the growth of a septum or membrane across a conical shell. This

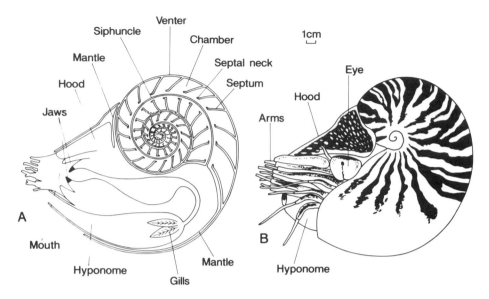

Figure 9.1   *General characteristics of the living, shelled, cephalopod* Nautilus. *A: Cross-section through shell and body. B: Exterior of the animal in life*

modification of the shell may have allowed the cephalopod ancestor to lift itself briefly from the substrate in search of food or safety. From this initial attempt at buoyancy developed a sophisticated system which characterises the class. In the living *Nautilus* the chambers are created by the soft body as the animal grows in a spiral (Figure 9.1). Each chamber is sealed off by the animal but is connected by a porous tube (**siphuncle**) which joins all the chambers with the animal. The chambers each contain some liquid (**cameral liquid**), but are mostly filled with gas at a pressure of less than 1 atmosphere, ranging from 0.3 to 0.9 atmospheres. In *Nautilus* the proportions of liquid to gas in the chambers are altered by the siphuncle, and this influences the relative density of the shell and therefore the buoyancy. Simply, *Nautilus* acts as a submarine does, pumping greater or lesser amounts of liqiud into the chambers to vary its position in the water column, although this process takes many hours to achieve.

Locomotion through 'jet propulsion' is achieved through the modification of the mantle and respiratory apparatus. Oxygenated water is taken into the mantle cavity to bathe the gills, and through muscular contraction of this cavity the spent water is expelled through a single siphon, the **hyponome**, created by a fold in the mantle. Therefore, motion of the cephalopods is predominantly backwards, as the jet of water is forced out anteriorly through the hyponome by the mantle muscle pump. In some cephalopods, such as the cuttlefish *Sepia*, backward motion is supplemented by fins capable of propelling the cuttlefish forwards.

In the majority of fossil cephalopods the shell is external (**ectocochleate**) and is characteristically chambered. Many ectocochleate shells are coiled and their chambered form is an important aid in distinguishing cephalopods from

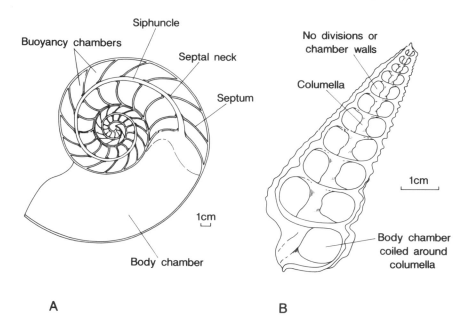

Figure 9.2 *Comparison of sectioned cephalopod and gastropod shells. The cephalopod (**A**) has buoyancy chambers, while the gastropod (**B**) has a single body chamber with no divisions or chamber walls*

gastropods (Figure 9.2). Unlike cephalopods, gastropods have no chambers, having instead a single body cavity for the soft parts which extends from the aperture to the top of the spire. Other cephalopods have an internal (**endocochleate**) shell which is chambered in some forms, but which is reduced to a vestige in others. Cuttlefish, for example, have a reduced chambered shell, the cuttlebone, while squid have drastically reduced their internal skeleton to an organic support known as the pen.

Cephalopods feed through active hunting or scavenging. Prey is captured by the multiple arms which may be equipped with suckers or hooks. In some cases pairs of arms may be modified into retractable tentacles which may be rapidly extended to capture prey. Once the victim has been ensnared it is drawn towards the centre of the crown of arms and into the mouth. Cephalopods are equipped with beak-like jaws which dispatch the prey.

9.1.2 Cephalopod Classification

The Cephalopoda is a class of the phylum Mollusca. A break-down of its classification is given below. Classification of cephalopods is dependent on the nature of shell and soft parts, and in particular the number of gills, two (**dibranchiate**) or four (**tetrabranchiate**); number of arms, eight, ten or multiple; and other small, rarely preserved skeletal elements such as the radula.

Phylum Mollusca Linnaeus, 1758
Class Cephalopoda Cuvier, 1797 (Cambrian–Recent)
Fully marine, free-swimming and self-buoyant molluscs adapted to a hunting mode of life.

Subclass Nautiloidea Agassiz, 1847 (Cambrian–Recent)
Cephalopods with coiled or straight ectocochleate shells with simple chamber walls; siphuncle central; living examples with multiple arms. Tetrabranchiate. Other classifications recognise that the 'nautiloids' are a large and diverse grouping, and separate them at subclass level into Endoceratoidea, Actinoceratoidea, Orthoceratoidea, as well as the Nautiloidea.

Subclass Coleoidea Bather, 1888 (Devonian–Recent)
Cephalopods with endocochleate shells; chambered in some, reduced in others; ten or eight arms grouped around mouth. Dibranchiate. Includes the internally shelled belemnoids as well as the soft-bodied squid and octopus.

Subclass Ammonoidea Zittel, 1884 (Devonian–Cretaceous)
Cepalopods with mostly coiled ectocochleate shells with complex suture walls; siphuncle marginal; number of arms unknown. Number of gills unknown. Includes the earliest ammonoids, the bactritids, which have straight shells, as well as the first coiled ammonoids, the clymenids, goniatites and ceratites, and the ammonites proper, the phylloceratids, lytoceratids and ammonitids.

9.2 CEPHALOPOD SHELL MORPHOLOGY

The cephalopods fall into two broad types: those with the soft body contained within an external or ectocochleate shell; and those with an internal or endo-cochleate shell contained within the soft body. Ectocochleate cephalopods include the ammonites and the nautiloids, and are represented today solely by *Nautilus* itself. The subclass Coleoidea encompasses all the endocochleate cephalopods, and contains a great diversity of shell types, from coiled chambered shells in *Spirula*, to the much reduced, organic, non-chambered supports found in squid and octopods.

9.2.1 Basic Components of Ectocochleate Cephalopod Shells

Ectocochleate cephalopods have complex shells built both to withstand water pressure and to act as a buoyancy aid. The shell comprises a cone which may or may not be coiled. This cone has an outer wall which is composed of a series of aragonite layers with an outer coating of organic material known as the **epithelium**. Externally, the shell may be ornamented by a variety of surface features, ranging from colour patterns through to a range of ribs and nodes (Figure 9.1). Internally, the shell is chambered. There are two types of chamber: buoyancy chambers or **camerae** (singular: **camera**); and a body chamber housing the head and other soft parts. The part of the shell which contains buoyancy chambers is known as the **phragmocone**. In the phragmocone, the camerae are regularly spaced and are separated from each other by chamber walls known as **septa** (singular: **septum**) (Figure 9.1). The septa are constructed from multiple layers like the remainder of the shell and are built to withstand pressure, conforming to a strong, domed shape resembling a watch-glass. The junction or **suture** of each septum with the internal surface of the shell wall has to withstand great pressures and varies from a relatively simple junction to one buttressed with a complexity of flutes. The form of this junction, the **suture line**, has been much studied and is of value in taxonomy. Each chamber is interconnected by a porous pipe known as the **siphuncle** (Fig. 9.1). The siphuncle passes through each septum by means of a type of bottle-neck arrangement, known as the **septal neck**, and the siphuncle passes from one neck to another. Ultimately, the siphuncle connects all chambers with the soft parts of the organism. There are two major types of ectocochleate cephalopods: **nautiloids** and **ammonoids**.

1. *Nautiloids* (Figure 9.3). Nautiloids were the first ectocochleate cephalopods. Nautiloids may be straight cones (**orthocones**) or coiled, with a range of morphologies between. As a result, the nautiloids have been subject to subdivision into major groups on the basis of their shell morphology and structure. However, nautiloids possess the following generalised characteristics:
  • siphuncle central to the septum
  • a simple suture line.
Nautiloids are relatively complex internally. They possess a range of characters designed to maintain the head in horizontal attitude in the water column. In orthocones, this is manifest in a series of structural additions to the camerae and siphuncle to act as counterbalances to the relatively weighty soft parts. Such

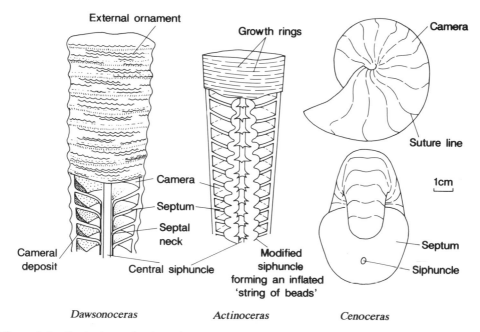

Figure 9.3 *Typical nautiloids: orthoconic* Dawsonoceras *from the Silurian and* Actinoceras *from the Ordovician; coiled* Cenoceras *from the Jurassic*

features are special calcareous deposits developed in the camerae (**cameral deposits**) or as modifications and additions to the siphuncle (Figure 9.3). Coiling, as in *Nautilus*, also achieved this, as it placed the centre of buoyancy directly above the body, positioned in the horizontal plane (Figure 9.1).

2. *Ammonoids* (Figure 9.4). Ammonoids are the most diverse of all ectocochleate cephalopods. For the most part, the ammonoids have developed a coiled phragmocone. The coils (whorls) of the phragmocone may overlap the preceding ones almost completely (**involute**) or not at all, resembling a coiled snake (**evolute**). This is determined by the diameter of the early whorls left showing after overlap, the **umbilicus** (Figure 9.4). A variety of shapes and sizes, with many ornament types, characterise the ammonoids, and often it is possible to obtain a great range of variation even within a single species. A great variety of terms have been evolved to describe the shape of the ammonoid conch. Typical examples are **oxycone**, reflective of a laterally compressed ammonite shell; **serpenticone**, referring to a loosely coiled, evolute ammonoid resembling a coiled snake; and **cadicone**, illustrating a ventrally flattened, and therefore fat, shell. Many more types exist. It has been considered that these different shapes may reflect different swimming speeds and styles, but this is probably an oversimplification (Figure 9.5). Modelling of ammonoid swimming suggests that 'streamlining' is unlikely to have made much difference to an animal dependent on buoyancy and a style of locomotion which would have created a slow rocking action. One group of

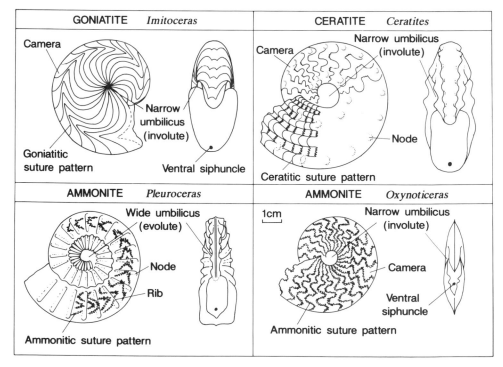

Figure 9.4 *Typical ammonoids: the goniatite* Imitoceras *from the Carboniferous; the ceratite* Ceratites *from the Triassic; and the ammonites* Pleuroceras *and* Oxynoticeras *from the Jurassic*

Figure 9.5 *The idea that streamlined ammonoids were faster swimmers than fatter, more ornamented, animals is likely to be a gross oversimplification, as it is probable that all ammonoids were sluggish swimmers [Modified from: Dartout-Bompis* et al. *(1989)* Bibliothèque de Travail: Les Ammonites **2**, p. 20]

ammonoids, the **heteromorphs**, are often bizarre in form and may have adopted a benthonic mode of life (Figure 9.6). Typical heteromorphs are orthoconic (e.g. *Baculites*), turretted (e.g. *Turrilites*) or complexly folded and bizzare (e.g. *Nipponites*) forms. Ammonoids possess the following generalised characteristics:

- siphuncle close to the outer (ventral) margin
- a complex suture line.

The suture line is known to have evolved in complexity through time (Figure 9.7). The convention is to describe inflections in the sutures as **saddles** (pointing towards the aperture) or **lobes** (pointing away from the aperture). This is demonstrated in the simple zigzag of most early ammonoids (**agoniatitic** and **goniatitic sutures**), lobes modified with some frills in the ceratites (**ceratitic suture**) and completely frilled lobes and saddles in the ammonites themselves (**ammonitic suture**) (Figure 9.7). This contrasts with the simplicity of the nautiloid suture, which has only simple deflections and no pronounced lobes or saddles. The development of the suture line is complex, and, although probably reflective of the need to maintain the structural strength of what is effectively a pressure vessel, there is no simple relationship. Ammonites were long considered to have possessed a lid or operculum to close off the shell in times of attack. These **aptychi** have been reconsidered in the light of discoveries in the body chambers of well-preserved ammonites, and are now thought to represent the lower jaw of the

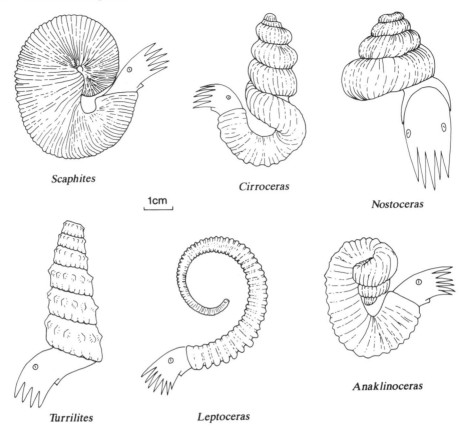

Scaphites

Cirroceras

1cm

Nostoceras

Turrilites

Leptoceras

Anaklinoceras

Figure 9.6 *Examples of heteromorph ammonites exhibiting coiling in several different planes. With the exception of the Jurassic genus* Leptoceras, *all are Cretaceous in age*

ammonite, acting like a scoop. This has fuelled a lively debate as to whether the ammonites fed mostly from the sea bottom, the lower jaw scooping up food.

9.2.2 Basic Components of Endocochleate Cephalopod Shells

Endocochleate cephalopods have modified shells for greater efficiency in swimming. Modifications include the development of a ventrally open body chamber. This permits greater flexibility of the mantle muscle and therefore greater propulsion capability, as more water can be taken into an expandable mantle no longer constrained by a shell. Three groups can be recognised: **belemnites**; **cuttlefish**, and **squid**.

1. *Belemnites* are common Mesozoic endocochleate cephalopods. They have a three part shell: the phragmocone, pro-ostracum and rostrum (Figures 9.8 and 9.9). The chambered shell or **phragmocone** has an open body chamber, with a

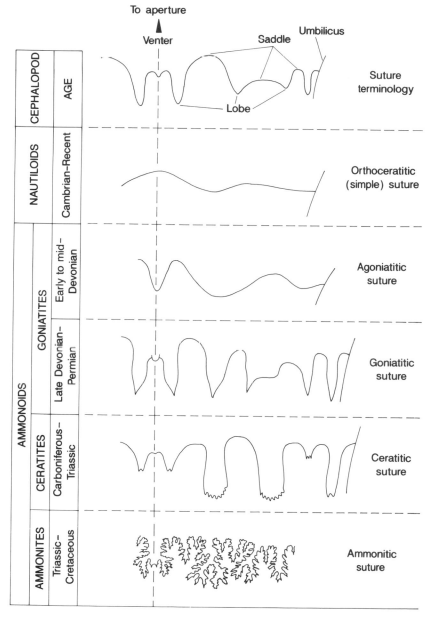

Figure 9.7 *Morphology of typical suture patterns in ectocochleate cephalopods [Modified from: Pojeta* et al. *(1987)* In *Boardman* et al. Fossil Invertebrates, *Blackwell, Fig. 14.51, p. 336]*

spatula-like support, the **pro-ostracum**. The phragmocone is contained in a solid bullet or club-shaped structure known as the guard, or more properly, the **rostrum** (Figure 9.9). The rostrum probably acted as a counterbalance to the head and arms, with the buoyant phragmocone acting as a pivot. This is a logical extension of the buoyancy adaptations of the orthoconic nautiloids. The phragmocone is

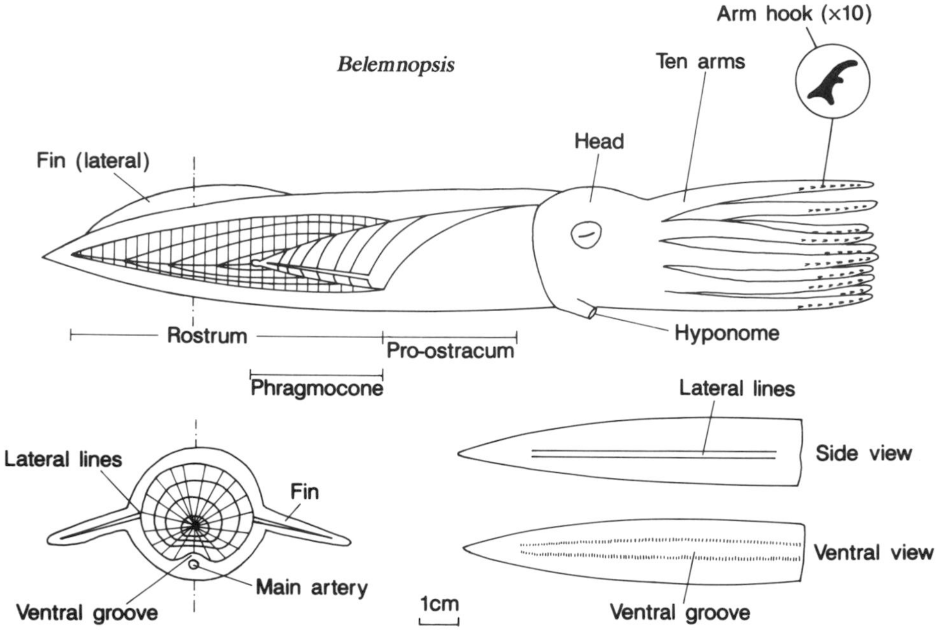

Figure 9.8 *Morphology of a typical belemnite showing position of shell and soft parts, cross-section through the body and rostrum, and a typical belemnite rostrum genus* Belemnopsis

constructed in much the same manner as that of the ectocochleate cephalopods. The rostrum is constructed in concentric layers of low-magnesium calcite inter-layered with organic-rich layers, each layer being added externally as new chambers were added to the phragmocone.

2. *Cuttlefish* and related endocochleate cephalopods have a ventrally open phragmocone and no rostrum. The familiar cuttlebone is the phragmocone, and consists of many closely spaced chambers. Buoyancy is achieved through liquid and gas as in the other chambered cephalopods, but here the need for a siphuncle is dispensed with, and variation in the gas–liquid proportion is achieved through equilibrium with the body.

3. *Squid* have a highly modified shell which no longer has chambers (Figure 9.10). This shell, calcitic in the Mesozoic and organic in the Cenozoic, serves as a support for the body, and buoyancy in these cephalopods is achieved either through constant swimming activity or through the development of a 'swim bladder' filled with an ammonia-rich fluid which has a lower specific gravity than water. Squids possess the ability to expel an inky substance in order to hide their escape if threatened by a potential predator. There is considerable evidence from the fossil stomach contents of large marine reptiles that squid and other soft-bodied cephalopods, including belemnites, were an enjoyable meal in the geological past (Figure 2.2) Squid fossils are relatively uncommon, but are preserved in exceptional circumstances, often with their ink sac intact (Figure 9.10).

Figure 9.9 *The belemnite* Cylindroteuthis *from the Jurassic Oxford Clay of England, showing rostrum, phragmocone and pro-ostracum preserved intact*

9.3 CEPHALOPOD EVOLUTION

The evolutionary development of the cephalopods is associated, initially at least, with the development of buoyancy. The earliest potential cephalopods appeared in the Cambrian, and, although there is considerable debate as to the oldest occurring example, it is clear that the development of chambering in an otherwise unremarkable conical shell may have led to an adaptive advantage, and to the

A

B

Figure 9.10   *Shells of fossil squids. **A:** Jeletzkyteuthis from the Lower Jurassic of England, showing internal support and ink sac. **B:** Trachyteuthis from the Upper Jurassic of Antarctica. It is possible that this actually represents a fossil cuttlefish 'bone' [Photographs: P. Doyle]*

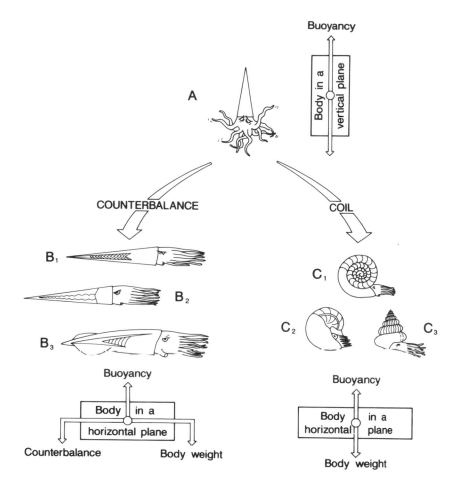

Figure 9.11 *Buoyancy in cephalopods. From the earlier ancestor (**A**) evolved two mechanisms to maintain the body in a horizontal position within the water column. The first to appear was the counterbalancing method, exhibited by the orthoconic nautiloids (**B₁** and **B₂**), and later the belemnoids (**B₃**). Coiling method used by both nautiloids and ammonoids (**C₁**–**C₃**)*

radiation of the nautiloids in the late Cambrian. At this point the cephalopods had developed the ability to maintain a horizontal position in the water column, either through counterbalancing, as in most of the straight-shelled cephalopods, or by coiling (Figure 9.11).

Most of the early nautiloids were straight-shelled. The earliest are the endoceratids, primitive nautiloids with wide siphuncles. The endoceratids display a variety of structures in their siphuncles – additional shell layers and the like – which may have enabled these nautiloids to maintain their position in the water column (Figure 9.3). The orthoceratids and actinoceratids appeared and diversified in the late Cambrian–Ordovician, and display a wide variety of skeletal modification, including deposits within the chambers (**cameral deposits**) to allow their attainment of a horizontal position in the water column. The endoceratids, orthoceratids and actinoceratids diversified in the Ordovician, but were depleted by the end-Ordovician extinction event, lingering on into the Carboniferous, and, in the case of the orthoceratids, into the Triassic (Figure 9.12). The nautilids themselves appeared in the Ordovician and were largely coiled, attaining the ability to place their body in the horizontal plane with their buoyancy above, rather like a balloon. The nautilids declined to their present-day level gradually throughout the remainder of the Phanerozoic.

The ammonoids developed from straight-shelled cephalopods, the bactritids, in the Devonian. The ammonoids were broadly successful and mostly utilised

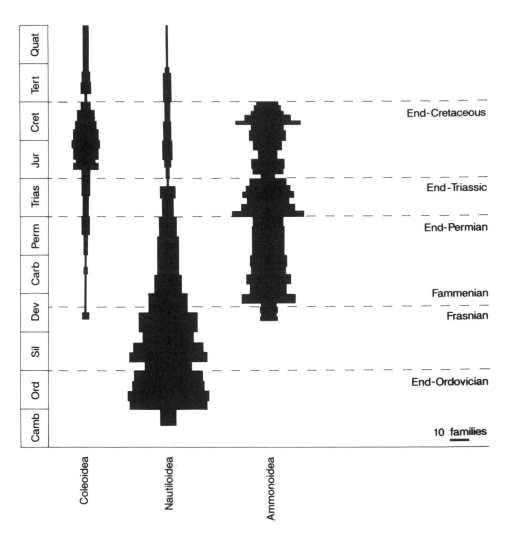

Figure 9.12 *The diversity of cephalopod families through geological time. The main extinction events are indicated [Compiled by A.L. Holder from: Benton (1993) The Fossil Record 2, Chapman & Hall]*

coiling in maintaining their horizontal body position. A pattern of evolutionary development is usually mapped out with reference to the suture line. Broadly, the Palaeozoic ammonoids had the simplest sutures, and most were extinguished in the Permian event. These were replaced by the ceratites, and notably the ammonites proper – the phylloceratids and lytoceratids – with extremely complex sutures, in the Triassic. The ammonoids were all extinguished at the end of the Cretaceous (Figure 9.12).

The colcoids represent the logical development of the horizontal, counterbalancing mode of life in cephalopods (Figure 9.11). The belemnoids developed from the bactritids, like the ammonites, and recent studies have suggested that ammonoids may have much in common with coleoids, particularly the form of the radula or rasping tongue, which has the same number of skeletal elements in both groups. The coleoids developed in the Devonian and were effectively analogous to the orthocone nautiloids, except that they had for the first time an internal skeleton, contained within a sheath-like soft body. The belemnites proper appeared in the Jurassic (or late Triassic on the basis of new information from China) and dispensed with the enclosed body chamber, thereby increasing the efficiency of the mantle pump for locomotion. All these early coleoids increased their counterbalancing efficiency through the development of the rostrum at the posterior. Squid and cuttlefish appeared in the Jurassic and represented a departure from the need for counterbalancing; squid lost their chambered buoyancy, while cuttlefish modified theirs to allow for a mobile, semi-benthonic life. The oldest confirmed octopods are known from a Cretaceous conservation Lagerstätte in the Lebanon. Like the ammonites, the belemnoids were extinguished at the end of the Cretaceous, leaving the squid, cuttlefish and octopods to diversify in the Cenozoic (Figure 9.12).

9.4 CEPHALOPOD APPLICATIONS

9.4.1 Palaeobiology

Functional Morphology

Ammonites have been the subject of several studies on functional morphology, largely associated with the form and function of the shell in buoyancy and locomotion. Although *Nautilus* is the only living ectocochleate cephalopod, it serves as an analogue for other extinct cephalopods, in that it possesses the siphuncle, camerae and other skeletal features. Most importantly, *Nautilus* has been used to determine the depth at which cephalopod shells collapse or **implode** with increasing water pressure. Modern *Nautilus* commonly lives at depths of 100–500 m and implodes at depths in excess of 800 m. The implosion depth is a function of the strength of the component parts, the engineered joins between septa and shell, and the strength of the siphuncle. Calculations based on living *Nautilus* have been extrapolated in comparison with fossil shells, and an implosion index to estimate the strengths of fossil cephalopods has been determined (Figure 9.13). This index

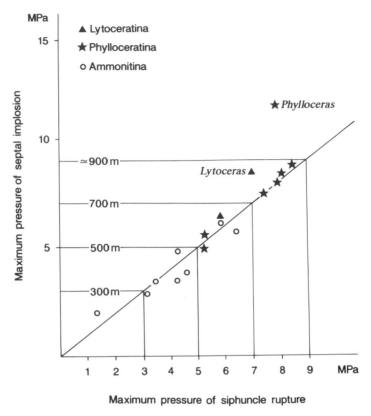

Figure 9.13   *The calculation of implosion depths for typical ammonite groups based on the strength of the septa and siphuncle to withstand water pressure [Modified from: Westermann (1990) In Pallini et al. (Eds) Fossili, Evoluzione, Ambiente, Comitato, Centenario Raffaele Piccinini, Fig. 3, p. 469]*

is a test of strength of two characters: the rupture strength of the siphuncle and the rupture strength of the septal buttresses or flutes. This has shown that ammonites and other chambered cephalopods were constrained by an implosion depth, with the majority being limited to shelf-depth waters.

Most famous is the discovery of sexual dimorphism in ammonites. Detailed collecting in the Jurassic clays of England in the 1920s demonstrated that there were several parallel lineages of large and small ammonites. Detailed examination of early ontogenetic stages demonstrated that in many cases large (**macroconch**) and small (**microconch**) ammonite 'species' were just morphological types, belonging in fact to one biological species, and representing differences in size between the sexes. This discovery was substantiated by the overall similarity of the early growth stages of the macro- and microconchs, the adult stage being represented by the addition of new features, such as size and shape differences, or the addition of shell features such as lappets, spike-like extensions to the aperture. Sexual dimorphism is now widely recognised throughout the ammonoids, and has been recognised on the same principles in a limited way in the belemnites too.

Evolution

Cephalopods have figured in many of the early studies on evolution. Ammonites have a special place in the history of the development of thought on evolution, but have not figured much in recent developments. This may be a function of the fact that many of these early studies have been discredited by later workers, particularly the so-called 'biogenic law' of Ernst Haeckel (1838–1902) which stated that 'ontogeny recapitulates phylogeny'. Put simply, Haeckel and others believed that the successive growth stages of an individual could demonstrate the evolutionary history of the fossil group, as new characters are added in the last growth stage. Taken apart, an ammonite could be expected to display a series of 'ancestors' in the successive growth stages of its individual life history, called its **ontogeny**. This 'law' came to dominate evolutionary, and even stratigraphical studies of ammonites in the early part of the twentieth century, such that specimens could be placed in an 'evolutionary series' through comparison with the growth stages observed in single descendant ammonites (Figure 9.14). In some cases this was done without recourse to stratigraphical information, and the whole edifice became unstable when detailed stratigraphical collecting showed that some characters first appeared in the early stages of ontogeny and were later spread to the adults of stratigraphically higher species – the exact reverse of the

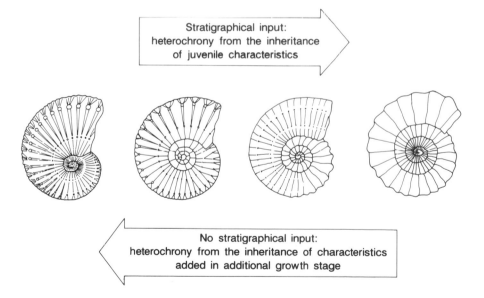

Figure 9.14 *Competing modes of heterochrony in the evolution of liparoceratid ammonites from the Lower Jurassic of England. Early authors believed in the biogenic law ('ontogeny recapitulates phylogeny') of Ernst Haeckel and tried to place taxa in an evolutionary series purely by a study of ontogeny, without detailed collecting and a proper stratigraphy. Later work based on stratigraphical studies demonstrated that the reverse was true, and that evolution of the group had proceeded by the inheritance of juvenile characteristics [Modified from: Kennedy (1977) In Hallam (Ed.) Patterns of Evolution, as Illustrated by the Fossil Record, Elsevier, Fig. 14, p. 266]*

predictions of the biogenic law as then understood. We now know that new characters may be developed in a species by the addition of an extra ontogenetic growth stage, or by the interruption of ontogeny and the loss of a growth stage. This concept – now called **heterochrony**, further discussed in Box 4.3 – is now thought to be of great importance in the development of some new characters, and it can be clearly demonstrated in some ammonites, particularly because, in common with all molluscs, they preserve the growth stages within the shell.

One of the most important studies in ammonite evolution is that of the Middle Jurassic ammonite *Kosmoceras* in the 1920s. In a classic study, Ronald Brinkman collected over 3000 specimens from a 14 metre succession of the Jurassic Oxford Clay in the English Midlands. For each ammonite he measured a range of characters, and recognised that there were five parallel evolving lineages of *Kosmoceras*, which he assigned to separate subgenera. The validity of this work has been questioned, especially as it is now known that some of the so-called subgenera actually represent separate sexes of species of *Kosmoceras*, and because Brinkman discarded his specimens, so that his results are difficult to reproduce. Despite this, recent evaluation has shown that seven characters vary in *Kosmoceras* through the section, and that these may be representative of gradual change in a nektonic organism (Figure 9.15).

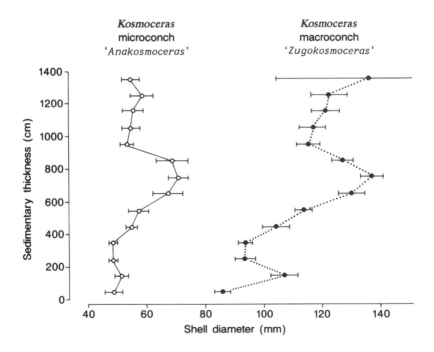

Figure 9.15 *Evolution of shell diameter in the ammonite* Kosmoceras *from the Oxford Clay of England. The micro- and macroconchs of this species were originally described as separate subgenera ('*Anakosmoceras' *and '*Zugokosmoceras'*) [Modified from: Raup and Crick (1981) Palaeobiology,* **7***, Fig. 3, p. 204]*

9.4.2 Palaeoenvironmental Analysis

Cephalopods are all fully marine, nektonic organisms limited primarily by four factors: salinity; temperature; water depth; and food supply (Table 9.1). Of these, salinity is of greatest importance, as cephalopods cannot survive in brackish or highly saline waters. Temperature is a limiting factor in some living cephalopod distributions, but squid and other endocochleates are found in marine waters from Equatorial to polar regions. Water depth is a prime control in ectocochleate cephalopods. As discussed above, the siphuncle and septa of ectocochleates can rupture with the pressures associated with water depth. However, squid and other endocochleates have greater depth freedom, as they are not limited by the implosion of the shell. Some squids are known to inhabit bathyal depths as a consequence. As predators, food supply is an extremely important limiter of cephalopods. Commonly, living endocochleates are restricted to shelf areas where crustaceans and other food sources are plentiful. In general this limits the distribution pattern of squid and octopods and, as a consequence, squid-fisheries target the feeding grounds of important genera such as *Loligo*.

Table 9.1 *Cephalopod limiting factors*

Temperature	Cephalopods have broad ranges and are found from the Equator to the polar regions.
Oxygenation	Cephalopods are commonest in fully oxygenated waters, although as free-swimming nektonic organisms they can inhabit the upper, oxygenated levels above the anoxic layer of a stratified water mass.
Salinity	Cephalopods are limited to fully marine conditions with normal salinities of $35^o/_{oo}$.
Depth	Cephalopods inhabit a range of water depths. Ectocochleates are limited by their implosion depth, which can be as much as 900 m.
Substrate	As nektonic organisms, most cephalopods are largely unaffected by substrate. However, some cephalopods are limited by their food source which may be substrate-dependent, such as crustaceans.
Turbulence	Cephalopods are adapted to moderate to low turbulence levels.

Cephalopod shells have been most commonly used in the determination of drift patterns and shoreline indicators. For example, straight-shelled cephalopod accumulations have been used as current indicators, the orientation of the shells being parallel to the current direction, the velocity of the current aligning the shells. In some cases these accumulations have been recognised as indicators of ancient strandings on shorelines or as accumulations after mass deaths which commonly occur after the mating that takes place at specific times in the life cycle of living cephalopods (Figure 9.16). In some cases, the implosion depth of cephalopods has been used to calculate the depth of deposition of the sedimentary sequence within which they occur, as unimploded shells would indicate that the depth of deposition did not exceed the depth at which implosion occurred. The discovery of imploded nautiloids *Simplicioceras* and *Euciphoceras* in the

Figure 9.16   *Mass accumulation of belemnites from the Lower Jurassic of England. Such accumulations can be interpreted as the result of mass mortality after mating, although this assemblage probably represents the regurgitated stomach contents of a large vertebrate (see Figure 2.2) [Photograph: P. Doyle]*

Eocene London Clay Formation suggests a water depth for the London Basin of around 300 m, which is the calculated septal implosion depth of these genera.

As nektonic organisms, cephalopods have most use in the determination of biogeographical patterns within ancient oceans. This is of primary importance for the Mesozoic, a time when there were two great marine realms, which are identified mostly on the basis of ammonites and belemnites. A **realm** is a large biogeographical unit based upon the overall similarity of the contained fauna, mainly at higher taxonomic levels of family and above. These Mesozoic realms, the Boreal and Tethyan, have a boundary in Europe which has been shown to have fluctuated in position through time. Traditional explanations have suggested climatic gradients, effectively a temperature variation, to explain the very clear provinciality of the faunas. Belemnites are particularly important in this respect as the two main groupings, the suborders Belemnitina and Belemnopseina, appear to be restricted to the Boreal and Tethyan realms, respectively. Recent study has suggested that a simple climatic story is not sufficient to explain the clear division of the two realms in Europe, the periodic intermingling of belemnites from northern and southern regions, and an observed increase in belemnite diversity northwards away from Europe. This evidence suggests that geographical controls rather than temperature differences may have been of paramount importance in delimiting belemnite distributions, and it is probable that Europe was a region of restricted seaways with uncertain environmental conditions. Mingling of northern and southern belemnite faunas is coincident with flooding episodes that may have allowed free passage southwards and northwards.

9.4.3 Stratigraphy

Cephalopods, particularly ammonites, have the greatest application in stratigraphy. Quite simply, ammonites are of paramount importance because they satisfy all of the criteria for a good guide fossil. Ammonites are widespread and independent of facies, because they were free-swimming and could cross oceans; were fast to evolve, with ammonite species often lasting no more than 0.5–1 million years from appearance to extinction; were readily preserved and are abundant as a consequence, and are easily recognised. Given these advantages, ammonites are the supreme example of a guide fossil, and 74, mostly total range, biozones have been erected for the Jurassic alone. This is complicated by the geographical restriction of some groups in the late Jurassic, but still remains one of the best and mostly highly developed biozonation schemes for any part of the stratigraphical column. This is discussed futher in Chapter 23. Belemnites also have potential, but are not widely used as they are less diverse and poorly known.

9.5 SUGGESTED READING

Detailed taxonomic studies of the cephalopods can be found in the relevant parts of the *Treatise on Invertebrate Paleontology* (Moore, 1957; 1959), while Clarkson (1993) and Pojeta *et al.* (1987) provide an accessible overview. House (1985) illustrates many of the most common fossil cephalopods. Kennedy and Cobban (1976), House and Senior (1981) and Lehman (1981) are highly recommended for their treatment of the ammonites, and Holland (1986) presents a worthy overview of the nautiloids. The fossil record of the family groups of cephalopods is given by Doyle (1993), Hewitt *et al.* (1993), King (1993) and Page (1993). Functional morphology studies worthy of examination, particularly in relation to ammonite implosion and morphotypes, are Westermann (1973; 1990) and Jacobs (1992). Sexual dimorphism in ammonites is dealt with in the classic paper by Callomon (1963), while sexual dimorphism in belemnites is discussed by Doyle (1985). Kennedy (1977) gives a review of the role of ammonites in microevolution, and Landman (1988) treats heterochrony in ammonites. An interesting historical discussion of the role of the 'biogenic law' in shaping ammonite evolutionary studies in the early part of the twentieth century is given in Donovan (1973). The paper by Raup and Crick (1981) is a measured re-evaluation of Ronald Brinkman's classic *Kosmoceras* study. The use of ammonites and belemnites in biogeography are discussed by Kennedy and Cobban (1976) and Doyle (1987). Reyment (1968), Batt (1993) and Doyle and Macdonald (1993) all give accounts of cephalopods in palaeoecology. An example of the depth of deposition of sedimentary sequences from implosion data is given by Hewitt (1988). The use of cephalopods in stratigraphy are discussed in the reviews by Kennedy and Cobban (1976) and House and Senior (1981).

Batt, R. 1993. Ammonite morphotypes as indicators of oxygenation in a Cretaceous epicontinental sea. *Lethaia*, **26**, 49–63.

Callomon, J.H. 1963. Sexual dimorphism in Jurassic ammonites. *Transactions of the Leicester Literary and Philosophical Society*, **57**, 21–56.

Clarkson, E.N.K. 1993. *Invertebrate Palaeontology and Evolution*. Third edition. Chapman & Hall, London.

Donovan, D.T. 1973. The influence of theoretical ideas in ammonite classification from Hyatt to Trueman. *University of Kansas Paleontological Contributions*, **62**, 1–16.

Doyle, P. 1985. Sexual dimorphism in the belemnite *Youngibelus* from the Lower Jurassic of Yorkshire. *Palaeontology*, **28**, 133–146.

Doyle, P. 1987. Lower Jurassic – Lower Cretaceous belemnite biogeography and the origin of the Mesozoic Boreal Realm. *Palaeogeography, Palaeoclimatology, Palaeoecology*, **61**, 237–254.

Doyle, P. 1993. Mollusca: Cephalopoda (Coleoidea). *In* Benton, M.J. (ed.), *The Fossil Record 2*. Chapman & Hall, London, 229–236.

Doyle, P. & Macdonald, D.I.M. 1993. Belemnite battlefields. *Lethaia*, **26**, 65–80.

Hewitt, R.H. 1988. Nautiloid shell taphonomy: interpretations based upon water pressure. *Palaeogeography, Palaeoclimatology, Palaeoecology*, **63**, 15–25.

Hewitt, R.H., Kullman, J., House, M.R., Glenister, B.F. & Wang Y.-G. 1993. Mollusca: Cephalopoda (pre-Jurassic Ammonoidea). *In* Benton, M.J. (ed.), *The Fossil Record 2*. Chapman & Hall, London, 189–212.

Holland, C.H. 1986. The nautiloid cephalopods: a strange success. *Journal of the Geological Society, London*, **144**, 1–15.

House, M.R., 1985. Cephalopoda. *In* Murray, J.W. (ed.), *Atlas of Invertebrate Macrofossils*, Longman, London, 114–152.

House, M.R. & Senior, J.R. (eds) 1981. *The Ammonoidea. The Evolution, Classification, Mode of Life, and Geological Usefulness of a Major Fossil Group*. Systematics Association Special Publication 18. Academic Press, London.

Jacobs, D.K. 1992. Shape, drag, and power in ammonoid swimming. *Paleobiology*, **18**, 203–220.

Kennedy, W.J. 1977. Ammonite evolution. *In* Hallam, A. (ed.), *Patterns of Evolution as Illustrated by the Fossil Record*. Elsevier, Amsterdam, 251–304.

Kennedy, W.J. and Cobban, W.A. 1976. *Aspects of Ammonite Biology, Biogeography and Biostratigraphy*. Special Papers in Palaeontology 17. Palaeontological Association, London.

King, A.H. 1993. Mollusca: Cephalopoda (Nautiloidea). *In* Benton, M.J. (ed.), *The Fossil Record 2*. Chapman & Hall, London, 169–188.

Landman, N.H. 1988. Heterochrony in ammonites. *In* McKinney, M.L. (ed.), *Heterochrony in Evolution*. Plenum, New York, 159–182.

Lehman, U. 1981. *The Ammonites – Their Life and Their World*. Cambridge University Press, Cambridge.

Moore, R.C. (ed.) 1957. *Treatise on Invertebrate Paleontology, Part L, Mollusca 4*. Geological Society of America and University of Kansas Press, Lawrence, KS.

Moore, R.C. (ed.) 1969. *Treatise on Invertebrate Paleontology, Part K, Mollusca 3*. Geological Society of America and University of Kansas Press, Lawrence, KS.

Page, K.N. 1993. Mollusca: Cephalopoda (Ammonoidea: Phylloceratina, Lytoceratina, Ammonitina and Ancyloceratina). *In* Benton, M.J. (ed.), *The Fossil Record 2*. Chapman & Hall, London, 213–228.

Pojeta, J., Runnegar, B., Peel, J.S. & Gordon, M. 1987. Phylum Mollusca. *In* Boardman, R.S., Cheetham, A.H. & Rowell, A.J. (eds), *Fossil invertebrates*. Blackwell Scientific Publications, Palo Alto, CA, 270–435.

Raup, D.M. & Crick, R.E. 1981. Evolution of single characters in the Jurassic ammonite *Kosmoceras*. *Paleobiology*, **7**, 200–215.

Reyment, R.A. 1968. Orthoconic nautiloids as indicators of shoreline surface currents. *Journal of Sedimentary Petrology*, **38**, 1387–1389.

Westermann, G.E.G. 1973. Strength of concave septa and depth limits of fossil cephalopods. *Lethaia*, **6**, 383–403.

Westermann, G.E.G. 1990. New developments in the ecology of Jurassic–Cretaceous ammonoids. *In* Pallini, G. *et al.* (eds), *Atti del secondo convegno internazionale fossili, evoluzione, ambiente.* Pergola, 459–478.

10
Brachiopods

10.1 BRACHIOPOD TAXONOMY

Brachiopods are marine shellfish with a fossil record which spans almost the whole of the Phanerozoic. They are mostly surface-dwelling animals which have a complex food-gathering mechanism housed within a hinged calcareous shell. Brachiopods have two-halved shells, but are unrelated to the molluscs because of the nature of their suspension feeding system, which is quite unlike that existing in the otherwise similar members of the class Bivalvia (Chapter 8). Although common in the geological record, brachiopods are now much less familiar as living organisms because of a drastic decline in diversity after the mass extinction in the Permian. Brachiopods achieved their peak in diversity when they were the dominant members of the Palaeozoic evolutionary fauna, monopolising the shallow marine environments of the early and late Palaeozoic. Because of this, brachiopods are particularly important fossils in Palaeozoic marine sediments, and have great value in palaeoenvironmental studies.

10.1.1 General Characteristics of Brachiopods

In many ways, brachiopods resemble bivalve molluscs, as both mostly possess an external calcareous shell consisting of two valves, and both are mostly benthic filter feeders. This is where the similarities end, however, as bivalves and brachiopods are distinguished through the orientation and symmetry of their bivalved shells (Figure 8.2) and, most importantly, through the nature of their internal organs. Brachiopods possess a special feeding organ known as the **lophophore** (Figure 10.1). This is complex and consists, in living representatives, of a large number of sticky filaments grouped on a ribbon-like axis and supported by a complex calcareous support or 'bracket' which extends inside the shell

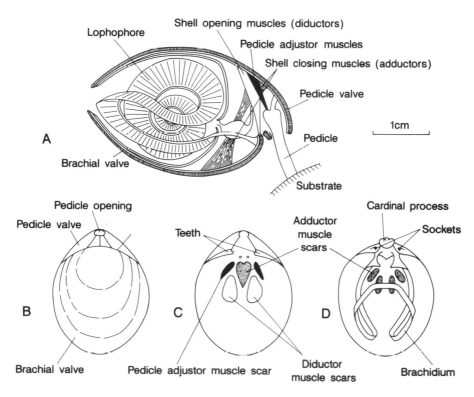

Figure 10.1 *General characteristics of brachiopods. A: Cross-section through a generalised living brachiopod. B–D: General characteristics of the shell. B: Shell exterior. C: Interior of the pedicle valve. D: Interior of the brachial valve [Modified from: Black (1988),* Elements of Palaeontology, *Fig. 78, p. 125]*

cavity. Brachiopods are sessile, mostly attached to their substrate by a fleshy stalk, the **pedicle,** which passes from the body cavity through an opening in the shell (Figure 10.1). However, others may be free-living, lying directly on the substrate, while a few live in specially constructed burrows.

10.1.2 Brachiopod Classification

Brachiopods constitute a separate phylum of the animal kingdom. Currently there are three classes, divided on the nature of shell structure (particularly the hinge mechanism) and chemistry. In particular, shell chemistry has formed the basis for much recent debate, which dispenses with the traditional grouping of brachiopods into articulate and inarticulate groups, and identifies two classes of the phylum: class Lingulata, comprising all brachiopods with a phosphatic shell; and class Calciata, comprising all brachiopods with a calcareous shell, which includes some 'inarticulate' brachiopods with the articulates. A more traditional classification is used here which retains the articulate–inarticulate division.

Phylum Brachiopoda Dumeril, 1806
Class Lingulata Gorjansky and Popov, 1985 (Cambrian–Recent)
Brachiopods with valves not hinged with teeth and sockets, and with organic (chitinophosphatic) shells. Includes lingulids and related burrowing brachiopods with organic shells.

Class Inarticulata Huxley, 1869 (Cambrian–Recent)
Brachiopods with valves not hinged by teeth and sockets, and with calcareous shells. Includes the craniaceans and other squat brachiopods with calcareous shells.

Class Articulata Huxley, 1869 (Cambrian–Recent)
Brachiopods with valves hinged by teeth and sockets, with calcareous shells. Comprises the numerically most diverse and abundant brachiopod groups. Subdivided into several orders, the most important of which are the Orthida, Strophomenida, Spiriferida, Pentamerida, Rhynchonellida and Terebratulida.

10.2 BRACHIOPOD SHELL MORPHOLOGY

The two main natural groups, the inarticulates (including the Lingulata and In-articulata) and articulates are very different in structure. The inarticulates are found as both surface-dwelling brachiopods with calcitic shells and short pedicles, and as deep-burrowing brachiopods with symmetrical, organic shells. This difference in shell chemistry has led to the separation of the inarticulates into those with organic shells living in burrows (Lingulata) and those with calcareous shells (Inarticulata). The valves are poorly articulated and are held together with a complexity of muscles. The Articulata are more complex, and have calcitic shells which are articulated with a series of complex muscles, as well as a tooth and socket joint arrangement.

10.2.1 Basic Components of Articulate Brachiopod Shells

Articulate brachiopods possess two valves which are unequal in size. The largest valve, the **pedicle valve**, contains the opening through which the fleshy pedicle passes (Figure 10.1). This valve is sometimes known as the **ventral valve** because of a convention of illustrating brachiopods with the largest valve lowermost. The smaller valve has attached to it the shelly internal lophophore supports, known as the **brachidium** (plural: **brachidia**). This valve is known as the **brachial valve** but is sometimes referred to as the **dorsal valve**. Brachiopods are therefore not **equivalve** (with two equal valves) but are characterised by the fact that each valve is **equilateral**, that is, each valve is symmetrical along an axis from its anterior to its posterior (Figures 8.2 and 10.1).

Articulate brachiopods are usually found with both valves clamped shut (Figure 10.2). This is because there is no natural spring acting against the muscles to open the shell; instead, the valves are shut through a complexity of muscles working both to open and close the shell. Brachiopods therefore not only have **adductor** muscles, which close the shell on contraction and which are connected to the interior of both valves, but also **diductor** muscles which act against the

Figure 10.2 *Fossil brachiopods in a shell bed from the Miocene of southern Spain, lens cap 50 mm. The brachiopods are found intact with both valves closed. This contrasts with the disarticulated bivalves which comprise much of the shell bed [Photograph: P. Doyle]*

adductors to open the shell. The diductor muscles are attached to the interior of the pedicle valve and converge on a knob called the **cardinal process** within the brachial valve (Figure 10.1). On the death of the brachiopod, the muscles decay and the shell remains naturally shut. Six main groups of articulate brachiopods can be distinguished on the combination of some limited shell characters: **hinge margin**; **shell convexity**; **pedicle opening**; and **brachidium type**. These characters are discussed below.

The hinge margin is of use as articulate brachiopods can be grouped for convenience into those with straight (**strophic**) hinge margins and those with curved (**astrophic**) hinge margins. This grouping is not necessarily reflective of the evolutionary development of the brachiopods, but represents a means to identify the commonly occurring groups through geological time. Strophic brachiopods include the orders Orthida, Strophomenida and Spiriferida. The order Spiriferida also includes some astrophic brachiopods, however, although some authorities include these in a separate order, the Atrypida. Astrophic brachiopods include the orders Pentamerida, Terebratulida and Rhynchonellida. Shell convexity is important in creating a robust or specially adapted shell form. Shells may be composed of two convex (**biconvex**) valves, or a convex pedicle valve and a concave brachial valve (**concavo-convex**). The pedicle opening may occur in one of two basic states: a triangular or diamond-shaped opening known as the **delthyrium**, sometimes later partially closed by **deltidial plates**; or a rounded opening or pedicle **foramen**. In other brachiopods the pedicle opening may be absent.

The brachidium is important in supporting the lophophore. Although some brachiopods do not appear to have possessed pronounced calcareous brachidia, others have well-developed examples. Simple brachidia are small bracket-like supports (**crura**); more complex are loops or spirals (**spiralia**) (Figure 10.3). Examination of brachidium type is generally impossible without either X-ray techniques or the destruction of the brachiopod through serial sectioning, a method of internal examination which involves slicing the shell into fine layers millimetre by millimetre. Serial sectioning is a commonly used method in the determination of brachiopod taxa (Figure 10.4). This is especially important since brachiopods of very different ancestry may resemble each other in external appearance. This is largely because of the phenomenon of **homeomorphy** which is common in brachiopods (Figure 10.5). Homeomorphs are organisms which resemble each other in shape and form, but which are derived from different ancestors and are therefore not directly related. The basic external brachiopod form is relatively simple, and it is common to find the same shape used more than once (Figure 10.5). It is therefore particularly important in all brachiopods to examine all their characteristics, including their internal features, to confirm any identification.

It is convenient to divide articulate brachiopods into two groupings, strophic and astrophic, according to the nature of their hinge line. This grouping aids in the practical identification of the brachiopod groups in the field, but in all cases further study is needed to determine the true nature of each brachiopod. The characteristics of these groups are discussed below.

1. *Strophic brachiopods* are all characterised by the possession of a straight hinge margin (Figure 10.6). The strophic brachiopods include the earliest articulates, and comprise three orders: Orthida, Strophomenida and Spiriferida. Their most important identifying features are given below, and illustrated in Figure 10.6.

Orthids (order Orthida, Cambrian to Permian or early Triassic) have the following characteristics:

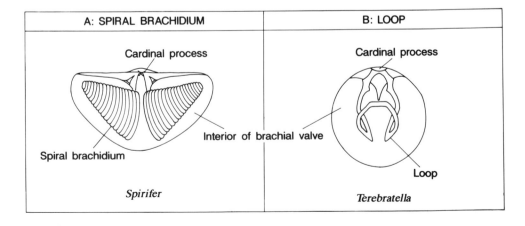

Figure 10.3 *Typical examples of complex lophophore supports (brachidia) in brachiopods*

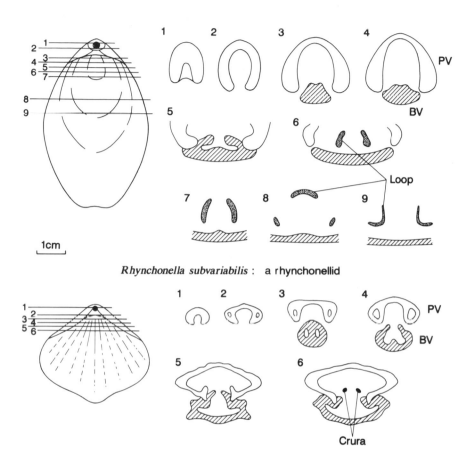

Rouillieria ovoides : a terebratulid

1cm

Rhynchonella subvariabilis : a rhynchonellid

Figure 10.4 *The technique of serial sectioning. This technique enables the examination of internal structures through the systematic sectioning of the brachiopod shell. Each of the numbered slices picks out differences in the lophophore supports and valve structures. PV pedicle valve; BV brachial valve [Modified from: Ager (1971) Proceedings of the Geologists' Association, **82**, Figs 1 and 2, pp. 398 and 400]*

- small, semi-circular shells (the width of the hinge margin does not exceed that of the widest part of the shell)
- both valves convex
- both valves densely ribbed
- an open delthyrium present for the pedicle
- the absence of a calcified brachidium.

Orthids are common Palaeozoic fossils. Their shells are characteristically small and finely ribbed. Some larger species can resemble the spiriferids, but are distinguished by the absence of a spiral brachidium, and a shorter hinge margin than the spiriferids. The delthyrium may be diamond-shaped, with corresponding

A   B

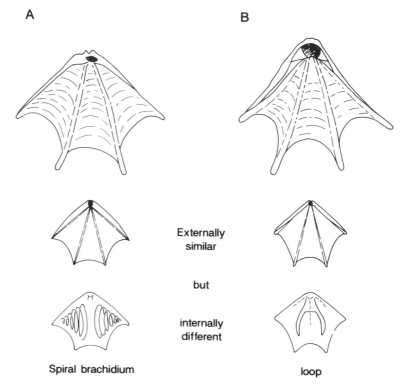

Externally
similar

but

internally
different

Spiral brachidium   loop

Figure 10.5   *Homeomorphy in brachiopods. These two brachiopods are externally similar, but internally have different lophophore supports. A: Tetractinella, a spiriferid from the Palaeozoic. B: Cheirothyris, a terebratulid from the Mesozoic*

openings in both pedicle and brachial valves, sometimes partially closed with deltidial plates, as with *Mimella* illustrated in Figure 10.6.

Strophomenids (order Strophomenida, Ordovician–Permian) have:
- large concavo-convex shells
- no pedicle opening, as the shell is supported upon the larger ('pedicle') valve, sometimes by large extended spines
- the absence of a calcified brachidium.

Strophomenids are characterised by their concavo-convex shell form and their lack of a pedicle opening. Strophomenids were free-living, supported on their larger ('pedicle') valve, sometimes with spines as anchors or supports.

Spiriferids (order Spiriferida, Ordovician–Recent) are characterised by:
- elongate, 'butterfly'-shaped shells (the hinge margin is the widest part of the shell)
- both valves convex, usually with strongly developed, pronounced ribs
- an open delthyrium
- a spiral brachidium.

The 'butterfly' shape and shell convexity are reflective of the need to contain a complex spiral brachidium which is characteristic of this group, but is restricted to

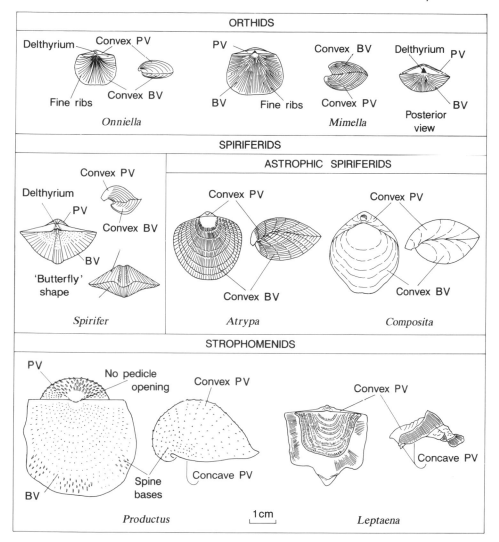

Figure 10.6 *Morphology of typical strophic articulate brachiopods. PV pedicle valve; BV brachial valve. All taxa are Palaeozoic in age*

approximately 80% of the spiriferids (gathered in the suborder, the Spiriferidina). The remaining 20% are composed of groups with astrophic hinge lines.

The suborders Atrypidina, Athyridina and Retziidina all possess a spiral brachidium which may be directed laterally, as in the Spiriferida proper, or into the brachial valve. The latter case is common in the genus *Atrypa* (Atrypidina) (Figure 10.6) which possesses a flattened pedicle valve and a domed brachial valve as a consequence. Members of all three groups are difficult to distinguish from astrophic brachiopods, with homeomorphy common (Figure 10.5). For example, *Composita* is a Carboniferous athyrid which closely resembles several

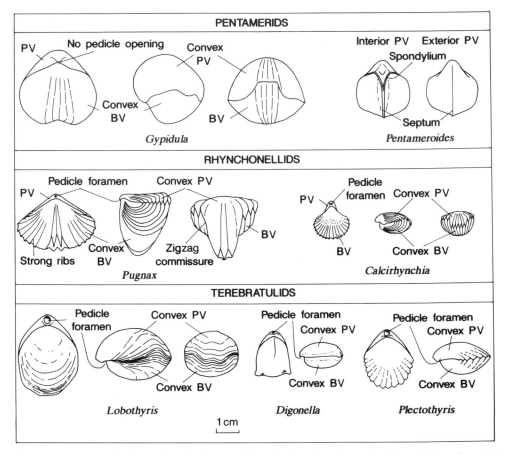

Figure 10.7   *Morphology of typical astrophic articulate brachiopods. PV pedicle valve; BV brachial valve. The pentamerids are early Palaeozoic in age. Of the rhynchonellids,* Pugnax *is Palaeozoic (Carboniferous) and* Calcirhynchia *is Mesozoic (Jurassic). The terebratulids are all Mesozoic (Jurassic) in age*

terebratulid genera; *Hustedia* is a Permian retziidinid which has a strongly ribbed shell, externally resembling many rhynchonellids. Both may only be distinguished by serial sectioning, which would reveal their spiralium.

2. *Astrophic brachiopods* are all characterised by a rounded hinge margin. They comprise three orders: Pentamerida, Rhynchonellida and Terebratulida. Their most important features are given below, and illustrated in Figure 10.7.

Pentamerids (order Pentamerida, Cambrian–Devonian) are characterised by:

• large, extremely robust biconvex shells
• no pedicle opening
• the absence of a calcified brachidium.

The robustness and convexity of the shell is characteristic of pentamerids, but so too is the development of additional internal shell features, the **spondylium** and **cruralium** (Figure 10.7). These extend into the shell cavity, forming a septum or internal wall, and were attachment points for the musculature needed to close and open the shell. Pentamerids may often be split along the line of their septum, or be preserved as characteristic internal moulds.

Rhynchonellids (order Rhynchonellida, Ordovician–Recent) generally have:
- a biconvex shell, in which the pedicle valve is relatively flat, but in which the brachial valve may be extended into a shape resembling a fox's head (this is clearly developed in the most extreme examples)
- usually coarsely ribbed (although some are smooth)
- no punctae
- a pedicle foramen, with deltidial plates closing the relict delthyrium
- a brachidium developed solely as a pair of bracket-like crura.

Rhynchonellids characteristically have a sulcus or dip in their commissure (the join between the two valves) which may have acted as a mechanism to regulate water flow into and out of the brachiopod. There is a great variation in the nature of this feature.

Terebratulids (order Terebratulida, Silurian–Recent) are characterised by:
- a biconvex shell which resembles the shape of a Roman lamp, with the pedicle valve extended anteriorly beyond the brachial
- a pedicle foramen, with deltidial plates closing the relict delthyrium
- a smooth shell, although well-preserved examples, display a microscopic 'orange peel' texture (this is created by the many regular holes (**punctae**) which penetrate the shell. Other exceptions include relatively rare ribbed species)
- a brachidium developed in the form of a short or long loop.

Terebratulids are often smooth-shelled and are commonly identified by their loop, foramen and punctae.

10.2.2 Basic Components of Inarticulate Brachiopod Shells

Inarticulate brachiopods comprise a heterogeneous group of brachiopods with at least two separate divisions, the **lingulates**, and the **inarticulates** proper, typified by the genus **Orbiculoidea** (Figure 10.8). Both are characterised by their complex musclature rather than teeth and sockets to hold the valves together. The lingulates, characterised by the genus *Lingula*, have phosphatic, bilaterally symmetrical and almost equivalve shells. They live in burrows in which the pedicle extends into the sediment and the anterior margin of the shell is positioned at the opening of the burrow. The pedicle is capable of retracting the shell into the burrow. *Lingula* inhabits intertidal environments of the present day; its ancestors, almost identical as far back as the early Palaeozoic and little different from living examples, probably inhabited the same environment. The inarticulates are very different. Living and fossil representatives have shells which are strongly inequivalve and are composed largely of protein and calcium carbonate. They live today, as in the past, as surface dwellers, with short pedicles to attach them to the substrate.

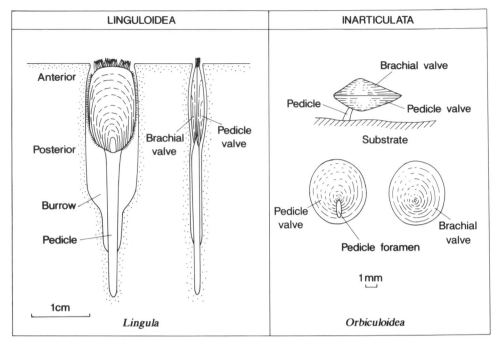

Figure 10.8 *The morphology and mode of life of typical inarticulate brachiopods*

10.3 BRACHIOPOD EVOLUTION

The brachiopods first appeared in the early Cambrian, and the first groups to appear were the organic-shelled Lingulata and the articulate order Orthida (Figure 10.9). This has raised questions of a polyphyletic (multiple-ancestor) origin for the Brachiopoda, as it is hard to determine whether the articulates arose from the inarticulates, or vice versa, given their co-occurrence. It may be, for example, that the articulates form one natural monophyletic (single-ancestor) evolutionary grouping, and the various inarticulates at least one other.

The evolutionary history of the inarticulate groups is fairly straightforward. From their first appearance the Lingulata have remained remarkably stable, inhabiting the shallow marine, brackish intertidal environments in which they occur today. Their maximum diversity was in the Ordovician, during which time the first of the calcareous-shelled Inarticulata appeared. The diversity of both groups has remained relatively static through to the present day (Figure 10.9).

The articulate brachiopods played an extremely important role in the Palaeozoic shelly faunas and their evolutionary history can be closely associated with major events in the development of the shallow marine ecosystem. The first articulates were the orthids, which can be traced to the earliest Cambrian. The orthids are ancestral to all other articulate brachiopods (Figure 10.10). The greatest expansion of the brachiopods took place in the Ordovician, when brachiopods became the dominant component of the Palaeozoic evolutionary fauna (Fig. 10.9).

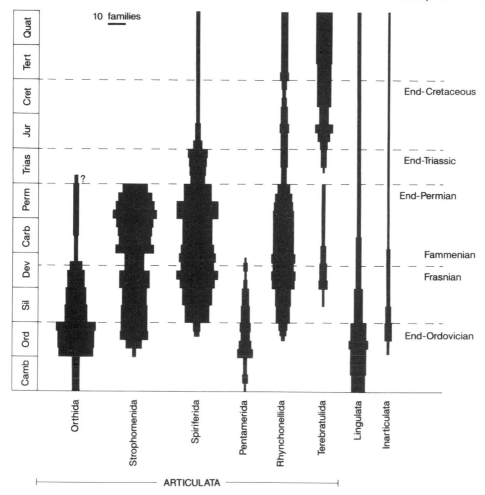

Figure 10.9 *The diversity of brachiopod families through geological time. The main extinc-tion events are indicated [Compiled by A.L. Holder from: Benton (1993)* The Fossil Record 2, *Chapman & Hall]*

At this time, the orthids radiated and were joined by the strophomenids and rhynchonellids. The spiriferids appeared later in the Ordovician. The pentamerids appeared in the late Cambrian, and also radiated. The Ordovician shallow marine ecosystem was therefore stocked by five of the six major orders of articulate brachiopods. Although the end-Ordovician extinctions depleted the orthids (which declined in diversity up to their extinction) and the strophomenids, the brachiopod-dominated ecosytem remained until the close of the Palaeozoic at the end of the Permian. Radiation of the spiriferids and strophomenids took place in the Devonian and Carboniferous, respectively, and the sixth order, the terebratulids, appeared in the Silurian (Figure 10.9). The end-Permian and end-Triassic extinctions largely extinguished the brachiopod-dominated marine eco-system, so that for the most part the Mesozoic–Recent brachiopod fauna is limited

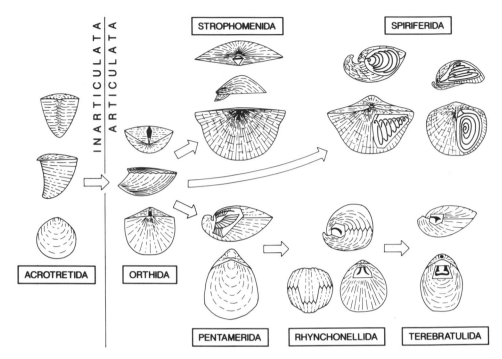

Figure 10.10   *The evolution of the articulate brachiopods from an inarticulate ancestor [Modified from: Rudwick (1970)* Living and Fossil Brachiopods, *Hutchinson, Fig. 4, p. 22]*

to the inarticulates and to the terebratulid and rhynchonellid articulate orders. Some authorities believe that a group of small, enigmatic articulates alive today, the thecideaceans, are actually living spiriferids (Figure 10.9).

10.4 BRACHIOPOD APPLICATIONS

10.4.1 Palaeobiology

Functional Morphology

Brachiopods are ideal test beds for functional studies. There is sufficient variation in living brachiopods (inarticulates, rhynchonellids, terebratulids plus minor groups) to provide a taxonomic uniformitarian base. Despite this, there are several features which are uncommon or non-existent in living populations: for example, the spiral brachidia of the spiriferids, the internal shell divisions of the pentamerids, and the spines of the strophomenids. These have entailed the development of functional models in order to determine their use and value to the brachiopod. To take two examples, the use of spines in the strophomenids and the origin of the zigzag join of the valves in rhynchonellids will demonstrate the mechanics of the process and the level of study.

Spines occur commonly in many strophomenids, particularly in the super-family Productacea, common in the Carboniferous. The productid brachiopods are typical strophomenids; they have strophic hinge lines, no pedicle opening, and a concavo-convex shell. The larger or pedicle valve commonly bears a range of spines, usually preserved only as spine bases, but preserved intact in some exceptional circumstances. As with all strophomenids, the commissure or join between the valves is seen to be deflected as a 'trail' away from the pedicle valve, almost at right angles to the brachial valve. This is interpreted as a functional adaptation to a soft substrate, with the brachiopod resting on its large pedicle valve, the trail providing a mechanism to prevent fouling of the lophophore. In this case, what would be the function of the spines? On hard substrates, spines could be interpreted as a proxy for the pedicle, this time providing a cradle-like support. In soft substrates, the spines could act as an anchor, anchoring the pedicle valve in the manner of roots in the soft substrate.

Rhynchonellids commonly have a zigzag join in their commissure. This is re-lated to the coarsely ribbed nature of the rhynchonellid shell, so that the termina-tion of each rib is a prominent point, and the termination of each groove is a corresponding 'V' in the shell. On closure this gives the impression of a tightly bound shell, but in a partially open feeding position the commissure would present a complex, zigzag baffled entry for the feeding currents (Figure 10.11). The zigzag is further divided on the basis of the median sulcus or deflection in the commissure, which is seen in many brachiopods. Functional interpretation of the sulcus from living brachiopods is that it helps separate the inhalent and exhalent currents serving the lophophore. Interpretation of the zigzag pattern of the rhynchonellid commissure shows a further subtlety; the lophophore is a delicate feature which could easily be damaged by the intake of large sedimentary parti-cles. The zigzag could trap such particles and prevent them from entering the mantle cavity and causing damage. This model is further confirmed by the de-velopment of interlocking spines at the termination of each rib in some rhynchonellids. This would clearly permit a greater degree of precision in sieving, allowing finer particles in and excluding larger, damaging grains (Figure 10.11).

Evolution

Brachiopods have not figured heavily in the development of evolutionary con-cepts. However, they have provided an important study material in the deter-mination of the functional significance of their shell and its architecture, and in the study of ancient biomolecules. Living and fossil brachiopods are known to con-tain proteins, lipids and possibly carbohydrates within the calcite crystals which form their shells, and which were created by the soft body or mantle. The incor-poration of these molecules into stable calcite crystals which are capable of retain-ing their original form for hundreds of millions of years provides an important protection. This means that the inevitable decay of these molecules with advanc-ing age would take place *in situ* within the crystal, away from outside influence. This contrasts with molecules which occur in the spaces between the crystals and which are prone to rapid decay and infection. As such, amino acids and lipids can

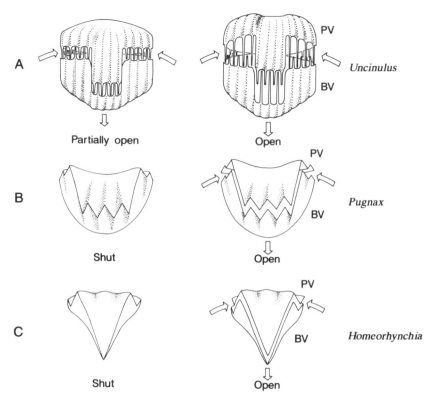

Figure 10.11   *The function of the zigzag commissure in rhynchonellid brachiopods in separating inhalent and exhalent currents and in preventing the ingress of sediment. **A:** Uncinulus from the Lower Palaeozoic (Devonian). **B:** Pugnax from the Upper Palaeozoic (Carboniferous). **C:** Homeorhynchia from the Mesozoic (Jurassic) [**A** modified from: Rudwick (1970) Living and Fossil Brachiopods, Hutchinson, Fig. 65, p. 116]*

be recovered from Mesozoic or even Palaeozoic brachiopods. The presence of such molecules creates the possibility that the true relationships between brachiopods could be determined at the molecular level, and this would have great bearing on the determination of accurate evolutionary histories. Much further work is needed to achieve this aim, however, and research in this field continues.

10.4.2 Palaeoenvironmental Analysis

As sessile organisms, brachiopods have their greatest role in the determination of ancient environments, at all scales from community analysis to global palaebiogeography. Brachiopods are useful in palaeoenvironmental analysis because they are common and are found in a great variety of shallow marine sedimentary facies. Importantly, there are still living representatives from which we can infer mode of life, function and limiting factors for extinct forms.

All living brachiopods are limited by substrate, oxygen levels and salinity (Table 10.1). Brachiopods are largely limited to a firm substrate to allow pedicle attachment, although some brachiopods, such as the strophomenids, may have been adapted to softer sediments. Most brachiopods are limited to fully oxygenated waters and normal marine salinities, as only *Lingula* and related lingulate brachiopods which can survive in the intertidal, brackish water environment. This adaptive advantage possessed by *Lingula* has meant that it has remained within the shallow intertidal habitat since the Palaeozoic, and is a reliable indicator of this environment in the geological past. Living articulates are limited to an epifaunal mode of life and are greatly affected by sedimentation rate and energy levels of the water activity through currents and the like. As attached suspension feeders with a delicate lophophore, the articulates are susceptible to sedimentation, as an increase in sedimentation could lead to burial. This is particularly important where brachiopods secondarily reduced their pedicle and became free-living, as with the strophomenids. Sediment fouling of the lophophore is also a limiting factor, although living brachiopods appear to be tolerant of turbidity. As discussed above, the zigzag nature of the commissure may have served to prevent access by large particles that the lophophore could not process (Figure 10.11).

One of the most important contributions of brachiopods to palaeoenvironmental studies has been the mapping of ancient shoreline distributions, particularly at the leading edge of marine transgressions. This is particularly important in Palaeozoic rocks, and several studies have mapped out a brachiopod depth-related zonation, with lingulates at the leading edge of the transgression in the intertidal zone, and a succession of orthids, pentamerids, strophomenids, spiriferids and other taxa at various depths offshore (Figure 10.12). In Mesozoic–Recent sediments brachiopods are less abundant, but still have application in shoreline studies, as in some cases a stable shoreline has been demonstrated by the offshore transition from whole to comminuted brachiopod shells.

In both Palaeozoic and Mesozoic–Recent successions brachiopods have proved to be of great value in palaeobiogeographical studies. Limited by depth, salinity and oxygenation, brachiopods can be grouped into faunal provinces linked by like taxa. These distribution patterns provide a useful tool in the determination of

Table 10.1 *Brachiopod limiting factors*

Temperature	Brachiopods are not closely limited by temperature today.
Oxygenation	Brachiopods are commonest in fully oxygenated waters, although individual opportunist species may be found at low oxygen levels.
Salinity	Brachiopods mostly live in near-normal marine salinities of 30–40‰. The lingulates can tolerate much reduced salinities.
Depth	Brachiopods are most abundant in shallow depths.
Substrate	Most brachiopods today are associated with firm substrates, attached by their pedicle. Fossil brachiopods may be found in a greater range of substrates.
Turbulence	Brachiopods are mostly limited today to conditions of moderate to high turbulence where suspended food particles are abundant.

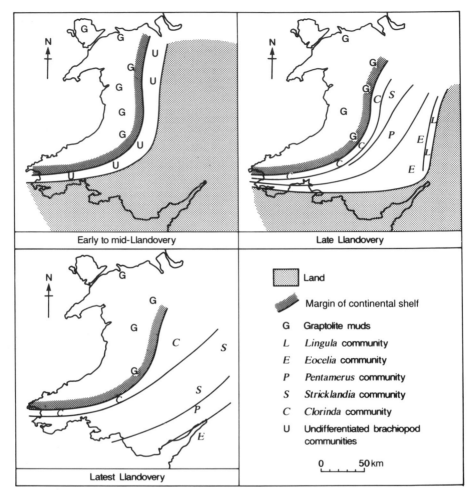

Figure 10.12   *Early Palaeozoic shorelines in Wales deduced from brachiopod assemblages. The maps depict a progressive transgression in the Llandovery [Modified from: Ziegler (1965) Nature **207**, Figs 1–3, pp. 270–271]*

ancient geographies, primarily because brachiopod distributions are limited simply by the nature of the local environment, and by their sedentary mode of life which restricts movement and migration to a short-lived free-floating larval stage. Because of this, the occurrence of brachiopod taxa has great significance, and can be used to determine the development of both oceanic links and the development of small-scale faunal restrictions.

10.4.3 Stratigraphy

Brachiopods have limited value in stratigraphy because of their strong facies relationship. This characteristic, which is an advantage in using brachiopods as environmental tools, is extremely limiting in stratigraphy. As a consequence, although brachiopods are abundant, readily preserved and easily recognisable, they are not independent of specific environments, and are not therefore as widespread as planktonic or free-swimming organisms. In addition, the rate of their evolutionary development is slow relative to other potential guide fossils. Nevertheless, brachiopods have some value in correlating local successions, particularly where like environments are to be correlated. This is true of the original coral–brachiopod biozonation of the British Lower Carboniferous, worked out in the early part of the twentieth century, and refined to the present day (Box 5.2).

10.5 SUGGESTED READING

A detailed taxonomic study of the brachiopods is given in the *Treatise on Invertebrate Paleontology* (Moore, 1965) which is soon to be updated, and a discussion of the recent revision of brachiopod higher taxa is provided by Popov *et al.* (1993). Rowell and Grant (1987) and Clarkson (1993) provide an accessible overview of the phylum, while Cocks (1985) illustrates many of the most important taxa. The fossil record of the family groups of brachiopods is given by Harper *et al.* (1993), and the evolution of the group as a whole is discussed by Williams and Hurst (1977). Brachiopod form and function have received much attention, and an excellent review is given by Rudwick (1970), who uses the taxonomic uniformitarian approach in his interpretation of functional morphology. The function of the zigzag commissure in rhynchonellids is discussed by Rudwick (1964). The paper by Curry *et al.* (1991) gives an up-to-date account of the value of brachiopods in molecular palaeontological studies. Brachiopod palaeoecology is reviewed in a straightforward manner by Ager (1967), with interesting papers on the subject by Hallam (1961), Ziegler *et al.* (1968), Lockley (1983) and Curry (1982). The importance of brachiopods in the interpretation of ancient shorelines is given by Ferguson (1962), Middlemiss (1962) and Ziegler (1965), while examples of large- and small-scale brachiopod biogeographies are given by Sandy (1991) and Prosser (1993). The use of brachiopods in stratigraphy is demonstrated in the classic paper by Vaughan (1905), brought up to date by Riley (1993), and is reviewed by Waterhouse (1977).

Ager, D.V. 1967. Brachiopod palaeoecology. *Earth Science Reviews*, **3**, 157–195.

Clarkson, E.N.K. 1993. *Invertebrate Palaeontology and Evolution*. Third edition. Chapman & Hall, London.

Cocks, L.R.M. 1985. Brachiopoda. *In* Murray, J.W. (ed.), *Atlas of Invertebrate Macrofossils*. Longman, London, 53–78.

Curry, G.B. 1982. Ecology and population structure of the Recent brachiopod *Terebratulina* from Scotland. *Palaeontology*, **25**, 227–246.

Curry, G.B., Lusack, M., Walton, D., Endo, K., Clegg, H., Abbott, G. & Armstrong, H. 1991. Biogeochemistry of brachiopod intracrystalline molecules. *Philosophical Transactions of the Royal Society of London, Series B*, **333**, 359–366.

Ferguson, L. 1962. The palaeoecology of a Lower Carboniferous marine transgression. *Journal of Paleontology*, **36**, 1090–1107.

Hallam, A. 1961. Brachiopod life-assemblages from the Marlstone Rock-Bed of Leicestershire. *Palaeontology*, **4**, 653–659.

Harper, D.A.T., Brunton, C.H.C., Cocks, L.R.M., Copper, P., Doyle, E.N., Jeffrey, A.L., Owen, E.F., Parkes, M.A., Popov, L.E. & Prosser, C.D. 1993. Brachiopoda. *In* Benton, M.J. (ed.), *The Fossil Record 2*, Chapman & Hall, London, 427–462.

Lockley, M.G. 1983. A review of brachiopod dominated palaeocommunities from the type Ordovician. *Palaeontology*, **26**, 111–145.

Middlemiss, F.A. 1962. Brachiopod ecology and Lower Greensand palaeogeography. *Palaeontology*, **5**, 253–267.

Moore, R.C. (ed.) 1965. *Treatise on Invertebrate Paleontology, Part H, Brachiopoda*. Geological Society of America and University of Kansas Press, Lawrence, KS.

Popov, L.E., Bassett, M.G., Holmer, L.E. & Laurie, J. 1993. Phylogenetic analysis of higher taxa of Brachiopoda. *Lethaia*, **26**, 1–5.

Prosser, C.D. 1993. Aalenian and Bajocian (Middle Jurassic) rhynchonellid biogeography in southern England. *Palaeogeography, Palaeoclimatology, Palaeoecology*, **100**, 147–158.

Riley, N.J. 1993. Dinantian (Lower Carboniferous) biostratigraphy and chronostratigraphy in the British Isles. *Journal of the Geological Society of London*, **150**, 427–446.

Rowell, A.J. & Grant, R.E. 1987. Phylum Brachiopoda. *In* Boardman, R.S., Cheetham, A.H. & Rowell, A.J. (eds), *Fossil Invertebrates*. Blackwell Scientific Publications, Palo Alto, CA, 445–496.

Rudwick, M.J.S. 1964. The function of zigzag deflections in the commissures of fossil brachiopods. *Palaeontology*, **7**, 135–171.

Rudwick, M.J.S. 1970. *Living and Fossil Brachiopods*. Hutchinson, London.

Sandy, M.R. 1991. Aspects of middle–late Jurassic-Cretaceous Tethyan brachiopod biogeography in relation to tectonic and paleoceanographic developments. *Palaeogeography, Palaeoclimatology, Palaeoecology*, **87**, 137–154.

Vaughan, A. 1905. The palaeontological sequence in the Carboniferous Limestone of the Bristol area. *Quarterly Journal of the Geological Society of London*, **61**, 181–307.

Waterhouse, J.B. 1977. The chronologic, ecologic and evolutionary significance of the phylum Brachiopoda. *In* Kauffman, E.G. & Hazel, J.E. (eds), *Concepts and Methods of Biostratigraphy*. Dowden, Hutchinson & Ross, Stroudsberg, PA, 497–518.

Williams, A. & Hurst, J.M. 1977. Brachiopod evolution. *In* Hallam, A. (ed.), *Patterns of Evolution as Illustrated by the Fossil Record*. Elsevier, Amsterdam, 79–121.

Ziegler, A.M. 1965. Silurian marine communities and their environmental significance. *Nature*, **207**, 270–272.

Ziegler, A.M., Cocks, R.M. & Bambach, R.K. 1968. The composition and structure of Lower Silurian marine communities. *Lethaia*, **1**, 1–27.

11
Echinoderms

11.1 ECHINODERM TAXONOMY

Echinoderms comprise a diverse range of organisms with a fossil record which extends back to the early Cambrian. Today, the most familiar echinoderms are the 'spiny-skinned' starfish (asteroids) and sea urchins (echinoids), while sea cucumbers (holothurians) are a common food delicacy in parts of Asia. An important characteristic of all living echinoderms is that they are fully marine, and as such are good indicators of marine conditions in the geological past. The echinoderms are integral members of the Palaeozoic evolutionary fauna. Geologically, echinoderm skeletons are important as rock-builders – some limestones (e.g. crinoidal limestone) may be composed almost excusively of the remains of echinoderms (Figure 11.1).

11.1.1 General Characteristics of Echinoderms

Echinoderms are characterised by their unique skeleton or **test** which occurs most commonly in the form of a 'box' of interlocking calcite plates (Figure 11.2). This box contains the vital organs, but is strictly speaking an internal skeleton, covered with a fine spiny skin. In extreme cases, such as the soft-bodied holothurians, the calcitic skeleton is reduced to small skeletal plates within the soft body of the animal. The echinoderm skeleton is also remarkable as for the most part it is based upon a five-ray symmetry (Figure 11.2). The most obvious expression of this is in the starfish, which is an echinoderm characterised by five equal limbs. In most cases, the interlocking calcite plates which comprise the echinoderm test display a similar pentameral symmetry, and this is pervasive through the skeletal elements of most members of the group.

Figure 11.1 *Crinoidal limestone from the Carboniferous of northern England. The fabric of the limestone is mostly composed of broken and disarticulated crinoid stems. Lens cap 50 mm*
[Photograph: P. Doyle]

Echinoderm fragments are easily recognised in the rock record. This is a function of the fact that each plate of the echinoderm skeleton appears to be a single crystal of calcite, displaying all the characteristics of this mineral under the microscope, or in hand specimen. This is especially noticeable in fragmentary specimens where the characteristic rhombic cleavage of calcite is displayed. In fact, echinoderm plates have a more complex structure, consisting of a network of struts and girders known as the **stereom**. This is usually masked during diagenesis of the fossil, when the network is overgrown by a filling of secondary calcite which is uniform with the primary calcite of the original structure, thereby creating the interlocked crystals of calcite.

Apart from the five-ray symmetry, echinoderms are unique in their possession of a respiratory, locomotion and feeding apparatus based upon water pressure, the **water-vascular system** (Figure 11.2). This system is controlled through the maintenance of a constant water pressure within the test. Water is drawn into the test through a porous opening, and is distributed via a complex plumbing system. The purpose of this system is to operate a series of **tube feet** which communicate with the water column through a series of pores in the test wall (Figure 11.2). The tube feet are prehensile, able to grasp through extension and retraction according to water pressure, and through the application of a sucker cup at the end of each tube foot. Tube feet are used in locomotion, in passing food to the mouth and in respiration; oxygen is gained by osmosis through the tube feet. The water-vascular system is therefore one of the most important components of the echinoderms.

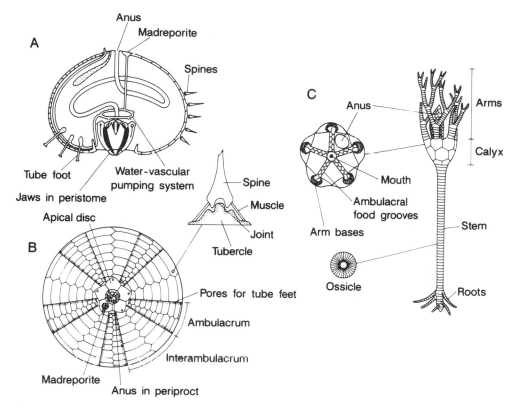

Figure 11.2 *General characteristics of echinoid (**A,B**) and crinoid (**C**) skeletons [Modified from: Black (1988)* The Elements of Palaeontology, *Cambridge University Press, Figs 106 and 123, pp. 175 and 198]*

Echinoderms are diverse and reflective of an equally diverse range of habitats and feeding approaches. For example, sea urchins are important echinoderms adapted to a surface-dwelling, grazing or scavenging mode of life, or to a burrowing condition with feeding through the capture of suspended particles, passed to the mouth by the tube feet.

11.1.2 Echinoderm Classification

The echinoderms represent a separate phylum of the animal kingdom, and in many ways one of the most bizarre. Their organisation and water-vascular system are unique to the phylum. The phylum Echinodermata is a diverse group of organisms ranging from the soft-bodied holothurians through to the echinoids, crinoids and asteroids, common as fossils and alive today. Classification is based upon the nature of the skeleton and in particular its division between fixed and free-living organisms. This classification is still under discussion, but a working example recognises two distinct subphyla and many classes. Only some of these classes are listed, two of which, the echinoids (Echinoidea) and crinoids (Crinoidea) are discussed.

Phylum Echinodermata Bruguière, 1791
Subphylum Eleutherozoa Bell, 1891 (Cambrian–Recent)
Free-living echinoderms with a radiate skeleton.

Class Echinoidea Leske, 1778 (Ordovician–Recent)
Echinoderms with globular to flattened tests without arms or stalks, and having numerous plates displaying pentameral symmetry, some with superimposed bilateral symmetry.

Class Holothuroidea de Blainville, 1834 (Ordovician–Recent)
Echinoderms with a cylindrical body with skeleton reduced to widely separated plates (sclerites).

Class Asteroidea de Blainville, 1830 (Ordovician–Recent)
Star-shaped echinoderms with five arms bearing ambulacral grooves, with the mouth on the lower surface.

Subphylum Pelmatozoa Leuckart, 1848 (Cambrian–Recent)
Stalked echinoderms with their body contained within a cup or calyx.

Class Crinoidea Miller, 1821 (Cambrian–Recent)
Echinoderms with a globular calyx with mouth central to the upper surface, surrounded by a series of arms; mostly attached to the substrate through a stem.

Class Blastoidea Say, 1825 (Silurian–Permian)
Echinoderms with a globular calyx with small arms (brachioles) mounted on specialised ambulacral areas; mostly attached to the substrate through a stem.

11.2 ECHINOID MORPHOLOGY

The echinoid test consists of a hemispherical box composed of interlocking calcite plates (Figure 11.2). There are two broad groups of echinoids, referred to as **regular** and **irregular**. Regular echinoids are faithful to the hemispherical shape, and have a strong radial symmetry. They represent the primary echinoid condition, although primitive forms may have been less symmetrical. Regular echinoids are surface-dwellers and live by grazing on a firm substrate, or by scavenging from dead organisms. Irregular echinoids represent a departure from the hemispherical form in order to develop a burrowing habit (Figure 11.3). Shallow-burrowing echinoids are flattened (**sand dollars** – so named after their resemblance to the large, American silver dollar), while deeper-burrowing echinoids often have developed a heart shape, the so-called **heart urchins** (Figure 11.3). Both types of irregular echinoid have developed a strong bilateral symmetry which is superimposed upon the radial symmetry.

All echinoids have a test composed of two parts, the **apical system** and the **corona**. The apical system is situated upon the upper (dorsal) surface of the test and is composed of a rosette of calcite plates (Figure 11.2). In regular echinoids the apical system also contains the anus, situated in a fleshy membraneous area known as the **periproct**. The apical system is arranged radially around the periproct and contains a porous plate which is the regulator of the water-vascular system, the **madreporite**, as well as pores for the release of gametes by the genitals. The corona comprises the rest of the test and is composed of ten radially arranged columns of paired plates. These columns extend from the apical system

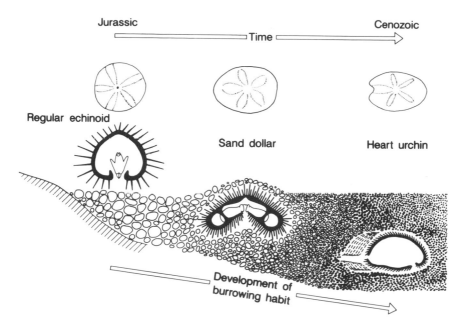

Figure 11.3 *The evolution of echinoids from regular echinoids to sand dollars and heart urchins, and the effective colonisation of finer-grained substrates [Modified from: McNamara (1990) In McNamara (Ed.) Evolutionary Trends, Belhaven, Fig. 9.6, p. 217]*

to the lower (ventral) surface, and can be divided into two types, with a total of five of each. **Ambulacra** (singular: **ambulacrum**) are the narrowest and comprise five columns composed of interlocking pairs of pentagonal plates (Figure 11.2). The ambulacra are significant as it is through a **pore pair** in each plate that the tube feet extrude. The pore pairs are arranged at the outer margin of the ambulacral columns. The five other columns are generally wider, and are called the **interambulacra** (singular: **interambulacrum**). The interambulacra do not possess pore pairs. Both ambulacra and interambulacra are ornamented with small, circular tubercles which acted in life as the attachment areas for the spines which are characteristic of echinoderms (meaning literally 'spiny skin'). These tubercles consist of a mound for the attachment of muscles, and a knob for the rotational movement, as in a ball-and-socket joint, of the attached spine (Figure 11.2). After death the spines become detached and are usually lost from the test, often incorporated as shell debris into the rock record.

The ventral (lower) surface of regular echinoids contains the mouth. This is complex and is set in the centre of a large notched hole known as the **peristome** (Figure 11.2). In regular echinoids, living as grazers, the peristome is large to allow the extrusion of a large set of jaws which articulate together into a structure resembling a hanging lantern (Figure 11.4). This 'lantern' contains a set of five jaws which operate together in a rasping action, each ending in a chisel-like tip. Traces of such rasping jaws are commonly encountered in the shallow marine environment, particularly on rocky coastlines. The jaws are supported by bracket-like structures which form a kind of girdle inside the peristome. The notching of

Figure 11.4   *A regular echinoid from the Cretaceous Chalk of southern England, preserved with its jaw apparatus present in its peristome [Photograph: D. Bates]*

the peristome area also allows for the extrusion of a series of feathery gills which supplement the actions of the tube feet in respiration.

Irregular echinoids represent a modification of the primary regular shape, notably the repositioning of the anus and periproct outside the apical system. This is an extremely important adaptation designed to prevent the fouling of the burrow by excrement. In most echinoids the apical system is in the uppermost position on the test. Within a burrow, this would be closest to the shaft which allows communication with the surface and with the supply of fresh, oxygenated and food-enriched marine waters. The position of the periproct in regular echinoids is clearly disadvantageous to a burrowing habit. Early irregular echinoids, such as *Pygaster* and *Holectypus* from the Jurassic, display the periproct still on the upper surface, but 'frozen' almost in the act of moving from the apical system to the posterior. The final destination of the periproct is the lower or ventral surface of the test, where fouling is less likely. The peristome remains on the ventral surface, but is repositioned, so that mouth and anus are located at opposite ends, anterior and posterior, of the test.

Adaption to burrowing also brought with it a change in feeding. For shallow-burrowing echinoids, prone to being washed out of their burrows, and adapted to a semi-active mode of life, the mouth still possesses jaws. These are much reduced but of similar pattern to those of the regular echinoids. In deep-burrowing echinoids, the peristome no longer has jaws, and instead of being a food gatherer, has been adapted as a passive food receiver, with food passed to it by the tube feet of the anterior ambulacrum. Such food particles are gathered by tube feet extruded through the burrow opening, and in some cases are passed along the tube feet through a string of exuded mucus. In order to guide the food to the mouth, the anterior ambulacrum is located within a deep groove which passes down a notch in the anterior of the test to the mouth. To avoid spillage, the peristome opening commonly develops a calcitic lip or **labrum** in order further to guide the food home.

The general characteristics can be identified in the three main functional groupings which form a convenient basis for identification of echinoderm groups: regular echinoids; shallow-burrowing irregular echinoids (sand dollars); and deep-burrowing irregular echinoids (heart urchins). These are discussed below.

1. *Regular echinoids* are adapted to a surface-dwelling habitat (Figure 11.5). Regular echinoids commonly possess:
- a hemispherical shape
- radial symmetry
- the periproct on the dorsal surface in the apical system
- a large, central peristome on the ventral surface
- the regular distribution of spine bases across the test.

The hemispherical shape and symmetrical form of regular echinoids is reflective of their mode of life as surface grazers or scavengers. To this end, the positioning of the anus on top of the test, and the mouth on the lower surface, is most efficient. The mouth houses a large jaw apparatus, as is appropriate for a grazer and scavenger. The regular distribution of spine bases is to serve a great range of spines which both protect the test and enable anchoring and movement (Figure 11.5).

2. *Sand dollars* are irregular echinoids adapted to a shallow-burrowing habitat (Figure 11.6). Shallow-burrowing echinoids possess:
- a flattened shape with internally buttressed margins
- weak to strong bilateral symmetry
- petal-like ambulacra
- the periproct on the ventral surface, close to the peristome
- a sub-central peristome with jaw apparatus on the ventral surface
- spine bases reduced in size
- specialist adaptions, such as holes or frills in the test margin.

The flattened shape of the sand dollar is perfectly adapted to a shallow-burrowing life in shifting sediments and allows the animal the means of recreating its burrow rapidly. The buttressed margins are to give the shell extra support in what is potentially a high-energy environment. The positioning of the anus on the lower surface, together with the mouth, is to increase the efficiency of the burrowing

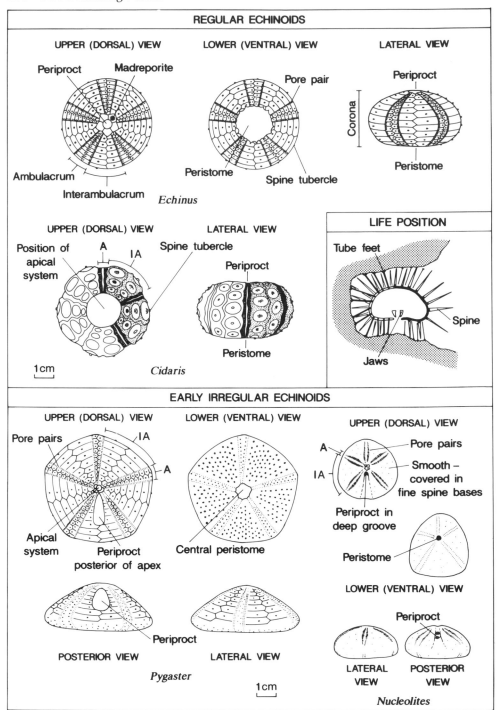

Figure 11.5   *Morphology of typical regular and early irregular echinoids.* Echinus *is a living species;* Cidaris, Pygaster *and* Nucleolites *are all Jurassic in age. A, ambulacrum; IA, interambulacrum*

organism and to prevent fouling the upper surface of the test in a burrow. The spines are much reduced because of the need for less drag in the burrow. Ambulacra are petal-like, restricted to the upper surface for greater respiratory efficiency. Holes (**lunules**) through the test, and frilled margins, provide a mechanism for passing sediment and food particles from the test surface to the mouth, and for passing excreta out of the burrow. They may also function in stabilising the shell during periods when it is flipped over by currents or wave action. Food grooves take the place of the ambulacra on the ventral surface, tube feet passing food from the lunules to the mouth (Figure 11.6).

3. *Heart urchins* are irregular echinoids adapted to a deep-burrowing habitat (Figure 11.6). Deep burrowing echinoids commonly possess:

- a heart shape which often has a wedged profile
- strong bilateral symmetry
- petal-like ambulacra
- the periproct situated in the posterior, isolated on the posterior, vertical surface
- the peristome on the ventral surface, located at the anterior margin
- an irregular distribution of different sizes of spine base
- the development of fascioles (see below).

Heart urchins are specially adapted to a deep-burrowing habitat. They have abandoned grazing for a passive method of feeding reliant upon the ambulacra and tube feet, which pass food particles to the mouth. The wedged heart shape is most efficient in burrowing, which is achieved through a persistent rocking action. The heart shape itself is reflective of the development of a groove containing the anterior ambulacrum. This 'food groove' acts in passing food particles to the mouth situated at the anterior of the ventral surface. This ambulacrum is the largest, and the remainder may be grouped close to the apical disc. This increases the efficiency of the ambulacra, with specially adapted tube feet maintaining the burrow opening, for respiration and for feeding. The mouth is situated at the anterior margin of the ventral suface, and the anus at the posterior, often on the vertical slope from the ventral to dorsal surfaces (Figure 11.6). In many cases there is a specially created sanitary burrow in which excrement is accumulated. The spines are of variable size, adapted to carry out a variety of duties: those at the anterior, for example, help with burrowing; those on the lower surface, in a shield-like area known as the **plastron**, with locomotion. Some areas are designated as **fascioles**, and here specially adapted spines covered in beating cilia help with sanitary cleaning to prevent fouling of the burrow (Figure 11.6).

11.3 CRINOID MORPHOLOGY

Crinoids share many of the characteristics of the echinoids, as they have their vital organs housed within a box made of interlocking calcite plates with five-ray symmetry. However, crinoids are either sessile, attached to the substrate by a flexible, skeletal column, or secondarily free-floating and planktonic.

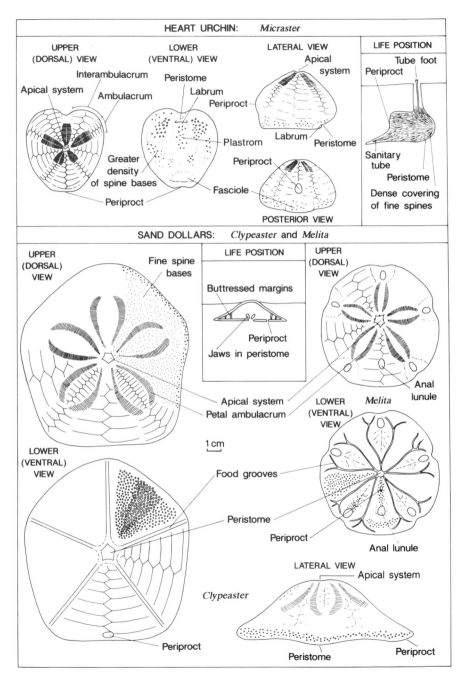

Figure 11.6   *Morphology of typical heart urchins and sand dollars.* Micraster *is Cretaceous in age;* Clypeaster *and* Melita *are Neogene in age*

Crinoids are common in the fossil record and are composed of three basic structural elements: **stem**, **cup** or **calyx**, and **arms** (Figure 11.2). The stem is flexible and consists of a series of interconnecting and articulating plates called **ossicles**. Ossicles are often circular, with articulating facets, but they may also demonstrate a five-ray symmetry in the shape of a star (Figure 11.7). In some cases, small offshoots from the base of the stem are developed as a kind of root to bed the crinoid into a soft substrate or cement it to a hard one. The cup or calyx is built of a series of plates, usually with four layers of interconnected, pentameral calcite plates. The upper surface of the cup contains the mouth, situated in its centre, and the anus, on the periphery. In some cases, the anus is developed at the top of a column of small plates designed as an anti-fouling 'chimney' (Figure 11.2). Five multiply branching arms are situated at the margins of the upper surface of the cup. These arms are composed of smaller ossicles than the stem, and have small cilia arranged on their inner surface, designed to gather food, passing it down the inner surface of the arms to ambulacra situated over the top surface of the calyx, and thence to the mouth. On death, the crinoid skeleton is prone to disarticulation, and while it is common to find bioclastic limestones composed almost exclusively of crinoid ossicles and plates (Figure 11.1), it is relatively difficult to find perfectly preserved examples of crinoids preserved *in situ* and intact.

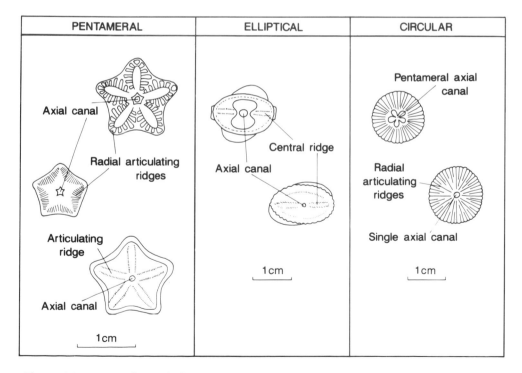

Figure 11.7   *Typical morphologies of crinoid ossicles [Modified from: Moore et al. (1952) Invertebrate Fossils, McGraw-Hill, Fig. 18.4, p. 612]*

11.4 ECHINODERM EVOLUTION

The evolution of the echinoderms is the subject of a great deal of study, and new phylogenies are constantly being constructed which then have considerable bearing on the higher classification of the group as a whole. The broad pattern of evolution is now relatively clear.

The earliest echinoderms appeared in the early Cambrian, although it has been suggested that the enigmatic Ediacaran organism *Tribrachidium* could represent a Proterozoic forerunner of the Echinodermata (Figure 7.4). The earliest groups of Cambrian echinoderms are chararcterised by their calcareous plated tests, but the first evolutionary radiation of the echinoderms took place in the Ordovician, when the echinoids, holothurians and asteroids appeared (Figure 11.8). The crinoids have a longer evolutionary history, traceable back to the late Cambrian. The echinoderms most characteristic of the Palaeozoic evolutionary fauna are the crinoids, which, although affected by the end-Ordovician and end-Devonian extinctions, were the most diverse and numerous of all echinoderms at this time. The end-Permian extinction had a devastating effect on all echinoderms, and the stemmed crinoids in particular were reduced to a handful of taxa (Figure 11.8). The Permian–Triassic interval has very few echinoderms, and it is only following the effects of the end-Triassic extinction that diversity increased. The echinoids in particular radiated in the Jurassic (with the first appearance of the irregular echinoids), in the Cretaceous and again in the Cenozoic (Figure 11.8). Crinoids recovered in the Jurassic and Cretaceous, but never reached the diversity that they had achieved in the Palaeozoic.

11.5 ECHINODERM APPLICATIONS

11.5.1 Palaeobiology

Functional Morphology

The abundance of living echinoids provides a perfect test bed for the interpretation of the functional morphology of fossil echinoids, particularly in relation to burrowing activity and associated structures in the heart urchins and sand dollars. For example, recent field studies of living spatangoid urchins have demonstrated the mechanism of burrow creation which can be used to interpret function in fossil occurrences (Figure 11.9).

In these studies it was found that differently shaped Recent spatangoids created different burrows. The burrowing urchins were found to conform to one of three shapes: flat, globular and wedge-shaped. Observation of living animals in the field and aquaria has demonstrated that burrows are created by the movement of spines, the different shapes of the urchins giving different attitudes to the spines. Flat urchins live close to the sediment surface in coarser sand, and burrow through the activity of their anterior spines loosening the sediment, and those low on each of the flanks pushing the sediment to one side (Figure 11.9). The flat

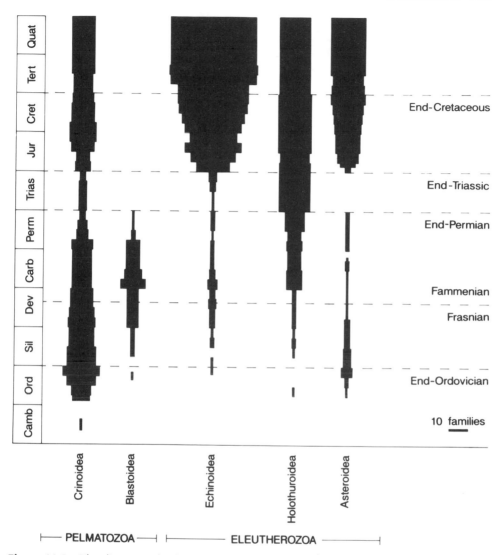

Figure 11.8 *The diversity of echinoderm families through geological time. The main extinction events are indicated [Compiled by A.L. Holder from: Benton (1993)* The Fossil Record 2, *Chapman & Hall]*

shape, as with all sand dollars, allows the urchin to remain stable against burrow disturbance. Globular urchins live in fine- to medium-grained sand and burrow by excavating frontal sediment with their anterior spines, the plastron spines providing the forward movement, and the spines low on each of the flanks moving the sediment from the anterior, accumulating it on their backs. The globular shape helps to support a greater weight of sediment and therefore allows the urchin to live in deeper burrows (Figure 11.9). Wedge-shaped urchins are common in soft mud, and burrow using a rocking action. During burrowing, the plastron spines provide the forward motion, while the anterior spines do most of

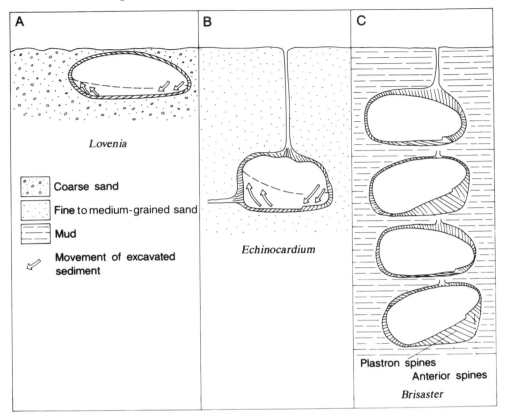

Figure 11.9 *Burrowing behaviour in Recent irregular echinoids.* **A:** *Flat type.* **B:** *Globular type.* **C:** *Wedge-shaped type [Modified from: Kanazawa (1992)* Palaeontology *35, Fig. 5, p. 739]*

the excavating when the animal is at an oblique angle within the burrow, and sediment is passed back to the posterior as small mud pellets. The wedge shape provides the ability of the animal to carry out the rocking action (Figure 11.9). This study has obvious implications for the interpretation of fossil echinoids, as the three test shapes may be commonly identified in a range of extinct species.

Evolution

Echinoids have long been the subject of detailed microevolutionary studies. This is primarily a function of their abundance in some successions, and of the relative complexity of their shell which records detailed morphological changes through time. As discussed in Chapter 4, since the late nineteenth century the genus *Micraster*, for example, has been the focus of much attention. In one of the earliest documented evolutionary lineages, Arthur Rowe was able to demonstrate that *Micraster* underwent several shape changes through geological time, with the successive species, *M. leskei*, *M. decipiens* and *M. coranguinum* (Figure 4.6). In this lineage the following changes were most obvious: the test became broader; the anterior groove containing the anterior ambulacrum deepened; the mouth moved to the anterior and developed a lip or labrum. As with all 'classic' lineages, the perceived gradual evolution of *Micraster* has been reassessed in the light of the punctuated equilibrium debate (Figure 4.6). Particularly important is the fact that the stratigraphical ranges of two of the species of this lineage, *M. decipiens* and *M. coranguinum*, overlap in stratigraphical range. This suggests that gradualism through anagenesis (transition from one species to the next through intermediates) is unlikely to have been the mode of evolution. Allopatric speciation would allow overlapping ranges, as the isolated population undergoing speciation is isolated from the contemporary parent population, before it reinvades and causes extinction.

Gradualism has, however, been convincingly demonstrated in the Cretaceous *Infulaster–Hagenowa* echinoid lineage, in which the test undergoes elongation of the apex to create an extremely bizarre shape. Many intermediates are known between the end members *Infulaster excentricus* and *Hagenowa blackmorei*, and no overlap is evident among them, suggesting successive replacement in an evolving anagenetic lineage. Clearly, in both *Micraster* and *Infulaster–Hagenowa* lineages, the echinoid test provides the perfect test bed for microevolutionary studies.

11.5.2 Palaeoenvironmental Analysis

Echinoderms are limited largely by salinity, substrate and oxygenation (Table 11.1). For the most part, echinoderms are fully marine and occur in normal salinity and fully oxygenated environments; they can be an important indicator of a range of environmental conditions. However, it is relatively rare to find echinoderms intact; this is a function of their construction, primarily as a series of plates loosely held together by the external skin. It is exceptionally rare, for instance, to find echinoids intact with their spines and their jaw apparatus, and it is even more exceptional to find holothurians as anything other than individual plates (sclerites). However, the level of intactness of echinoderm skeletons has also a palaeoenvironmental significance, as the possibility of intact preservation is determined by sedimentation rate and energetic levels. Five grades of preservation have been recognised, which equate with different environmental conditions (Table 11.2).

Table 11.1 Echinoderm limiting factors

Temperature	Echinoderms can tolerate a wide temperature range.
Oxygenation	Echinoderms are commonest in fully oxygenated waters, although individual opportunist species may be found at low oxygen levels.
Salinity	Echinoderms are restricted to near-normal marine salinity levels of around $35^0/_{00}$. Abundant echinoderms are found only in normal marine salinities.
Depth	Echinoderms are found in a range of water depths, down to abyssal levels.
Substrate	Echinoderms are associated with a range of substrates, with crinoids and echinoids occuring in both soft and hard substrate types.
Turbulence	Some echinoids are adapted to life in fairly turbulent conditions.

Table 11.2   *Preservational states and environmental conditions in echinoderms*

1. Near-perfect preservation	Skeletal plates, etc., intact. Demonstrative of instant death and burial through smothering, caused by rapid sedimentation.
2. Disassociation	Skeletal parts are separated but identifiable as members of single individuals. Illustrative of low turbulence and high sedimentation rate.
3. Incomplete preservation	The commonest preservation state for echinoids. May occur in a range of conditions.
4. Abundant disarticulated skeletal parts	Typical of crinoidal limestones, for example. Usually associated with higher-energy conditions than preservation state 2.
5. Rare or microscopic skeletal parts	Common in small echinoderms that readily fragment, such as holothurians. Associated with a wide range of environmental conditions.

Echinoids may live in a range of shallow marine environments, ranging from the rocky intertidal zone pools inhabited by regular echinoids, through shallow sand environments colonised by sand dollars, to the finer-grained offshore sediments in which the heart urchins construct their burrows. Echinoids are therefore limited by substrate and energy levels, with specialist adaption from high- to low-energy conditions. In general, irregular echinoids are more often encountered in the fossil record quite simply because they inhabit lower-energy environments, burrows, or are constructed to withstand the destructive nature of the shallow-water environment. As a rule, sand dollars are a common indicator of high energy levels and are a component of shallow marine carbonate sequences from the Mesozoic onwards. Heart urchins are more often preserved *in situ* and are demonstrative of the finer-grained facies. Regular echinoids are only rarely preserved intact, although their calcite plates and spines are a common bioclastic element in limestones.

Crinoids are a common component of Palaeozoic successions and, to a certain extent, later Jurassic and Cretaceous successions. Crinoids are limited by salinity and energy levels. In the Palaeozoic, crinoids were a common component of bioherms, a kind of organic build-up, and these are represented in the fossil record by crinoidal limestone banks illustrative of the density of crinoid thickets in the Carboniferous. Crinoids are important in demonstrating the nature of the oxygenation state of the Lower Jurassic succession in southern Germany, or of the salinity levels in the Late Jurassic Solnhofen lagoon. At Holzmaden, the giant crinoid *Seirocrinus* may have adopted a secondary planktonic (pseudoplanktonic) mode of life, floating above a stagnant bottom, or alternatively, growing through the low-oxygen bottom layer to reach more oxygenated conditions (Figure 2.22). In Solnhofen, the crinoid *Saccocoma* is perfectly preserved and is demonstrative of the periodic washing in of fully marine organisms into a saline lagoon (Figure 11.10). Both examples are demonstrative of environmental interpretations based on perfectly preserved crinoids in conservation Lagerstätten (preservational state

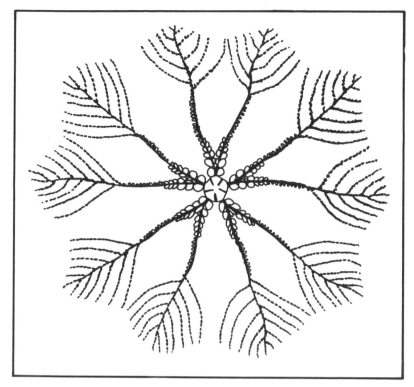

Figure 11.10 *The crinoid* Saccocoma, *showing the feather-like arms.* Saccocoma *is common in the Solnhofen Limestone of southern Germany [Drawing by H.E. Clark, modified from: Barthel et al. (1994)* Solnhofen. A study in Mesozoic Palaeontology, *Cambridge University Press, Fig. 7.50, p. 155]*

2; Table 11.2), but show what information can be derived from their presence in rock sequences.

11.5.3 Stratigraphy

As facies fossils, echinoderms have only limited application in the field of bio-stratigraphy. Nevertheless, the Upper Cretaceous chalks of England and northern France are successfully zoned on the basis of both burrowing heart urchins such as *Micraster* and pelagic crinoids such as *Marsupites*. In the Upper Cretaceous chalk sequences of northern Europe echinoids are still commonly used as guide fossils, particularly from the *Micraster* lineage first determined in the last part of the nineteenth century. Echinoids are strongly facies-related, with an extremely narrow range of adaptation to specific substrates. Regular echinoids are commonest in hard to firm substrates; irregular echinoids are abundant in sand, marl and stable, non-turbulent calcareous muds. Given the nature of the echinoid test, preservation potential is linked to substrate, with irregular, burrowing echinoids more likely to be preserved intact. In addition, although echinoids are mobile organisms, their wider distribution is limited by the spread of their free-floating larval stage. Echinoids have the advantage, however, in being fast-evolving, abundant and easily recognisable.

11.6 SUGGESTED READING

The detailed taxonomy of the Echinodermata is given in the relevant parts of the *Treatise on Invertebrate Paleontology* (Moore, 1966; 1967; Moore and Teichert, 1978). A recent revision of the echinoderm classification is given by Smith (1984b). More accessible overviews of the group are provided by Sprinkle and Keir (1987) and Clarkson (1993), while Smith and Murray (1985) illustrate many of the commonest echinoderm taxa. Simms *et al.* (1993) document the stratigraphical ranges of all known echinoderm families. Smith's (1984a) book is an excellent overview of echinoid palaeobiology, including microevolution and ecology. The *Micraster* lineage is documented by the classic papers of Rowe (1899), Kermack (1954), Nichols (1959) and Stokes (1977). Brief discussion of several other echinoid lineages, including *Infulaster–Hagenowa*, is given in Smith (1984a), and a discussion of the evolution of the irregular echinoids by Kier (1982). The *Infulaster–Hagenowa* lineage is further discussed by Gale and Smith (1982). Examples of functional morphological studies in echinoids in general are given by Smith (1984a), and in sand dollars in particular by Seilacher (1979) and Smith and Ghiold (1982). Kanazawa (1992) is an important paper documenting the burrowing activity of Recent spatangoid echinoids. Examples of functional morphology studies in crinoids are given by Seilacher *et al.* (1968), Simms (1986) and Milsom (1994). Palaeoenvironmental studies using echinoderms include those of Milsom (1994), Milsom and Sharpe (1995) and Seilacher *et al.* (1968), while the use of echinoids in biostratigraphy is demonstrated by the classic paper by Rowe (1900) and is nicely reviewed by Ernst and Seibertz (1977).

Clarkson, E.N.K. 1993. *Invertebrate Palaeontology and Evolution*. Third edition. Chapman & Hall, London.
Ernst, G. & Seibertz, E. 1977. Concepts and methods of echinoid biostratigraphy. *In* Kauffman, E.G. and Hazel, J.E. (eds), *Concepts and Methods in Biostratigraphy*. Dowden, Hutchinson & Ross, Stroudsberg, PA, 541–563.
Gale, A.S. & Smith, A.B. 1982. The palaeobiology of the Cretaceous irregular echinoids *Infulaster* and *Hagenowa*. *Palaeontology*, **25**, 11–42.
Kanazawa, K. 1992. Adaptation of test shape for burrowing and locomotion in spatangoid echinoids. *Palaeontology*, **35**, 733–750.
Kermack, K.A. 1954. A biometric study of *Micraster coranguinum* and *M. (Isomicraster) senonensis. Philosophical Transactions of the Royal Society*, **B237**, 375–428.
Kier, P.M. 1982. Rapid evolution in echinoids. *Palaeontology*, **25**, 1–9.
Milsom, C.V. 1994. *Saccocoma*: a benthic crinoid from the Jurassic Solnhofen limestone. *Palaeontology*, **37**, 121–129.
Milsom, C.V. & Sharpe, T. 1995. Jurassic lagoon: salt or soup? *Geology Today*, **11**, 22–26.
Moore, R.C. (ed.) 1966. *Treatise on Invertebrate Paleontology, Part U, Echinodermata 3*. Geological Society of America and University of Kansas Press, Lawrence, KS.
Moore, R.C. (ed.) 1967. *Treatise on Invertebrate Paleontology, Part S, Echinodermata 1*. Geological Society of America and University of Kansas Press, Lawrence, KS.

Moore, R.C. & Teichert, C. (eds) 1978. *Treatise on Invertebrate Paleontology, Part T, Echinodermata 2*. Geological Society of America and University of Kansas Press, Lawrence, KS.

Nichols, D. 1959. Changes in the heart-urchin *Micraster* interpreted in relation to living forms. *Philosophical Transactions of the Royal Society*, **B242**, 347–437.

Rowe, A.W. 1899. An analysis of the genus *Micraster*, as determined by rigid zonal collecting from the zone of *Rhynchonella Cuvieri* to that of *Micraster cor-anguinum*. *Quarterly Journal of the Geological Society of London*, **55**, 494–547.

Rowe, A.W. 1900. The zones of the White Chalk of the English coast. Part 1. Kent and Sussex. *Proceedings of the Geologists' Association*, **16**, 289–368.

Seilacher, A. 1979. Constructional morphology of sand dollars. *Paleobiology*, **5**, 191–222.

Seilacher, A., Drzozewski, G. & Haude, R. 1968. Form and function of the stem in a pseudoplanktonic crinoid (*Seirocrinus*). *Palaeontology*, **11**, 275–282.

Simms, M.J. 1986. Contrasting lifestyles in Lower Jurassic crinoids: a comparison of benthic and pseudopelagic isocrinida. *Palaeontology*, **29**, 475–493.

Simms, M.J., Gale, A.S., Gilliland, P., Rose, E.P.F. & Sevastopulo, G.D. 1993. Echinodermata. *In* Benton, M.J. (ed.), *The Fossil Record 2*. Chapman & Hall, London, 491–528.

Smith, A.B. 1984a. *Echinoid Palaeobiology*. Unwin Hyman, London.

Smith, A.B. 1984b. Classification of the Echinodermata. *Palaeontology*, **27**, 431–459.

Smith, A.B. & Ghiold, J. 1982. Roles for holes in sand-dollars (Echinoidea): a review of lunule function and evolution. *Paleobiology*, **8**, 242–253.

Smith, A.B. & Murray, J.W. 1985. Echinodermata. *In* Murray, J.W. (ed.), *Atlas of Invertebrate Macrofossils*. Longman, London, 153–190.

Sprinkle, J. & Keir, P.M. 1987. Phylum Echinodermata. *In* Boardman, R.S., Cheetham, A.H. & Rowell, A.J. (eds), *Fossil Invertebrates*. Blackwell Scientific Publications, Palo Alto, CA, 550–611.

Stokes, R.B. 1977. The echinoids *Micraster* and *Epiaster* from the Turonian and Senonian of England. *Palaeontology*, **20**, 805–821.

12
Trilobites

12.1 TRILOBITE TAXONOMY

Trilobites are extremely important fossil organisms in Palaeozoic rocks. Resembling modern-day, land-dwelling woodlice and other crustaceans with a jointed external skeleton, trilobites are extinct aquatic animals adapted to fully marine conditions. Their closest living relative is a 'living fossil' itself: the king crab *Limulus* which has a large shield-like external skeleton and a tail extended into a spine. *Limulus* today lives in a relatively limited environment; from study of the sediments which contain them, it is clear that trilobites lived in a diverse range of shallow marine environments and dominated the earliest or Cambrian evolutionary fauna.

12.1.1 General Characteristics

Trilobites are presently thought to constitute a separate phylum or subphylum, the Trilobita, but are closely related to one of the most successful animal groups living today, the insects. Grouped together as the Arthropoda, forming either a phylum or an even larger grouping, a superphylum, the insects, crabs, ostracods (Chapter 17), and trilobites have several important characteristics in common: all have a hard dorsal exoskeleton which is shed in **moults** as the organism grows, and all possess **jointed appendages** – legs, antennae, and so on. Many arthropods, for example the insects, have a skeleton composed of **chitin** and organic material related to cellulose. Trilobites, however, possessed an exoskeleton which was composed of calcite in life.

Trilobites are in the main characterised by their exoskeleton, which is characteristically divisible into three sections or **lobes** (Figure 12.1). Three lateral lobes are identifiable because of a central raised area (the **axis**) which runs the length of the trilobite from head to tail. Three other sections are present in the trilobite skeleton: these are the head (**cephalon**), body (**thorax**) and tail (**pygidium**). In common with all other arthropods, trilobites are known to have periodically shed their exoskeleton during growth. In this way, most trilobite fossils are moults, rather than the remains of dead bodies. Moults are the physical evidence of the need for the organism to shed its external skeleton during growth. During the process of moulting (**ecdysis**) the three-lobed skeleton is disintegrated and it is usual and common to find the head and tail as separate entities, and the flexible thorax broken into its component parts (Figure 12.2).

As organisms with an arthropod body plan, trilobites had jointed appendages. It is known that trilobite appendages were **biramous**, consisting of two branches, one above the other, with one pair on either side of the central axis per thoracic segment (Figure 12.1). In each pair, the lower appendage formed the walking limb, while the upper one supported a gill for respiration. Actual fossil appendages are rare, mostly only preserved in conservation Lagerstätten such as the Burgess Shale, but the physical traces of the motion of trilobites may be determined through the presence of the tracks and traces of moving, feeding and resting trilobites, now found as trace fossils. Among other lines of evidence, these traces illustrate that trilobites had a diverse mode of life. For the most part, they lived on the sediment surface in the shallow marine environment, probably

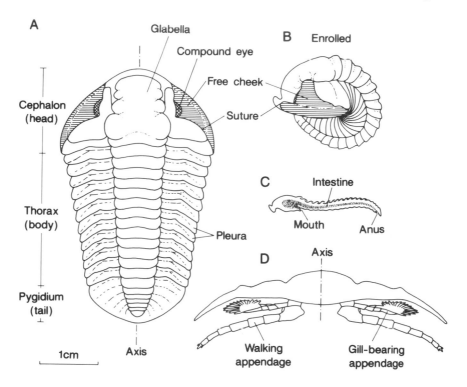

Figure 12.1 *Morphology of a typical trilobite,* Calymene, *of Silurian age [Modified from: Black (1988)* The Elements of Palaeontology, *Cambridge University Press, Fig. 86, p. 145]*

Figure 12.2   *Moulting in the Ordovician trilobite* Platycalymene. *The animal has cast aside its redundant moult which has been gently disturbed by current activity before burial [Photograph: P. Sheldon]*

feeding as scavengers on the organic components of sediments, or perhaps as predators in some cases. Other trilobites are known to have lived as pelagic or planktonic organisms, floating within the deeper marine setting.

12.1.2 Trilobite Classification

Trilobites are variously considered to be a phylum of the animal kingdom in their own right, albeit forming part of a larger group of arthropods, or as a subphylum of the Arthropoda. In both cases, the trilobites are gathered into a single class, subdivided at order level. Classification is based largely upon shell morphology.

Class Trilobita Walch, 1871 (Cambrian–Permian)
Marine arthropods with a calcitic exoskeleton divided into three longitudinal lobes and possessing a distinct head, thorax and tail. The trilobites are divided at order level, distinguished by a combination of features. Important orders include the Cambrian–Ordovician Agnostida (small trilobites with head and tail of similar size and form and few thoracic segments); the Cambrian Redlichiida (typifying the Cambrian trilobites with large head and tiny tail); the Ordovician–Devonian Phacopida (typical post-Cambrian trilobites with enrolment capability and well-developed eyes); the Cambrian–Silurian Asaphida, which includes the Ordovician trinucleids, a family of trilobites with no eyes, probable sensory apparatus in their cephalic fringe, and with enrolment capability. The classification of the trilobites is still a matter for debate.

12.2 TRILOBITE MORPHOLOGY

The trilobite exoskeleton is divisible into three components, cephalon, thorax and pygidium (Figure 12.1). The skeleton was flexible, with the greatest flexibility achieved in the thorax, which was composed of a series of articulating segments, known as the **pleura** (singular: **pleuron**). Both the cephalon and the pygidium comprise single plates of fused segments, with the articulating segments of the thorax between them.

The cephalon is the most complex part of the exoskeleton as it is here that many of the diagnostic features and the sensory apparatus were housed. The cephalon has a basic shield or arched shape. It has a central bulbous raised area, the **glabella**, under which were housed many of the vital organs of the trilobite (Figure 12.1). These were protected on the lower surface by an equally bulbous feature, the **hypostome**, which forms a small shield-like feature joined to the anterior margin of the cephalon, but which is rarely seen as it is lost during moulting. The glabella may preserve the relics of the fused components of a segmented ancestor in the form of a series of small ridges and furrows. Adjacent to the glabella, and either side of it, are the **cheeks** (Figure 12.1). These are usually traversed by two very definite lines of suture, one on each cheek. These **suture lines** are extremely important to the trilobite as it is along these lines that the cephalon is split during ecdysis, in order that the next growth stage may emerge. Because of this the suture line takes on a twofold importance: firstly, it has been important in the classification of the trilobites; and secondly, it is important in understanding the mechanism of moulting in individual trilobite groups. Commonly, trilobite fossils are a result of moulting rather than death, and it is usual to find exoskeletons which are incomplete because of this. The cheeks are therefore usually divided into two: the **fixed cheeks** immediately adjacent to and either side of the glabella; and the **free cheeks** which are lost when the suture line splits. Together, the fixed cheeks and glabella make up the **cranidium** (Figure 12.1).

Trilobite sutures were previously important in classification. There are four basic states, divisible on the line of the suture as it transgresses over the cephalon. In general this is measured through reference to the outer margin of the cephalon, and in particular the angle (**genal angle**) created by the rounding of the posterior margins of the head shield, sometimes developed as spines (**genal spines**). This classification is illustrated in Figure 12.3. In **opisthoparian** trilobites the suture line cuts the posterior margin of the cephalon. **Proparian** trilobites have the suture line anterior of the genal angle or spine. **Gonatoparian** trilobites, a minority, have the suture line dissecting the genal angle, while in some trilobites sutures are **marginal** and run around the outer edge of the cephalon.

The cephalon is also important as it houses the sensory apparatus, particularly eyes. Similar to living insects, trilobite eyes are compound (**holochroal**), composed of densely crowded cylinders of calcite. Given that calcite promotes double vision – through the cystallographic effect of double refraction – experiments have shown that trilobites were able to combat this in a variety of ways, in particular by arranging the main crystallographic axis of the lens so that it was perpendicular to the ocular surface (Figure 12.4). Other trilobites developed

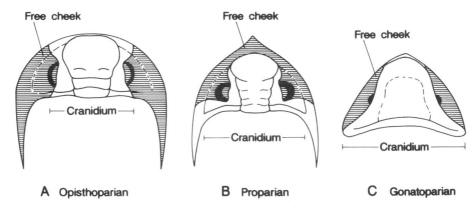

A Opisthoparian   **B** Proparian   **C** Gonatoparian

Figure 12.3   *Facial suture patterns of typical trilobites.* **A:** Paradoxides *from the Cambrian.* **B:**
Dalmanites *from the Silurian.* **C:** Trimerus *from the Silurian*

specialised lenses composed of two interlocking crystals which allow for correction of the refraction effect, in much the same way that an optician corrects short sight with spectacles. In trilobites the sutures generally divide the eye from its supporting base, thus allowing the development of fresh eyes beneath the old. Other trilobites lack eyes. In many cases, these trilobites have pits and **terraces** – concentric raised areas bordering the cephalon – which may have housed hairs or other sensory apparatus.

The thorax and pygidium are more straightforward. The thorax is composed of the articulating pleurae, and these individually protected the walking leg and a gill-bearing arm of the appendage pair. The pygidium is relatively simple, although like the glabella it may preserve those vestiges of its formerly segmented past in the form of ridges and furrows.

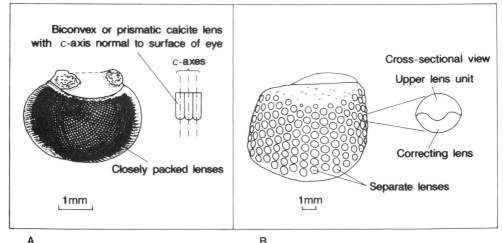

Figure 12.4   *Trilobite eyes. The majority of trilobites have holochroal eyes composed of closely packed lenses (**A**). Some later trilobites (e.g.* Phacops*) possess the advanced schizochroal eye, with separate, corrected lenses (**B**)*

Trilobites were diverse and filled a great many ecological roles in the Palaeozoic seas. Their morphology is complex, and a large number of functional adaptations to a specific mode of life have been identified for trilobite genera and species. However, it is convenient to group trilobites morphologically into two broad groups which correspond with the broad macroevolutionary development of the group: **Cambrian** trilobites and **post-Cambrian** trilobites.

1. *Cambrian trilobites* (Figure 12.5). Cambrian trilobites were an extremely important component of the Cambrian Fauna, inhabiting a range of different habitats. Cambrian trilobites are broadly characterised by :
- large cephalons
- small pygidia, in some cases greatly reduced
- a flattened, low-relief exoskeleton
- a variable number of pleura in the thorax.

For the most part Cambrian trilobites are characteristically of low relief, with a relatively smooth exoskeleton. The cephalon is large, and the pygidium much smaller. Most Cambrian trilobites have opisthoparian or marginal sutures (Figure 12.5). In some genera, such as *Paradoxides* or *Olenellus,* the pygidium consists only of a small plate; while in others, such as *Elrathia,* the pygidium is larger and more regularly developed. This disparity means that enrolment is not practical. The eyes are standard holochroal compound eyes but are often of low relief. The facial suture completely surrounds the eyes in many Cambrian trilobites such that the eye component of the moult is lost completely.

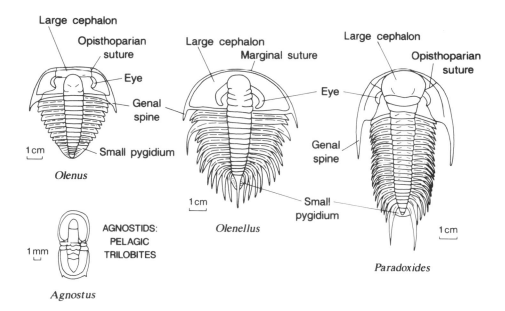

Figure 12.5 *Morphology of typical Cambrian trilobites*

There are some Cambrian trilobites which do not conform to the norm: the *agnostids* (Figures 12.5 and 12.6). These have the following characteristics:

- an extremely small body size
- a large cephalon and pygidium of equivalent size and shape
- a thorax of relatively few pleurae (two or three)
- no eyes.

These fossils have a debatable position within the trilobites proper. They were probably planktonic, explaining the unusual body plan which was not designed for bottom-dwelling.

2. *Post-Cambrian trilobites* (Figure 12.7). Post-Cambrian trilobites display greater range of variation and form than Cambrian trilobites. Broadly, this reflects a greater morphological diversity associated with radiation in the aftermath of the end-Cambrian extinction event. Although diverse, post-Cambrian trilobites may be recognised by the following general characteristics:

Figure 12.6　*A typical agnostid trilobite from the Cambrian of Wales. Length of specimen 7 mm [Photograph: D. Bates]*

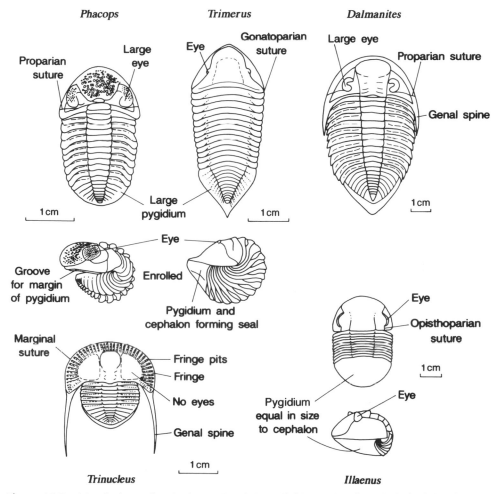

Figure 12.7 *Morphology of typical post-Cambrian trilobites.* Trinucleus *is Ordovician in age; the remainder are all typically Silurian*

- cephalons and pygidia often of the same or similar size
- a diverse range of morphologies with greater surface relief
- the possession of well-developed eyes or other sensory apparatus
- the potential for enrolment.

The post-Cambrian trilobites are characterised by a greater range of morphological adaptions (Figure 12.8). Most post-Cambrian trilobites could enrol into a ball, often with **coaptative structures**. These structures are effectively features of the anterior of the cephalon and posterior of the pygidium which allow these skeletal elements to lock together, thereby protecting the soft body from predators (Figure 12.9). For example, trilobites such as *Calymene* could adopt a spheroidal shape on enrolment (Figure 12.1). This was assisted by the development of similar-sized cephalons and pygidia which helped encompass the soft parts between the enrolled hard parts. However, this is not always the case. The trinucleids had relatively small tails; it is envisaged that the tail and thorax could bend back upon itself almost 90°, flexing only the first few segments of the thorax in order to protect the soft body (Figure 12.10). Protection was enabled also through the development of large genal spines, which appear to have been an effective countermeasure for protection against predators.

Spines had been present in other trilobites since the Cambrian, and could represent a mechanism for spreading body mass in soft sediment. Certainly this is so for many extremely spinose trilobites, such as *Leonaspis*. Other shapes developed in the post-Cambrian trilobites and are probably specifically associated with certain environmental settings. The illaenids, for example, developed an exceptionally smooth cephalon and pygidium, and an overall domed relief, suggesting a shallow-burrowing mode of life, the smooth surface reflecting the need to reduce surface drag (Figure 12.7).

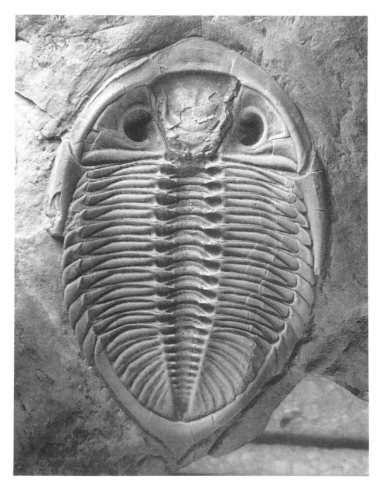

Figure 12.8 *The interior of the exoskeleton of a typical post-Cambrian trilobite,* Dalmanites, *from the Silurian of central England [Photograph: D. Bates]*

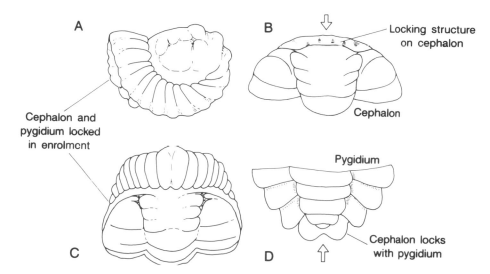

Figure 12.9 *Enrolment structures in the Ordovician trilobite* Placoparia. *In this genus structures on the cephalon and pygidium lock together to protect the trilobite when enrolled [Based on: Henry & Clarkson (1975)* Fossils and Strata **4**, *Plate 2]*

Figure 12.10 *Enrolment in a trinucleid trilobite from the Ordovician of Wales [Photograph: P. Sheldon]*

Eye types diversified in the post-Cambrian; the holochroal state was joined by a new eye with individual lenses, the **schizochroal** eye, in the phacopid trilobites (e.g. *Phacops*) (Figure 12.4). Eyes are also more prominent; in some trilobites this appears to have permitted almost 360° vision. In some (e.g. *Encrinurus*), eyes were developed on individual stalks; in others (e.g. *Cyclopyge*), eyes became extremely large relative to the rest of the body, suggesting a potential planktonic mode of life (Figure 12.11). In other trilobites different sensory apparatuses were developed. In the trinucleid trilobites (e.g. *Trinucleus, Onnia*) the cephalon developed a broad **fringe** with a series of pits (Figure 12.10). Although the function of these pits is still the subject of debate, it has been suggested that they contained sensory hairs. This contrasts with the fact that the trinucleids had no eyes. The harpids (e.g. *Harpes*) possess a similar structure on a more pronounced shield-like fringe.

12.3 TRILOBITE EVOLUTION

Trilobites are one of the most important invertebrate groups of the Palaeozoic. Trilobites first appeared in the earliest Cambrian and radiated to fill a wide range

Figure 12.11   *The large holochroal eyes of the pelagic trilobite* Cyclopyge *from the Ordovician of Wales [Photograph: P. Sheldon]*

of habitats. The rapid appearance of trilobites in the early Cambrian has long puzzled scientists, among them Darwin, who postulated in his *Origin of Species* that: 'Cambrian . . . trilobites are descended from some one crustacean, which must have lived long before the Cambrian age'. The origin of trilobites may be some worm-like Proterozoic ancestor, which developed a hard exoskeleton over its segmented body. Certainly *Spriggina*, from the Ediacaran Biota, has some resemblances to trilobites, especially in the development of a discrete head.

The early Cambrian trilobite radiation is correlated with the creation of wide shelf areas through continental flooding associated with the end of the Proterozoic ice age. The end of 'ice house' conditions may also have stimulated greater levels of free circulation in the oceans, and the resultant release of nutrients from the deep oceans into the newly created shelf areas may have provided the impetus for shell creation through mineralisation in a range of organisms, trilobites included. Trilobites were quickly able to fill much of the ecospace created, their hard exoskeleton providing protection, and their jointed appendages allowing mobility. Maximum diversity was reached in the late Cambrian when there were around 75 families living (Figure 12.12). It is generally agreed that the Cambrian trilobites retained a relatively limited range of variation, and this may reflect an absence of competition for ecospace, or may simply reflect the success of the group in colonising the available habitat space.

At the close of the Cambrian the trilobites suffered a major extinction event which effectively halved the total number of families (Figure 12.12). As with all extinction events, the search for a cause is difficult, but contenders are the reduction in area of continental shelves, and the development of new predators. Certainly there were a number of regressions at the close of the Cambrian which would have reduced ecospace and increased competition among the trilobite families inhabiting them. This is coincident with the rise of nautiloids, mobile predators which may have added to the selection pressure on the unspecialised Cambrian trilobite groups. What is clear is that the trilobites gained new constructional themes in the Ordovician which were to remain largely unchanged until the final extinction of the trilobites in the end-Permian event (Figure 12.12). These themes – efficient enrolment, the development of larger eyes or new forms of sensory apparatus (terrace pits, for example), greater variation in exoskeleton form, and so on – enabled trilobites to combat the new predators effectively and to colonise new environments: reefs, for example. However, the trilobites were unable to re-establish their dominance in the shallow seas, and extinctions at the close of the Ordovician and Devonian intervals effectively reduced their diversity to less than five families, all of which were finished off in the end-Permian extinction event (Figure 12.12).

12.4 TRILOBITE APPLICATIONS

12.4.1 Palaeobiology

Trilobites have fascinated students of evolution, ontogeny and functional morphology, largely because of the information captured in the hard exoskeleton.

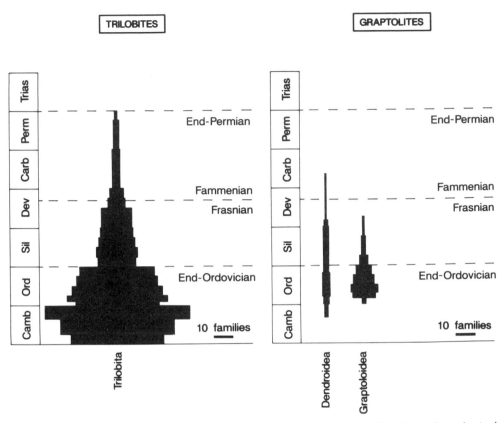

Figure 12.12   *The diversity of trilobite and graptolite (Chapter 14) families through geological time. The main extinction events are indicated [Compiled by A.L. Holder from: Benton (1993) The Fossil Record 2, Chapman & Hall]*

Functional Morphology

Trilobite ontogeny, the life history of individuals in a species, has long been of interest to trilobite researchers. Each trilobite is known to have undergone several growth stages, each with a moult which has a preservation potential. The succession of moult stages has been identified and includes three phases: **protaspid**, in which the trilobite skeleton forms little more than an undifferentiated disc; **meraspid**, in which cephalon and pygidium can be recognised; and **holaspid**, when the full number of thoracic segments has been reached. Ontogenetic studies are of great importance as they allow researchers to consider whether some phylogenetic changes may be related to paedomorphosis – the carrying of juvenile characteristics on into the adult stage and beyond, as a sucessful adaptation which is passed through a population. The origin of some of the trilobite characters, such as eyes or suture types, may be related to this process.

Trilobite functional morphological studies are almost too numerous to mention, and include the function of the compound eye, the form and function of the jointed appendages, and the development of locking coaptative stuctures on the pygidium and cephalon to aid in enrolment (Figure 12.9).

Evolution

Evolutionary studies have centred on the macroevolution of the group, associated with the initial radiation event and subsequent extinctions. The great diversity of the Cambrian trilobites and the morphological diversity of the Ordovician trilobites have been studied in relation to global events such as relative sea-level changes and consequent effects upon the shallow marine environment.

Trilobites have been the subject of much attention in microevolutionary studies, and have helped in the development of both punctuated equilibrium and phyletic gradualism models. Niles Eldredge, one of the authors of the punctuated equilibrium model, based his hypothesis in part on the evolutionary development of one trilobite species, *Phacops rana*, from the Devonian of North America. Eldredge recognised that there were several contemporaneous subspecies of *P. rana* geographically separated within the Devonian of the eastern United States. Each of these underwent little morphological change, and upon extinction of the parent population in the east the subspecies invaded the vacant niche. This combination of stasis and rapid morphological shifts following reinvasion from a peripheral population is a central concept in the punctuated equilibrium theory. This contrasts with a recent study by Peter Sheldon, who demonstrated that over an estimated period of 3 million years, eight separate trilobite lineages underwent gradual change in the Ordovician of central Wales. This study has helped redefine the status of phyletic gradualism as illustrated by the fossil record, and is one of the most important recent additions to our knowledge in this field. It is further discussed in Chapter 21.

12.4.2 Palaeoenvironmental Analysis

As extinct organisms unlikely to lend themselves to an accurate taxonomic uniformitarian approach, trilobites should be relatively difficult to use in palaeoenvironmental analysis. However, trilobites are abundant, and the presence of several typical arthropodan characteristics provides a fairly stable interpreter of trilobite ecology. Trilobites are commonest in shallow marine facies (limestones, shales and sandstones), with greatest diversity in those facies consistent with normal marine salinities. Trilobites were probably limited by salinity, substrate and oxygenation levels (Table 12.1). Trilobite-derived trace fossils are common in Palaeozoic shallow marine sequences, and demonstrate a range of behavioural activities, including resting (*Rusophycus*), movement through the sediment (*Cruziana*) and sideways crawling on the sediment surface (e.g. *Dimorphichnites*). These and other traces are of great importance in interpreting ancient ecologies.

On a broader scale, trilobites have been valuable tools in the reconstruction of Lower Palaeozoic palaeogeographies. The role of trilobites in this task is discussed further in Chapter 22, but the most famous use of trilobite distribution

Table 12.1 *Trilobite limiting factors*

Temperature	Temperature ranges are difficult to assess for trilobites, but as they appear to be widespread, this factor may not have been paramount.
Oxygenation	Trilobites are commonest in sediments formed under well-oxygenated conditions.
Salinity	Trilobites were probably limited to fully marine salinities (~ 35‰).
Depth	Trilobites were probably restricted to shelf depths.
Substrate	Trilobites are found in a variety of sediments. Functional interpretations of spines and other features suggest that individual trilobite groups may have been adapted to specific substrates, firm and soft.
Turbulence	Trilobites may have tolerated moderate to low turbulence levels.

patterns in solving palaeogeographic problems was in the discovery and reconstruction of the 'proto-Atlantic' or Iapetus Ocean in the early Palaeozoic (Box 3.6).

12.4.3 Stratigraphy

Trilobites have an important stratigraphical application. In particular, many evolved rapidly, were abundant and were readily preserved. Recognition is hampered in some cases by the process of moulting which separates the trilobite exoskeleton into head, tail and thoracic segments which may be individually difficult to recognise. However, although free-moving, they are not entirely independent of facies and are subject to provinciality, or restriction to certain geographic areas, which has made them important as interpreters of palaeogeography. However, they were able to spread freely along continental shelves, and this, together with their other advantages, makes them important guide fossils for early Palaeozoic sequences. Trilobites have also been used to determine much larger biostratigraphical units in the North American Upper Cambrian which have been called **biomeres** (Figure 12.13). These are actually equivalent to stages rather than biozones, and represent broad stratigraphical divisions characterised by the longevity of certain trilobite families, the boundaries of which are denoted by three mass extinction episodes.

12.5 SUGGESTED READING

The most detailed taxonomic review of the trilobites is given in the *Treatise on Invertebrate Paleontology* (Moore, 1959), but more accessible accounts are given by Clarkson (1993) and Robison and Kaesler (1987). The books by Levi-Setti (1975) and Whittington (1992) are highly recommended, both as photographic atlases of the range of trilobite types and as general readers on the subject. Additional information and photographic illustrations are given in Thomas and Fortey (1985), and the stratigraphical ranges of trilobite families are fully documented by

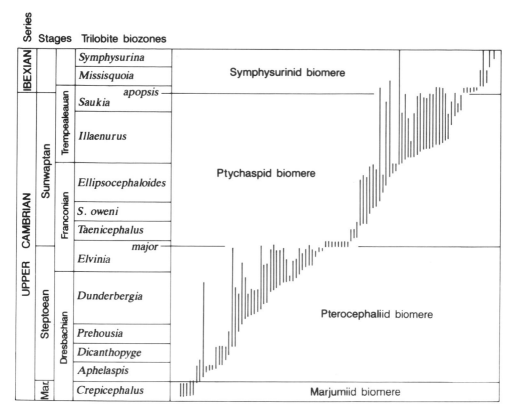

Figure 12.13 *The Upper Cambrian trilobite biomeres in North America. Each biomere is represented by the stratigraphical ranges of a number of trilobite genera and the boundaries are denoted by mass extinction events. These biomeres are important in broad-scale correlation across North America [Modified from: Westrop and Ludvigsen (1987) Palaeobiology, **13**, Fig. 1, p. 85]*

Romano *et al.* (1993). Trilobites in evolutionary studies are dealt with in the papers by Burrett and Richardson (1978) and Westrop (1988), examining the link between Cambrian trilobite diversity and flooding; Whittington (1966), documenting the changes over the Cambrian–Ordovician boundary; Eldredge (1972; 1977), in his discussion of *Phacops rana*; and Sheldon (1987), in his now classic paper documenting gradualism in Ordovician trilobites. Whittington (1957) gives a comprehensive account of trilobite ontogeny, and examples of functional morphology studies on trilobites are given in the papers by Cambell (1975), Clarkson (1975), Henry and Clarkson (1975) and Whittington (1975), all of which appeared in a special issue of the journal *Fossils and Strata* (Martinsson, 1975). Other examples of functional morphology studies are given by Schmalfuss (1981) and Westrop (1983). The palaeoecology and palaeogeographical implications of trilobite distributions are dealt with in the seminal paper by Wilson (1966), and in papers by Taylor (1977), Chatteron and Speyer (1989) and Cocks and Fortey (1990). Trilobite trace fossils are nicely discussed by Clarkson (1993). Taylor (1977) and

particularly Thomas *et al.* (1984) are useful reviews of the use of trilobites in stratigraphical correlation. The concept of biomeres is discussed by Palmer (1965) and
Westrop and Ludvigsen (1987).

Burrett, C.F. & Richardson, R.G. 1978. Cambrian trilobite diversity related to cratonic
    flooding. *Nature*, **272**, 717–719.
Cambell, K.S.W. 1975. The functional morphology of *Cryptolithus*. *Fossils and Strata*, **4**, 65–
    86.
Chatterton, B.D.E. & Speyer, S.E. 1989. Larval ecology, life history strategies, and patterns
    of extinction and survivorship among Ordovician trilobites. *Paleobiology*, **15**, 118–132.
Clarkson, E.N.K. 1975. The evolution of the eye in trilobites. *Fossils and Strata*, **4**, 7–31.
Clarkson, E.N.K. 1993. *Invertebrate Palaeontology and Evolution.* Third edition. Chapman &
    Hall, London.
Cocks, L.R.M & Fortey, R.A. 1990. Biogeography of Ordovician and Silurian faunas. *In*
    McKerrow, W.S. and Scotese, C.R. (eds), *Palaeozoic Palaeogeography and Biogeography*.
    Geological Society Memoir 12, 97–104.
Eldredge, N. 1972. Systematics and evolution of *Phacops rana* (Green 1832), and *Phacops
    iowensis* (Delo, 1935) (Trilobita) from the Middle Devonian of North America. *Bulletin
    of the American Museum of Natural History*, **147**, 49–113.
Eldredge, N. 1977. Trilobites and evolutionary patterns. *In* Hallam, A. (ed.), *Patterns of
    Evolution.* Elsevier, Amsterdam, 305–352.
Fortey, R.A. & Owens, R.M. 1990. Trilobites. *In* McNamara, K.J. (ed.), *Evolutionary Trends.*
    Belhaven Press, London, 121–142.
Henry, J.L. & Clarkson, E.N.K. 1975. Enrollment and coaptations in some species of the
    Ordovician trilobite genus *Placoparia*. *Fossils and Strata*, **4**, 87–96.
Levi-Setti, R. 1975. *Trilobites: A Photographic Atlas.* University of Chicago Press, Chicago.
Martinsson, A. (ed.) 1975. *Evolution and morphology of the Trilobita, Trilobitoidea and Mero-
    stomata.* Special issue of *Fossils and Strata*, **4**.
Moore, R.C. (ed.) 1959. *Treatise on Invertebrate Paleontology, Part O, Arthropoda 1.* Geological
    Society of America and University of Kansas Press, Lawrence, KS.
Palmer, A.R. 1965. Biomere – a new kind of biostratigraphic unit. *Journal of Paleontology*, **39**,
    149–153.
Robison, R.A. & Kaesler, R.L. 1987. Phylum Arthropoda. *In* Boardman, R.S., Cheetham,
    A.H. & Rowell, A.J. (eds), *Fossil Invertebrates.* Blackwell Scientific Publications, Oxford,
    205–269.
Romano, M., Chang, W.T., Dean, W.T., Edgecombe, G.D., Fortey, R.A., Holloway, D.J.,
    Lane, P.D., Owen, A.W., Owens, R.M., Palmer, A.R., Rushton, A.W.A., Shergold, J.H.,
    Siveter, D.J. and Whyte, M.A. 1993. Arthropoda (Trilobita). *In* Benton, M.J. (ed.), *The
    Fossil Record 2.* Chapman & Hall, London, 279–296.
Schmalfuss, H. 1981. Structure, patterns and function of cuticular terraces in trilobites.
    Lethaia, **14**, 331–341.
Sheldon, P.R. 1988. Parallel gradualistic evolution of Ordovician trilobites. *Nature*, **330**, 561–
    563.
Taylor, M.E. 1977. Late Cambrian of Western North America: trilobite biofacies, environ-
    mental significance and biostratigraphic implications. *In* Kauffman, E.G. and Hazel,
    J.E. (eds), *Concepts and Methods of Biostratigraphy*, Hutchinson, Dowden & Ross,
    Stroudsberg, PA, 397–426.
Thomas, A.T. & Fortey, R.A. 1985. Phylum Arthropoda, subphylum Trilobita. *In* Murray,
    J.W. (ed.), *Atlas of Invertebrate Macrofossils*, Longman, London, 207–229.
Thomas, A.T., Owens, R.M. & Rushton, A.W.A. 1984. Trilobites in British stratigraphy.
    Geological Society of London Special Reports, **16**, 78 pp.
Westrop, S.R. 1983. The life habits of the Ordovician illaenine trilobite *Bumastoides*. *Lethaia*,
    16, 15–24.

Westrop, S.R. 1988. Trilobite diversity patterns in an Upper Cambrian stage. *Paleobiology,* **14**, 401–409.

Westrop, S.R. & Ludvigsen, R. 1987. Biogeographic control of trilobite mass extinction at an Upper Cambrian 'biomere' boundary. *Paleobiology,* **13**, 84–99.

Whittington, H.B. 1957. The ontogeny of trilobites. *Biological Reviews,* **32**, 421–469.

Whittington, H.B. 1966. Phylogeny and distribution of Ordovician trilobites. *Journal of Paleontology,* **40**, 696–737.

Whittington, H.B. 1975. Trilobites with appendages from the Middle Cambrian Burgess Shale, British Columbia. *Fossils and Strata,* **4**, 97–136.

Whittington, H.B. 1992. *Trilobites.* Boydell Press, London.

Wilson, J.T. 1966. Did the Atlantic close and then re-open? *Nature,* **211**, 676–681.

13
Corals

13.1 CORAL TAXONOMY

Corals are fully marine organisms which are commonly encountered today in most tropical settings as the major components of reefs such as the Great Barrier Reef in Australia. A form of coral 'reef' first appeared in the early Palaeozoic, but as we know them today they first appeared in the Mesozoic. Corals are grouped with the sea anemones and jellyfish into the phylum Cnidaria on the basis of the simple construction of their soft bodies. However, unlike sea anemones and jellyfish, corals are common in the fossil record because of their construction of a hard calcareous skeleton. Because of their preservation potential corals are important fossils. In particular, they form part of the Palaeozoic evolutionary fauna, though the phylum as a whole has a long geological history, with several cnidarian taxa recognisable in the Ediacaran Biota. Corals are particularly important in geological studies in the determination of palaeoenvironments as they are limited by their narrow tolerance limits to a range of environmental parameters.

13.1.1 General Characteristics of Corals

The phylum Cnidaria comprises the sea anemones, corals, jellyfish and hydrozoans. This grouping reflects the nature of the soft body, which is one of the simplest of all metazoan (multicellular) organisms. Effectively, the soft body consists of a gut or body cavity (**enteron**) surrounded by tentacles which gather food suspended in the water column (Figure 13.1). Food is passed to the enteron through an opening which acts as both mouth and anus. Food is broken down and assimilated into the body through the internal wall of the gut, the **endoderm**. In order that this process is efficiently carried out, the endoderm is subject to a series of folds, known as

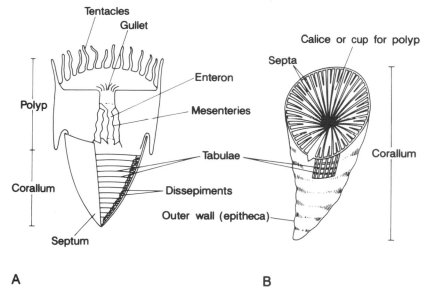

Figure 13.1 *Coral morphology. The rugose corals are the most complex of all corals. **A:** section through a hypothetical rugose coral in life. **B:** structure of a typical solitary rugose coral,* Zaphrentis *[**A** modified from: Black (1988)* The Elements of Palaeontology, *Cambridge University Press, Fig. 63a, p. 101]*

mesenteries, which increase the overall surface area of the gut wall. The outer wall of the polyp is known as the **ectoderm,** and between the ectoderm and endoderm cell walls is a jelly-like layer which contains a simple nervous system.

In primitive cnidarians (e.g. hydrozoans and some jellyfish) it is common for the life history of an individual to have successive cycles of attached **polyps** (typified by the sea anemone) and free-floating **medusae** (typified by the jellyfish), the polyp reproducing asexually to produce a medusa, the medusa reproducing sexually to produce the polyp, and so on. In some sea anemones and corals the medusoid phase of the life cycle has been suppressed, with the soft body developed only as a polyp. In sea anemones, the polyp attaches directly to the substrate, and therefore no hard support or skeleton is needed. In corals, the polyp is attached to a calcareous skeleton which it secretes as a support. Growth of the calcareous skeleton is continuous and regular, with a set number of growth periods per month. Corals are restricted to fully marine conditions today, with an extremely limited band of salinity, temperature and depth in which they can survive.

13.1.2 Coral Classification

The phylum Cnidaria contains a diverse range of organisms which includes the corals, and the higher classification of the group is largely dependent on the form of the soft body. Only the corals, which secrete hard body parts important in the geological record, are considered here. Detailed classification of the corals is based on the nature of the construction of the shell. The classification of the Cnidaria, and particularly the corals, varies greatly according to different authorities in the field. For example, the three geologically most important coral groups – the tabulates, rugosans and scleractinians – are variously considered as three separate subclasses of the Anthozoa, or as three separate orders of the Zoantharia. The latter is the classification used here.

Phylum Cnidaria Hatschek, 1888

Class Petalonamae Pflug, 1970 (Proterozoic (Vendian))
Leaf-like structures with a median line. Considered to constitute a separate phylum of the animal kingdom by some authorities. Includes the genera *Spriggina*, *Rangea* and *Charnia*. This group is not considered in detail here, but is included to demonstrate the antiquity of the phylum.

Class Anthozoa Ehrenberg, 1834 (Cambrian–Recent)
Exclusively marine cnidarians in which the polyps have a gullet leading into the enteron. Enteron divided by mesenteries. Includes sea pens and sea anemones as well as corals.

Subclass Zoantharia de Blainville, 1830 (Cambrian–Recent)
The Zoantharia is subdivided into several orders, of which the Tabulata (Ordovician–Permian), Rugosa (Ordovician–Permian) and Scleractinia (Triassic–Recent), are the most geologically important. The various coral groups are distinguished from each other on the basis of their skeletal structure.

13.2 CORAL MORPHOLOGY

Corals have mostly aragonitic skeletons, and these are more usually recrystallised to calcite in fossil representatives. Each coral skeleton, the **corallum,** is composed of relatively few characters, although the detailed development of these may be complex (Figure 13.1). Common to all corals is the outer wall or **epitheca**. This is often irregular in form and has a rough (**rugose**) texture, usually with a series of incremental growth bands on its surface. These growth bands are added by the polyp which secretes the shell at its junction with the top surface of the skeleton, the **calice**. Each calice is a cup-like depression which represents the junction in life between the polyp and the skeleton. In individual (**solitary**) corals an individual calice takes up the whole of the corallum surface (Figure 13.1). In colonial (**compound**) corals there may be many **corallites**, each with its own calice serving one of the many polyps of the colony. Coral shapes are variable. Solitary corals may be cone-shaped (usually called **horn corals**), disc-shaped (sometimes called **button corals**), or cylindrical. Compound corals are extremely variable in shape and form, with different colony types in each of the three main orders, but a typical form is the dome-like **brain-coral**.

The interior of the coral skeleton has several structural components, and these are not developed in all three coral orders. Common to all corals are the **tabulae** (singular: **tabula**). These approximate to the horizontal, although they may be concave-up, and are added as the coral grows upwards (Figure 13.1). They represent the development of successive calices as the coral grows. **Septa** (singular:

septum) are vertical walls which are radially arranged so that they extend inwards from the inner wall of the epitheca. Septa serve as a support for the mesenteries, the folded inner surface of the enteron. With growth, more septa are added radially, and the pattern of septal additions is important to the classification of coral type, discussed below. The most complex of all corals, the **rugose corals**, have two additional structural components to their skeleton: **dissepiments** and an **axial complex** (Figure 13.1). Dissepiments form small structural elements which are mostly restricted to the outermost part of the shell interior, close to the interior of the outer wall. Dissepiments probably serve as a junction between the tabulae and the interior of the epitheca, in order to improve the fit of the polyp to the calice. The axial complex is peculiar to rugose corals and comprises a range of features, from a single column of calcite (the **columella**) to a series of net-like and web-like structural elements. This occupies the central axis of the corallum to a greater or lesser degree.

There are three main coral groups which contribute to the fossil record: **tabulate** corals, **rugose** corals and **scleractinian** corals. The tabulate and rugose corals are characteristic of the Palaeozoic and were wiped out in the end-Permian extinction, to be replaced by the scleractinians in the Triassic which continue to the present day. The general characteristics of these fossil groups are given below:

1. *Tabulate* corals (Figure 13.2). Tabulate corals are wholly Palaeozoic corals belonging to the order Tabulata. They can be broadly characterised by relatively few features. Tabulate corals:
   - are always compound
   - possess only tabulae as major internal shell features
   - are relatively simple
   - have variable colony shapes, most commonly brain-coral-like (with polygonal or rounded corallites surrounded by a dense calcareous mass); picket-fence-like (with individual corallites joined in a kind of chain, forming the 'fence'); or forming simple branching corallites (Figure 13.2).

The tabulate corals are the simplest of the three main skeletal coral groups. They are always compound, the skeleton consisting of a range of small, open corallites. The tabulae are often domed. There are no septa, although some incipient 'spikes' have been identified in some genera, such as the brain-coral-like *Favosites*.

2. *Rugose* corals (Figure 13.3). Rugose corals are Palaeozoic corals belonging to the order Rugosa. Broadly, rugose corals:
   - are relatively complex
   - may be compound or solitary – compound corals may be brain-coral-like (massive) with polygonal corallites; branching; or composed of subparallel, cylindrical corallites
   - possess tabulae, septa, dissepiments and an axial complex
   - possess septae which are inserted in four specific areas, leading to the creation of gaps known as **fossulae** and the development of a bilateral symmetry
   - have dissepiments organised into a special area, the **dissepimentarium**
   - have a variable axial complex.

Rugose corals possess a greater amount of structural components to their corallum (Figure 13.3). Rugose corals can be solitary (horn corals) or compound, and

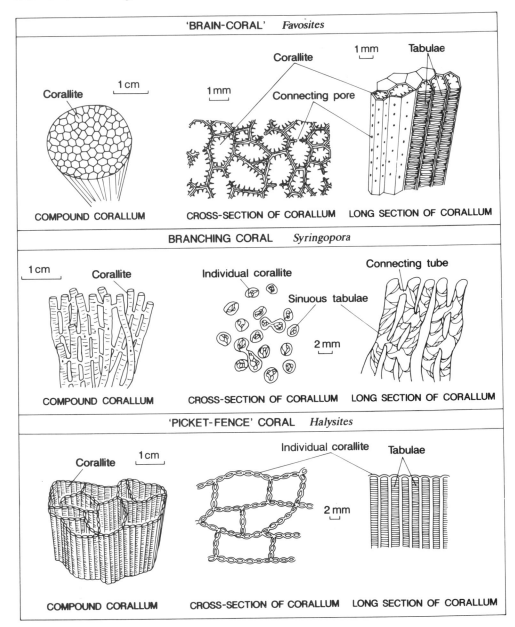

Figure 13.2 *Morphology of typical tabulate corals.* Favosites *and* Halysites *are Silurian in age, while* Syringopora *is common in Carboniferous rocks*

in some cases both forms can be found in a single genus, such as in the Carboniferous coral *Lonsdaleia*. As its name suggests, the rugose corallum possesses a rough-textured epitheca. Internally, the skeleton is composed of tabulae and septae, but the skeleton characteristically possesses an axial complex, and a zone of dissepiments (**dissepimentarium**) around the outer edge of each corallite (Figure 13.3). It is

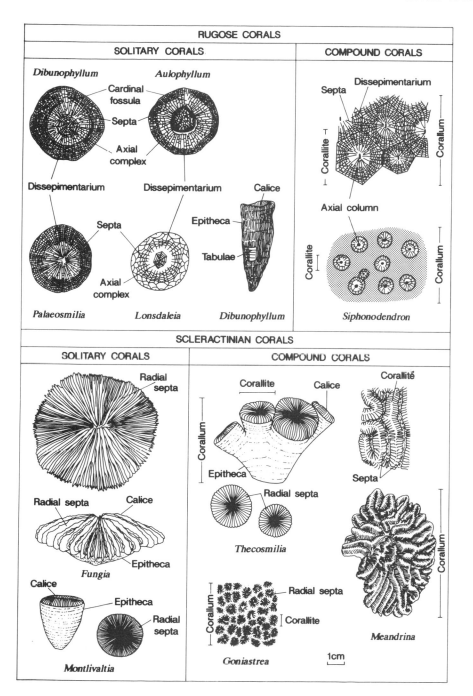

Figure 13.3 *Morphology of typical rugose and scleractinian corals. The rugose corals are all Carboniferous in age.* Thecosmilia *and* Montlivaltia *are Jurassic scleractinians, and the remainder are Recent [Modified from: Black (1988)* The Elements of Palaeontology, *Cambridge University Press, Figs 68 and 73, pp. 107 and 116]*

perhaps these two characteristics, more than any other, which help distinguish the rugose corals from the other two skeletal types. The axial complex is unique to rugose corals. It consists of modifications of the major septa to form a column (the **columella**) as in *Siphonodendron*, or modifications of the tabulae to form a broad axial zone, as in *Aulophyllum*. Dissepiments are found in scleractinians, but are only concentrated into a dissepimentarium in the rugose corals.

Each rugose corallum has a bilateral symmetry imposed by the mechanism of septal insertion through the growth or ontogeny of a single individual. As the coral grows, septa are inserted regularly at four specific points (Figure 13.4). The first septum created in the youngest coral is a single septum, the **proseptum**, which divides the corallite in two. With additional growth, the proseptum is divided into two: the **cardinal** and **counter** prosepta. Continued growth is along a set pattern with additional septa inserted, firstly, on either side of the cardinal septum (**alar** septa), and secondly, on either side of the counter septum (**counter-lateral** septa). Further insertions of smaller septa are then made adjacent to each of the four alar and counterlateral septa together. Insertion of further septa forces a readjustment of their position to make room, and crowding together in the four insertion points eventually leads to the creation of areas which are free from septa, the **fossulae** (Figure 13.4). Although it is often difficult to identify fossulae in many rugose corals, the most noticeable is the **cardinal fossula** adjacent to the cardinal septum, particularly well developed in the Carboniferous genus *Zaphrentis*. This pattern of septal insertion, leading to a strong bilateral symmetry, is unique to rugose corals, and distinguishes them from the scleractinians which have a radial pattern of septal insertion (Figure 13.4).

3. *Scleractinian* corals (Figure 13.3). Scleractinian corals are Mesozoic–Recent corals belonging to the order Scleractinia. Corals belonging to the order can be broadly characterised by the features given below. Scleractinians:

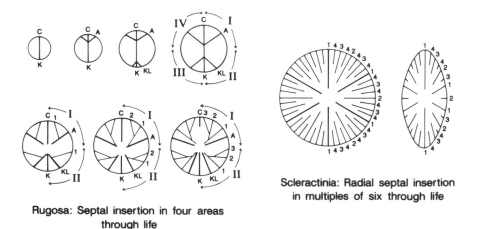

Rugosa: Septal insertion in four areas through life

Scleractinia: Radial septal insertion in multiples of six through life

Figure 13.4   *The mechanism of septal insertion in rugose and scleractinian corals [Modified from: Oliver and Coates (1987) In Boardman et al. (Eds) Fossil Invertebrates, Blackwells, Fig. 11.30, p. 178]*

- are compound or solitary – compound corals may be brain-coral-like (massive); arranged in linear series; branching; or composed of subparallel, cylindrical corallites
- possess tabulae and septa, but no dissepimentarium or axial complex
- have septa which are inserted radially in regular groups of six, with no fossulae.

Like rugose corals, scleractinians can be both solitary or compound (Figure 13.3). In many ways they have a less complex skeleton than that of the rugose coral which they otherwise resemble. Scleractinians possess tabulae and septae together with some dissepiments, but do not have an axial complex or dissepimentarium. Septal insertion is less complex than in the Rugosa; scleractinians are often referred to as 'hexacorals' because septal insertion is regular and in multiples of six (Figure 13.4). Septal insertion in sixes leads to the creation of a radially symmetrical corallite. The septa are closely associated with the messentaries of the endoderm.

13.3 CORAL EVOLUTION

The first cnidarians can be identified from the Ediacaran Biota, including the first jellyfish and hydrozoans, as well as taxa identified as representative of the Anthozoa (Figure 7.4). As with all interpretations of the Ediacaran Biota, these identifications are subject to question, and the first really recognisable cnidarian fossils are found in Cambrian rocks. The corals have a patchy record in the Cambrian; a few tabulae-bearing coral-like fossils have been found, but the first real evidence of the tabulate corals is found in the Ordovician, when they first radiated (Figure 13.5). The rugose corals also appeared in the Ordovician, and together the tabulate and rugose corals became common components of the Palaeozoic marine ecosystem. In general, Palaeozoic reefs were built predominantly by tabulates in conjunction with other reef-building, non-cnidarian organisms, such as stromatoporoids and bryozoans; rugose corals played a subordinate role. Both the tabulate and rugose coral faunas were severely affected by the end-Devonian extinction, but the rugose corals in particular recovered to become common in the Carboniferous (Figure 13.5). Both rugose and tabulate corals were completely extinguished at the end of the Permian when a major mass extinction event devastated a great many reef-dwelling organisms (Figure 13.5).

The first of the scleractinians appeared in the Triassic, replacing the rugose and tabulate corals, and remain the most important skeletal coral group today (Figure 13.5). Their origin is still debated, and involves two possible routes. The first involves direct derivation from the rugose corals. However, as yet there is no evidence of an intermediate between the two groups, and there is a considerable time gap from the last appearance of the rugosa in the late Permian to the first appearance of the scleractinians in the mid-Triassic (Figure 2.19). The second possibility is that the scleractinians were derived from a soft-bodied anthozoan ancestor, such as a sea anemone, via a route involving the creation of a mineralised skeleton. Little evidence exists to be able to substantiate either hypothesis. The scleractinians developed along two lines, the reef-building **hermatypic** corals

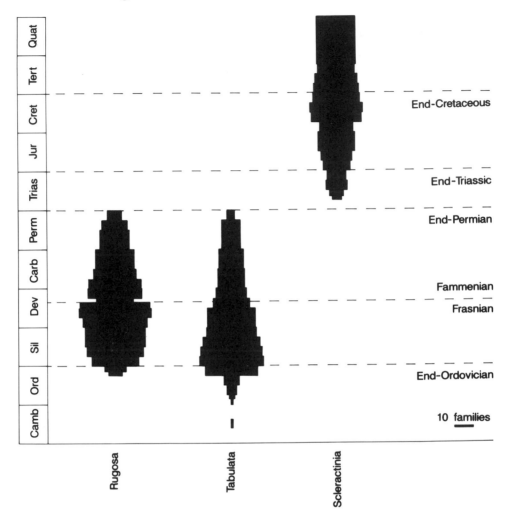

Figure 13.5 *The diversity of coral families through geological time. The main extinction events are indicated [Compiled by A.L. Holder from: Benton (1993)* The Fossil Record 2, *Chapman & Hall]*

living in symbiosis with algae, the zooxanthellae; and the deeper-water **aherma-typic** corals, without zooxanthellae. The hermatypic corals flourished in the later part of the Cenozoic, producing a great phase of reef development which has continued, with some interruption, to the present day.

13.4 CORAL APPLICATIONS

13.4.1 Palaeobiology

Corals have provided relatively few detailed studies of microevolution, despite their advantage in being durable fossils which are commonly preserved in the fossil record. Some classic studies have been carried out on a few rugose corals, particularly *Zaphrentis*, with documented changes in the form of the cardinal fossula, particularly well developed in this genus, and in the length of the septa. Although the trend demonstrated is clear, it has been criticised because there are distinct gaps in the faunal sequence, and because the same lineage has not been proven outside the original area of study in Scotland and northern England. Despite this criticism, it is clear that corals could provide an important tool in determining evolutionary lineages and the nature of variation in the coral skeleton through geological time.

13.4.2 Palaeoenvironmental Analysis

Corals are extremely important tools in palaeoenvironmental analysis, and this is particularly so because of their limited tolerance of the environmental parameters of salinity, depth (proportional to sunlight penetration) and temperature (Table 13.1). Hermatypic scleractinians require normal salinity, a temperature range of 18–29°C and a depth not greater than 200 m, the latter to allow light penetration for the process of photosynthesis carried out by their symbiotic zooxanthellae (Figure 13.6). Ahermatypic scleractinians have a greater ecological range, as they are not restricted by a symbiotic relationship, and although they require normal salinities, they can survive in much deeper and consequently colder waters. Clearly the ecological tolerances for living corals can be determined very accurately, but the reliability of such environmental modelling becomes suspect with increasing geological age, particularly so for Palaeozoic rocks which contain only tabulate and rugose corals which are entirely different to, and perhaps not even directly related to, living scleractinian forms.

Table 13.1   *Coral limiting factors*

Temperature	Living hermatypic corals are unable to withstand temperatures as low as 16–17°C, or as high as 40°C. Optimum growing temperatures are 25–29°C. Living ahermatypic corals can survive in the temperature range of 1–28°C. Rugose and tabulate corals may have displayed a similar range to living scleractinians, although this is difficult to confirm.
Oxygenation	Corals are found in fully oxygenated waters.
Salinity	Living corals (hermatypic and ahermatypic) are restricted to near-normal marine salinities of 34–36°/_{oo}, although they can tolerate a greater range of 27–48°/_{oo}.
Depth	Hermatypic corals are restricted to a water depth of less than 150 m, with best growth at around 15 m. Ahermatypic corals are not restricted by the presence of zooxanthellae, and can live at depths of up to 6000 m.
Substrate	All living corals require a hard substrate for firm attachment.
Turbulence	Living hermatypic corals require turbulent water because of the need for fully oxygenated, clear waters with an abundance of suspended food particles.

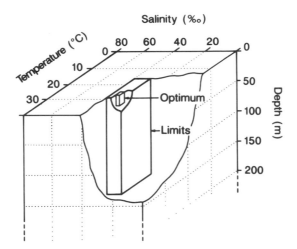

Figure 13.6   *The factors which limit the growth of hermatypic corals today [Modified from: Wells (1957) Geological Society of America Memoir **67**, Fig. 1, p. 1088]*

Rugose corals can, however, be broadly separated into two depth-related facies associations: shelf carbonates with structurally complex compound and solitary corals; and basinal muds with simple, solitary coral types. This may be analogous to the scleractinian division into hermatypic and ahermatypic coral groups, but it has so far not been confirmed whether rugose corals possessed zooxanthellae or not. If they did, then, as with the scleractinians, the presence of algae as symbionts within the polyp growth would effectively have limited them to the photic zone in order to continue photosynthesis. This would give a bathymetric significance to both scleractinian and rugose reef build-ups in the fossil record. Studies within fossil shelf carbonate sequences suggest that rugose corals may have had a bathymetric relationship. For example, in exhumed coral reefs of Devonian age in Western Australia, compound rugose corals tend to form the fore-reef flanks, and the reef platform is composed of a framework of non-coral stromatoporoids and algae. Tabulate corals are also found in this association, and often appeared alongside the rugosa in later Palaeozoic reef developments. However, in most Palaeozoic reefs, corals are subordinate to the stromatoporoids and other encrusting organisms, although in some cases they form the foundation for the development of the reef.

Corals are sufficiently geographically restricted to be of importance in palaeobiogeography and palaeogeography. Today, the optimum distribution of reef corals in the Pacific is largely restricted to a narrow belt straddling the Equator encompassing 46° of latitude, although their maximum north–south range is something like 70° of latitude. This distribution is primarily a function of sea surface temperature (SST) and the optimum northern and southern boundaries, at 23°N and 23°S, are coincident with a winter SST isotherm of 21°C (Figure 13.7). Most hermatypic scleractinians from the fossil record can be interpreted in the light of this, and reef corals are therefore a valuable indicator of latitude, and

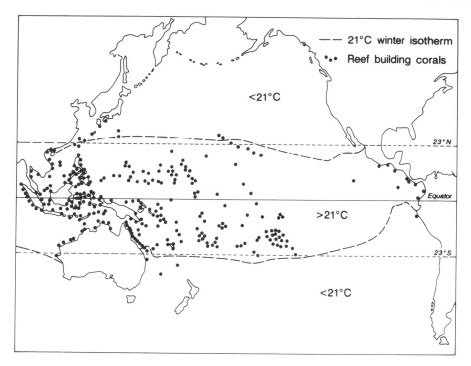

Figure 13.7 *The occurrence of coral reefs in the Pacific today, showing the dependence on temperature. Note also that the density of reefs decreases towards the east [Modified from: Ziegler (1983)* Introduction to Palaeobiology, *Ellis Horwood, Fig. 177, p. 153]*

particularly of the tropical belt, in the geological past. Distribution patterns of rugose corals plotted on palaeogeographic reconstructions show that these corals were subject to a similar latitudinal restriction.

Corals may also be of value in determining longitude. In the present-day Pacific, for example, there is a general eastward decline in the diversity of coral taxa, and this may be used as a measure of longitude, as the east–west range of a given living coral genus is never more than four times its north–south range. Sea surface temperature is known to decline eastwards across the present-day Pacific, and this most probably controlled the longitudinal pattern displayed by the corals. Recently, this has been used as a tool in determining the Permian palaeogeography of the ancient Pacific, using the probability that, like scleractinians, rugose corals will have the following constraints on their distribution: they will be largely restricted to the Equatorial belt; decline in diversity eastwards across the ancient Pacific; and decline in diversity to the north and south of the Equator. This has been used to determine the former location of coral-bearing terranes in the North American Cordillera. These terranes are small continental areas within the Pacific which have been swept up into the Cordillera during continental collisions and now form a collage or mosaic of unrelated blocks, each with its own stratigraphy and geological characteristics. Study of Permian coral distributions shows that the greatest diversity and concentration of the rugose corals was close to the South

China block, decreasing to the north, south and east as predicted by the three constraints. Studies of the Permian coral diversity of three terranes – Wrangellia, Stikinia and Eastern Klamath – shows that all three were up to 6700 km west of North America in the Permian Pacific Ocean, located no further north than 30°N palaeolatitude, with the Eastern Klamath terrane tied down to between 11° and 21°N. These examples clearly demonstrate the value of biogeographical studies in palaeogeographical reconstructions.

13.4.3 Stratigraphy

Corals are of limited value in stratigraphy because of their very specific habitat preferences, and they are very strongly facies-controlled. The distribution of corals is also limited to the brief, free-floating larval stage. The slow rate of evolution in some coral taxa is equally not advantageous to them as potential guide fossils. Nevertheless, corals are abundant, usually well preserved and generally easily recognisable, and they have been pressed into service in correlating like environments, particularly in the Lower Carboniferous limestones of Britain, Ireland and other parts of Europe, as well as in North America, and this biozonation continues to be refined today (Box 5.2; Figure 13.8).

Perhaps the most innovative use of corals as geochronometers has been the discovery of the value of the incremental growth bands preserved on the epitheca of some rugose corals. Detailed analysis of these growth bands suggests that, through comparison with similar bands on living scleractinian corals, they are yearly increments composed of finer, daily additions. Study of rugose coral banding demonstrates that there were an average of 400 days in the Devonian year, which is consistent with estimates that the rate of the Earth's rotation has been slowing by about 2 seconds per 100 000 years.

13.5 SUGGESTED READING

The details of coral taxonomy are given in the *Treatise of Invertebrate Paleontology* (Moore, 1956), and are summarised in an accessible form by Clarkson (1993) and Oliver and Coates (1987). Scrutton and Rosen (1985) illustrate many of the commonest coral taxa, while Nudds and Sepkoski (1993) give a detailed analysis of the stratigraphical range of all the commonest families. The classic story of evolution in *Zaphrentis* is given by Carruthers (1910), and Oliver (1980) discusses the evolutionary relationship of rugose and scleractinian corals. Copper (1985) demonstrates the presence of polyps in relation to tabulate coral skeletons in the fossil record. The palaeoecological significance of corals, particularly in relation to reef development and palaeobathymetry, is discussed by Wells (1957), Broadhurst and Simpson (1972), Playford (1980) and Perrin *et al.* (1995). Belasky and Runnegar (1994) discuss an innovative application of rugose corals in the reconstruction of Permian palaeogeography. The application of corals in biostratigraphy, particularly in relation to the Carboniferous successions, is discussed in the classic

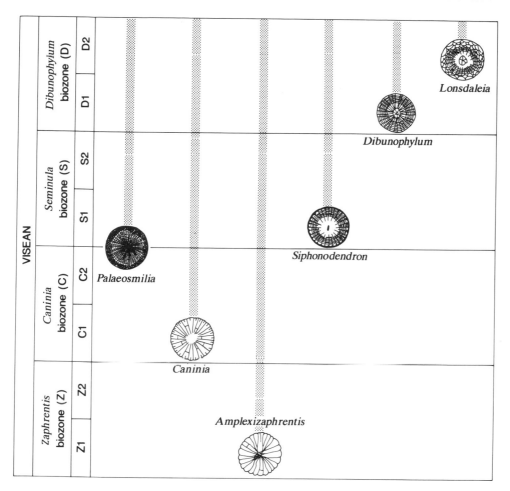

Figure 13.8 *Vaughan's coral–brachiopod biozones, with the stratigraphical ranges of import-ant coral genera illustrated [Modified from: Clarkson (1978)* Invertebrate Palaeontology and Evolution *(First Edition), Allen & Unwin, Fig. 5.14, p. 90]*

paper by Vaughan (1905), and more recently by Sando (1977), Mitchel (1989) and Riley (1993). Finally, the story of corals as geochronometers is given by Wells (1963) and Scrutton (1965).

Belasky, P. & Runnegar, B. 1994. Permian longitudes of Wrangellia, Stikinia and Eastern Klamath terranes based on coral biogeography. *Geology*, **22**, 1095–1098.

Broadhurst, F.M. & Simpson, I.M. 1972. Bathymetry on a Carboniferous reef. *Lethaia*, 6, 367–381.

Carruthers, R.G. 1910. On the evolution of *Zaphrentis delanouei* in Lower Carboniferous times. *Quarterly Journal of the Geological Society of London*, **66**, 523–536.

Clarkson, E.N.K. 1993. *Invertebrate Palaeontology and Evolution*. Third edition. Chapman & Hall, London.

Copper, P. 1985. Fossilised polyps in 430-Myr-old *Favosites* corals. *Nature*, **316**, 142–144.

Mitchel, M. 1989. Biostratigraphy of the Visean (Dinantian) rugose coral faunas in Britain. *Proceedings of the Yorkshire Geological Society*, **47**, 233–247.

Moore, R.C. (ed.) 1956. *Treatise on Invertebrate Paleontology, Part F, Coelenterata.* Geological Society of America and University of Kansas Press, Lawrence, KS.

Nudds, J.R. & Sepkoski, J.J. 1993. Coelenterata. *In* Benton, M.J. (ed.), *The Fossil Record 2.* Chapman & Hall, London, 101–124.

Oliver, W.A. 1980. The relationship of the scleractinian corals to the rugose corals. *Paleobiology*, **6**, 146–160.

Oliver, W.A. & Coates, A.G. 1987. Phylum Cnidaria. *In* Boardman, R.S., Cheetham, A.H. & Rowell, A.J. (eds), *Fossil Invertebrates.* Blackwell Scientific Publications, Palo Alto, CA, 140–193.

Perrin, C., Bosence, D.W.J. & Rosen, B. 1995. Quantitative approaches to palaeozonation and palaeobathymetry of corals and coralline algae in Cenozoic reefs. *In* Bosence, D.W.J. & Allison, P.A. (eds), *Marine Palaeoenvironmental Analysis from Fossils.* Geological Society Special Publication 83, London, 181–230.

Playford, P.E. 1980. Devonian 'Great Barrier Reef' of Canning Basin, Western Australia. *Bulletin of the American Association of Petroleum Geologists*, **64**, 814–840.

Riley, N.J. 1993. Dinantian (Lower Carboniferous) biostratigraphy and chronostratigraphy in the British Isles. *Journal of the Geological Society of London*, **150**, 427–446.

Sando, W.J. 1977. North American Mississippian coral biostratigraphy. *In* Kauffman, E.G. & Hazel, J.E. (eds), *Concepts and Methods of Biostratigraphy.* Dowden, Hutchinson & Ross, Stroudsberg, PA, 483–496.

Scrutton, C.T. 1965. Periodicity in Devonian coral growth. *Palaeontology*, **7**, 552–558.

Scrutton, C.T. & Rosen, B.R. 1985. Cnidaria. *In* Murray, J.W. (ed.), *Atlas of Invertebrate Macrofossils.* Longman, London, 11–46.

Vaughan, A. 1905. The palaeontological sequence in the Carboniferous limestone of the Bristol area. *Quarterly Journal of the Geological Society of London*, **61**, 181–307.

Wells, J.W. 1957. Corals. *In* Hedgepeth, J. (ed.), *Treatise on Marine Ecology and Paleoecology, Volume 2.* Memoir of the Geological Society of America 67, Lawrence, KS, 773–782.

Wells, J.W. 1963. Coral growth and geochronometry. *Nature*, **197**, 948–950.

14
Graptolites

14.1 GRAPTOLITE TAXONOMY

Graptolites are extinct colonial, marine organisms which mostly had a planktonic existence. The name 'graptolite' is derived from Greek words describing writing on stone, as they often appear like 'pencil-marks' written upon their enclosing matrix. In general terms, graptolites are sometimes unimpressive fossils, but this is in contrast with their extreme importance in geological studies, particularly as guide fossils in the early Palaeozoic. Graptolites formed an important part of the Palaeozoic Fauna and were an integral component of the marine ecosystem in the Palaeozoic. Graptolites are valuable guide fossils in Lower Palaeozoic rock sequences.

14.1.1 Graptolite General Characteristics

Graptolites probably had a mostly planktonic mode of life. Interpretation of their mode of life is possible through comparison with a living colonial animal, *Rhabdopleura*, which belongs to a phylum of animals distantly related to the chordates (which includes the vertebrates), the phylum Hemichordata (Figure 14.1). *Rhabdopleura* has a skeleton which is composed of a series of interconnected tubes constructed out of organic collagens, rather than calcite or other hard mineral substances (Figure 14.1). Each tube is constructed from half-rings of organic collagen which together build up the tube with a zigzag join, rather like layers of bandages on an Egyptian mummy. Each tube is connected to the next, and the inhabitants of each tube, the **zooids**, are similarly connected to each other by the connective tissue of the **stolon**. The stolon is a kind of nervous system and is homologous to the nerve chord of the chordates, making both *Rhabdopleura* and graptolites distant, colonial, relatives of vetebrates and other members of this animal phylum. Graptolites possess similar structural elements to *Rhabdopleura*: tubes (**thecae**) which probably housed the food-gathering zooids; a similar 'bandaged' skeletal construction, and the probable presence of a stolon, most convincingly identified in the dendroid graptolites, which runs from the initial theca and joins all the thecae in the colony (Figure 14.1). Detailed analysis of the graptolite skeletal stucture demonstrates considerable complexity. Each layer has an inner and outer part which together make up the **periderm**. The inner or **fusellar** layer is built in regular growth bands to form the interconnecting half-rings. The outer or **cortical** layer is more irregular, and consists of criss-crossings of thin bandage-like strips. These appear to have been plastered on the outside of each theca by the zooid, probably as a support.

Graptolites were probably suspension feeders and were mostly planktonic. Experimental studies using scale models of graptolite colonies suggest that many may have been able to spiral down with a corkscrew motion through the water column, and then exploit upward draughts to rise again. This would have the advantage of providing access to separate feeding areas for each zooid, so that during the spiralling action each part of the water column was not fed over more than once by the stacked zooids in the colony. Other studies have suggested that graptolites may have been capable of active swimming. In some graptolites, flotation aids have been recognised, such as vanes and floats. Others, particularly the dendroids, appear to possess holdfasts – anchors which would hold the graptolite colony firmly to the sea bottom, showing that some of the earliest graptolites may have been benthonic.

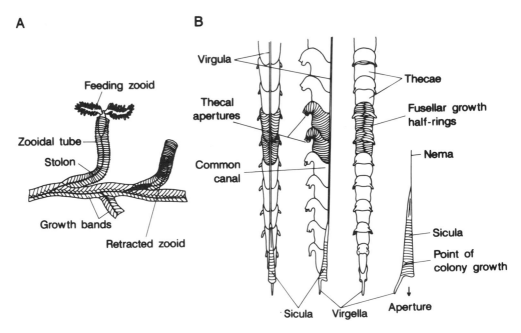

Figure 14.1 *Morphology of living and fossil hemichordates.* **A:** *The living genus* Rhabdopleura. **B:** *The fossil genus* Monograptus [Modified from: Berry (1987) In Boardman et al., (Eds) Fossil Invertebrates, *Blackwells, Figs 19.3 and 19.9, pp. 613 and 617]*

14.1.2 Graptolite Classification

Although previously classified with other colonial organisms such as the corals, since the detailed comparison with the hemichordate *Rhabdopleura* in the first half of the twentieth century, graptolites have been placed in the phylum Hemichordata. The hemichordates are ancestral to the chordates themselves, which include the vertebrates. The graptolites are contained within a single class of the phylum, and two important orders are recognised, the Dendroidea and the Graptoloidea.

Phylum Hemichordata Bateson, 1885
Class Graptolithina Bronn, 1846 (Cambrian–Carboniferous)
Colonial organisms consisting of tube-like thecae arranged on branching stipes, and with an organic skeleton composed of collagens in two separate layers. The class is divided into two important orders: the Cambrian–Carboniferous **Dendroidea**, which have multiple stipes, small theca of two types, and a sicula without a nema; and the Ordovician–Devonian **Graptoloidea**, which have fewer stipes, larger thecae and a sicula which possesses a nema.

14.2 GRAPTOLITE MORPHOLOGY

Graptolites were colonial organisms. The colony, or **rhabdosome**, can consist of one or more branches (**stipes**) which diverge from a single point (the **sicula**) (Figures 14.1 and 14.2). Each stipe has arranged upon it a series of tubes (**thecae**) which housed the zooids in life. In each case, the colony was started by growth from the first formed theca, the **sicula**. The sicula was secreted by the first zooid in the colony and forms an acute cone arranged vertically in life position, with the aperture pointing towards the sea bed as the sicula floated (Figure 14.1). A rod-like **nema** points away from the apex of the sicula and new thecae were grown through asexual budding in a complex manner from a special point on the sicula, the primary notch. Once the colony has developed in this way, the growth of one or more stipes commences. Stipes can grow upwards (called **scandent**), opposite to the direction in which the sicula aperture faces; downwards (**pendent**), in the same direction; or in any intermediate direction – sloping upwards (**reclined**); extended laterally (**horizontal**); or sloping downwards (**declined**) (Figures 14.1 and 14.2). Stipes may be separate (**uniserial**) or arranged back-to-back with the nema (now called the **virgula**) incorporated between them. In most cases only two stipes are involved (**biserial**), but in others there may be four stipes (**quadriserial**) arranged in a cross-like arrangement, as with the genus *Phyllograptus* (Figure 14.3).

The thecae are variable in shape and form. In the earliest graptolites, the dendroids, there are two types, the large **autothecae** and the smaller **bithecae** (Figure 14.2). These are regularly spaced on the stipes and may have housed different zooid types, perhaps even different sexes. In the later graptolites, the graptoloids, the thecae are of one type per stipe but may take on many different forms between species. Many are simple, having uncomplicated apertures, and are arranged so that they are closely touching or overlapping along the stipe. In some graptolites

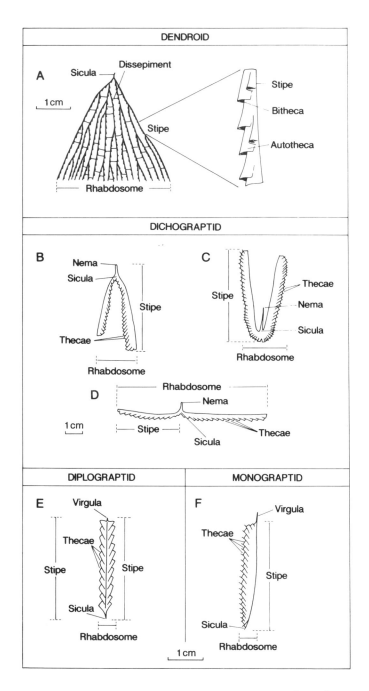

Figure 14.2 *Morphology of typical graptolites.* **A:** Dictyonema *from the Cambrian.* **B, D:** Didymograptus *from the Ordovician.* **C:** Isograptus *from the Ordovician.* **E:** Glyptograptus *from the Silurian.* **F:** Saetograptus *from the Silurian*

Figure 14.3 *The leaf like rhabdosome of the Silurian diplograptid* Petalolithus. *Length 10 mm*
[Photograph: D. Bates]

the thecae may be widely separated or **isolate**. Thecae may be more complex in other graptoloids, and have a variety of shapes, and a complexity of spines and apertural modifications. In both dendroids and graptoloids each theca is interconnected through the common canal which may have housed a stolon similar to that of *Rhabdopleura*.

Graptolites are complex organisms which display a great variety in shape and form. Two major divisions may be recognised: the dendroid graptolites of the order Dendroidea; and the graptoloids or 'true graptolites' of the order Graptoloidea. The general characteristics of these two groups are discussed below, and are illustrated in Figures 14.2–14.4.

1. *Dendroidea*. Dendroid graptolites belong to the order Dendroidea, and are characterised by:
- numerous stipes with connecting cross-bars (dissepiments)
- the possession of more than one type of theca: bithecae and autothecae (these are possibly representative of zooids of different sexes, and each is connected to a stolon system identifiable in well-preserved specimens)
- a sicula which lacks a nema.

The dendroids are characteristically multiply stiped (Figures 14.2 and 14.4). However, the rhabdosome is usually found broken up, and it is rare to find an intact colony. In life the dendroid colony may have had an open cone form, and it has been inferred to be either a bottom-attached colony or a floating, planktonic colony. The clearest identifier of dendroid graptolites are the cross-bars

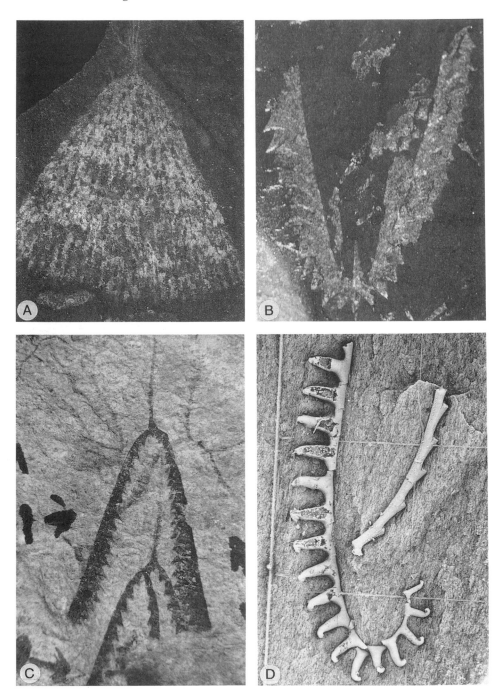

Figure 14.4   *Typical graptolites.* **A:** *The dendroid* Dictyonema *; rhabdosome length 22 mm.* **B:** *The dichograptid* Isograptus; *rhabdosome length 13 mm.* **C:** *The dichograptid* Tetragraptus; *length 6 mm.* **D:** *A monograptid with isolate thecae; length 4 mm [Photographs: D. Bates]*

(**dissepiments**) which act as spacers, and the number of stipes. The thecae are small and difficult to observe in hand specimen without the aid of a microscope. The dendroid graptolites were the longest-ranging graptolites, and may be found in suitable rocks of Cambrian to Carboniferous age.

2. *Graptoloids*. Graptoloids belong to the order Graptoloidea, linked by the following characters:

- rhabdosomes with few stipes (a maximum of eight)
- the possession of a single thecal type in most cases
- a sicula possessing a nema.

Graptoloids are mostly distiguished from dendroids by the small number of stipes, and the general absence of cross-bars or dissepiments joining them, although some have recently been identified in a rare instance. Graptoloids have a great importance in biostratigraphy, and, at the broadest level, four major faunal groups can be recognised: the **anisograptid fauna** (Ordovician: Tremadoc); the **dichograptid fauna** (Ordovician: Arenig); the **diplograptid fauna** (Ordovician–Silurian: Llanvirn–Llandovery); and the **monograptid fauna** (Silurian, Llandovery–Middle Devonian) (Figure 14.2). In the simplest (perhaps over-simplified) terms, these faunas have long been recognised as representing a model of decreasing numbers of stipes with increasing thecal complexity (Figure 14.2). It is on this basis that the faunas can be recognised. Their broad characteristics are given below and illustrated in Figures 14.2–14.4.

Anisograptids are often poorly preserved and difficult to identify, and represent the earliest of the true graptolites (order Graptoloidea). In general terms they may be characterised by:

- rhabdosomes often forming spreading, multiple branched colonies which lack dissepiments
- the presence of bithecae in addition to autothecae.

Anisograptids are in many ways intermediate between the dendroids (in the possession of two thecal types) and the graptoloids (in possessing relatively few thecae).

Dichograptids belong to the suborder Dichograptida, and are broadly characterised by:

- rhabdosomes which have stipes arranged in multiples of two
- pendent, scandent and extended stipes
- simple thecae with simple apertures.

The stipes of dichograptids (Figures 14.2–14.4) may be scandent or pendent, arranged according to their position relative to the sicula. Stipes may be back-to-back; *Phyllograptus* has a leaf-like shape with four scandent stipes arranged back-to-back giving a cross-like section to the rhabdosome, for example (Figure 14.3). Classic dichograptids include *Didymograptus*, the pendent 'tuning-fork' graptolite; and *Tetragraptus*, with four stipes in several different orientations with different species (Figures 14.2 and 14.4).

Diplograptids belong to the suborder Diplograptida, and are characterised by:

- rhabdosomes with two scandent stipes
- complex thecae with a range of aperture types.

Stipes may be developed back-to-back (biserial) or, more rarely, separated (uniserial). In some cases they may be partially back-to-back and partially separated.

The complexity of the thecal apertures and the nature of the stipes distinguish these graptolites from most others (Figures 14.2 and 14.3).

Monograptids belong to the suborder Monograptida, the last of the true graptolites. Monograptids are characterised by:

- rhabdosomes consisting of a single, uniserial scandent stipe
- complex thecae with a range of thecal apertures.

The monograptids are for the most part characterised by their single stipe of relatively complex thecae. There is a great range of thecal types and aperture developments. Typical thecal types include lobate (rounded like a lobe), hooked, triangulate and isolate (widely separated and elongate) (Figures 14.2 and 14.4).

14.3 GRAPTOLITE EVOLUTION

The graptolites suffer as fossil entities because, for the most part, they are compressed and the level of detail contained within their poorly preserved rhabdosomes is relatively limited. However, a general pattern of the evolution of the graptolite rhabdosome, and in particular of its changes in relative complexity, can be determined. The dendroid graptolites were the first graptolites to appear and the last to become extinct (Figure 12.12). Their rhabdosome is complex and has the only real evidence of the stolon system characteristic of the Hemichordata. The earliest dendroids were probably attached to the substrate and acted as an open, cone-like network with its zooids filtering food particles. Some representatives have been found with what appear to be holdfasts to retain the graptolite in this position. However, it is probable that other dendroids were able to float, this time with the apex of the cone pointing upwards rather than downwards. The anisograptids, the first of the true graptolites, appeared in the lowest Ordovician (Tremadoc) and are in many ways intermediate between the dendroids and the graptoloids, particularly in the possession of a spreading rhabdosome with two types of thecae. The latest anisograptids show a reduction in the importance of the bithecae, with the succeeding dichograptids possessing only autothecae.

The dichograptids radiated in the Ordovician (Figure 12.12), during the Arenig, creating many forms with up to eight stipes grouped in multiples of two. Typically, these stipes can be scandent (e.g. *Phyllograptus*), pendent (e.g. *Didymograptus*) or intermediately directed. Several web- or vane-like features have been found associated with dichograptid rhabdosomes showing an efficient flotation mechanism. The dichograptids were replaced in the later Ordovician, in the Llanvirn, by the diplograptids, twin-stiped scandent forms which probably evolved from a two-stiped dichograptid ancestor. The diplograptids were replaced in the Silurian by the monograptids, single-stiped, scandent graptolites which display an increasing complexity in thecal form throughout their geological history. The monograptids were extinguished in the mid-Devonian.

14.4 GRAPTOLITE APPLICATIONS

14.4.1 Palaeobiology

Functional Morphology

The graptolites have long been a focus for functional morphological studies as palaeontologists have struggled to interpret the form and function of imperfectly preserved colonies through comparison with the living hemichordate, *Rhabdopleura*. In many cases this has proven difficult; most graptolites are preserved solely as compressions with very little chance of interpretation. However, in limestones in particular, graptolites are recoverable through acid digestion of the rock, leaving the organic skeleton of the colony intact. This has allowed a detailed examination of the graptolite skeleton and, in particular, of the structure of its periderm. Recent advances have determined that the two parts of the graptolite periderm were constructed at different phases: the inner fusellar layer created in the intial stages of thecal development, the outer cortical layer laid down by the actions of the zooids themselves systematically adding the bandage-like stuctures over the fusellar layer in order to reinforce it.

Although studies on well-preserved rhabdosomes have greatly reinforced our understanding of graptolite form and function, the mode of life of planktonic graptolites has been revealed by the use of life-sized model versions of their colonies. The models were constructed of materials which can replicate the density of graptolite colonies and were allowed to fall through a column of water in order to determine the pattern of their behaviour. These experiments demonstrated that the graptolite colony was not simply a passive floater, but descended in a spiral motion through the water column, although the mechanism for returning up through the water column could only be speculated at. Clearly the positioning of the zooids relative to the stipes would be of importance, each zooid sampling from its own immediate water space, the spiral motion providing the most efficient pattern for harvesting the water column (Figure 14.5). These experiments have demonstrated that selection of rhabdosome types was at least in part controlled by feeding strategy. These recent experiments go some way in supporting earlier studies on graptolite feeding patterns. These studies suggested that from benthonic, dendroid ancestors graptolites evolved the ability to be automobile, actively moving through the water column by the action of ciliary feeding, although still effectively being passive planktonic floaters. This hypothesis has been the source of an active and lively debate which has continued for over 25 years.

Evolution

Graptolites have proved of value in some evolutionary studies, particularly associated with the detailed evolution of the Silurian–Devonian monograptids. In some cases, this is primarily because the progressive growth (**astogeny**) of the colony, theca by theca, records heterochronic changes. For example, in the classic

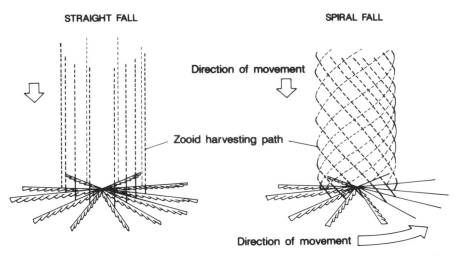

STRAIGHT FALL

SPIRAL FALL

Direction of movement

Zooid harvesting path

Direction of movement

Figure 14.5   *Two potential feeding patterns of the graptolite* Loganograptus *based on physical models. Spiral fall would represent a more efficient mechanism of zooidal feeding [Modified from: Rigby and Rickards (1989)* Paleobiology, **15**, *Fig. 4, p. 410]*

study of *Monograptus revolutus*, the final thecae added to the colony developed a simple shape very different from the preceding hooked form with apertural spines. The succeeding later representatives of the species *M. revolutus* are characterised by simple thecae, and an evolutionary relationship can be established whereby the development of simple thecae in late colony growth was selected as advantageous, eventually being passed to the descendant species. Graptolite studies have also contributed to the punctuated equilibrium debate. Recently, studies of *Monograptus hercynicus* have demonstrated the existence of stasis in colony form punctuated by rapid increase in sicula width, and are considered to be representative of the punctuational model of microevolution.

14.4.2 Palaeoenvironmental Analysis

Graptolites were for the most part planktonic colonial organisms of generally unlimited distribution (Table 14.1) and as such are of limited usefulness in benthic palaeoenvironmental analysis. In general, graptolites are most commonly associated with marine sediments of the outer shelf; and commonly, Lower Palaeozoic successions can be divided into inner, shelly facies and outer graptolitic muds. This has certainly been recognised in association with the depth-related brachiopod assemblages of the Ordovician and Silurian (Figure 10.12). In addition, it is possible to define 'inshore' and 'offshore' species of graptolites for various intervals of the early Palaeozoic. In general terms, it appears that the more robust species were commonest in shallower-water sediments. Although this could be a false impression given by the fact that only the strongest rhabdosomes could survive in the higher-energy inshore zone, these robust species, such as *Monograptus priodon, M. vomerinus* and *M. flemingii* in the Silurian, are uncommon in offshore muds.

Table 14.1 *Graptolite limiting factors*

Temperature	As planktonic organisms, graptolites may have tolerated a broad temperature range.
Oxygenation	Graptolites are commonly found in black shales, but as planktonic organisms they may have inhabited the upper, oxygenated levels of the water column.
Salinity	Graptolites probably inhabited normal marine waters.
Depth	As planktonic organisms, graptolites were not directly limited by water depth, although some taxa may have inhabited specific levels within the water column.
Substrate	Most graptolites were planktonic. Some dendroids may have been limited to firm sediments.
Turbulence	Graptolites probably lived in low-turbulence waters and would have been broken up in highly turbulent conditions.

Similar depth relationships can be recognised for other graptolite groups. In the early Ordovician, for instance, it is possible to recognise two broad graptolite assemblages associated with shallow- and deep-water facies. The didymograptid biofacies is recognised from both shallow- and deep-water facies, but the isograptid biofacies is recorded only from deep-water muds. This relationship suggests that these graptolite assemblages were living in different water masses. The didymograptids probably inhabited the uppermost part of the water column, and, as such, would be distributed across oceans in both shelf and basinal settings. The isograptids probably inhabited deeper waters beneath the didymograptids, with the two groups never substantially mingling. In this way the isograptids are rarely found in a shelf setting, except where major continental flooding through sea-level rise takes place. Clearly, the value of these depth studies is in the determination of continental flooding episodes, of transgressions, and of their subsequent regressive episodes. Another example is discussed in Chapter 22.

14.4.3 Stratigraphy

Graptolites have traditionally been considered to be one of the most important guide fossils in Lower Palaeozoic successions (Figure 14.6). Graptolites fulfil all the basic criteria of a good guide fossil: they are mostly planktonic and therefore widespread and independent of facies. This is not always the case, as some graptolites are unknown in the shallowest facies. However, the depth-related studies discussed above suggest that most graptolites lived in the upper part of the water column and were capable of being incorporated in both shelf and basinal facies. In addition, many graptolite species were fast-evolving and have the short stratigraphical ranges important for a guide fossil.

Although the graptolite skeleton is apparently relatively fragile, it was readily preserved and, as a consequence, graptolites are abundant. Most importantly, they are easy to recognise, perhaps surprisingly so, given the often unimpressive

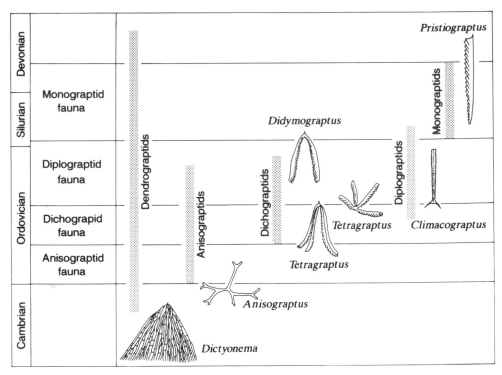

Figure 14.6 *The stratigraphical succession of graptolite faunas*

nature of the compressed and diagenetically replaced specimens most commonly found. However, even the most complex thecae can be broadly recognised in a compressed form, and this means that the subtle changes of some biozonation schemes can be determined in even the most deformed rock sequences. This is important in the correlation of Lower Palaeozoic sequences given their age and the increasing likelihood of tectonic activity with time. The use of graptolites in intercontinental correlation is further discussed in Chapter 23.

14.5 SUGGESTED READING

The details of graptolite taxonomy are given in the *Treatise on Invertebrate Paleontology* (Teichert, 1970). Readable overviews of the group are given by Berry (1987) and Clarkson (1993), with Palmer and Rickards (1991) representing a particularly well-written and well-illustrated account. Further illustrations of commonly occurring taxa are provided by Rickards (1985), and the stratigraphical ranges of the most important families are depicted in Rickards (1993). Graptolite functional morphology has recently received much attention; this is particularly well demonstrated by the papers by Rickards *et al.* (1982) on the structure of the graptolite periderm, and by the papers of Rigby and Rickards (1989) and Rigby (1991; 1992) on graptolite feeding. The case for graptolite automobility is summarised by Kirk (1969; 1990).

The classic evolutionary story of the development of various thecal types in the monograptids is given by Sudbury (1958), and an example of the contribution of graptolites to the punctuated equilibrium debate by Springer and Murphy (1994). The palaeoecology of graptolites is comprehensively reviewed by Rickards (1975). Other aspects of graptolite palaeoecology, including their value in depth studies and palaeobiogeography, are described by Finney (1986), Rickards *et al.* (1990), Cooper *et al.* (1991) and Underwood (1993). Finally, the use of graptolites as guide fossils is demonstrated in the classic papers by Lapworth (1878), in determining the structure of the Southern Uplands of Scotland; Elles and Wood (1922), in reviewing the most important graptolite guide fossils from Britain; and Bulman (1958), in describing the broad sequence of graptolite faunas. Fortey (1993) is a well-written essay which reaffirms the importance of Lapworth's work. Recent papers demonstrating the principles of graptolite biostratigraphy include Berry (1977), Berry and Wilde (1990) and Cooper and Lindholm (1990).

Berry, W.B.N. 1977. Graptolite biostratigraphy: a wedding of classical principles and current concepts. *In* Kauffman, E.G. & Hazel, J.E. (eds), *Concepts and Methods of Biostratigraphy*. Dowden, Hutchinson & Ross, Stroudsberg, PA, 321–338.

Berry, W.B.N. 1987. Phylum Hemichordata (including Graptolithina). *In* Boardman, R.S., Cheetham, A.H. & Rowell, A.J. (eds), *Fossil Invertebrates*. Blackwell Scientific Publications, Palo Alto, CA, 612–635.

Berry, W.B.N. & Wilde, P. 1990. Graptolite biogeography: implications for palaeogeography and palaeooceanography. *In* McKerrow, W.S. & Scotese, C.R. (eds), *Palaeozoic Palaeogeography and Biogeography*. Geological Society Memoir 12.

Bulman, O.M.B. 1958. The sequence of graptolite faunas. *Palaeontology*, **1**, 159–173.

Clarkson, E.N.K. 1993. *Invertebrate Palaeontology and Evolution*. Third edition. Chapman & Hall, London.

Cooper, R.A. & Lindholm, K. 1990. A precise worldwide correlation of early Ordovician graptolite sequences. *Geological Magazine*, **127**, 497–525.

Cooper, R.A., Fortey, R.A. & Lindholm, K. 1991. Latitudinal and depth zonation of early Ordovician graptolites. *Lethaia*, **24**, 199–218.

Elles, G.L. and Wood, E.M.R. 1922. *A Monograph of British Graptolites*. Monographs of the Palaeontographical Society, London.

Finney, S.C. 1986. Graptolite biofacies and correlation of eustatic, subsidence, and tectonic events in the Middle to Upper Ordovician of North America. *Palaios*, **1**, 435–461.

Fortey, R.A. 1993. Charles Lapworth and the biostratigraphic paradigm. *Journal of the Geological Society of London*, **150**, 209–218.

Kirk, N.H. 1969. Some thoughts on the ecology, mode of life and evolution of the Graptolithina. *Proceedings of the Geological Society of London*, **1659**, 273–292.

Kirk, N.H. 1990. Juvenile sessility, vertical automobility, and passive lateral transport as factors in graptoloid evolution. *Modern Geology*, **14**, 153–187.

Lapworth, C. 1878. The Moffat Series. *Quarterly Journal of the Geological Society of London*, **34**, 240–343.

Palmer, D. & Rickards, R.B. (eds) 1991. *Graptolites: Writing in the Rocks*. Boydell Press, London.

Rickards, R.B. 1975. Palaeoecology of the Graptolithina, an extinct class of the phylum Hemichordata. *Biological Reviews*, **50**, 397–436.

Rickards, R.B. 1985. Graptolithina. *In* Murray, J.W. (ed.), *Atlas of Invertebrate Macrofossils*. Longman, London, 191–198.

Rickards, R.B. 1993. Graptolithina. *In* Benton, M.J. (ed.), *The Fossil Record 2*. Chapman & Hall, London, 537–542.

Rickards, R.B., Crowther, P.R. & Chapman, A.J. 1982. Ultrastructural studies of graptolites – a review. *Geological Magazine*, **119**, 355–370.

Rickards, R.B., Rigby, S. & Harris, J.H. 1990. Graptoloid biogeography: recent progress, future hopes, in Palaeozoic palaeogeography and biogeography. *In* McKerrow, W.S. & Scotese, C.R. (eds), *Palaeozoic Palaeogeography and Biogeography*. Geological Society Memoir 12.

Rigby, S. 1991. Feeding strategies in graptoloids. *Palaeontology*, **34**, 797–814.

Rigby, S. 1992. Graptoloid feeding efficiency, rotation and astogeny. *Lethaia*, **25**, 51–69.

Rigby, S. & Rickards, R.B. 1989. New evidence for the life habit of graptoloids from physical modelling. *Paleobiology*, **15**, 402–413.

Springer, K.B. & Murphy, M.A. 1994. Punctuated stasis and collateral evolution in the Devonian lineage of *Monograptus hercynicus*. *Lethaia*, **27**, 119–128.

Sudbury, M. 1958. Triangulate monograptids from the *Monograptus gregarius* zone (Lower Llandovery) of the Rheidol Gorge (Cardiganshire). *Philosophical Transactions of the Royal Society, B*, **241**, 485–555.

Teichert, C. (ed.) 1970. *Treatise on Invertebrate Paleontology, Part V, Graptolithina (revised)*. Geological Society of America and University of Kansas Press, Lawrence, KS.

Underwood, C.J. 1993. The position of graptolites within Lower Palaeozoic planktic ecosystems. *Lethaia*, **26**, 189–202.

15
Bryozoans

15.1 BRYOZOAN TAXONOMY

Bryozoans are aquatic, colonial organisms which consist of numerous individuals most commonly housed within a calcareous skeleton. The majority of bryozoans are marine, although some rarer brackish-water and freshwater forms are also known. Bryozoans have a long geological record which extends back to the Ordovician, and are an important component of both the Palaeozoic and Modern evolutionary faunas. Bryozoans are important palaeoenvironmental indicators, but despite their relative abundance in the fossil record, they have often been overlooked.

15.1.1 General Characteristics of Bryozoans

Bryozoans represent the only animal phylum to be completely developed in a colonial habit. Cnidarians (corals and sea anemones) as well as hemichordates all have individual as well as colonial organisms contained within their phyla. Rugose and scleractinian corals, for example, are commonly developed in both colonial and solitary form (Chapter 13). Bryozoans are common elements of the shallow marine fauna, and although some bryozoans construct a non-calcareous skeleton, the majority secrete a calcareous skeleton (the **zoarium**) which in its simplest form comprises a series of simple compartments (the **zooecia**) which encompass the **zooids** (Figure 15.1). Each compartment contains the fluid-filled body cavity and the retractable, food-gathering arms of the zooid. Bryozoans are thought to be closely related to brachiopods, as, like them, each zooid has a complex food-gathering **lophophore**. The lophophore in bryozoans consists of a series of ten retractable tentacles armed with beating cilia which gather the food particles from the water column and pass them to the body cavity and mouth

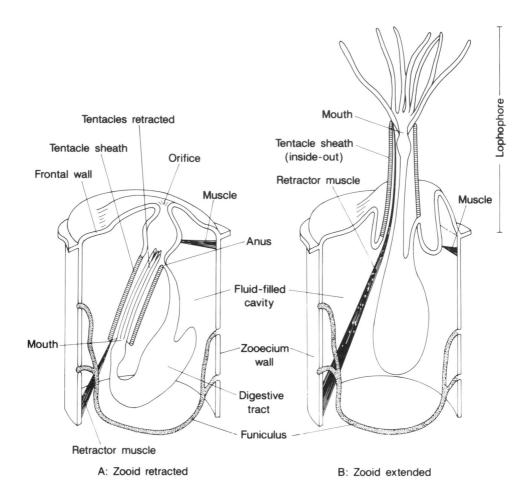

Figure 15.1   *General characteristics of a living bryozoan [Modified from: Boardman and Cheetham (1987)* In *Boardman* et al. *(Eds)* Fossil Invertebrates, *Blackwells, Fig. 17.2, p. 501]*

(Figure 15.1). Each zooid is interconnected in the colony by a stolon-type organ known as the **funiculus**.

Bryozoan colonies are highly variable in shape and form, and many of the major groups may develop each of the four major types (encrusting, erect, massive and free-living) of colony form. Most commonly, however, bryozoan colonies are developed as **encrusters**, forming mats or branched stem colonies attached to a hard rocky substrate, or, commonly, a discarded bivalve or other shell; or as **erect** colonies, forming branched, stick-like forms (Figure 15.2). Erect bryozoan colonies are most often confused with other calcareous colonial species, such as the corals. However, they may be distinguished by their lack of the complex internal calcareous structure of septa, tabulae and dissepiments which is encountered in the coral skeleton.

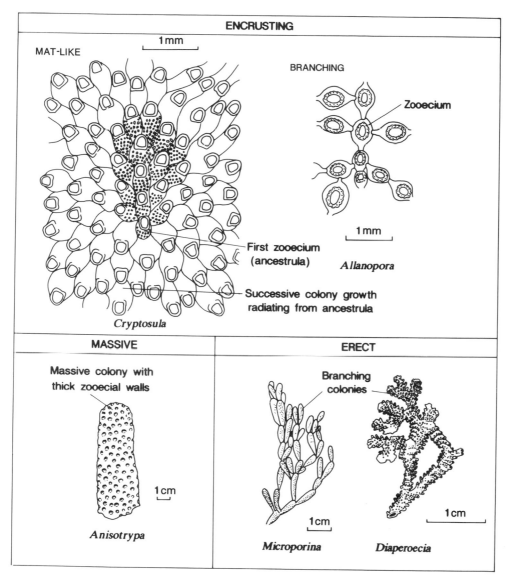

ENCRUSTING

MAT-LIKE

1mm

BRANCHING

Zooecium

First zooecium
(ancestrula)

Allanopora

Successive colony growth
radiating from ancestrula

Cryptosula

MASSIVE

Massive colony with
thick zooecial walls

1cm

Anisotrypa

ERECT

Branching
colonies

1cm

Microporina

1cm

Diaperoecia

Figure 15.2 *Typical colony form in living and fossil bryozoans*

15.1.2 Bryozoan Classification

Bryozoans were originally classified with the corals in the phylum Cnidaria (Chapter 13) because of their colonial habit. However, they were recognised as a complex and distinct animal phylum in the early nineteenth century. Bryozoans are classified on the nature of their shell structure and chemistry, and on the form of the zooecia, the compartments which contain the zooids.

Phylum Bryozoa Ehrenberg, 1831
(also called Polyzoa and Ectoprocta)

Class Stenolaemata Borg, 1920 (Ordovician–Recent)
Marine bryozoans with a calcareous skeleton. Skeleton has cylindrical, tube-like zooids at an angle to the direction of growth.

Class Gymnolaemata Allman, 1869 (Ordovician–Recent)
Mainly marine but sometimes brackish or freshwater bryozoans with a calcareous skeleton. Box-like or cylindrical zooids aligned in direction of growth and connected by funicular network.

Class Phylactolaemata Allman, 1856 (Cretaceous–Recent)
Freshwater bryozoans with a non-calcareous skeleton.

15.2 BRYOZOAN MORPHOLOGY

The calcareous skeleton (**zoarium**) which comprises most bryozoans is composed of a series of interconnected tubes or boxes (the **zooecia**) which contain the zooids (Figure 15.1). Each zooid forms part of the whole colonial organism. Each **zooecium** has an opening or **orifice** through which the zooid can extrude when feeding, and retract when resting (Figure 15.1). In more complex forms, the orifice may be closed off by a calcareous lid or **operculum**. Each zooecium is generally small, rarely more than 1 mm in average length. The walls of the zooecium are complex, and are important in defining the characteristics of individual bryozoan groups. Some bryozoans have special chambers (**brood chambers**) which contained the fertilised eggs until ready to hatch. These eggs, the product of sexual reproduction, are hatched into free-floating larvae which settle and develop into the first formed member of the colony, the **ancestrula**, and the later colony members develop from this pioneer through asexual budding.

Bryozoans are complex, and colony shape varies widely, even within the three classes. Typically though, bryozoan colonies fall into four colony types: **encrusting**, consisting of a single layer of zooecia in contact with the substrate; **massive**, consisting of multi-layered, nodular masses of zooecia; **erect**, consisting of branched colonies with an encrusting base; and **free-living**, forming an erect colony without firm attachment or anchorage (Figure 15.2). Marine bryozoans are usually found as encrusting, massive and erect colonies.

The most commonly encountered bryozoans in the fossil record are members of the marine classes Stenolaemata and Gymnolaemata. The general characteristics of the most important groups are given below, and illustrated in Figures 15.3 and 15.4.

1. *Stenolaemate* bryozoans possess elongate, tube-like zooecia (Figure 15.3). The class includes three bryozoan groups. *Cyclostomes* (order Cyclostomata, Ordovician–Recent), can be recognised by their:

- erect or encrusting colonies
- tubular zooecia with circular apertures.

Cyclostomes are a common component of shallow marine fossil assemblages and consist of simple branching encrusters or more complex 'mats' which grow concentrically from the first formed zooid. They are distinguished from other encrusting bryozoans by the simplicity of their zooecial structure.

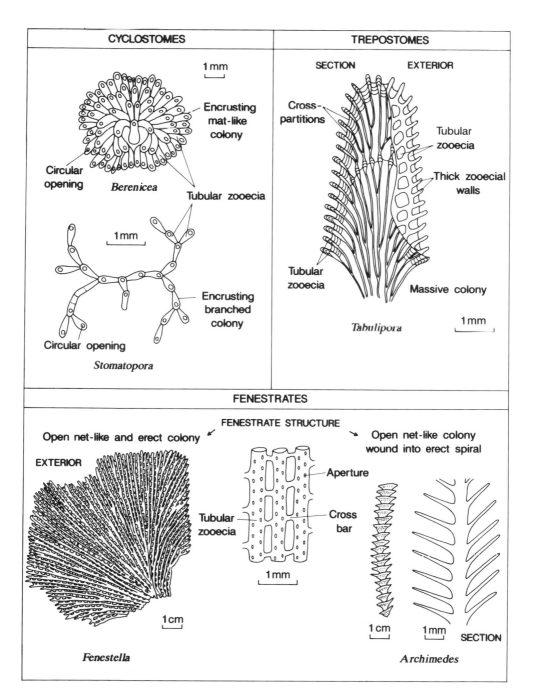

Figure 15.3 *Morphology of typical stenolaemate bryozoans. The cyclostomes are Mesozoic in age, while the trepostomes and fenestrates are Palaeozoic*

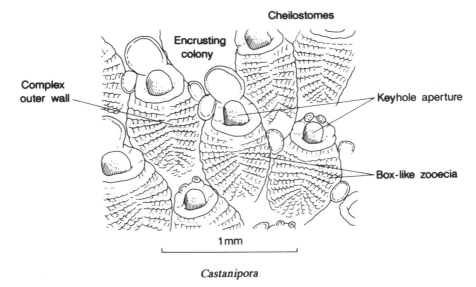

Figure 15.4   *Morphology of a typical gymnolaemate bryozoan from the Cenozoic*

Trepostomes (order Trepostomata, Ordovician–Permian), are broadly characterised by their:
- massive, coral-like colonies
- closely packed, tubular zooecia with cross-partitions, and often with smaller
  apertures between the larger ones.

Trepostomes have massive skeletons made up of a complex network of zooecia,
and are often referred to as 'stony' bryozoans because of it. They are sometimes
confused with tabulate coral colonies. However, they are distinguished by the
detail of their tubular zooecia, which are unlike the tabulate and corallite wall of
the corals.

Fenestrates (order Fenestrata, Ordovician–Permian), can be broadly characterised by their:
- erect, open, mesh-like colonies
- tubular zooecia arranged in branches with regularly spaced cross-bars.

Fenestrate bryozoans are an important component of the Palaeozoic shallow marine fauna, and are common in reef environments. They are readily recognised by
their open, net-like structure of regularly spaced tubular zooecia with intervening
cross-bars that give the colony its 'fenestrate' form, resembling regularly spaced
windows. These formed erect cone-like nets in life, as in the genus *Fenestella*, or
wound into a screw form, as in the aptly named *Archimedes*, named after the
simple helical screw of the same name.

2. *Gymnolaemate* bryozoans possess box-like zooecia (Figure 15.4). The most
important are the *cheilostomes* (order Cheilostomata, Ordovician-Recent), broadly
characterised by:
- commonly encrusting, but also erect colonies
- short, box-like zooecia with keyhole orifices and opercula

- a complex outer wall to the zooecium.

Cheilostomes are a common component of a range of shallow marine faunas, particularly from the Mesozoic to Recent interval. They have a strongly calcified skeleton with a complex, often encrusting habit. Cheilostomes often have brood chambers which contained fertilised eggs.

15.3 BRYOZOAN EVOLUTION

Bryozoans first appeared in the early Ordovician (Figure 15.5). The first group to appear was the Stenolaemata, which quickly diversified to become the dominant Palaeozoic bryozoans. The stenolaemates colonised a wide range of shallow marine habitats, including reefs. The fenestrate bryozoans in paticular are a common component of marine faunas in the Palaeozoic. The stenolaemates survived the end-Ordovician extinctions, but only one group, the cyclostomes, survived the end-Permian extinction, radiating in the Triassic to become the dominant group throughout the Mesozoic.

The fortunes of the Stenolaemata, and of the cyclostomes, changed following a great reduction in their abundance at the end of the Cretaceous. The cyclostomes were largely extinguished, and were replaced by the calcified Gymnolaemata, which radiated to fill most of the available habitat space vacated by the cyclostomes (Figure 15.5). Gymnolaemates remain the dominant bryozoans in modern seas.

15.4 BRYOZOAN APPLICATIONS

15.4.1 Palaeobiology

Functional Morphology

Functional morphology studies of bryozoans have proved inviting because of their colonial habit. The study of colonial groups brings added problems as they cannot simply be viewed as an amalgamation of individuals. In some cases, in both bryozoans and corals, there is differentiation between individuals as some take on certain specialised tasks. Detailed study of individuals in different areas of the colony is necessary to ascertain what morphological adaptations this involves.

As an example of functional studies, the morphology of fenestrate bryozoans has long interested palaeontologists because of their open network of zooecia with adjoining cross-bars. Functional studies have determined that the mesh created by the fenestrate skeleton improved feeding by filtering out food particles as currents of water passed through the fenestrae. This would provide an efficient feeding mechanism for the zooids, and would explain the success of this body plan in the Palaeozoic.

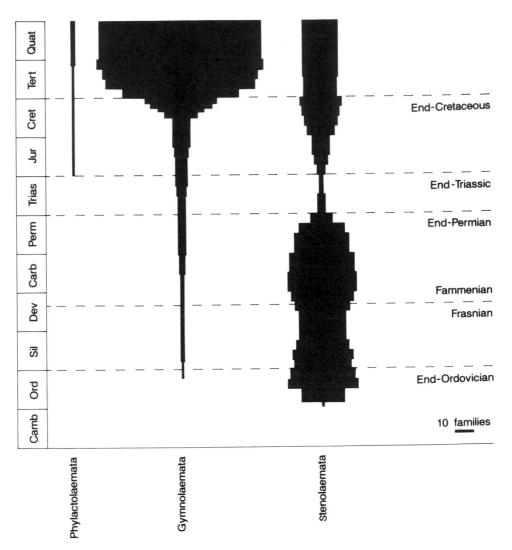

Figure 15.5 *The diversity of bryozoan families through geological time. The main extinction events are indicated [Compiled by A.L. Holder from: Benton (1993)* The Fossil Record 2, *Chapman & Hall]*

Evolutionary Studies

Recent studies on the morphological changes observable in the cheilostome bryozoan *Metrarabdotos* have proven to be of great value in the determination of stasis and punctuational events in the geological record. A discussion of the evolutionary implications of these studies is given in Chapter 21.

15.4.2 Palaeoenvironmental Analysis

There are four main controls on the distribution of bryozoans: temperature, salinity, wave energy, and substrate (Table 15.1). Although bryozoans have a broad temperature tolerance, the majority of bryozoan species are limited to a narrow range, and many are particularly associated with warm temperatures. Most bryozoans are fully marine, requiring normal salinity (around $36^o/_{oo}$) for optimum living conditions. This means that any significant drop in salinity levels will result in a corresponding drop in bryozoan diversity and density. Wave energy is an important limiting factor given the fragile nature of many bryozoan skeletons. Most species, therefore, live below the wave base or in quiet, shallow-water environments. In addition, substrate exerts a stong control on bryozoan diversity and distribution, in that a hard substrate (even if very small) is necessary as a point of attachment for most species. These four factors make bryozoans valuable as indicators of palaeoenvironments, in particular temperature and salinity (Figure 15.6). However, as it is clear that some bryzoans are at home in brackish and freshwater environments, detailed application of uniformitarian principles is necessary in any palaeoenvironmental interpretation.

Table 15.1 *Bryozoan limiting factors*

Temperature	Bryozoans have a broad temperature range, and are found from Equatorial to polar regions.
Oxygenation	Bryozoans are mostly limited to normal, oxygenated waters.
Salinity	Bryozoans live in a range of salinities from fresh water to hypersaline. Freshwater bryozoans belong solely to the class Phylactolaemata, which has an extremely limited fossil record. Most marine bryozoans are restricted to normal marine salinities of around $36^o/_{oo}$, with a sharp diversity decline in brackish waters.
Depth	Bryozoans have a large depth range, from intertidal to abyssal depths of over 8000 m. However, bryozoans are most abundant and diverse in depths of 20–80 m.
Substrate	Most bryozoans require a firm substrate.
Turbulence	Bryozoans are adapted to a range of water turbulence levels.

The range of life habits adopted by bryozoans is also specifically associated with environments, as certain morphologies are better suited to certain conditions. For example, the rare free-living forms are most commonly found on moving sand. Encrusting forms are the most robust, and are common elements of shallow-water faunas. Erect bryozoans have an advantage of presenting a greater surface area to food-laden currents, but may suffer breakage in stronger currents. Fragile forms tend to be restricted to quiet, shallow-water conditions, while more heavily calcified, erect forms can be found in higher-energy environments. Deep waters can also support bryozoan populations. Although the fine sediment characteristic of the sea-floor sediments at depths greater than 1000 m restricts

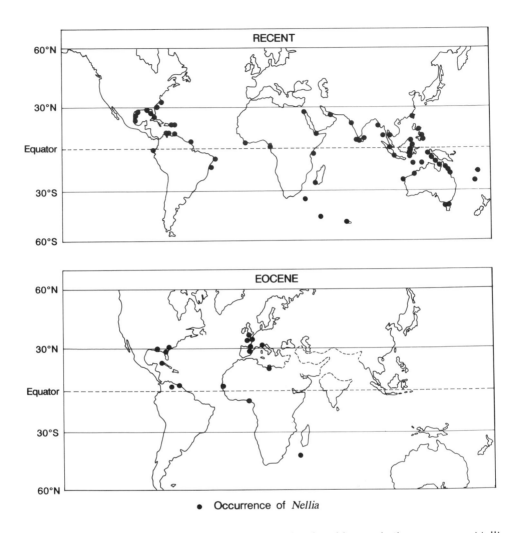

Figure 15.6   *The geographical distribution of the fossil and living cheilostome genus* Nellia. *This genus is largely restricted to the warm waters which straddle the Equator [Modified from: Boardman and Cheetham (1987)* In *Boardman et al. (Eds)* Fossil Invertebrates, *Blackwells, Fig. 17.50, p. 544]*

encrusting and erect forms, this is the preferred habitat of those rare species which can root into sediment for support.

Bryozoans have been important contributors to reefs through time. They were significant frame-builders in early Palaeozoic reefs. Fenestrate bryozoans, in particular, were common members of Palaeozoic reefs. Following the end-Permian extinction, they were less important reef components, but may still frequently be found as part of the fauna, often acting as sediment-binders enabling the creation of build-ups.

15.4.3 Stratigraphy

Bryozoans are fundamentally facies fossils, restricted to particular environments by their mode of attachment and growth. Although some could attach to floating large plankton or driftwood, for example, this restriction severely limits their value as guide fossils. This is compounded by the fact that many bryozoan species, especially Palaeozoic ones, are very long-ranging. However, in some facies, particularly shelf carbonates, they may be abundant, readily preserved and easily recognised, which means they could be of value in local correlations.

15.5 SUGGESTED READING

The *Treatise on Invertebrate Paleontology* (Robison, 1953) remains the invaluable reference work on the taxonomy of the phylum, while more accessible overviews are given by Boardman and Cheetham (1987) and Clarkson (1993). The edited volumes by Larwood (1973) and Larwood and Neilson (1981) provide many important papers on the group. Taylor (1985) illustrates many of the common taxa. Aspects of the functional morphology of certain groups of bryozoans are given by Cowen and Rider (1972) and Boardman and McKinney (1976). Smith (1995) comprehensively reviews the application of bryozoans in palaeoenvironmental analysis. An overview of bryozoan evolution is given by Schopf (1977) and McKinney and Jackson (1989).

Boardman, R.S. & Cheetham, A.H. 1987. Phylum Bryozoa. *In* Boardman, R.S., Cheetham, A.H. & Rowell, A.J. (eds), *Fossil Invertebrates*. Blackwell Scientific Publications, Palo Alto, CA, 497–549.

Boardman, R.S. & McKinney, F.K. 1976. Skeletal architecture and preserved organs of four-sided zooids in convergent genera of Palaeozoic Trepostomata (Bryozoa). *Journal of Paleontology*, **50**, 25–78.

Clarkson, E.N.K. 1993. *Invertebrate Palaeontology and Evolution*. Third Edition. Chapman & Hall, London.

Cowen, R. & Rider, J. 1972. Functional analysis of fenestellid bryozoan colonies. *Lethaia*, **5**, 147–164.

McKinney, F. K. & Jackson, J. 1989. *Bryozoan Evolution*. Unwin Hyman, London.

Larwood, G.P. (ed.) 1973. *Living and Fossil Bryozoans*. Academic Press, London.

Larwood, G.P. & Neilson, C. (eds) 1981. *Recent and Fossil Bryozoans*. Olsen and Olsen, Fredensborg.

Robison, R.A. (ed.) 1953. *Treatise on Invertebrate Palaeontology, Part G, Bryozoa*. Second Edition. Geological Society of America and University of Kansas Press, Lawrence, KS.

Schopf, T.J.M. 1977. Patterns of evolution in the Bryozoa. *In* Hallam, A. (ed.), *Patterns of Evolution as Demonstrated by the Fossil Record*. Elsevier, Amsterdam, 159–207.

Smith, A.M. 1995. Palaeoenvironmental interpretation using bryozoans: a review. *In* Bosence, D.W.J. & Allison, P.A. (eds), *Marine Palaeoenvironmental Analysis from Fossils*. Geological Society Special Publication 83, London, 231–244.

Taylor, P.D. 1985. Bryozoa. *In* Murray, J.W. (ed.), *Atlas of Invertebrate Macrofossils*. Longman, London, 47–52.

16
Microfossils: Foraminifera

16.1 FORAMINIFERAL TAXONOMY

Foraminifera are mostly microscopic, single-celled aquatic organisms which have a protective shell enclosing the soft body. Foraminifera are important elements of the Palaeozoic and Modern or Mesozoic–Cenozoic faunas. The majority are marine or marginal marine, but rare freshwater forms do occur. Benthonic foraminifera have a long geological history which extends back to the Cambrian. They are particularly useful in palaeoenvironmental analysis, but can also be of use in stratigraphical studies. Planktonic foraminifera evolved in the Mesozoic and are particularly important as guide fossils.

16.1.1 General Characteristics of Foraminifera

Foraminifera are small single-celled animals belonging to the phylum Protozoa. They are mostly microscopic in size, usually with a maximum length of less than 0.5 m, but examples are known with lengths of up to 100 mm. A microscope is therefore necessary to study the morphology of foraminifera and to carry out identifications; because of this they are included in an informal grouping of invertebrate fossils known as the **microfossils**, and their study forms part of micropalaeontology. Fossil groups included in micropalaeontology cover a wide range of taxa and include both plant remains, such as diatoms and calcareous algae, and animal remains, such as ostracods (Chapter 17) and radiolaria.

Foraminifera are made up of two basic units: the cell itself, consisting of the soft **cytoplasm** (a jellylike substance) which contains all the functional parts of the cell including the nucleus; and the shell or **test**, which can be very variable in form and construction (Figure 16.1). Although apparently simple, the single cell of foraminifera can carry out all the many functions necessary for life and

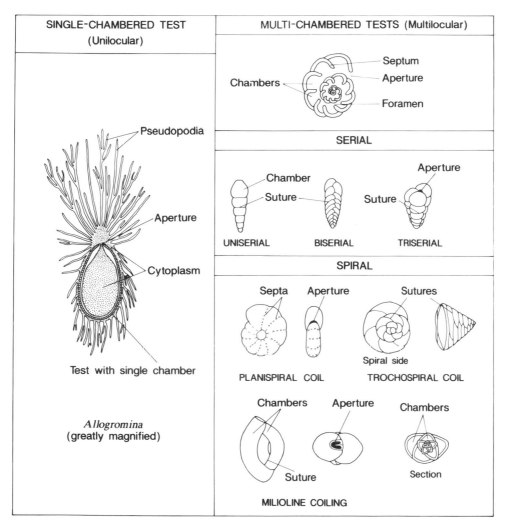

Figure 16.1 *Morphology of typical foraminiferal tests, greatly magnified. The living genus* Allogromina *is shown, together with its cytoplasm and pseudopodia [Modified from: Buzas et al. (1987) In Boardman et al. (Eds) Fossil Invertebrates, Blackwells, Figs 8.10 and 8.12, pp. 73 and 74]*

reproduction; functions normally carried out by many different cells in meta-zoans. In fossils, it is only the test which is commonly found preserved. The test can be flexible and made from organic compounds, or hard with a variable mineral composition.

Foraminifera are variable in life habit. All are aquatic, and different taxa inhabit a full range of marine and marginal marine environments, while a few species have been recorded from fresh water. The majority are benthonic, and most are free-moving, but a few live permanently cemented to hard substrates. Present-day free-moving forms have been found on many sedimentary substrates, as well as on plant material such as seaweed fronds, and occasionally from within the sediment itself. Benthonic foraminifera can use extensions of the cytoplasm called **pseudopodia** (literally meaning 'false feet') as a temporary means of attachment to the substrate (Figure 16.1). Relatively few foraminifera have adopted a planktonic mode of life. They are exclusively marine and float in the· surface waters of oceans, but may occur in vast numbers, and often contribute to ocean sediments, creating what are termed globigerinid oozes – limestones composed of planktonic foraminifera.

16.1.2 Foraminiferal Classification

Foraminifera comprise a single order of the phylum Protozoa, which includes the majority of single-celled organisms. Although the order Foraminiferida is defined on aspects of the soft parts, its further subdivision is based on the nature of the test. Of primary importance is test composition, and this forms the basis of the suborders listed below. Features used in the definition of superfamilies and lesser taxonomic categories include life habit; chamber number, shape and arrangement; aperture and other accessory structures. Only the more common and/or evolutionary important suborders are listed here.

Phylum Protozoa
Order Foraminiferida Eichwald, 1830 (Cambrian–Recent)
Single-celled organisms with a fine, complex network of pseudopodia (extrusions of the cytoplasm).

Suborder Allogromiina Loeblich and Tappan, 1961 (Cambrian–Recent)
Benthonic foraminifera with a single-chambered organic (membranous or proteinaceous) test.

Suborder Textulariina Delage and Herouard, 1896 (Cambrian–Recent)
Benthonic foraminifera with an agglutinated (sometimes referred to as arenaceous) test constructed of grains gathered from the host sediment and cemented together.

Suborder Fusulinina Wedekind, 1937 (Silurian–Permian)
Benthonic foraminifera with a microgranular test sometimes differentiated into two or more layers.

Suborder Miliolina Delage and Herouard, 1896 (Carboniferous–Recent)
Benthonic foraminifera with a milky-white (porcellaneous) test of high-magnesium calcite.

Suborder Rotaliina Delage and Herouard, 1896 (Triassic–Recent)
Benthonic foraminifera with a perforated test composed of multiple layers of glassy (hyaline) calcite in which the calcite crytals are either perpendicular to the test surface (radiate) or randomly orientated (granular).

Suborder Globigerinina Delage and Herouard, 1896 (Jurassic–Recent)
Planktonic foraminifera with a perforated two-layered (bilamellar) test of radiate glassy calcite.

16.2 FORAMINIFERAL MORPHOLOGY

The simplest foraminiferal test consists of an undivided chamber with a single simple opening or **aperture** to the exterior. This is described as a **unilocular** (one-chambered) test (Figure 16.1). **Multilocular** tests are made up of two or more chambers which are separated by partitions or **septa** (singular: **septum**), similar to those found in cephalopods (Chapter 9), but not used as buoyancy aids. The aperture is generally preserved internally as a **foramen** (plural: **foramina**) penetrating each septum and offering a means of communication between chambers (Figure 16.1). The first formed chamber is called the **proloculus**, and each chamber represents a growth stage. The number of chambers is highly variable.

Individual chambers can occur in a variety of shapes (e.g. spherical, tubular) and can be arranged in many ways. The two basic patterns are **serial**, like a string of beads, and **spiral**, like a coil of rope (Figure 16.1). Serial forms can be made more complex by the addition of a second (**biserial**) or third (**triserial**) series of chambers. Spiral forms may coil in a single plane (**planispiral**) or in a helical spiral (**trochospiral**) (Figure 16.1).

The test wall can be constructed in a number of ways (Figure 16.2). It is important as it offers support and protection to the soft parts. The simplest is a flexible **membraneous** wall which is secreted by the animal and consists of protein and sugar compounds. This simple structure is present in all foraminifera as a basal layer. **Agglutinated** or arenaceous walls are rigid and are constructed of sedimentary particles bound with a calcareous or ferruginous cement secreted by the organism (Figure 16.2). All other wall types are secreted and the majority are composed of calcite, although aragonite and opaline silica are also found. Calcitic walls are of three main types (Figure 16.2). Firstly, **microgranular** walls are constructed of one or more layers of small, equidimensional calcite grains which may be arranged randomly or at right angles to the surface, and therefore appear fibrous. Secondly, **porcellaneous** walls are constructed of three layers of calcite crystals arranged in such a way as to give the wall a milky, opaque appearance. Thirdly, **hyaline** walls have multiple perforations and appear translucent and glassy.

Two major foraminiferal groups may be recognised based on wall structure: **arenaceous** foraminifera and **calcareous** foraminifera. Both groups may be characterised as follows:

1. *Arenaceous* foraminifera (suborder Textulariina, Cambrian–Recent) have variable test morphology but are characterised by:
   - a test wall composed of arenaceous (sand) grains
   - an entirely benthonic mode of life.

The test wall of arenaceous foraminifera is sandy in appearance (Figure 16.3); any perforations that are present are very indistinct, so it appears solid. Arenaceous foraminifera can be of any shape or size, and can be quite complex. They have the widest geographical distribution of any foraminiferal group. This is because those with a ferruginous cement can survive below the carbonate compensation depth (a set depth in the deep ocean below which calcium carbonate dissolves), and they

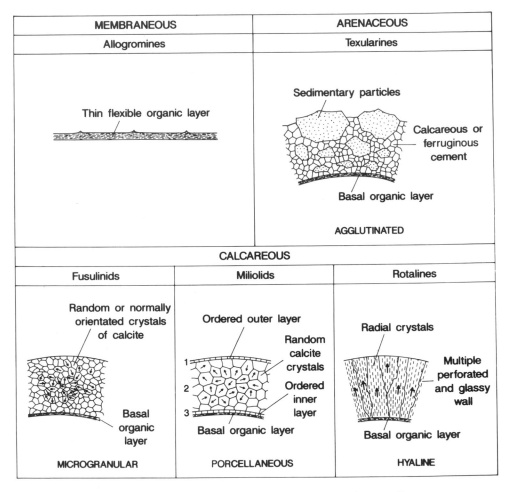

MEMBRANEOUS	ARENACEOUS
Allogromines	Texularines

Thin flexible organic layer

Sedimentary particles

Calcareous or ferruginous cement

Basal organic layer

AGGLUTINATED

CALCAREOUS		
Fusulinids	Miliolids	Rotalines

Random or normally orientated crystals of calcite

Basal organic layer

MICROGRANULAR

Ordered outer layer

Random calcite crystals

Ordered inner layer

Basal organic layer

PORCELLANEOUS

Radial crystals

Multiple perforated and glassy wall

Basal organic layer

HYALINE

Figure 16.2 *The structure of the foraminiferal test wall*

can therefore live in the deepest parts of the oceans, as well as in all other marine and marginal marine environments.

2. *Calcareous* foraminifera all have a secreted, rigid wall of calcium carbonate (Figure 16.3). The exact structure of this wall characterises the major groups.

Fusulinids (suborder Fusulinina, Silurian–Permian) possess:
- walls with a granular, sugary appearance
- larger examples which are commonly planispirally coiled and have a characteristic 'rugby-ball' shape
- an entirely benthonic mode of life.

Fusulinids are generally large and oval in shape. The wall appears very fine-grained and the apertures are often indistinct. Fusulinids may also have perforations in their test wall.

Miliolids (suborder Miliolina, Carboniferous–Recent) can be recognised by their:
- porcellaneous milky-white appearance

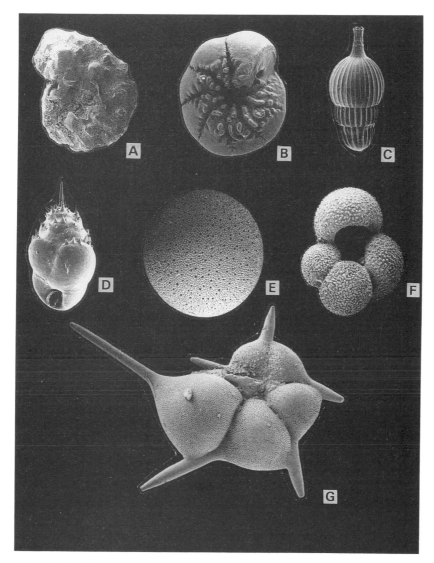

Figure 16.3 *Typical foraminifera.* **A:** *A Recent textularine,* Discammina, × 75. **B:** *A Pliocene rotaline,* Ammonia, × 75. **C:** *A Recent rotaline,* Amphicorna, × 75. **D:** *A Recent rotaline,* Bulminia, × 75. **E:** *A Recent globigerinid,* Orbulina, × 75. **F:** *A Pliocene globigerinid,* Globerigeroides, × 75. **G:** *An Eocene rotaline,* Hantkenina, × 120 *[Photographs: F.M.D. Lowry]*

- complex 'milioline' coiling
- entirely benthonic mode of life.

Miliolids have a pearly white wall which appears to be solid, with generally no perforations. Most miliolids are characterised by milioline coiling which consists of long, sausage-shaped chambers coiled with a constant angle between them (Figure 16.1). There are two main miliolid types. The first are the small, simpler forms with clear milioline coiling. These forms tend to have a single distinct aperture with a tooth attachment. The second group are the large oval forms superficially similar to fusulinids, with apertures which are small and indistinct.

Rotalines (suborder Rotaliina, Triassic–Recent) are very variable in form, but are characterised by:
- a hyaline or 'glassy' appearance
- a perforated wall
- an entirely benthonic mode of life.

The rotalines are the most diverse group of the foraminifera, and are mainly distinguished by their perforated, glassy wall. In all other obvious features, such as size and shape, they exhibit a high degree of variability.

Globigerinids (suborder Globigerinina, Jurassic–Recent) are broadly similar to rotalines in wall structure and are characterised by:
- a hyaline wall structure
- a perforated wall
- a multilocular test
- chambers which are commonly spirally coiled
- the presence of multiple apertures
- an entirely planktonic mode of life.

This group may be difficult to distinguish from the benthonic rotalines as their wall structure is similar. Many do exhibit features adapted to their planktonic mode of life, however. Frequently the chambers are bulbous and inflated, the perforations in the wall are distinct, and the apertures are large and may be numerous. Most globigerinids are either trochospiral or planispiral; serial forms are relatively rare.

16.3 FORAMINIFERAL EVOLUTION

The earliest reliable records of foraminifera are from the early Cambrian; Precambrian examples have been claimed, but these are generally poorly preserved fossils in thin section or the residues from acid-treated preparations. The earliest forms were allogromids with simple membraneous tests. The first hard-walled foraminifera appeared in the Cambrian with the addition of a simple arenaceous coating: the early textulariids (Figure 16.4). However, the early fossil record of foraminifera remains poor until the Devonian with the appearance of the first calcareous tests; these were the fusulines which may have evolved from allogromids in the Silurian, and which dominated the Palaeozoic until they disappeared in the end-Permian extinction (Figure 16.4).

Shortly after their first appearance, the fusulines gave rise to the first foraminifera with a simple calcitic hyaline wall. These became dominant after the demise of the fusulines, and the Triassic saw a major radiation, with the appearance of many of the major benthonic groups (Figure 16.4). By the Cretaceous, the rotalines were the most important foraminifera in shelf settings. It is believed that they evolved from a relatively minor group of aragonitic foraminifera, the robertinids, which also gave rise to the only group to adopt a planktonic mode of life, the globigerinids. The multilamellar, hyaline test of both of these groups is advantageous to the organism as it is strong and yet allows light

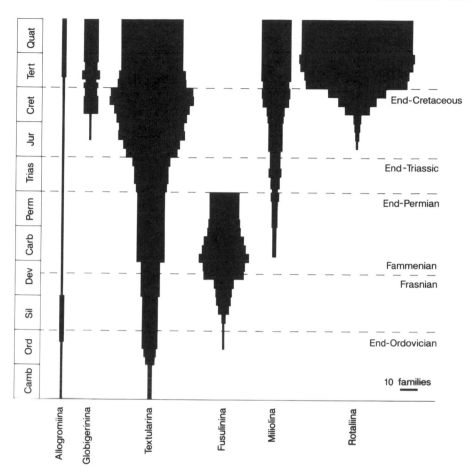

Figure 16.4 *The diversity of foraminiferal families through geological time. The main extinction events are indicated [Compiled by A.L. Holder from: Benton (1993) The Fossil Record 2, Chapman & Hall]*

to pass easily to the interior of the test. Right up to the present day rotalines remain the dominant benthonic foraminiferal group, with the globigerinids the sole planktonic group. However, the end-Cretaceous extinction event had a dramatic effect on the planktonic foraminifera. The diverse Cretaceous assemblage was wiped out, with the exception of a few minor genera, but was able to recover in an adaptive radiation in the early Palaeogene (Figure 16.4).

16.4 APPLICATIONS

16.4.1 Palaeobiology

Foraminifera have long been of importance in evolutionary studies. The record of evolutionary change of planktonic foraminifera in the expanded deep-sea

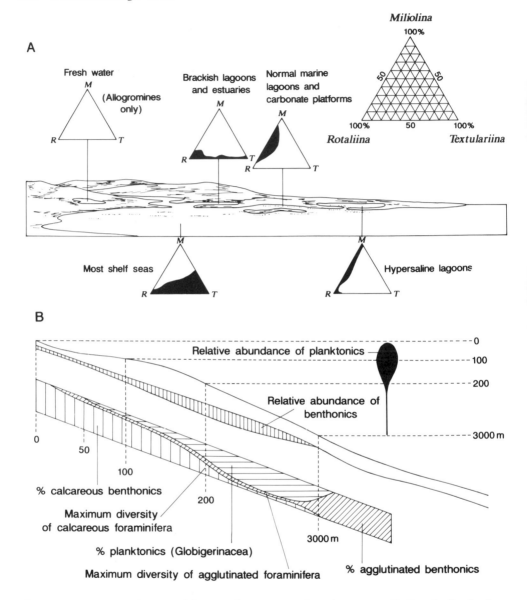

Figure 16.5 *A: Distribution of foraminifera in typical environments. B: Depth distribution [Modified from: Brasier (1980)* Microfossils, *Chapman & Hall, Fig. 13.10, p. 101]*

sequences offers an excellent opportunity to test evolutionary models (Figure 4.8). For example, detailed studies of Cretaceous genera such as *Rotalipora* and *Ticinella* have demonstrated change in a number of separate morphological characteristics. The development of a keel, a thickened ridge around the periphery of the test, appears to have played an important role in positioning the animal in the water column. Changes in the aperture are also documented, and clearly, as the primary connection between the interior and exterior of the test, this is important to a range of functions. The study of Neogene planktonic foraminifera from the southwest Pacific has demonstrated phyletic gradualism in the *Globorotalia inflata* lineage, while both modes of evolution have been determined in a subgenus of *Globorotalia*, *Globoconella* (Box 4.7). Given their relative abundance and diversity in many successions, foraminifera have also been used as an important test as to the effect of extinction events, such as the end-Cretaceous mass extinction (Chapter 21).

16.4.2 Palaeoenvironmental Analysis

The majority of foraminifera are found in marine conditions, where populations can be very diverse (Figure 16.4). Foraminifera are largely limited by temperature, salinity, oxygen levels and substrate (Table 16.1). Marginal marine environments such as lagoons, estuaries and marshes can also support dense populations, but the diversity tends to be much reduced (Figure 16.4). Some foraminifera, particularly larger forms and some planktonic forms, have symbiotic algae living within the cytoplasm. These algae require light to enable them to photosynthesise, and so their distribution is restricted to the photic zone. Benthonic foraminifera, like many benthonic groups, are strongly influenced by substrate as well as water chemistry, salinity and temperature. Planktonic forms will only survive in water of normal marine salinity, and are also sensitive to water chemistry and temperature. Modern faunas are latitudinally distributed with clearly defined polar, temperate and tropical faunas. The temperature sensitivity has led to their use in interpreting changing palaeoclimates through the geological record, especially in

Table 16.1 *Foraminiferal limiting factors*

Temperature	Foraminifera are very tolerant of temperature variations and are known from tropical to polar regions. However, individual groups may have limited tolerances. Planktonic species, in particular, may be temperature-controlled, and several characteristics may be seen to vary with temperature, including shape and size changes.
Oxygenation	Foraminifera are mostly limited to normal oxygenated waters, although they can survive low-oxygen conditions.
Salinity	Foraminifera are present in a wide range of salinities, from fresh water to hypersaline conditions of up to 90°/$_{oo}$. However, freshwater foraminifera are rare, and most planktonic species are known solely from near-normal marine salinities of 30–40°/$_{oo}$, with ornament and shell thickness varying with salinity changes.
Depth	Foraminifera are found from sea level to below 10 000 m. Most calcareous forms are unknown below 3000 m because the solubility of $CaCO_3$ increases at this depth. The relative proportion of planktonic to benthonic species varies according to depth, with the shallowest waters having 0% and the deepest, below 1000 m, 100%.
Substrate	The influence of substrate is difficult to assess, although agglutinating foraminifera prefer a sand substrate for test construction.
Turbulence	Foraminifera are mostly adapted to low-turbulence conditions.

the Quaternary. Detailed studies of North Atlantic Quaternary sediments have enabled the construction of temperature curves. This work is aided by the addition of oxygen isotope data collected by analysing the isotopic composition of oxygen atoms within the carbonate tests of foraminifera.

16.4.3 Stratigraphy

Planktonic foraminifera are an ideal group for biostratigraphy. They have many of the characteristics necessary for good guide fossils: widespread distribution due to their planktonic mode of life, abundance and small size (a small sample can yield numerous specimens), rapid evolution and distinctive species (to the practised eye at least). Detailed biozones for different latitudes have been erected from the early Cretaceous, when they first became widespread, up to the present day.

Benthonic foraminifera have also proved useful in stratigraphical studies. Although they are facies-controlled, they can be of great use in certain circumstances. Detailed local biozones have been constructed where evolutionary rates are high and/or other groups of fossils are rare. For example, fusuline foraminifera have been used as zonal fossils in the British Carboniferous. The Upper Palaeozoic is characterised by abundant and evolving fusulinids, enabling a relatively detailed biozonation of sixteen zones world-wide. Large milioline foraminifera, such as *Alveolina*, have been successfully used to zone the Palaeogene of the Mediterranean; and benthonic foraminiferal schemes are commonly used by oil exploration companies in the Palaeogene of the North Sea. In all cases, biozonation schemes based on benthonic foraminifera are influenced by facies. World-wide schemes may be possible, but it is rare to find all taxa in one place and therefore the schemes can only be partially applied.

16.5 SUGGESTED READING

Loeblich and Tappan (1988) is the most complete taxonomic study of the group, and includes illustrations and descriptions of all genera recorded at that time. Much simplified versions are given in Brasier (1980), Haynes (1981), Bignot (1985) and Buzas *et al.* (1987). Haynes is an excellent and accessible overview of all aspects of foraminifera. Murray (1991) covers many aspects of palaeoenvironmental applications as well as modern ecological data on benthonic groups. Bé (1977) provides similar coverage for planktonic foraminifera. Other palaeoenvironmental papers include Bernhard (1986). The palaeoclimatic significance of foraminifera in the Quaternary is summarised by Bradley (1985). Stratigraphical applications within the British Isles are covered by Jenkins and Murray (1989). Wider stratigraphical applications and evolutionary relationships of the planktonic foraminifera are given in great detail by Blow (1977), and in more accessible form in Bolli and Saunders (1985), Caron (1985), Iaccarino (1985), Jenkins (1985), and Toumarkine and Luterbacher (1985), all of which will be found in the same volume. Stratigraphical treatments are also described by Kellogg *et al.*

(1978) and Robasynski *et al.* (1984). Evolutionary topics are covered in a variety of ways by Malmgren and Kennett (1981; 1983), Banner and Lowry (1985), Buzas & Culver (1989), Collins (1989), Gaskell (1991) and a number of others.

Banner, F.T. & Lowry, F.M.D. 1985. The stratigraphic record of planktonic foraminifera: evolutionary implications. *Special Papers in Palaeontology*, **33**, 117–130.

Bé, A.W.H. 1977. An ecological, zoogeographic and taxonomic review of Recent planktonic foraminifera. *In* Ramsey, A.T.S. (ed.), *Oceanic micropalaeontology*, Volume 1. Academic Press, London, 1–100.

Bernhard, J.M. 1986. Characteristic assemblages and morphologies of benthic foraminifera from anoxic, organic-rich deposits: Jurassic through Holocene. *Journal of Foraminiferal Research*, **16**, 207–215.

Bignot, G. 1985. *Elements of Micropalaeontology*. Graham and Trotman, London.

Blow, W.H. 1979. *The Cainozoic Globigerinida*. E.J. Brill, Leiden.

Bolli, H.M. & Saunders, J.B. 1985. Oligocene to Holocene low latitude planktic foraminifera. *In* Bolli, H.M., Saunders, J.B. & Perch-Nielsen, K. (eds), *Plankton Stratigraphy*, Volume 1. Cambridge University Press, Cambridge, 155–262.

Bradley, R.S. 1985. *Quaternary Paleoclimatology. Methods of Paleoclimatic Reconstruction*. Allen & Unwin, Boston.

Brasier, M. 1980. *Microfossils*. Allen & Unwin, London.

Buzas, M.A. & Culver, S.J. 1989. Biogeographic and evolutionary patterns of continental benthic foraminifera. *Paleobiology*, **15**, 11–19.

Buzas, M.A., Douglass, R.C. & Smith, C.C. 1987. Kingdom Protista. *In* Boardman, R.S., Cheetham, A.H. & Rowell, A.J. (eds), *Fossil Invertebrates*, Blackwell Scientific Publications, Palo Alto, CA, 67–106.

Caron, M. 1985. Cretaceous planktic foraminifera. *In* Bolli, H.M., Saunders, J.B. & Perch-Nielsen, K. (eds), *Plankton Stratigraphy*, Volume 1. Cambridge University Press, Cambridge, 17–86.

Collins, L.S. 1989. Evolutionary rates of a rapid radiation: the Paleogene planktic foraminifera. *Palaios*, **4**, 251–263.

Gaskell, B.A. 1991. Extinction patterns in Paleogene benthic foraminiferal faunas: relationship to climate and sea level. *Palaios*, **6**, 2–16.

Haynes, J.R. 1981. *Foraminifera*. Macmillan, London.

Iaccarino, S. 1985. Mediterranean Miocene and Pliocene planktic foraminifera. *In* Bolli, H.M., Saunders, J.B. & Perch-Nielsen, K. (eds), *Plankton Stratigraphy*, Volume 1. Cambridge University Press, Cambridge, 283–314.

Jenkins, D.G. 1985. Southern mid-latitude Paleocene to Holocene planktic foraminifera. *In* Bolli, H.M., Saunders, J.B. & Perch-Nielsen, K. (eds), *Plankton Stratigraphy*, Volume 1. Cambridge University Press, Cambridge, 263–282.

Jenkins, D.G. & Murray, J.W. 1989. *Stratigraphical Atlas of Fossil Foraminifera*. Second Edition. BMS/Ellis Horwood, London.

Kellogg, T.B., Duplessy, J.C. & Shackleton, N.J. 1978. Planktonic foraminiferal and oxygen isotopic stratigraphy and paleoclimatology of Norwegian Sea deep-sea cores. *Boreas*, **7**, 61–73.

Loeblich, A.R. & Tappan, H. 1988. *Foraminiferal Genera and Their Classification*. Van Nostrand Reinhold, New York.

Malmgren, B.A. & Kennett, J.P. 1981. Phyletic gradualism in a Late Cenozoic planktonic foraminiferal lineage: DSDP Site 284, southwest Pacific. *Paleobiology*, **7**, 230–240.

Malmgren, B.A. & Kennett, J.P. 1983. Phyletic gradualism in the *Globorotalia inflata* lineage vindicated. *Paleobiology*, **9**, 427–428.

Murray, J.W. 1991. *Ecology and Palaeoecology of Benthic Foraminifera*. Longman, Harlow.

Robasynski, F., Caron, M., Gonzalez, J.M. & Wonders, A. 1984. Atlas of late Cretaceous planktonic foraminifera. *Revue de Micropaléontologie*, **26**, 145–305.

Toumarkine, M. & Luterbacher, H. 1985. Paleocene and Eocene planktic foraminifera. *In* Bolli, H.M., Saunders, J.B. and Perch-Nielsen, K. (eds), *Plankton Stratigraphy*, Volume 1. Cambridge University Press, Cambridge, 87–154.

17
Microfossils: Ostracods

17.1 OSTRACOD TAXONOMY

Ostracods are small bivalved crustaceans found today in all aquatic environments including marine, brackish and freshwater. They have a long stratigraphical record extending back to the Cambrian, and are common elements of the Palaeozoic and Mesozoic–Cenozoic evolutionary faunas. The majority are benthonic and are therefore facies-controlled. They are of great palaeoenvironmental importance, but of more limited biostratigraphical use.

17.1.1 General Characteristics of Ostracods

Ostracods are generally small in size and, like foraminifera (Chapter 16), are considered in the informal grouping of microfossils. However, although they are frequently found associated with foraminifera in microfossil assemblages, they are considerably more complex than these single-celled organisms, and are more closely related to trilobites (Chapter 12) as both are arthropods, possessing a hard exoskeleton and jointed appendages. Ostracods are superficially similar to bivalves and brachiopods in that their shell or **carapace** consists of two hinged valves enclosing the soft body parts (Figure 17.1). However, ostracods may be distinguished as they are generally much smaller, differ in details of the hinge and imprints left on the interior of the valves by attached muscles, have two valves which are generally asymmetrical, and lack growth lines. Ostracod valves lack growth lines due to their process of moulting during growth, which involves the shedding of old valves as the soft parts outgrow them.

The ostracod body comprises an anterior **head**, and a **thorax**, although this differentiation is much less obvious than in the trilobites (Figure 17.1). Ostracods possess a mouth and usually one eye situated on the head, and an anus to the posterior. As in all crustaceans, the body bears seven pairs of ventral **limbs** which

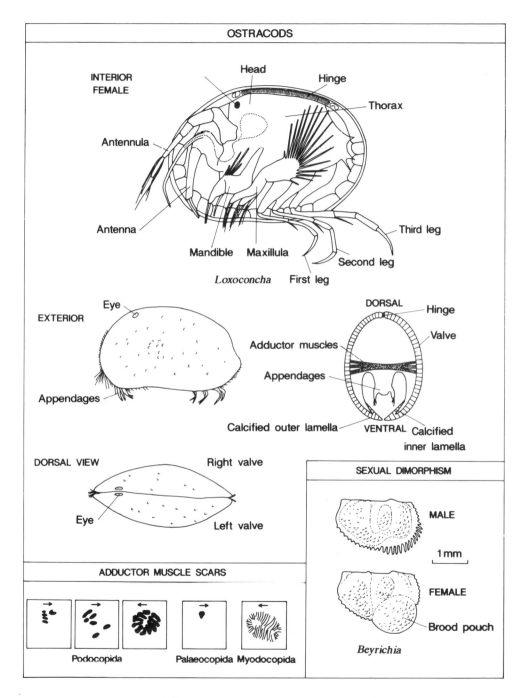

OSTRACODS

INTERIOR FEMALE

Head

Hinge

Thorax

Antennula

Antenna

Mandible Maxillula

Second leg

Third leg

Loxoconcha First leg

EXTERIOR

Eye

Appendages

DORSAL

Hinge

Valve

Adductor muscles

Appendages

Calcified outer lamella

VENTRAL Calcified inner lamella

DORSAL VIEW

Right valve

Eye

Left valve

ADDUCTOR MUSCLE SCARS

Podocopida

Palaeocopida Myodocopida

SEXUAL DIMORPHISM

MALE

1 mm

FEMALE

Brood pouch

Beyrichia

Figure 17.1 *Morphology of the living ostracod* Loxoconcha. *Adductor muscle scars on the interior of the carapaces of typical groups are also illustrated, together with an example of sexual dimorphism in the palaeocopid genus* Beyrichia *[Mostly based on an original drawing by D. Horne]*

Figure 17.2 *Exceptionally preserved ostracod from the Cretaceous Santana Formation of Brazil, exhibiting a full set of appendages. Greatly magnified [Photograph: D. Martill]*

carry sensitive bristles or **setae** and terminal **claws**. The limbs are variously adapted (Figures 17.1 and 17.2). The anterior set are the **antennules** which are used in feeding and in movement. The second set are the **antennae** which are primarily used in movement. Both of these sets are in front of the mouth. The next set are beside the mouth and are the **mandibles**. The **maxillae** are behind the mouth and both of these sets are involved in feeding, by assisting in the chewing of food. The final three sets of limbs are positioned on the thorax and have a variety of functions including movement (Figures 17.1 and 17.2).

Ostracods do not possess gills as larger crustaceans do, but respire by absorbing oxygen directly from the surrounding water. The limbs assist in this process by wafting currents of water around the valves. They open and close the valves by a set of adductor muscles which are attached centrally to the interior of each valve. Ostracods reproduce sexually, and differences in the shells of the two sexes are common. The females may lay the fertilised eggs or they may retain them in a **brood pouch** in the posterior part of the carapace (Figure 17.1). Once the young ostracods emerge, growth takes place in stages. At intervals the valve is cast off or **moulted**, and a new, larger shell is created. These growth stages are called **instars**. The presence of sexual dimorphs and a range of instars is important when considering the shell morphology of ostracods.

17.1.2 Ostracod Classification

Ostracods form a class of the phylum Crustacea within the broader context of the Arthropoda (Chapter 12). The ostracods are a varied group of predominantly marine arthropods which have highly differentiated limbs. The main characteristics used in classification are valve shape, details of the hinge, and the arrangement of muscle scars.

Phylum Crustacea Pennant, 1777
Class Ostracoda Latreille, 1806 (Cambrian–Recent)
Laterally compressed, bivalved crustaceans with dorsal hinge.

Order Archaeocopida Sylvester–Bradley, 1961 (Cambrian–Ordovician)
Long, straight or sinuous hinge-line. Carapace flexible, slightly calcified.

Order Leperditicopida Scott, 1961 (Cambrian–Devonian)
Long, straight hinge; heavily calcified, unequal to subequal valves with a large muscle
scar composed of numerous elements.

Order Palaeocopida Henningsmoen, 1953 (Ordovician–Permian)
Long straight dorsal margin, with no calcareous inner lamella in the shell.

Order Myodocopida Sars, 1866 (Ordovician–Recent)
All marine. Subequal valves, may have anterior 'beak' or rostrum.

Order Podocopida Sars, 1866 (Ordovician–Recent)
Curved or short straight dorsal margin, with prominent muscle scars.

17.2 OSTRACOD MORPHOLOGY

The ostracod shell (carapace) is composed of two **valves** which articulate by a dorsal **hinge**, and may consist either of an arrangement of teeth and sockets, or of ridges and grooves (Figure 17.1). The valves are asymmetrical as they are rarely similar in shape although they may be of the same size. Each valve is constructed of two lamellae or layers: an external, entirely calcified lamella, and an internal chitinous, sometimes partially calcified lamella (Figure 17.1). The external lamella is penetrated by **pore canals** which exit externally through a **pore** which may contain a **sieve plate**. In life, these pores contain sensitive hairs, **setae**, which provide information about the surrounding environment. A second set of pore canals called **marginal pores** run along the plane of attachment of internal and external lamellae around the marginal area of the valve. These also contain sensitive hair-like setae. The muscles of attachment are not normally preserved, but scars are found either centrally on each valve or towards the anterior end. The number and arrangement of these scars is variable between taxa, although uniform within a group. Sexual dimorphism is common in the carapaces of some taxa. Where brood care is practised, the female may have an inflated posterior section to the carapace which would have housed the brood pouch in life (Figure 17.1). In other forms, eggs are laid. Most eggs are highly resistant to drying out (desiccation) and other environmental changes. In this way, populations of ostracods can survive in temporary water bodies.

The most common ostracod groups are: the **Palaeocopida**; the **Podocopida**; and the **Myodocopida**. The characteristic features of these groups are given below, and are illustrated in Figures 17.3–17.5.

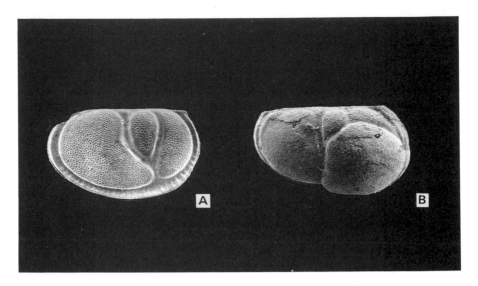

Figure 17.3 *A typical palaeocopid genus,* Macrypsilon, *from the Silurian, showing strong sexual dimorphism.* **A:** *Male, right valve.* **B:** *Female, right valve. Note inflated brood chamber*
[Photographs: D.J. Siveter]

1. *Palaeocopida* (Ordovician–Permian) were the dominant Palaeozoic ostracods, and are characterised by:
  • a long straight hinge line
  • valves sculpted into ridges, sulci (depressions) and lobes
  • common sexual dimorphism.
Palaeocopid ostracods demonstrate the strongest sexual dimorphism; females were generally larger than males, and had brood pouches and more strongly developed lobes (Figure 17.3). Members of this group lived mainly on or in the sediment, but some were probably free-swimming.

2. *Podocopida* (Ordovician–Recent) are the dominant ostracods in the Mesozoic–Cenozoic evolutionary fauna and are common today (Figures 17.4 and 17.5). They have the following characteristics:
  • a convex dorsal margin and straight or concave ventral margin
  • shell ornament common, but sulci and lobes rare
  • clearly developed muscle scars.
The muscle scars in the Podocopida are very distinct and are of importance in the separation of the suborders and superfamilies. Commonly occurring groups include three from the suborder Podocopina.

Bairdiaceans (superfamily Bairdacea) (Ordovician–Recent) are characterised by:
  • a smooth, thick shell
  • a muscle scar pattern consisting of between six and 15 elongate scars variously arranged, but commonly radial
  • an entirely marine habitat.
Bairdiaceans tend to have a distinctive shape with a very strongly convex dorsal

Figure 17.4 *Typical podocopid ostracods. **A:** A Cretaceous bairdacean, Bairdoppilata, left valve, × 50. **B:** A Cretaceous cypridean, Macrosarisa, right valve, × 32. **C:** A Cretaceous cytheracean, Cythereis, right valve, × 54 [Photographs: I.J. Slipper]*

margin and a slightly convex ventral margin (Figure 17.3). They tend to have weak hinges.

Cypridaceans (superfamily Cypridacea) (Devonian–Recent) can be recognised by:

- their smooth, thin shell
- their mostly simple hinge
- a 'pawprint' muscle-scar pattern often consisting of a large dorsal element and five smaller elements
- they are common in fresh water, and are rarely marine.

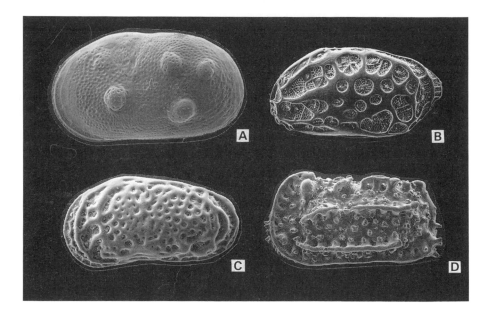

Figure 17.5   *Typical podocopid ostracods.* **A:** *A Recent, brackish-water cypridean,* Cyprideis. **B:** *A Recent marine cytheracean.* Hemicytherura. **C:** *A Pleistocene marine cytheracean,* Callistocythere. **D:** *A Recent marine cytheracean,* Carinocythereis. *All greatly magnified [Photographs: D. Horne]*

This group contains most of the freshwater ostracods. The carapaces tend to show little variation and modern forms are distinguished on details of the appendages, although this is obviously not generally possible in fossils (Figures 17.3 and 17.4).

Cytheraceans (superfamily Cytheracea) (Ordovician–Recent) are of variable morphology but can be recognised by their:
- usually well-developed hinge
- widespread distribution
- distinctive muscle scar pattern of four or five vertically aligned elements with several other elements arranged to the anterior.

Cytheraceans are one of the most varied groups in terms of morphology and ecology (Figures 17.3 and 17.4). It is difficult to distinguish the group clearly if the all-important muscle-scar pattern is not visible.

3. *Myodocopida* (Ordovician–Recent) are long-ranging but are better known from the Palaeozoic Fauna. They are characterised by their:
- planktonic, or partially planktonic, mode of life
- weakly developed hinge.

Myodocopid ostracods are a common element of the Palaeozoic Fauna and rare in the Modern Fauna as later forms have thin carapaces.

17.3 OSTRACOD EVOLUTION

The earliest recorded ostracods have been found in Lower Cambrian sediments, and belong to the Order Archaeocopida. More common are the Leperditicopida, however, which dominated the early Palaeozoic until the Ordovician (Figure 17.6). The Ordovician was a time of rapid expansion, with all the major orders appearing at this time. The Palaeocopida were dominant in the Ordovician, but their numbers declined until their eventual extinction at the end of the Permian. The myodocopids were the most common group in the Carboniferous, but through Mesozoic times until the present day, the Podocopida diversified and radiated (Figure 17.6).

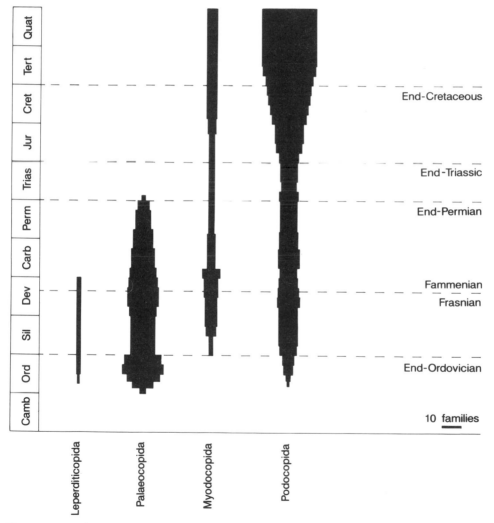

Figure 17.6 *The diversity of ostracod families through geological time. The main extinction events are indicated [Compiled by A.L. Holder from: Benton (1993)* The Fossil Record 2, *Chapman & Hall]*

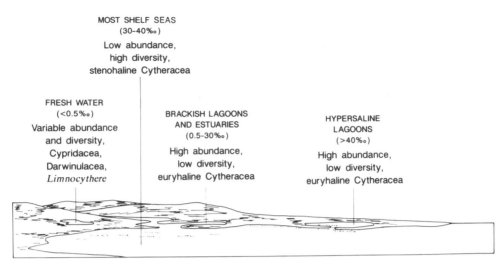

MOST SHELF SEAS
(30–40‰)
Low abundance,
high diversity,
stenohaline Cytheracea

FRESH WATER
(<0.5‰)
Variable abundance
and diversity,
Cypridacea,
Darwinulacea,
Limnocythere

BRACKISH LAGOONS
AND ESTUARIES
(0.5–30‰)
High abundance,
low diversity,
euryhaline Cytheracea

HYPERSALINE
LAGOONS
(>40‰)
High abundance,
low diversity,
euryhaline Cytheracea

Figure 17.7 *Distribution of ostracods in common non-marine and marginal marine environments [Modified from: Brasier (1980)* Microfossils, *Chapman & Hall, Fig. 14.7, p. 129]*

Ostracods were affected by both the end-Permian and, to a lesser extent, the end-Cretaceous extinction events. For example, the Palaeocopida and one group of the Podocopida became extinct at the end of the Permian, although both show a gradual decline from the end of the Devonian. The effect of the Cretaceous–Tertiary boundary extinction event was less marked (Figure 17.6).

17.4 OSTRACOD APPLICATIONS

17.4.1 Palaeobiology

Ostracods are abundant and widespread today, and therefore provide many possibilities for taxonomic uniformitarian studies. For example, some freshwater ostracods are relatively easily kept and bred in laboratory conditions, and recent studies have shed much light on their feeding habits and reproduction. Such results can be applied to fossils and a clearer understanding of functional morphology gained. In evolutionary studies, several macroevolutionary trends can be recognised. For example, there has been a decrease in size from the giants of the Palaeozoic; the number of adductor muscle scars has also been reduced, while the complexity of the hinge has increased. These studies have added to our understanding of the evolutionary process.

17.4.2 Palaeoenvironmental Analysis

Ostracods are of great importance to palaeoenvironmental analysis for three reasons: firstly, they occur today in a wide range of aqueous environments, and have done so since the Mesozoic; secondly, there has been a great deal of study of the ecology of living ostracods; and thirdly, it is often possible to determine population size, dynamics and taphonomy from the fossil record, through examination of the age structure of the assemblage. Ostracods are therefore perfect examples of the potential for palaeoenvironmental interpretations from the fossil record.

Ostracods are predominantly benthonic and are therefore facies-controlled and strongly influenced by various palaeoenvironmental factors. In particular, ostracods are limited by salinity and substrate (Table 17.1). Although many species are highly tolerant of variation, others are limited by such parameters as temperature, salinity, substrate, water chemistry, water depth and light penetration (as ostracods have eyes). Their common occurrence in non-marine conditions, as well as the full range of marine environments from shoreline to abyssal depths, makes them very useful environmental indicators (Figure 17.6). They have successfully been used as highly sensitive salinity indicators, and have recently been used as possible indicators of water pollution levels.

Table 17.1 *Ostracod limiting factors*

Temperature	Ostracods are found in all normal marine temperature ranges.
Oxygenation	Ostracods are found in normal levels of oxygenation but are also present in low-oxygen conditions.
Salinity	Ostracods are known from freshwater ($2^{0}/_{00}$), brackish (2–$20^{0}/_{00}$), fully marine (20–$40^{0}/_{00}$) and even hypersaline (over $80^{0}/_{00}$) conditions. Many taxa have specific tolerances, with many characters, such as shell ornament, varying with salinity level. Ostracods are the commonest fossils in brackish-water conditions.
Depth	Ostracods are known from all depths, but are commonest in shallow waters. Several characters are known to vary with depth; size and number of spines, for example, both increase with depth.
Substrate	Ostracod morphology and mode of life have a direct link with the type of substrate: free-swimmers have thin shells, benthonic ostracods are more ornamented, for example.
Turbulence	Ostracods are adapted to moderate to low turbulence levels.

17.4.3 Stratigraphy

Ostracods traditionally lag behind certain other microfossil groups in biostratigraphical utility. As predominantly benthonic organisms, facies control is a problem in interpreting their temporal distribution. They can, however, be extremely useful, particularly in marginal marine or saline lagoon facies. This is particularly important in the late Jurassic to early Cretaceous Purbeck–Wealden facies of southern England, where suitable guide fossils have been hard to find. Ostracods have two main strengths over other groups: they extend over a very long period of geological time and they inhabit all aquatic environments. They have been very effectively applied to the stratigraphy of non-marine sequences where other fossil groups may be rare or excluded entirely. Tentative long-distance correlations have been published for such environments, for example for the late Jurassic to early Cretaceous of Brazil and West Africa.

In most marine situations, the strong provincialism exhibited by ostracods limits their use in long-distance correlation. They can be of value in smaller areas, however, and within provinces, and this has been convincingly demonstrated in various Palaeozoic examples and in the Upper Cretaceous of the Middle East.

17.5 SUGGESTED READING

Moore's (1961) *Treatise on Invertebrate Paleontology* provides a full, if dated, taxonomy of the Ostracoda. Brasier (1980), Bignot (1985) and Robison and Kaesler (1987) offer simplified taxonomic treatments as well as short reviews on other aspects of the group. There are several texts and compendia of papers which deal with the geological applications of ostracods. Most important are De Deckker *et al.* (1988), Van Morkhoven (1962), Neale (1969), Maddocks (1982), and Whatley and Maybury (1990). Loffler and Danielopol (1978) is a general text covering many aspects of the palaeoenvironmental applications; other papers cover individual aspects, such as Benson (1981) and Benson *et al.* (1984). Bate (1972) is of interest due to the description of rare fossil appendages. The stratigraphical ranges and applications of ostracods are reviewed in Anderson (1973; 1985), Bate and Robinson (1978), Bate *et al.* (1982), Keen (1982) and Van Harten and Van Hinte (1984).

Anderson, F.W. 1973. The Jurassic–Cretaceous transition: the non-marine ostracod faunas. *Geological Journal* (special issue), **5**, 101–110.

Anderson, F.W. 1985. Ostracod faunas in the Purbeck and Wealden of England. *Journal of Micropalaeontology*, **4**, 1–68.

Bate, R.H. 1972. Phosphatized ostracods with appendages from the Lower Cretaceous. *Palaeontology*, **15**, 379–393.

Bate, R.H. & Robinson, E. (eds) 1978. *A Stratigraphic Index of British Ostracoda*. Seel House Press, Liverpool.

Bate, R.H., Robinson, E. & Sheppard, L.M. (eds) 1982. *Fossil and Recent Ostracods*. Ellis Horwood, Chichester.

Benson, R.H. 1981. Form, function and architecture in ostracode shells. *Annual Reviews, Earth and Planetary Sciences*, **9**, 398–413.

Benson, R.H., Chapman, R.E. and Deck, L.T. 1984. Paleoceanographic events and deep-sea ostracodes. *Science*, **224**, 1334–1336.

Bignot, G. 1985. *Elements of Micropalaeontology*. Graham & Trotman, London.

Brasier, M. 1980. *Microfossils*. Allen & Unwin, London.

De Deckker, P., Colin, J.-P. & Peypouquet, J.-P. (eds) 1988. *Ostracoda in the Earth Sciences*. Elsevier, Amsterdam.

Keen, M.C. 1982. Ostracods and Tertiary biostratigraphy. *In* Maddocks, R.F. (ed.) *Applications of Ostracoda*. University of Houston Geosciences, Houston, TX, 78–95.

Loffler, H. & Danielopol, D.L. (eds) 1978. *Aspects of the Ecology and Zoogeography of Recent and Fossil Ostracoda*. Junk, The Hague.

Maddocks, R.F. (ed.) 1982. *Applications of Ostracoda*. University of Houston Geosciences, Houston, TX.

Moore, R.C. (ed.) 1961. *Treatise on Invertebrate Palaeontology, Part Q, Arthropoda 3 – Crustacea – Ostracoda*. Geological Society of America and University of Kansas Press, Lawrence, KS.

Neale, J.W. (ed.) 1969. *The Taxonomy, Morphology and Ecology of Recent Ostracoda*. Oliver and Boyd, Edinburgh.

Robison, R.A. & Kaesler, R.L. 1987. Phylum Arthropoda. *In* Boardman, R.S., Cheetham, A.H. & Rowell, A.J. (eds), *Fossil Invertebrates*. Blackwell Scientific Publications, Palo Alto, CA, 205–269.

Van Harten, D. & Van Hinte, J. E. 1984. Ostracod range charts as a chronoecologic tool. *Marine Micropalaeontology*, **8**, 425–433.

Van Morkhoven, F.P.C.M. 1962. *Post-Palaeozoic Ostracoda. Their Morphology, Taxonomy and Economic Use*. Elsevier, Amsterdam.

Whatley, R. & Maybury, C. 1990. *Ostracoda and Global Events*. Chapman & Hall, London.

18
Trace Fossils

18.1 INTRODUCTION TO TRACE FOSSILS

Today animals and plants interact with the sedimentary environment to create a range of tracks and traces which demonstrate their one-time presence (Figure 18.1). On any modern beach, for example, a casual observer might be expected to see the footprints of wading birds, and of humans and their dogs. From these data an observer can make deductions about the nature of the trace producer (bird, dog, human) and about their behaviour (wading, walking and running). Further examination would reveal the activity of burrowing organisms such as worms or bivalves in the creation of a dwelling burrow, or the movement of snails in grazing patches of seaweed on rocky shores. These traces provide a wealth of information about the nature of the inhabitants of the beach environment and their lives which is easy to interpret because of the well-known habitats of modern trace producers. The geological record of trace fossils provides a tantalising glimpse of the nature and behaviour of ancient ecologies which can only be partially gleaned from the body fossil record. Trace fossils are extremely important as they provide the interface between two important parts of palaeoenvironmental interpretation: sedimentology and palaeontology. Trace fossils have an exceptionally long fossil record, and some of the evidence of the earliest metazoans is derived from trace fossils.

18.2 TRACE FOSSIL TAXONOMY

Trace fossils are sometimes referred to as **ichnofossils**, from the Greek word *ichnos*, meaning footprint or track. Trace fossils are the tracks, trails and other structures, such as rootlet traces, left in or on the substrate by a range of organisms. Trace fossils are fundamentally different from **body fossils** in that they are the result of an organism's behaviour, rather than parts of an organism's body or shell.

Figure 18.1   *Dinosaur footprint as a paddling pool. This demonstrates the motion of some of the largest animals on earth, the sauropods [From: Colbert (1945) The Dinosaur Book, American Museum of Natural History, p. 29]*

Trace fossils can be classified according to: Linnaean taxonomy; inferred life history and behaviour of the trace-producing organisms, known as **ethology**; or preservational type.

18.2.1 Linnaean Classification

This involves the utilisation of a binomial system of nomenclature somewhat similar to that employed for body fossils and living plant and animal species. The formal acceptance of the binomial system for traces finally came about through the introduction of **ichnotaxa**, including species (**ichnospecies**) and genera (**ichnogenera**) in the latest edition of the *International Code on Zoological Nomenclature*, published in 1985. Ichnogenera and ichnospecies are simply used as mechanisms to define morphological differences. The ichnogenus is therefore a convenient identifier of a range of characters which are then divisible into smaller morphological subgroups. This is potentially confusing, however, as it is tempting to call trace-producing organisms and traces by the same name. An example of this would be the common use of the genus name of the rock-boring bivalve *Lithophaga* for the borings themselves (*Lithophaga*-borings). Although this is generally acceptable where there is a clearly defined relationship between trace producer and trace, in many cases a direct relationship is difficult to prove, and therefore an independent name, effectively acting as an identifier for a particular *trace morphology* rather than an association with a particular organism, is desirable. In our example, the trace producer would be the genus *Lithophaga* while the produced trace would be the ichnogenus *Gastrochaenolites*, describing the bulb-shaped morphology of the boring. This separation is particularly important considering that it is possible for some traces to have been created by organisms belonging to different animal phyla, such as crustaceans and worms in producing the U-tube ichnogenus *Diplocraterion*.

18.2.2 Ethological Classification

The ethological (behavioural) classification is the one most commonly used in trace fossils and is primarily a mechanism for distinguishing groups of traces on the basis of the behaviour of a given set of organisms. It is an entirely separate classification from Linnaean ichnotaxa which serves only to denote morphological groupings, and is therefore objective. Ethology requires a greater element of subjectivity as it involves the interpretation of trace fossils as the result of a particular behavioural process, and it seeks to link several objective ichnogenera on the basis of the interpretation of the inferred behaviour of their trace producer.

Several categories have been identified (Figures 3.5 and 18.2). This list is not comprehensive, as other trace fossil types have been and continue to be recognised, such as fossil faeces or coprolites, but the main types include: resting traces (**cubichnia**), created by active organisms while at rest or in the process of concealment from prey; locomotion traces (**repichnia**), tracks and trails created by organisms moving across the sediment surface; dwelling traces (**domichnia**), three-dimensional dwelling structures created by an organism as a burrow; grazing traces (**pascichnia**), horizontal feeding traces on the surface of the substrate; and feeding burrows (**fodinichnia**), shafts and networks (vertical or horizontal) cut in the sediment by deposit feeders.

18.2.3 Preservational Classification

Trace fossils can be classified according to the nature of their preservation, particularly according to the relationship of the trace with the sedimentary surface –

for example, whether the trace is on the sediment surface (exogenic), or whether it is contained within the body of the sediment itself (endogenic) (Figure 2.17). This can be further refined on the nature of the casting medium, as traces can be found whole with **full relief**, with the boundaries of circular burrows, for example, clearly defined within the enclosing sediment; or with **semirelief**, with one part of the trace being fully defined, either on the upper surface of a given sedimentary layer as **epirelief**, or on the lower surface of a sedimentary layer as **hyporelief**, in both cases preserving a concave or convex trace as appropriate.

18.3 TRACE FOSSIL MORPHOLOGIES

Trace fossils are usually identified using a combination of the three classifications. The Linnaean classification provides a shorthand illustration of the morphology of the trace fossil itself. The preservational classification allows for the interpretation of the relationship of the trace producer with the sediment, and the ethological classification provides a framework with which to interpret the mechanism and mode of creation of the traces. The ethological classification is used below to provide a basis for discussion and identification of commonly encountered trace fossil groups, and typical traces are illustrated in Figures 18.2–18.9.

1. *Resting traces* (Figure 18.2). Resting traces may be recognised by their:
- following bedding planes, and being preserved in semirelief
- having a shape which is reflective of the body outline of the producer
- possessing well-defined features which mimic the lower part of the producer.

Typical resting traces include the ichnogenera *Rusophycus* and *Asteriacites*. *Rusophycus* is a trace commonly associated with trilobites. In common with other resting traces, it has the potential to grade into a locomotion trace, in this case, *Cruziana*. *Rusophycus* conforms to a basic trilobite shape and commonly bears features of the lower surface of the animal, such as the position of the limbs. *Asteriacites* is a well-known resting trace left by a starfish: it has a well-defined, five-ray symmetry and an association of features indicative of the lower surface of the starfish (Figure 18.2).

2. *Locomotion traces* (Figures 18.2 and 18.3). Locomotion traces may be recognised by the following criteria:
- traces follow bedding planes, and are preserved in semirelief
- the motion of the producer is random or directional rather than systematic
- traces are usually associated with prod marks or impressions left by the producer.

Typical terrestrial traces are footprints left by a variety of organisms (Figures 18.1 and 18.3). An example of a marine locomotion trace is *Cruziana*, which is created as a simple burrow by the trace producer ploughing through the sediment (Figure 18.2). *Cruziana* is generally produced as a positive relief on the base of a sedimentary layer (convex hyporelief), and it displays a simple linear path and paired plough marks left by the trace producer's limbs and appendages. *Gyrochorte* is a similar trace preserved in positive relief on the upper surface of a sedimentary layer (convex epirelief), and is created when the trace producer ploughs through

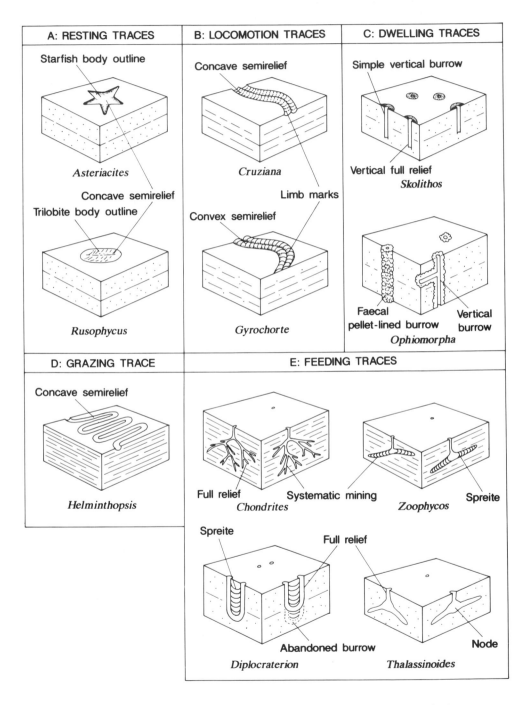

Figure 18.2   *The ethological classification of trace fossils illustrating typical ichnogenera*

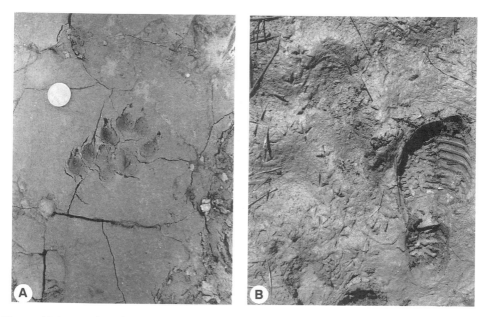

Figure 18.3 *Modern locomotion traces.* **A:** *Dog footprints.* **B:** *Human and bird footprints*
[*Photographs: P. Doyle*]

the sediment at a very shallow depth (Figure 18.2). The structure of the trace is created by the sediments which pass over the upper surface of the animal.

3. *Dwelling traces* (Figures 18.2, 18.4 and 18.5). Dwelling traces may be recognised by the following criteria:

- they may be vertical or horizontal preserved in full relief
- they are usually cylindrical, and may be simple vertical tubes, U-tubes or more complex branching systems
- they may bear evidence of scratch or prod marks left by appendages, or of cemented or lined walls.

Typical dwelling traces include *Skolithos* and *Ophiomorpha*. *Skolithos* comprises a simple, unpaired pipe (Figures 18.2 and 18.4). *Ophiomorpha* is often associated with shrimps and other crustaceans in the present day, and is lined with faecal pellets, displaying as a consequence a nodular outer surface to the burrow (Figure 18.2). Other dwelling traces include *Teredolites* and *Gastrochaenolites* which are bivalve borings cut into driftwood and firm or rock substrates, respectively (Figure 18.5).

4. *Grazing traces* (Figures 18.2 and 18.6). Grazing traces commonly possess the following characteristics:

- they are preserved on the bedding plane surface in semirelief
- they are meandering and systematic, usually with a regular system of switchbacks with regular spacing.

Typical grazing traces include: *Nereites*, *Spiroraphe*, *Helminthopsis* and *Paleodictyon*. *Nereites* and *Spiroraphe* are preserved as regular, spirally induced grazing patterns on the sediment surface. *Helminthopsis* comprises a complex series of grazing

Figure 18.4   Skolithos, a dwelling trace. **A:** From the Jurassic of England. **B:** From the Miocene of southern Spain [Photographs: P. Doyle]

Figure 18.5 Gastrochaenolites, a dwelling trace formed as a rock boring. This boulder formed part of a nearshore environment during the Miocene in southern Spain [Photograph: P. Doyle]

switchbacks (Figure 18.2). *Paleodictyon* forms an almost bizarre pattern composed of a network of regular polygons demonstrating systematic feeding (Figure 18.6).

5. *Feeding burrows* (Figures 18.2 and 18.7–18.9). Feeding burrows are complex but can be grouped on the basis of their feeding process. Typically, feeding burrows are:

- penetrative into the sediment, and preserved in full relief
- illustrative of progressive or systematic mining of the sediment
- more complex examples are characterised by back-filling features known as spreite.

Feeding burrows include the downward-branching *Chondrites*, the complex downward-spiralling *Zoophycos* (Figures 18.2 and 18.7) and the feeding/dwelling traces made by *Diplocraterion*, *Rhizocorallium* and *Thalassinoides*. Both *Diplocraterion* and *Rhizocorallium* form U-burrows (Figures 18.2 and 18.8), *Diplocraterion* with a vertical U-burrow and *Rhizocorallium* a vertical and then horizontal U-burrow. Both ichnotaxa commonly have scratch marks from claws on the burrow sides, and spreite representing an equilibrium of the trace producer with the rate of sedimentation. *Thalassinoides* is usually associated with shrimps and commonly displays a network of vertical and horizontal tubes which are interconnected at nodes or 'triple junctions' of passages, which may have functioned as turning circles for the trace producers (Figures 18.2 and 18.9).

Figure 18.6   *Grazing traces of* Nereites *ichnofacies from the Miocene of sourthern Spain.* **A:** Paleodictyodon. **B:** Helminthopsis *[Photographs: M.R. Bennett]*

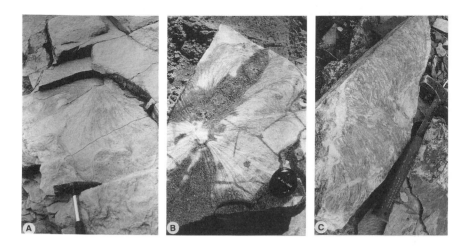

Figure 18.7 *The complex feeding trace Zoophycos. **A, B:** From the Cretaceous of northern Spain. **C:** From the Cretaceous of Argentina [Photographs: P. Doyle]*

Figure 18.8 *The U-shaped feeding burrow Diplocraterion from the Jurassic of southern England [Photograph: P. Doyle]*

Figure 18.9   *The branched feeding trace* Thalassinoides, *showing the typical triple junction branching.* **A:** *From the Cretaceous of Argentina.* **B:** *From the Miocene of southern Spain* [Photographs: P. Doyle]

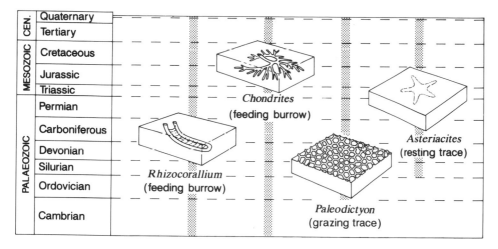

Figure 18.10 *The stratigraphical range of typical trace fossils. Trace fossil taxa often have ranges which span the whole of the Phanerozoic [Modified from: Ziegler (1983) Introduction to palaeobiology, Ellis Horwood, Fig. 168, p. 145]*

18.4 TRACE FOSSIL APPLICATIONS

18.4.1 General Concepts

The importance of trace fossils to geology rests on five very important concepts:

1. **Long time range.** Trace fossil 'taxa' have remained remarkably constant throughout geological time, such that similar taxa occur in present-day environments much as they did early in the Phanerozoic (Figure 18.10). This has three important implications: firstly, that similar traces may be produced by a range of organisms, although usually members of the same phylum; secondly, that the association of traces with substrates has remained remarkably constant throughout geological time; and thirdly, that the long time range effectively restricts the value and use of trace fossils in stratigraphy.

2. **Narrow facies range.** From detailed analysis it is clear that trace fossils have remained remarkably constrained by facies, such that certain traces are found in close association with certain substrate and therefore facies types. This means that trace fossils have a close association with their environment and are therefore good environmental indices.

3. **No reworking.** It is extremely rare for trace fossils to be reworked into younger sedimentary successions. This is because traces themselves are usually part of the fabric of a sedimentary rock unit, so that when such sediments are eroded the traces themselves are also cut through and destroyed, rather than released as a clast and reworked as often happens with body fossils.

4. **Occurrence in unfossiliferous rocks.** Often, traces are found where there are no body fossils. This is especially the case in early Palaeozoic/Precambrian successions; deep- or shallow-water successions; and hostile environments. In all these

cases, trace fossils give an important insight into the nature of the sedimentary environment, and in some cases may be of value in stratigraphy (Chapter 23).

5. **Creation by soft-bodied taxa.** Many traces have been made by soft-bodied organisms which are not otherwise recorded within the sedimentary record. This is particularly important in demonstrating: the presence of soft-bodied taxa in a hostile environment which precludes other organisms; the function of the soft-bodied taxa through their interaction with the sedimentary record; and the existence of metazoans prior to the evolution of hard body parts in the Precambrian.

18.4.2 Applications in Palaeobiology

Functional Morphology

Trace fossils have considerable applications in palaeobiology, and, in particular, in functional morphology and locomotion studies. Particular attention has been paid to the trilobite resting and locomotion traces, for example, which demonstrate a range of activities. These include resting partially buried in sediment (*Rusophycus*), moving through the sediment with a ploughing action (*Cruziana*), walking ahead on 'tiptoe' (*Protichnites*), or moving obliquely across the sediment surface (*Dimorphichnites*). In some cases, it is possible to observe the transition from one track or trace to another – *Rusophycus* to *Cruziana* or *Protichnites*, for example. On a larger scale, trace fossils are important in vertebrate locomotion studies, as the speed at which dinosaurs moved has in many cases been calculated from the spread of footprints in a trackway.

In some cases the trace producer for an individual trace will be something of a mystery, especially where no modern analogue can be found. In the case of *Zoophycos*, authors variously described it as a resting trace, or as a complex feeding trace, the *spreite* providing evidence of complex mining activity. Recently, comparison with the traces left by deep-sea surface-feeding worms (echiurans) has suggested that the complex spiral form of *Zoophycos* may represent nothing more than a 'cesspit' for the faecal pellets of similar deep-sea worms.

Evolution

Trace fossils are valuable in providing evidence of the existence and evolution of soft-bodied taxa not represented in the fossil record by body fossils. This is of particular importance in the Precambrian-Cambrian transition, where the first traces of *Phycodes* penetrating the sediment suggest the evolution of burrowing organisms which may have helped reduce the diversity of stromatolites and other algal mats.

18.4.3 Applications in Palaeoenvironmental Analysis

Trace fossils have their greatest application in palaeoenvironmental analysis. In a general sense, trace fossils may be used as indicators of the rate of sedimentation, since hardground assemblages (associated with a slow or reduced sedimentation rate) will be very different from shelf sediment associations, commonly with U- and simple burrows endeavouring to retain an equilibrium of burrow depth within the increasing sedimentary pile.

The depth relationship of trace fossil assemblages (ichnofacies) has already been introduced in Chapter 3. This relationship was first determined in the late 1960s, with a basic onshore–offshore pattern demonstrated by the succession of ichnofacies: *Skolithos – Cruziana – Zoophycos – Nereites* (Box 3.7). Although some of these traces are found in deeper (*Skolithos*) and shallower (*Zoophycos*) settings dependent on the nature of the substrate, in the main these trace assemblages have been shown to be reliable indicators of ancient water depths. In other cases, the diversity of trace fossils, and the nature of the colonisation history of the substrate, have proven to be of value in determination of environmental parameters such as salinity and oxygen levels. In general, the diversity of trace fossil assemblages falls with increased or decreased salinity levels, or with decreased oxygen levels. **Tiering**, the vertical stacking of traces within a sedimentary pile, can also give an indication of change in conditions (Figure 18.11). In fully oxygenated conditions, for example, several trace-producing organisms will colonise the sedimentary pile and inhabit different levels within it, their entry and exit burrows cross-cutting the first formed traces in the colonisation. With decreasing oxygen levels, there will be fewer traces found in this cross-cutting relationship. A detailed case history of the use of trace fossils in palaeoenvironmental studies is given in Chapter 22.

18.4.4 Applications in Stratigraphy

Trace fossils have limited application in stratigraphy because, for the most part, individual taxa are extremely long-ranging, the whole of the Phanerozoic in some

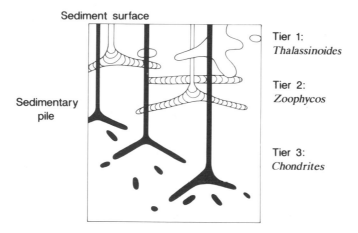

Figure 18.11 *The concept of tiering in trace fossils. The three trace fossils illustrated penetrate to different levels (tiers) in the sedimentary pile in order to feed*

extreme cases. However, trace fossils can help in the determination of **event horizons**, that is, stratigraphical units which are associated with specific geological events. For example, distinct trace fossil colonisation events are associated with hardgrounds (semi-lithified sediment associated with reduced sedimentation rate), or rhythmic sedimentation associated with climate change (Milankovich cycles). Erosion of tiered trace fossil sequences has also been suggested as a yardstick for determining the completeness of the fossil record. Erosion of the trace tiers in a stack of burrowed units is often obvious, and therefore a calculation of the amount of sedimentary thickness lost on the basis of these tiers is possible. However, perhaps the most important trace fossil application in stratigraphy is the determination of the Cambrian–Precambrian boundary, an event horizon associated with the first infaunal colonisation of the sedimentary record. This application is fully discussed in Chapter 23.

18.5 SUGGESTED READING

A great many books have been produced which provide excellent introductions to the nature and range of the subject. The most important are Frey (1975) and Bromley (1990), while Crimes and Harper (1970; 1977), Basan (1978) and Ekdale *et al.* (1984) are useful compilations. Short introductions to trace fossils are given by Osgood (1987) and Pemberton *et al.* (1990). Individual identification of ichnotaxa is possible with the aid of the appropriate part of the *Treatise on Invertebrate Paleontology* (Teichert, 1975). The concept of depth-related ichnofacies is introduced by Seilacher (1967) and re-examined by Frey and Seilacher (1980). The application of trace fossils in palaeobiology is discussed in general by Osgood (1975) and is demonstrated by the papers on *Zoophycos* by Kotake (1989; 1992). Examples of papers which discuss the application of trace fossils in palaeoenvironmental and sedimentological studies are: Howard (1975), Rhoads (1975), Bromley and Ekdale (1986) and Droser and Bottjer (1987). In particular, the concept of tiering is discussed by Bromley and Ekdale (1986) and Bromley (1990). The use of trace fossils in stratigraphy is discussed by Crimes (1975; 1987) and Wetzel and Aigner (1986).

Basan, P.B. (ed.) 1978. *Trace Fossil Concepts*. SEPM Short Course 5.
Bromley, R.G. 1990. *Trace Fossils. Biology and Taphonomy*. Unwin Hyman, London.
Bromley, R.G. & Ekdale, A.A. 1986. Composite ichnofabrics and tiering of burrows. *Geological Magazine*, **123**, 59–65.
Crimes, T.P. 1975. The stratigraphical significance of trace fossils. *In* Frey, R.W. (ed.), *The Study of Trace Fossils*. Springer-Verlag, Berlin, 109–130.
Crimes, T.P. 1987. Trace fossils and correlation of late Precambrian and early Cambrian strata. *Geological Magazine*, **124**, 97–189.
Crimes, T.P. & Harper, J.C. (eds) 1970. *Trace Fossils*. Seel House Press, Liverpool.
Crimes, T.P. & Harper, J.C. (eds) 1977. *Trace Fossils 2*. Seel House Press, Liverpool.
Droser, M.L. & Bottjer, D.J. 1987. A semiquantative field-classification of ichnofabric. *Journal of Sedimentary Petrology* , **56**, 13–27.
Ekdale, A.A., Bromley, R.G. & Pemberton, S.G. 1984. *Ichnology. The Use of Trace Fossils in Sedimentology and Stratigraphy*. SEPM Short Course 15.

Frey, R.W. (ed.) 1975. *The Study of Trace Fossils*. Springer-Verlag, Berlin.

Frey, R.W. & Seilacher, A. 1980. Uniformity in marine invertebrate ichnology. *Lethaia*, **13**, 183–208.

Howard, J.D. 1975. The sedimentological significance of trace fossils. *In* Frey, R.W. (ed.), *The Study of Trace Fossils*. Springer-Verlag, Berlin, 131–146.

Kotake, N. 1989. Paleoecology of the *Zoophycos* producers. *Lethaia*, **22**, 327–341.

Kotake, N. 1992. Deep-sea echiurans: possible producers of *Zoophycos*. *Lethaia*, **25**, 311–316.

Osgood, R.G. 1975. The paleontological significance of trace fossils. *In* Frey, R.W. (ed.), *The Study of Trace Fossils*. Springer-Verlag, Berlin, 87–108.

Osgood, R.G. 1987. Trace fossils. *In* Boardman, R.S., Cheetham, A.H. & Rowell, A.J. (eds), *Fossil Invertebrates*. Blackwell Scientific Publications, Palo Alto, CA, 663–674.

Pemberton, S.G., Frey, R.W. & Saunders, T.D.A. 1990. Trace fossils. *In* Briggs, D.E.G. & Crowther, P.R. (eds), *Palaeobiology – A Synthesis*. Blackwell Scientific Publications, Oxford, 355–362.

Rhoads, D.C. 1975. The paleoecological and environmental significance of trace fossils. *In* Frey, R.W. (ed.), *The Study of Trace Fossils*. Springer-Verlag, Berlin, 147–160.

Seilacher, A. 1967. Bathymetry of trace fossils. *Marine Geology*, **5**, 413–428.

Teichert, C. (ed.) 1975. *Treatise on Invertebrate Paleontology, Part W, Miscellanea, Supplement 1*. Geological Society of America and the University of Kansas Press, Lawrence, KS.

Wetzel, A. & Aigner, T. 1986. Stratigraphic completeness: tiered trace fossils provide a measuring stick. *Geology*, **14**, 234–237.

19
Summary of Part II

In Part II the characteristics and applications of the main invertebrate fossil groups were examined. These fossil groups are among the most common ones encountered and are the most abundant invertebrate fossils found within most marine sequences. This chapter summarises the geological applications of these common fossil groups.

19.1 THE GEOLOGICAL RECORD OF THE MARINE INVERTEBRATES

The main invertebrate fossil groups can be considered as part of the three evolutionary faunas which developed during the Phanerozoic – the interval of 'evident life' which extends from the beginning of the Cambrian, some 560 million years ago, to the present day. The three evolutionary faunas are: the Cambrian Fauna, largely dominated by the trilobites; the Palaeozoic Fauna, largely dominated by the brachiopods; and the Modern or Mesozoic-Cenozoic Fauna, mostly dominated by the molluscs. Each of these faunas comprises a group of higher taxa which have similar histories of diversification and evolution, and which dominated the marine record for a significant period of geological time. The main fossil groups considered in Part II can be referred to these evolutionary faunas, and these are sumarised in Table 19.1.

19.2 APPLICATION OF THE MAIN FOSSIL GROUPS IN PALAEOBIOLOGY

Palaeobiology can be simply defined as the study of fossils as once living organisms. Like its sister subject, biology, the range of palaeobiology is vast, but there

Table 19.1 *The fossil record of the main invertebrate groups*

Group	First appearance	Last appearance	Greatest diversity
Cambrian Fauna			
Trilobites	Early Cambrian	Latest Permian	Cambrian
Palaeozoic Fauna			
Brachiopods	Early Cambrian	Extant	Ordovician–Permian
Cephalopods	Cambrian	Extant	
Tabulate/rugose corals	Ordovician	Permian	Ordovician–Permian
Stenolaemate bryozoans	Ordovician	Extant	Ordovician–Triassic
Graptolites	Cambrian	Permian	Ordovician–Silurian
Crinoids	Cambrian	Extant	Ordovician–Permian
Ostracods	Cambrian	Extant	Cambrian–Recent
Foraminifera	Cambrian	Extant	Cambrian–Recent
Modern Fauna			
Bivalves	Cambrian	Extant	Jurassic–Recent
Gastropods	Cambrian	Extant	Palaeogene–Recent
Echinoids	Ordovician	Extant	Jurassic–Recent
Scleractinian corals	Triassic	Extant	Cretaceous–Recent
Gymnolaemate bryozoans	Ordovician	Extant	Jurassic–Recent

are two fields of information which may be most commonly gained from the fossil record: functional morphology and evolution. The allied subject of palaeoecology is considered in Section 19.3 below.

Functional morphology involves interpretation of the form and function of the skeleton or skeletal parts of a fossil organism. This is achieved through three processes: taxonomic uniformitarianism, the direct comparison of fossils with living relatives; comparative anatomy, the interpretation of the function of broadly similar features in unrelated organisms; or physical modelling using scale models of organisms in a variety of environmental conditions.

The reliability of the interpretation of the functional morphology of an organism is directly related to the recency of its extinction. As a general rule, the confidence with which taxonomic uniformitarianism can be applied decreases with advancing age. Even in the case of the so-called 'living fossils' (e.g. the brachiopod *Lingula* and the cephalopod *Nautilus*), which have remained morphologically similar through a great tract of geological time, there must be some doubt. This is because although it is likely that ecological tolerances may have remained stable in some groups (e.g in *Lingula*), this may not be the case in others. Examples of the functional morphological studies discussed in Part II are summarised in Table 19.2.

Fossils are important in the determination of the pattern, mode and rate of evolution. Macroevolution is the evolution of characters above the species level and involves the development of the major features and patterns of the fossil record as a whole. Microevolution is the documentation of changes in an

Table 19.2 *Examples of functional morphology studies in fossils*

Group	Morphological approach	Summary of outcome
Rudist bivalves (Cretaceous)	Comparative anatomy	Interpretation of reef formation and feeding strategy
Frilled gastropods (Silurian)	Taxonomic uniformitarianism	Interpretation of the function of frills as supports
Ammonites (Mesozoic)	Taxonomic uniformitarianism and comparative anatomy	Calculation of the water depth at which ammonite shells collapsed with increased pressure
Rhynchonellid brachiopods (Palaeozoic–Mesozoic)	Taxonomic uniformitarianism and comparative anatomy	Interpretation of the zigzag join of the rhynchonellid commissure as a filtering device
Irregular echinoids (heart urchins) (Mesozoic)	Taxonomic uniformitarianism	Determination of the burrowing activity of heart urchins with different test shapes
Trilobites (Ordovician–Silurian)	Comparative anatomy	Interpretation of terrace lines as sensory apparatus
Graptolites (Ordovician–Devonian)	Physical modelling	Interpretation of the mode of feeding in planktonic graptolites
Zoophycos Feeding trace	Comparative anatomy	Interpretation of the trace producer

organism on a generation-to-generation basis, leading to the development of a new species. Macroevolutionary patterns are mostly determined through the compilation of data on the stratigraphical range and diversity of fossil groups at family level, although detailed studies such as species extinctions are needed to determine the nature of mass extinction event horizons. Microevolutionary patterns are mostly determined by the compilation of morphological changes within a single species through geological time. This is usually developed by detailed collecting from the most complete stratigraphical successions possible, in order to plot the evolutionary lineage and determine species-to-species transitions. Although macroevolutionary patterns are one of the most important contributions made by palaeontology to evolutionary studies, detailed studies at the species level have done much to determine the existence of twin modes of evolution: punctuated equilibrium and phyletic gradualism. Further work has suggested the existence in tandem of gradual morphological change punctuated by rapid morphological shifts: punctuated anagenesis. Examples of evolutionary patterns demonstrated by the fossil groups discussed in Part II are given in Table 19.3.

Table 19.3 *Examples of microevolutionary studies in individual fossil groups*

Group	Mode of evolution	Summary
Gyphaea (Jurassic bivalve)	Punctuated equilibrium or punctuated anagenesis	Reinterpretation of a classic example of gradualism as punctuated equilibrium with an overall size increase
Kosmoceras (Jurassic ammonite)	Phyletic gradualism	Gradual change, with some reversals, in a range of characters
Micraster (Cretaceous echinoid)	Punctuated equilibrium	Reinterpretation of gradualism as punctuation in a classic lineage
Infulaster–Hagenowa (Cretaceous echinoids)	Phyletic gradualism	Gradual elongation of the apical region in an echinoid lineage
Ordovician trilobites	Phyletic gradualism	Gradualistic changes, with reversals, in a number of Ordovician trilobite genera
Zaphrentis (Carboniferous rugose coral)	?Phyletic gradualism	Classic study in need of re-evaluation
Monograptus (Silurian graptolite)	Punctuated anagenesis	Overall shape changes with rapid sicula width increases
Metrarabdotos (Bryozoan)	Punctuated equilibrium	Changes in aperture and shape

19.3 APPLICATION OF FOSSILS IN PALAEOENVIRONMENTAL ANALYSIS

Fossils are important environmental indicators because, as living organisms, their distribution, diversity and abundance were controlled by a series of environmental parameters, such as light, temperature, salinity, substrate, and so on. Taxonomic uniformitarianism is the tool for determining the ecological tolerances of once living organisms through comparison with what is known about their living relatives. Application of this tool further allows interpretation of the nature of the ancient environment, for it follows that where fossils can be assumed to be in their life position, the nature of the environment around them must have been within the acceptable tolerance limits of the individual organisms. This is often complicated by partial preservation of a fauna, removal of organisms from their original life position, or the survival of organisms at the limits of their tolerance in an otherwise hostile environment. However, in these cases, it is often apparent when the fossils have been reworked, as they may be gathered together and aligned by a prevailing current, or damaged; and in most cases, communities of organisms living at the limits of their tolerance levels will not be diverse, although individual species may be abundant. A guide to the environmental significance of fossil organisms is given in Table 19.4. This guide is approximate and subject to the ecological tolerances of individual species.

Table 19.4   *Environmental significance of selected fossil groups*

Group	Main limiters	Environmental significance
Benthonic species		
Bivalves	depth, substrate, oxygen, salinity	Bivalves are important environmental indicators in substrate type, oxygenation and salinity studies; they are mostly neritic
Brachiopods	substrate, oxygen, salinity	Brachiopods are mostly neritic species limited to a firm substrate and fully marine environments
Echinoderms	salinity, substrate, oxygen	Echinoderms are neritic to abyssal organisms limited to fully marine environments
Trilobites	?salinity, substrate, oxygen	Trilobites were probably mostly neritic organisms, although they may have had some oceanic, planktonic species. They are found in a range of fully marine facies
Corals	salinity, depth, temperature	Modern hermatypic species are neritic, limited to a narrow temperature, depth and salinity range. Ahermatypic species can survive in abyssal depths. Rugose corals may have had a similar environmental range to modern corals
Bryozoans	temperature, salinity, substrate, energy	Some bryozoans live in fresh waters, but most are marine, neritic species living in normal salinity ranges
Benthonic foraminifera	temperature, salinity, substrate	Benthonic foraminifera are mostly marine, living in normal salinity ranges
Ostracods	salinity, substrate	Ostracods are mostly benthonic and are found in a wide range of salinities
Nektonic species		
Cephalopods	salinity, temperature, depth, food supply	Cephalopods are fully marine and are mostly neritic
Planktonic species		
Graptolites	salinity, depth	Graptolites were fully marine neritic to oceanic organisms. Some species may have inhabited specific depths in the water column
Planktonic foraminifera	temperature, salinity	Planktonic foraminifera are fully marine neritic to oceanic organisms, sensitive to temperature variation

19.4 APPLICATIONS OF FOSSILS IN STRATIGRAPHY

To have the greatest application as guide fossils in stratigraphy, fossils must satisfy at least the more important of the six main criteria. Guide fossils must be: independent of their environment; fast-evolving; geographically widespread; abundant; readily preserved; and readily identifiable. In practice, this means that nektonic or planktonic organisms have the greatest application as guide fossils, as they are widespread and independent of a particular facies. However, in many cases benthonic organisms may be pressed into service where correlation is on a local scale, or where they have some limited dispersal capability. In these examples, an increased rate of evolution, from first appearance to extinction, is the most important factor in their use as guide fossils. The stratigraphical potential of the main fossil groups is summarised in Table 19.5.

Table 19.5 *Applications in stratigraphy*

Group	Guide fossil criteria					
	Inde-pendent of facies	Wide-spread	Fast-evolving	Abun-dant	Readily preserved	Readily identi-fiable
Planktonic species						
Planktonic foraminifera	yes	yes	yes	yes	yes	yes
Graptolites	yes	yes	yes	yes	yes	yes
Planktonic gastropods	yes	yes	no	no	yes	yes
Nektonic species						
Cephalopods	yes	yes	yes	yes	yes	yes
Benthonic species						
Bivalves	no	no	rarely	yes	yes	yes
Gastropods	no	no	no	yes	yes	yes
Brachiopods	no	no	no	yes	yes	yes
Trilobites	rarely	mostly	mostly	yes	yes	mostly
Corals	no	no	rarely	yes	yes	yes
Bryozoans	no	no	mostly	yes	yes	yes
Benthonic foraminifera	no	mostly	yes	yes	yes	yes
Ostracods	no	mostly	yes	yes	yes	yes
Trace fossils	no	no	no	yes	yes	yes

Part III
FOSSILS AS INFORMATION

20
Data from the Fossil Record

In Part III the concept that fossils are primarily sources of information is reinforced, and their role in the three main areas of applied palaeontology – palaeobiology, palaeoenvironmental interpretation and stratigraphy – is explored. It is important to realise that it is rare indeed for fossils to be found in isolation. In most cases, fossils form part of assemblages of many different taxa, each with its own environmental signal or stratigraphical relevance. In this chapter and the chapters that follow the mechanics of the interpretation of these fossil assemblages is discussed through the examination of detailed case histories.

20.1 FOSSILS AND SEDIMENTS

Fossils are a constituent part of the rock record. They are most commonly encountered in the sedimentary rocks, the end products of a range of processes operating in a great diversity of both marine and terrestrial environments, but they may also be found in igneous and metamorphic rocks. For example, fossils are sometimes incorporated within lava flows. Charred tree stumps have been discovered in the basalt lava flows of Palaeogene age on the Isle of Mull in northwest Scotland, and provide direct evidence of the movement of the lava over the ancient land surface. In addition, fossils are relatively common in rocks metamorphosed by regional tectonic activity. In these cases, the resulting deformed fossils in slates and similar metamorphic rock types are important tools in determining the nature of deformation, as they provide a basis for calculation of the amount of stress required to distort the fossil from its original shape (Box 2.5).

Most sedimentary rocks contain fossils in one form or another. By virtue of their small size and production in huge numbers, microfossils are the most common biological components of the rock record and are encountered in the sedimentary products of almost all environments. In some cases, such as the wind-blown pollen and spores of terrestrial plants, the same microfossils may be distributed in both terrestrial and marine environments, but this is rare. Macrofossils are encountered in a range of sedimentary environments, and may be preserved both *in situ* as autochthonous fossils, or transported and found as allochthonous accumulates. In most cases, the majority of fossils are found in clusters which may be related with varying degrees of confidence to the once living community. As discussed in Chapter 3, a living community is a cluster of living, interacting organisms with a distinctive composition and definite geographical boundaries, and it is often difficult to determine just how much a fossil assemblage can be considered truly representative of such a living community. In general, an estimation of the degree of transport and reworking of individual components of an assemblage or association is essential in determining community structure. For example, fossils preserved in life position may be considered as autochthonous inhabitants of the particular environment, while cumulates of individual groups in shell beds may represent a greater or lesser amount of reworking. In view of these limitations, fossil assemblages can be considered only as an approximation of the original community.

Separate from fossil assemblages, sediments can be classified on the basis of their internal characteristics and macrofossil occurrences into 12 types of fossiliferous deposit (Table 20.1). Marine sediments (types 1–8) have the commonest macrofossils, and here fossils range from perfectly preserved shells to microscopic fragments. *In situ* and reworked fossils are found in all marine sediments to a greater or lesser degree. Autochthonous and intact benthonic organisms are most commonly encountered in build-ups (type 1), characterised by reef-forming organisms; well-laminated sediments (type 3) preserved *in situ* in a low-oxygen environment; and hardgrounds (type 7), where there are abundant encrusting and boring organisms. Semi-autochthonous benthonic organisms are most commonly encountered in well-stratified and poorly stratified shelf sediments (types 2 and 4), where the sedimentary processes are active in exhuming burrowing organisms and transporting shell debris. Allochthonous organisms, whether benthonic, nektonic or planktonic, are commonly encountered in mass flows (type 5), where sediments containing fossils have been remobilised; and lag concentrates and hardgrounds (types 6 and 7), which are fossil accumulates gathered over a considerable period of geological time, during periods of reduced sedimentation rate. Faunas of laminated shales (type 3) and nodular limestones (type 8) are often mostly planktonic or nektonic organisms which after death have fallen through the water column into low-oxygen and deep-water settings. Terrestrial fauna and flora are represented in deposit types 9–12. Trace fossils form an important component of all deposit types, although their diversity and abundance differ according to the nature of the sedimentary environment. In general, then, traces are commonest in marine settings (types 1–8); and are most diverse in shelf sediments (types 2 and 4). Hard substrates (types 1, 6 and 7) will have a distinct trace fauna of rock borers, for example; while well-laminated sediments (type 3) will, by definition, be characterised by a very limited trace fauna, precluded by low oxygen levels.

Table 20.1 *The Goldring classification of fossiliferous deposits*

Deposit type	Sedimentary characteristics	Nature of fossil occurrence
1. Build-ups	Build-ups of carbonate deposits, usually, but not entirely in the photic zone. Some build-ups are associated with bathyal settings	Build-ups are almost entirely of organic origin and composed of corals, algae, bivalves, bryozoans, etc.
2. Well-stratified sediments	Bioclastic limestones and sandstones; storm beds; tuffs, etc., mostly from shelf settings	Fossils common in these mostly neritic sediments; can be fragmentary
3. Well-laminated marine sediments	Bituminous mudrocks (black shales), thinly bedded limestones	Fossils common and well preserved; often composed of nekton or plankton. Trace fossils rare or absent
4. Poorly stratified sediments	Poorly stratified, bioturbated shelf sandstones, mudstones and limestones	Fossil occurrences grade from concentrates to sparsely fossiliferous. Traces common
5. Mass flows	Mass or debris flows in a deep-water setting with floating clasts and fossils derived from shelf settings	Rapid burial often leads to exceptional preservation; in other cases, fossils can be abraded, ecologically mixed and allochthonous
6. Lag concentrates	Associated with erosional surfaces and unconformities in shelf settings	Fossils accumulated over large time interval; often abraded; encrusters and borers common
7. Hardgrounds	Associated with low sedimentation rate; planed and cemented surface	Fossil occurrences as for lag concentrates; encrusters and borers common
8. Nodular limestones	Associated with condensed deposits	Often packed with nektonic organisms such as ammonites
9. Fluvial sediments	Well-stratified and associated with channel-fills and river point bars	Plant fossils often abundant; also non-marine molluscs and ostracods
10. Coals	Peats, lignites and coals	Composed of plant debris
11. Fossil forests	Tree stumps and rootlet beds	Trees and plant material *in situ*
12. Volcanic associations	Lavas, tuffs and volcanic sediments	Variable; includes fossils preserved by mineralising hot springs

Modified from: Goldring, R. (1991) *Fossils in the field*, Longman, Harlow

These fossil deposits provide unique insights into the nature of the sedimentary record, but the level of information provided by them varies. Fossiliferous deposits provide the basis for a range of interpretative studies, and are the main repository of information for the three main palaeontological applications of palaeobiology, palaeoenvironmental analysis and stratigraphy. For example, build-ups (type 1) provide crucial information on the nature, changing constituents and evolution of reefs throughout the Phanerozoic (palaeobiology), as well as helping define the environmental parameters of water depth, salinity and temperature for at least part of the interval (palaeoenvironmental analysis). Equally, both well-stratified (type 2) and poorly stratified (type 4) shelf sandstones and limestones present vast storehouses of information with their rich fauna. These deposits are most commonly the basis for the determination of evolutionary lineages, ecological associations and stratigraphical ranges.

In each case, the value of each fossil or fossil assemblage in providing palaeobiological, palaeoenvironmental or stratigraphical information is dependent upon the nature of the sampling and data collection. For example, for evolutionary work it is necessary to sample fossil assemblages comprehensively from an extended stratigraphical sequence in order to determine any morphological changes; while in palaeoecological work it is necessary to determine from a bedding-plane assemblage which fossils are autochthonous (in place) or allochthonous (transported), and so on.

20.2 DATA RETRIEVAL FROM THE FOSSIL RECORD

The sedimentary record is the primary repository of palaeontological information; once a fossil is liberated from it, the majority of the retrievable information is lost. Typical of this are museums, which have largely historical collections with limited supplementary information (Figure 20.1). This mostly results from the early days of the subject, when collectors often extracted the most perfectly preserved specimens from a given locality, with relatively little regard for detailed stratigraphical horizon, exact geographical location, association with other fossil organisms, the nature of the sedimentary environment, and so on. These specimens provide a relatively limited resource for the full range of palaeontological study. Clearly, then, the actual fossils themselves represent a fraction of the data that can be retrieved from the record, and in collecting fossils we should aim to gather enough associated data to allow us to investigate palaeobiology and stratigraphy and to conduct palaeoenvironmental analysis. The remainder of this section discusses the principles and practice of primary data collection and sampling in palaeontology.

20.2.1 General Principles

The mechanism for primary data collection in palaeontology is of extreme importance, and should not be underestimated. In particular, there are three general principles which need to be observed in all field-based studies in palaeontology.

First, no collecting should be carried out until the stratigraphical succession has been carefully **mapped** and **logged**. Mapping entails the recording of the surface distribution of lithological units on an appropriate topographical base map, usually at a scale of 1:10 000, or on an overlay to an aerial photograph. This provides

Figure 20.1 *The mammal gallery of a late Victorian natural history museum. The Museo Nacional de La Plata in Argentina is an excellent example of a museum which is well laid out and curated. However, in common with all such repositories across the world, most of the geological specimens were collected at a time when stratigraphical information and accurate location details were not routinely collected [Photograph: P. Doyle]*

an understanding of the lateral extent of the geological unit to be studied and is very important in complex folded and faulted areas. Logging is the process whereby the nature of the sedimentary succession is carefully recorded, bed by bed, with particular regard to grain-size variation, sedimentary structures, *in situ* occurrence of fossils, fossil accumulations, bedding associations, contacts and boundaries between beds, and so on (Figure 20.2). The most commonly employed method is the **graphic log**, which is a scaled, accurate but pictorial representation of the sedimentary succession, showing lithology, grain-size variation and/or carbonate content, the nature of boundaries, fossil content and sedimentary structures denoted by symbols (Figures 20.3 and 20.4).

Second, collecting should be carried out according to a set sampling strategy designed for the specific purpose. Without exception, the following elementary

Figure 20.2 *Geologists at work logging sections in the field using measuring tapes and levelling equipment. For safety reasons it is advisable that a hard hat is worn when carrying out such work [Photograph: P. Doyle]*

information is necessary: **geographical location**, accurate to eight-figure national grid coordinates within the British Isles, and to the same level of accuracy where national topographic maps of equivalent quality are available in other parts of the world, or otherwise global latitude and longitude data; **lithological description** of the rock unit containing the sample; **sample position** relative to a stratigraphical height in a succession, a numbered bedding system (again with stratigraphical height), or location on a measured log of the succession; **sample attitude**, that is, whether the fossil is interpreted as in life position or otherwise, or, in the case of an assemblage of fossils, whether there is a preferred attitude or orientation; **facies association**, that is, the association with specific sedimentological features such as hardgrounds or with particular sedimentary structures; and **palaeoecological association**, that is the association of one fossil with another or with a group of individuals.

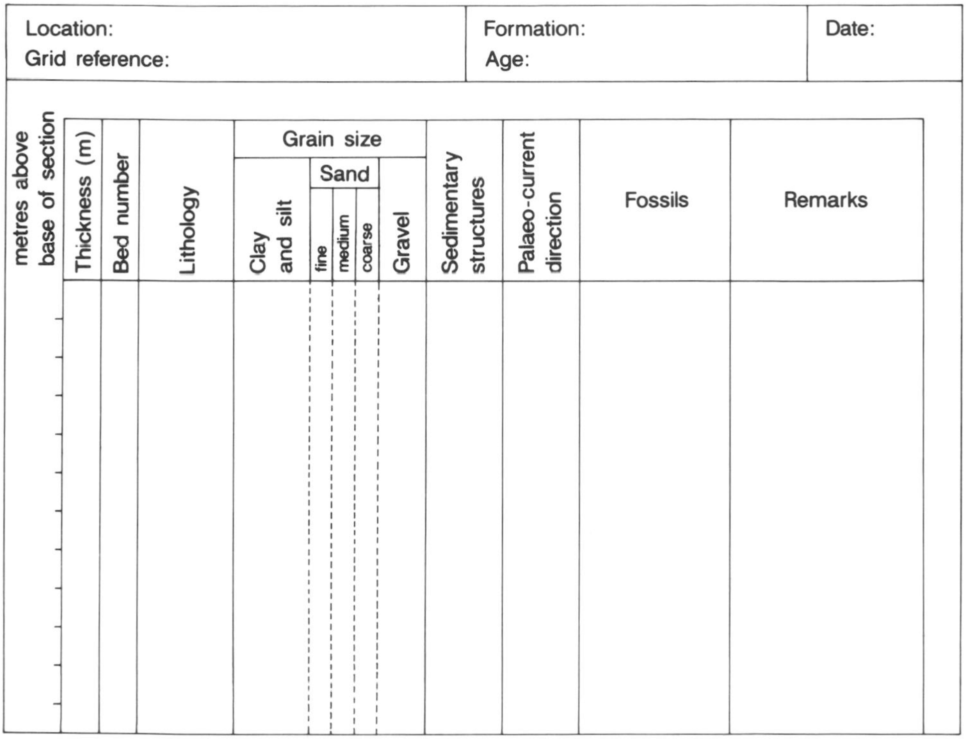

| Location: | | | | | | | Formation: | | | Date: |
| Grid reference: | | | | | | | Age: | | | |

metres above base of section	Thickness (m)	Bed number	Lithology	Grain size					Sedimentary structures	Palaeo-current direction	Fossils	Remarks
				Clay and silt	Sand			Gravel				
					fine	medium	coarse					

Figure 20.3 An example of a graphic logging sheet [Modified from: Tucker (1982) Field Description of Sedimentary Rocks, *Open University Press, Fig. 2.1, p. 13*]

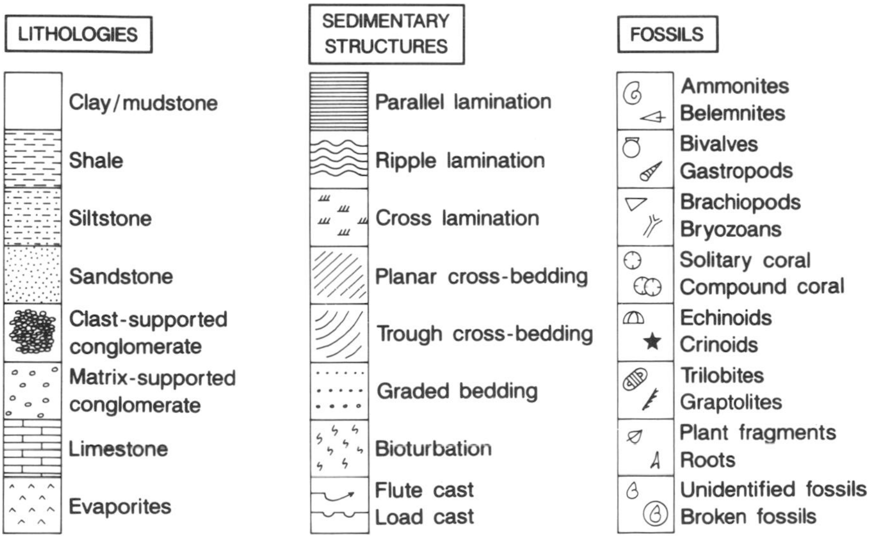

LITHOLOGIES	SEDIMENTARY STRUCTURES	FOSSILS
Clay/mudstone	Parallel lamination	Ammonites / Belemnites
Shale	Ripple lamination	Bivalves / Gastropods
Siltstone	Cross lamination	Brachiopods / Bryozoans
Sandstone	Planar cross-bedding	Solitary coral / Compound coral
Clast-supported conglomerate	Trough cross-bedding	Echinoids / Crinoids
Matrix-supported conglomerate	Graded bedding	Trilobites / Graptolites
Limestone	Bioturbation	Plant fragments / Roots
Evaporites	Flute cast / Load cast	Unidentified fossils / Broken fossils

Figure 20.4 Examples of symbols to be used on the graphic logging sheet [Modified from: Tucker (1982) Field Description of Sedimentary Rocks, *Open University Press, Fig. 2.2, p. 14*]

Third, fossils recovered from scree ('float') or other surface deposits weathered or eroded from the sedimentary succession can provide important information about the range of morphological variation of a fossil group, but cannot be viewed in the same light as *in situ* fossils. This is simply because loose specimens cannot be located accurately relative to a detailed log, and are removed from their sedimentological and stratigraphical setting. In all such cases, the only information that can be retrieved is that of functional morphology and species variation, and even then it is of limited practical use.

20.2.2 Sampling

The process of sampling in palaeontological study is important as it directly influences the relevance of the data set in palaeobiological, palaeoenvironmental and stratigraphical studies. In particular, many studies have suffered from a perceived 'collector bias', which can be variously ascribed to picking out the best specimens, the largest specimens, the smallest specimens, and so on. Many palaeontological studies have been called into question by the status of the sampling and therefore it is extremely important that any sampling is carried out relative to a particular strategy designed to meet the particular demands of the study. There are three basic types of sampling strategy: **search sampling**, defined as the search for specific organisms or horizons within a given rock succession; **systematic sampling**, defined as regular sampling at specific intervals through a stratigraphical column; and **random sampling**, defined as the sampling at random intervals through a stratigraphical succession. Search sampling is most likely to create collector bias, as the search will be most likely to result in a selective collection. However, search sampling is appropriate where, for example, stratigraphical correlation is the aim of the sampling. Systematic and random sampling are more likely to result in a statistically significant result, especially where these techniques are used together. Where the object of the exercise is to develop a stratigraphical succession for an individual species, for example in the development of a lineage relationship, or in the development of a biozonation scheme, systematic and search sampling are the most appropriate. Palaeoenvironmental studies of diversity and abundance are best served through a statistically valid approach, and random sampling allows rigour to be attached with the minimum of bias.

20.2.3 Collecting

Different collecting techniques are appropriate for different fossil groups. Invertebrate macrofossils are most commonly collected in the field using a hammer and chisel, or a trowel in soft sediments. In each case, samples should be carefully wrapped in an appropriate wrapping material, usually soft paper, and placed in separate sealable bags. Each bag should be annotated using an indelible marker with location, bed number, sample number and date, and this information should be transcribed into an appropriate field notebook (Figure 20.5). Sample numbers

Figure 20.5 *Author's field collection from the Jurassic rocks of the Antarctic Peninsula. The collection is laid our for sorting prior to wrapping. Each specimen is protected by sticky fabric tape upon which the location and individual specimen number has been written. These samples were located stratigraphically on a graphic log [Photograph: P. Doyle]*

should ideally be noted on the graphic log adjacent to the sampled unit. Further work may be needed to extract the fossil from its matrix. This should be carried out in the laboratory using appropriate tools. In such cases, retention of the matrix is valuable as it may yield microfossils.

Microfossils are, for the most part, difficult to detect with the naked eye, and the nature of the sampling is such that a bulk sediment sample is collected for processing back at the laboratory. It is essential that the interval from which the bulk sample is collected is clean and clear from potential contamination from other sources of microfossils. It is also very important to remove weathered surface material which is unlikely to contain microfossils as they are easily dissolved. In general, ostracods and foraminifera are commonest in mudrocks and limestones, and in these lithologies, around 200–500 g of sediments should be collected to yield sufficient specimens from each sample site. In fact, only half of each sample collected will be examined, as the other half should be kept in reserve in case of problems in extracting the microfossils in the laboratory. As with macrofossils, appropriate data should be recorded in indelible ink upon the plastic bag containing the sample, and the bag should be firmly sealed. In many cases, it is important to obtain both macro-and microfossil samples from the same horizons for detailed palaeoecological work or stratigraphical comparison. As with macrofossils, sample numbers should be noted alongside the appropriate bed on the graphic log sheet.

It is usually inappropriate to collect trace fossils, as they form part and parcel of the fabric of the sedimentary rock. In most cases, detailed sketches, photographs and measurements taken in the field are the most important recording media. In some cases, intensity of burrowing (ichnofabric) can be estimated semi-quantitatively in the field using the published guides, and the interrelationship of burrows in the sedimentary record (tiering) should also be noted. Records should be made both on the graphic log (as part of the fabric of the sedimentary record) and in the field notebook, together with such data as the frame number of any photograph taken.

20.3 DATA RETRIEVAL FROM THE PUBLISHED RECORD

The publication of stratigraphical, range, palaeoecological association and other data provides a significant source of secondary information in the determination of aspects of the fossil record. This is most appropriate in the compilations of extinction data at the family level which have fuelled much of the debate about periodicity of extinctions in the fossil record in recent years (further discussed in Chapter 21). It is also important in the determination of the geographical range of individual taxa, which is necessarily reliant on the published literature documenting its distribution across the world. In both cases, the data set has been severely criticised as being of unequal quality and therefore of questionable scientific relevance. However, it is clear that the compilation of bibliographic sources is an important source of cumulative data in the palaeontological record, and is sufficient at least to suggest major trends and distribution patterns. This forms the basis for most palaeobiogeographical studies, an example of which is discussed in Chapter 22.

20.4 SUMMARY OF KEY POINTS

- Most sedimentary rocks contain fossils, and sedimentary deposits can be classified into 12 types, according to the nature of the fossil occurrence. Marine sediments contain the commonest fossils which vary from autochthonous build-ups through semi-authochthonous shelf associations to allochthonous assemblages associated with mass flows (Table 20.1).
- Once a fossil is removed from its containing sedimentary rock, the majority of the retrievable information is lost. Care must be taken to gather as much information before collection as is necessary to allow the interpretation of palaeobiology, palaeoenvironment and stratigraphical value.
- Three general principles govern primary data collection. Firstly, every fossil-bearing succession should be **logged** prior to collection. Secondly, collecting should be carried out according to a set strategy. Finally, loose specimens should be avoided unless considered valuable for determining morphological variation.
- Sampling can be **random** or **systematic**, or it can involve the simple **search** for specific fossil types. Random sampling is most applicable in palaeoenvironmental studies; systematic and search sampling are most applicable in

palaeobiology and stratigraphy. Collecting should be carried out with appropriate equipment and techniques.
- Data may also be retrieved from the published record. In general, this is less reliable than primary data, but it is valuable in the interpretation of broad patterns in palaeontology.

20.5 SUGGESTED READING

Goldring's (1991) book is almost unique in providing a guide to palaeontological data collection in the field. Tucker (1982) is a good field guide to sedimentological logging and other techniques, while Barnes (1988) provides basic information on field mapping. Raup and Stanley (1978) is an important source of information for all palaeontological studies. Kummel and Raup (1965), although old, has a useful section on the nature of sampling strategies in palaeontology, and contains many papers on individual laboratory techniques. Briggs and Crowther (1990) also has a section on laboratory techniques. Haynes (1981) devotes a chapter to the collection and preparation of microfossils. Horowitz and Potter (1971) is an invaluable reference to the identification of fossil fragments in sedimentary rock thin sections. Finally, Hughes (1989) provides a new, if unconventional, perspective on the way in which palaeontological data should be collected and recorded without bias.

Barnes, J. 1988. *Basic Geological Mapping.* Geological Society Handbook. Open University Press, Milton Keynes.
Briggs, D.E.G. & Crowther, P.E. (eds) 1990. *Palaeobiology – A Synthesis.* Blackwell Scientific Publications, Oxford.
Goldring, R. 1991. *Fossils in the Field.* Longman, Harlow.
Haynes, J.R. 1981. *Foraminifera.* Macmillan, London.
Horowitz, A.S. & Potter, P.E. 1971. *Introductory Petrography of Fossils.* Springer-Verlag, Berlin.
Hughes, N.F. 1989. *Fossils as Information.* Cambridge University Press, Cambridge.
Kummel, B. & Raup, D. (eds) 1965. *Handbook of Paleontological Techniques.* W.H. Freeman, San Francisco.
Raup, D. & Stanley, S.M. 1978. *Principles of Paleontology.* Second edition. W.H. Freeman, San Francisco.
Tucker, M.E. 1982. *The Field Description of Sedimentary Rocks.* Geological Society Handbook. Open University Press, Milton Keynes.

21
Studies in Palaeobiology

This chapter deals with case studies in the application of fossils in palaeobiological studies; in particular, it concentrates on the role of fossils and the fossil record in determining evolutionary patterns.

21.1 GENERAL CONSIDERATIONS

In determining evolutionary patterns from the geological record, four factors are of extreme importance: the stratigraphical completeness of the interval sampled; the sampling procedure; the range in variation of the organisms under study; and the nature of the data compilation. These are explored below.

1. **Stratigraphical completeness**. As discussed in Chapter 2, the nature and completeness of the stratigraphical record have long been debated by geologists and palaeontologists. Many early estimates of the age of the Earth were based on simple calculations of the thickest sedimentary successions multiplied by the rate of accumulation as observed in a variety of settings. This method was flawed simply because the sedimentary record is a result of the cumulative effect of both deposition and removal of sediment. In fact, the longer the time span, the more likely it is that the stratigraphical record is incomplete. Similarly, sedimentary thickness is not an accurate proxy for time as in deeper-water environments; away from the eroding and depositional influences of wave action, the sedimentary record may be subject to sparse sedimentation, but relatively little erosion. The sedimentary record in such environments may therefore be thin but relatively complete. In shallow-water environments, where wave and other high-energy activity is present, sediments may be relatively thick but incomplete, with numerous gaps, a function of high erosion and depositional rates. In general terms, the most complete stratigraphical

sequences are those which are subject to continuous sedimentation but which are away from the eroding powers of waves. Typical locations are in offshore shelf, deep-sea and lacustrine settings. For all settings, estimates of stratigraphical completeness may be determined by the application of simple calculations. These may be based on absolute dating techniques, and detailed comparison of the sedimentation rate in present-day environments with the thickness of the ancient sedimentary record (Box 21.1). Such calculations are important in providing an estimate of the resolving power of the stratigraphical record in the determination of evolutionary patterns.

2. **Sampling procedure**. The aim of evolutionary studies is to plot the morphological changes in a lineage or group of lineages through geological time. The effectiveness of such a study is related to the nature of the stratigraphical record. Put simply, an imperfect stratigraphical record will give a microevolutionary pattern which is deceptive. This is particularly important where the determination of gradualistic or punctuated patterns is required, since it has long been argued that the sedimentary record would naturally favour a punctuated pattern. For microevolutionary studies, samples need to satisfy two criteria: firstly, each sample must be sufficiently vertically constrained that it might represent an approximation to a living population; and secondly, sampling must be carried out at sufficient closely spaced intervals to enable the rate and mode of change within the sedimentary sequence to be determined. Clearly, an appreciation of the nature and completeness of the stratigraphical record is essential before a microevolutionary study can be undertaken. In the main, then, a systematic sampling procedure is the most appropriate. Sample size is constrained by the abundance of the fossil group within the deposit.

3. **Range of variation in morphology**. Morphological change is most clearly demonstrated where a range of morphological features can be measured, and therefore any observed changes can be quantified. Morphological variation in a species may be demonstrated with respect to two axes: horizontally, representing the actual morphological variation within a species for a given time period; and vertically, representing shifts in morphology through geological time (Figure 21.1). Clearly it is important to establish the range in morphology for a given time plane, in order that lineage shifts, whether gradual or rapid, can be evaluated. This has had increased importance with the demonstration of reversals in morphological characteristics through geological time.

4. **The nature of the data compilation**. For macroevolutionary patterns in particular, which rely on the compilation of a number of data, it is important that there was a uniform standard in the original data collection. Often, this is impossible to achieve given the number of scientists involved, and there are three major problems. Firstly, inaccurate or incomplete recording of stratigraphical position and age can lead to the extension or contraction of the actual range of the taxon under study, and give rise to pseudo-appearances or extinctions. Such phenomena are clearly an artefact of imperfect plotting and recording of geological ranges of species, genera, families, and so on. A second problem is misidentification, and the tendency for assignment of fossils to 'balloon taxa' which have flexible morphological boundaries, the definition of

BOX 21.1: RESOLUTION ANALYSIS

The resolving power of the stratigraphical record can be calculated using three factors:

1. Total time (T) to deposit a rock sequence of given thickness (X). This is obtained through absolute dating methods of the upper and lower limits of the sequence.
2. Estimated time (m) taken for the deposition of an individual sedimentary layer of a given thickness (i). Two estimates may be made. The longer estimate is based upon the minimum rate of sedimentation (m_{min}) and is calculated by the following equation:

$$m_{min} = \frac{iT}{X}$$

For example, a 1 metre thick bed (i) in a 12 metre thick sequence (X) known to have been deposited over an interval of 1500 years (T) would have an estimated time of deposition of 125 years (m_{min}). The shorter estimate (m_{max}) is based upon the observed time taken for the same thickness of sediment to be deposited in an equivalent environmental setting today. This estimate is calculated using the equation:

$$m_{max} = \frac{ic}{s}$$

where i is the thickness of the bed, c is a measure of the compaction of the sediment after deposition, and s is the rate of deposition of an equivalent uncompacted thickness of sediment today. For example, if the compaction of our 1 metre thick bed was at a rate of 1:1, and if the deposition rate for a similar sedimentary environment today is 17 metres per 10 000 years, then the shortest estimate of deposition would be 58.8 years.
3. Stratigraphical completeness (S). This is the proportion of a time interval which is represented by a thickness of strata, as opposed to that which is lost by erosion. This may be calculated by the equation:

$$S = \frac{Xc}{sT} \times 100\%$$

For our hypothetical example, where X is 12 metres, c is 1, s is 17 metres per 10 000 years and T is 1500 years, estimated stratigraphical completeness would be 47%.

These three factors allow palaeontologists to determine the relative time represented by the stratigraphical record, in order that a clear idea of the resolution available in determining microevolutionary patterns can be gained.

Sources: Schindel, P.E. (1982) Resolution analysis: a new approach to the gaps in the fossil record. *Paleobiology*, 8, 340–353. Skelton, P.W. (1993) The fossil record of evolution in species. *In* Skelton, P.W. (ed.), *Evolution: a Biological and Palaeontological Approach*. Addison-Wesley, Wokingham, 445–509.

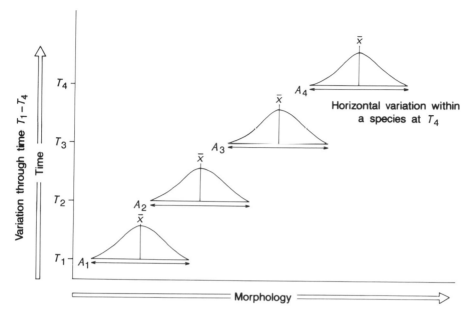

Horizontal variation within
a species at T_4

Figure 21.1 *The range in variation of morphology within a species. Morphological variation may be demonstrated with respect to two axes. The horizontal axis represents the variation for a given time period. The vertical axis represents morphological shifts through geological time*

which may be continuously 'inflated' by the assignment of dubious represent-atives to them. Finally, there is a tendency for names of taxa to change at major stratigraphical boundaries, where one expert's experience stops and another's begins.

The following case histories demonstrate how, with accurate collecting and rigorous analysis, it is possible to determine evolutionary patterns from the fossil record.

21.2 STASIS AND PUNCTUATION IN BRYOZOANS
(Cheetham, 1986)

1. Introduction

The punctuated equilibrium model was developed in the early 1970s by Step-hen Gould and Niles Eldredge (Eldredge and Gould 1972) primarily because they felt that the evolutionary record of most fossil groups was not a smooth curve of gradual change, but actually staccato, a record of long periods of morphological stasis interrupted by rapid change. In general, the authors of the punctuational model felt that the construction of evolutionary lineages from the fossil record was underlined by an expectation that there would be some gradual change, and little or no expectation that species would remain mor-phologically static for large periods of geological time. Following Eldredge and

Gould's seminal paper, few studies have demonstrated either gradual change or stasis without some doubt. In 1986, Alan Cheetham published a study of evolution in a Neogene bryozoan based on rigorous collecting and analysis which convincingly demonstrated the existence of evolutionary stasis.

In his study, Cheetham defined the difference between the gradualistic and punctuational models of evolution on the basis of the time scale of morphological change, and, in particular, whether the rate of change within the morphological boundaries of an individual species was equivalent to or greater than that across the species boundaries. In other words, in the gradualistic model new species could expect to be created by a gradual and relatively constant rate of change, and in practice it should be difficult to determine definite boundaries between ancestor and descendant. In the punctuated model, on the other hand, morphological change within a species would be minimal, and the development of new species recorded by rapid morphological shifts. In such cases, ancestor and descendant can be clearly distinguished.

2. The Neogene Bryozoan *Metrarabdotos*

The Neogene cheilostome bryozoan *Metrarabdotos* formed the basis for Cheetham's study. In bryozoans, there are sufficient differences between zooids to give an indication of the range of variation within a species that can be encountered, and this provides an estimate of the level of morphological resolution above which species-level distinctions, characterising new species, can be made. In cheilostome bryozoans there is a strong correspondence between skeletal and soft-part morphology which implies that changes in the skeleton reflect overall changes in the organism as a whole.

Metrarabdotos is an ideal genus for this type of study. Specimens were sampled from Upper Miocene to Lower Pliocene deposits of the Dominican Republic, spanning the interval from 3.5 to 8 million years ago (Figure 21.2). During this interval, *Metrarabdotos* was diverse and widely dispersed, and detailed collections can be made from the sedimentary sequence between these two datum points. Estimates of the stratigraphical completeness (Box 21.1) for the interval as a whole demonstrated that it was remarkably complete, with preservation of up to 63% of the record. In addition, based upon comparison of sedimentary thickness and present-day accumulation rates (Box 21.1), Cheetham determined that the mean estimated interval between each horizon sampled was in the order of 160 000 years, with a range of 20 000 to 1 million years.

3. Rate of Change in Evolving *Metrarabdotos*

For each sampled interval, 46 morphological characters were measured from each *Metrarabdotos* population. Not all of these characters were sufficient to distinguish between species, so Cheetham weighted characters on the basis of their ability to distinguish species. Fifteen characters of the original 46 were selected for detailed analysis. Twelve *Metrarabdotos* species were recognised within the sampled interval (Figure 21.2). The resolution of sampling, every 160 000 years, was adequate for nine comparisons of rates of change of the 15 characters within and across species boundaries. In every case, the variance in the rate of change was significantly greater across the species boundaries than

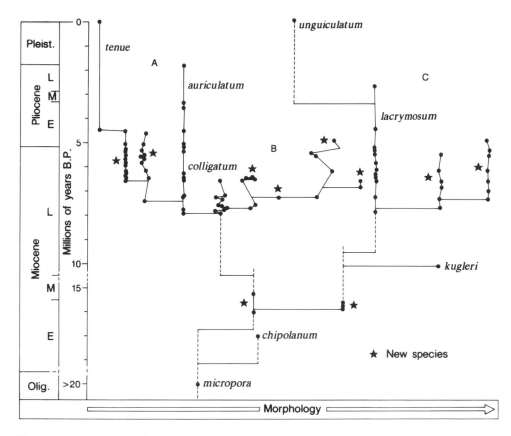

Figure 21.2 *Punctuated equilibrium in the Neogene bryozoan* Metrarabdotos. *The diagram represents species developed during rapid morphological shifts separated by periods of no morphological change [Modified from: Cheetham (1986)* Paleobiology **12**, *Fig. 5, p. 196]*

within individual species. In fact, in most cases, the rate of change within species was found to be practically zero, with the ratio of within-species variation to across-species variation being less than 0.3. This study provides direct evidence of stasis in the fossil record, with species distinguishable because of the strong morphological shift between them (Figure 21.2). This mode of evolution was supported by the fact that the species ranges were seen to overlap, which is consistent with the punctuational model, but not with a gradual transition from one species to another.

4. Comment

The validity of Cheetham's study is based on three factors: the stratigraphical resolution and sampling interval; the range of morphological variation; and the rigour of the statistical analysis. The stratigraphical resolution determined the sampling interval, and the range in morphological characters, together with their biological relevance to the organisms and their rigorous analysis, led to the determination of the detailed pattern of microevolution.

5. References

Cheetham, A.H. 1986. Tempo of evolution in a Neogene bryozoan: rates of morphologic change within and across species boundaries. *Paleobiology*, **12**, 190–202.

Eldredge, N. and Gould, S.J. 1972. Punctuated equilibria: an alternative to phyletic gradualism. *In* Schopf, T.J. (ed.), *Models in Paleobiology*. Freeman Cooper, San Francisco, 82–115.

21.3 GRADUALISM AND REVERSALS IN TRILOBITES
(Sheldon, 1987)

1. Introduction

It has been argued that in the main, the stratigraphical record favours the model of punctuated equilibrium (Fortey, 1985), and that gradualism, as interpreted as unidirectional, straight-line change in morphology, would be difficult to determine in what is considered to be a fossil record of extreme imperfection. One of the most convincing modern studies of gradualism in the fossil record is Sheldon's (1987) study of some 15 000 trilobites collected from the Ordovician sediments of central Wales.

2. The Trilobites of Builth, Central Wales

Trilobites from the Builth inlier in central Wales are among the best-known and most abundant of all trilobites from the British Isles. Trilobites belonging to eight generic groupings were collected systematically by Sheldon from the Teretiusculus Shales, belonging to the Llandeilo Series of the Ordovician. The total thickness of these shales is in the region of 500 m, probably deposited over a time span of some 2 million years within a single graptolite biozone. Samples were collected from 380 levels, each with an average stratigraphical thickness of 23 cm, and through comparison with sedimentation in similar environments today, Sheldon estimated that the actual time span for each interval was probably no greater than 900 years.

3. Parallel Gradualistic Lineages

Sheldon had originally set out to identify the well-described trilobite fauna of the single graptolite biozone, but had recognised that the existing species definitions were based on characters which seemed to vary throughout the section studied. In *Ogygiocarella*, for example, the species *O. debuchii* and *O. angustissima* were originally thought to be distinguishable on the basis of ribs on the pygidium – the former having 11, the latter 13. Detailed collecting by Sheldon demonstrated that in fact there were numerous intermediates between the two 'species', and that in practice it was extremely hard to draw a boundary between them (Figure 21.3). This position was replicated with other genera, particularly *Cnemidopyge* (Figure 21.4) and *Platycalymene*, and a total of eight lineages were identified in which there was a net increase in the number of pygidial ribs. Perhaps even more surprisingly, there were times when the lineages showed temporary reversals in the trend, with a reduction in the number of ribs (Figure 21.3).

4. Comment

This example clearly demonstrates gradualism in a rapidly deposited, uniform shelf environment. The function of the ribs is unknown, but their variance through the section was clearly demonstrated by the accuracy of the collecting. The reversals demonstrated by Sheldon could be argued to reflect small-scale gaps in the record masking the true pattern, but in a later paper Sheldon (1993) demonstrated that with further accuracy of collecting, the *Cnemidopyge* lineage shows an overall trend in rib increase, with a large number of superimposed reversals, probably a true reflection of the nature of evolution in these benthonic organisms (Figure 21.3). Sheldon's study clearly illustrates the necessity for accurate and closely spaced collecting to define the nature of the evolutionary lineages, and for a fossil record free from obvious breaks in which the resolving power is high, in this case to within 900 years per collection interval.

5. References

Fortey, R.A. 1985. Gradualism and punctuated equilibria as competing and complementary theories. *In* Cope, J.C.W & Skelton, P.W. (eds), *Evolutionary Case Histories from the Fossil Record*, Special Papers in Palaeontology 33, London, 17–28.

Sheldon, P.R. 1987. Parallel gradualistic evolution of Ordovician trilobites. *Nature*, **330**, 561–563.

Sheldon, P.R. 1993. Making sense of microevolutionary patterns. *In* Lees, D.R. & Edwards, D. (eds), *Evolutionary Patterns and Processes*. Linnaean Society Symposium, Volume 14. Academic Press, London, 19–31.

21.4 THE NATURE OF AN EXTINCTION BOUNDARY
(Keller, 1988; Keller and Barrera, 1990)

1. Introduction

The nature and causes of the mass extinction at the Cretaceous–Tertiary boundary have proven to be one of the most hotly debated scientific issues of the late twentieth century. This debate has arisen partly because of interest in the extinction of the dinosaurs and other large reptiles, and partly because of the recent hypothesis that a large extra-terrestrial body impacted with the Earth at this time. The impact hypothesis, first developed by Alvarez *et al.* (1980) and the subject of a great body of research since that paper, was primarily based on the geochemical enrichment of the element iridium within a 'boundary-clay' layer at several sites across the world. Iridium is an element which is common only in meteorites and in the Earth's mantle, and levels of iridium in the 'boundary clay' were found to be several times the normally expected background concentrations. Other evidence, such as the presence of quartz grains displaying shock-induced fracturing, has led to the belief that a large meteorite, some 10 km in diameter, may have impacted with the Earth at the close of the Cretaceous and created a failure in the global ecosystem.

In fact, it can be argued that the fossil record provides relatively little evidence of a geologically instantaneous mass extinction event which coincides

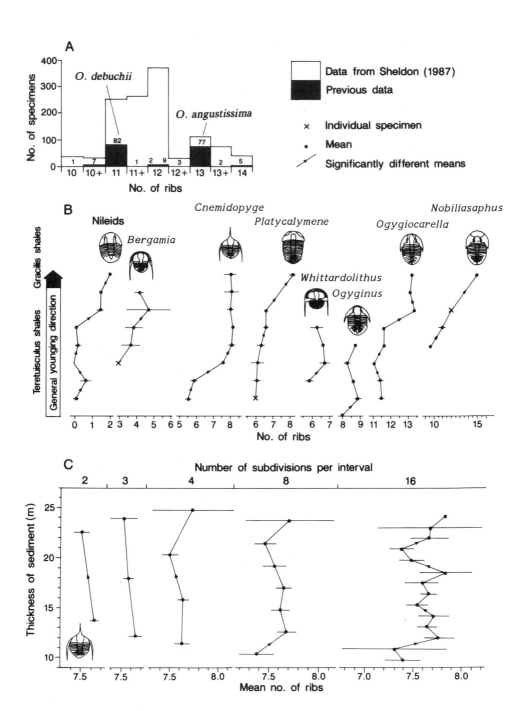

Figure 21.4 *The Ordovician trilobite* Cnemidopyge *[Photograph: P. Sheldon]*

Figure 21.3 (opposite) *Phyletic gradualism in Ordovician trilobites.* **A:** *The traditional separation of two species of* Ogygiocarella *is on the basis of the number of ribs. Sheldon's collecting demonstrated that both species fall within the range of variation of a single species.* **B:** *Gradual changes in the number of ribs on the pygidia of eight trilobite genera. Some of these lineages show both increases and decreases in the number of ribs.* **C:** *Changes in the number of pygidial ribs in the* Cnemidopyge *lineage. With finer sampling intervals per section, the pattern of increase and decrease in rib numbers becomes more marked [A, B modified from: Sheldon (1987)* Nature **330***, Figs 2 and 4, pp. 561 and 562;* **C** *modified from: Sheldon (1993) In* Lees & Edwards (Eds) Evolutionary Patterns and Processes, *Academic Press, Fig. 1, p. 23]*

with the iridium-rich boundary-clay layer. Each of the fossil groups so far investigated appears to show a gradual decline which began an estimated 300 000 to 400 000 years before the end of the Cretaceous, although there is an accelerated rate in extinctions at the boundary itself. The extinctions at the end of the Cretaceous may well have been the result of a global catastrophe, but they may also have been directly influenced by more local events, or by sea-level or climatic changes, for example. Clearly, the key to understanding the nature of these extinctions is a sedimentary sequence estimated to have a high level of stratigraphical completeness. This is not quite as easy as it seems, as around 90% of all Cretaceous–Tertiary boundary sections are extremely thin, and have abundant gaps, associated with a major regressive phase at the end of the Cretaceous. Recently, however, some expanded sections known to have had high rates of sedimentation have been sampled on a centimetre scale for foraminifera, in order that the effects of both local and catastrophic extinction events can be disentangled.

2. The Cretaceous–Tertiary Boundary at El Kef, Tunisia

Until recently, it was felt that the only hope of a complete stratigraphical record spanning the Cretaceous–Tertiary boundary was in cores obtained from drilling in the deep-ocean, which are characterised by both steady rates of sedimentation and limited chance of erosion from currents and waves, characteristic of inshore waters. The deep ocean record recovered showed a clear transition from foraminifera-rich carbonates to a thin, carbonate-poor layer devoid of foraminifera. In fact, close comparison of the deep-ocean record with sequences deposited in shallow waters in Spain, Tunisia and Texas using guide fossils has shown that there is a gap in the stratigraphical record coincident with the boundary in most deep-water successions. The most complete section so far discovered is that of El Kef in Tunisia. Here the Cretaceous–Tertiary boundary section is contained within the marls of the El Haria Formation, and the boundary is denoted by a 2–3 millimetre thick, rust-coloured layer at the base of a black clay which has been shown to be enriched in iridium (Figure 21.5).

In her study of the foraminifera of the marl sequence at El Kef, Keller (1988) used samples collected with reference to the clearly denoted boundary layer. A programme of systematic sampling was carried out. The section was sampled up to 4 m below, and up to 10 m above, the boundary layer. Below the boundary, sampling was carried out at 20 cm intervals. Above the boundary clay, systematic sampling was carried out at 5 cm intervals for the first 1.6 m, 20 cm intervals for the next 1.4 m, and at 50 cm intervals between 3 and 10 m above the boundary.

3. Foraminifera from El Kef

At El Kef, the diversity of the latest Cretaceous planktonic foraminifera is constant at around 50 species, with an average of 15–20 species above the boundary layer, a decline of around 78% in the total species diversity (Figure 21.5). This decline is rapid and commenced 25 cm below the boundary layer, reaching a maximum of seven species (86% decline in diversity) at 7 cm above the boundary. Total species diversity remains very low (ten species or less) in the first 50 cm of clay above the boundary layer, increasing to a maximum of 15–20 species above this level (Figure 21.5).

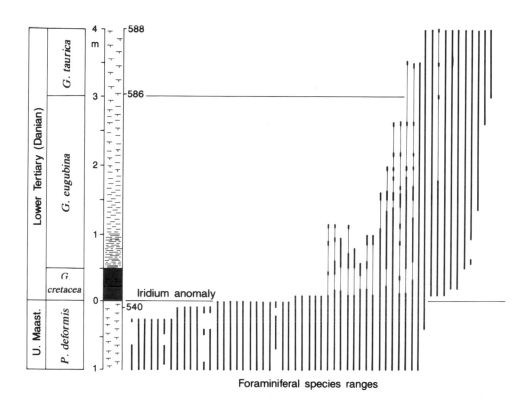

Figure 21.5 *Changes in the foraminiferal species diversity across the Cretaceous–Tertiary boundary at El Kef, Tunisia. Note that extinctions took place both before and after the iridium event [Modified from: Keller and Barrera (1990)* Geological Society of America, Special Paper, **247**, *Fig. 1, p. 567]*

4. Extinctions at the Cretaceous–Tertiary Boundary

The planktonic foraminifera at El Kef show an extended extinction pattern which straddles the Cretaceous–Tertiary boundary section. About 13 species (29%) disappear between 25 and 7 cm below the boundary layer. Twelve species (26%) disappear at the boundary, while five species (11%) disappear 15 cm above the boundary, eight (17%) linger on into the overlying black clay, and a further eight (17%) survive the extinction event (Figure 21.5). Clearly, the detailed collecting in the El Kef section demonstrates a more complex extinction pattern than simple mass mortality at the base of the iridium-rich clay layer, and similarly complex patterns of extinction have been demonstrated in the Brazos River region in Texas. In fact, Keller and Barrera (1990) interpret the record at El Kef as displaying three extinction events with different causes: a pre-boundary extinction (29%) probably associated with environmental changes such as sea-level fall; boundary extinctions (26%) associated with the iridium anomaly, and therefore possibly affected by the postulated impact; and post-boundary extinctions (28%) associated with the black clay, indicating environmentally stressed conditions, perhaps associated with a loss in primary oceanic productivity.

6. Comment
This example clearly demonstrates the importance of systematic sampling techniques in determining the nature of major events in Earth history, such as a mass extinction. Previous studies on incomplete sections have shown that there was an instantaneous and catastrophic extinction of planktonic foraminifera at the Cretaceous–Tertiary boundary. Systematic studies of expanded sequences show that the extinction was complex, with events before, during and after what is generally accepted as a major catastrophic event. This allows us to determine the complex nature of such events for the first time, and therefore to develop an adequate basis on which to build models of causal mechanisms.

6. References
Alvarez, L.W., Alvarez, W., Asaro, F. & Michel, H.V. 1980. Extraterrestrial cause for the Cretaceous–Tertiary extinction. *Science*, **208**, 1095–1108.

Keller, G. 1988. Extinction, survivorship and evolution of planktic foraminifera across the Cretaceous/Tertiary boundary at El Kef, Tunisia. *Marine Micropaleontology*, **13**, 239–263.

Keller, G. & Barrera, E. 1990. The Cretaceous/Tertiary boundary impact hypothesis and the paleontological record. *In* Sharpton, V.L. & Ward, P.D. (eds), *Global Catastrophes in Earth History: An Interdisciplinary Conference on Impacts, Volcanism and Mass Mortality*. Geological Society of America Special Paper 247, Boulder, CO, 563–575.

21.5 THE PERIODICITY OF EXTINCTIONS
(Raup and Sepkoski, 1984; 1986; Patterson and Smith, 1987)

1. Introduction
It is now well accepted that a number of major mass extinction episodes, times when the standing diversity of the Earth's biota fell dramatically over a geologically rapid interval, have occurred throughout the geological past. In order to assess more accurately the nature and timing of these extinction events, two palaeontologists, David Raup and John Sepkoski, embarked upon the mammoth task of compiling the stratigraphical ranges of all known marine families, and latterly, genera, from published records. This work has clearly identified major extinction events; but, more controversially, Raup and Sepkoski (1984; 1986) have claimed that on the basis of detailed statistical analyses, there appears to have been a clear periodicity in extinctions, with a major event every 26 million years (Figure 21.6). However, this pattern has been questioned by other palaeontologists, particularly with respect to the nature of the data set.

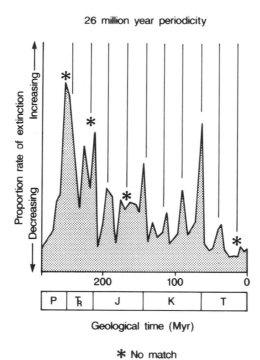

26 million year periodicity

Geological time (Myr)

∗ No match

Figure 21.6   *The periodicity of extinctions in the geological past. Asterisks illustrate that the 26 million year periodicity is approximate in some cases [Modified from: Sepkoski (1982) Geological Society of America Special Paper 190]*

2. The 26 Million Year Periodicity of Extinctions

In their initial analysis, Raup and Sepkoski (1984) compiled family range data for only the latter part of the Phanerozoic, spanning the late Permian to the middle Miocene. They excluded living families (i.e. families which were not extinct), all families where last stratigraphical appearances were not precisely known, and all families which had questionable status, either taxonomically or in stratigraphical position. In this way, Raup and Sepkoski hoped to reduce the inevitable inaccuracy of a compendium of many other people's data. In total, 567 families were analysed. Twelve statistically significant extinction peaks were found, with eight of the major peaks separated by a regular interval of approximately 26 million years (Figure 21.6). Later analyses with more data (Raup and Sepkoski, 1986), especially genera, reconfirmed that extinction appeared to follow a definite cycle every 26 million years.

3. The Data Set Questioned

The data set used by Raup and Sepkoski is necessarily second-hand, as it would be an impossible task to try to verify the accuracy of the stratigraphical ranges of all known taxa for the whole of the Phanerozoic. However, work by Patterson and Smith (1987) has questioned not so much the nature of the longevity of each family group, but rather whether each family itself is a valid biological entity. They examined the data used by Raup and Sepkoski for the fishes and echinoderms, and used this to construct a criticism of the periodicity hypothesis.

Patterson and Smith applied a strict cladistic approach in defining families (Box 3.2). They maintained that only monophyletic groups (in which all members of the family have a single ancestor) have validity in a biological classification, and excluded all paraphyletic groups (which are monophyletic taxa which do not contain all the descendants of a single ancestor) which are mainly human perceptions drawn up to encompass a matter of opinion rather than biological truth. Patterson and Smith carried out their own analyses, and determined that the total set of fish and echinoderm data showed correspondence with Raup and Sepkoski's observed periodicity, with five out of eight peaks corresponding (Figure 21.7). However, detailed analysis of the data set revealed two basic data types. The first type is 'signal' data, composed of monophyletic families containing two or more species which have accurate range data. The second is 'noise' data, which is composed of: paraphyletic 'families', arbitrary groupings which often form an 'ancestral group' characterised by the possession of primitive features; polyphyletic 'families', composed of unrelated taxa; and monotypic 'families', which contain just a single species (Figure 21.7). Noise data, forming some 75% of the data set for fishes and echinoderms, are based upon groupings which are largely arbitrary or inaccurate, do not represent the true macroevolutionary pattern, and therefore strongly bias the record. Interestingly, Patterson and Smith's exercise demonstrated that, in fact, in the case of fishes and echinoderms at least, it is the inaccurate noise rather than the accurate signal data which display the periodicity – a concept that is difficult to explain (Figure 21.7).

4. **Comment**

Raup and Sepkoski's analysis clearly demonstrates that the compilation of secondary data in palaeontology can potentially be as important in determining patterns of evolution in the fossil record as smaller-scale, field-based studies. However, it is clear that the data set may be flawed because of inaccurate recording or reporting of stratigraphical ranges. In their re-evaluation of parts of the periodicity data, Patterson and Smith have convincingly shown that, in general, accuracy in determining monophyletic groups is perhaps even more important.

5. **References**

Patterson, C. & Smith, A.B. 1987. Is the periodicity of extinctions a taxonomic artefact? *Nature*, **330**, 248–252.

Raup, D.M. & Sepkoski, J.J. 1984. Periodicity of extinctions in the geologic past. *Proceedings of the National Academy of Sciences, USA,* **81**, 801–805.

Raup, D.M. & Sepkoski, J.J. 1986. Periodic extinction of families and genera. *Science*, **231**, 833–836.

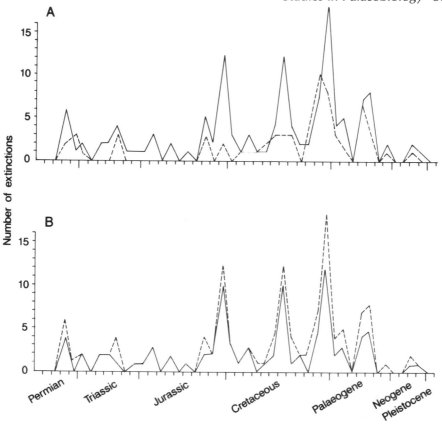

Figure 21.7 *Extinctions in echinoderm and fish families, from the Permian to the Recent. A: solid line – extinctions recognised by Sepkoski; broken line – extinctions of monophyletic groups as recognised by Patterson and Smith. B: Plot of the Sepkoski data (broken line) and the noise data recognised by Patterson and Smith (solid line). Note that the noise data correspond closely to the 26 million year periodicity [Modified from: Patterson and Smith (1987)* Nature*, 330, Fig. 2, p. 250]*

21.6 SUMMARY OF KEY POINTS

Four factors are important in determining evolutionary patterns from the fossil record: the stratigraphical completeness of the interval sampled; the nature and resolution of the sampling procedure; the range in variation of the organisms under study; and the nature of the data compilation.

- **Stratigraphical completeness** is of paramount importance as it determines the value of the interpretation: the greater the imperfection, the less viable is the interpretation of evolutionary pattern. This is demonstrated in the determination of evolutionary patterns in the bryozoan *Metrarabdotos*, in Sheldon's trlobites, and in the macroevolutionary story of the extinction of foraminifera at El Kef. Here, the relative completeness of the successions sampled was important in accurately demonstrating evolutionary stasis, gradualism and a stepped extinction pattern which might otherwise have been lost. This is also bound up in the nature of the sampling procedure utilised, which was at the level of centimetre accuracy for all these examples.

- Determining the **range in variation** within a given species at a given time interval is essential in order to be able to demonstrate the nature of the evolutionary changes within a species through time. In *Metrarabdotos*, for example, the range in morphology was determined within a species, and its rate of change through time assessed. In this case, the rate of change exceeded that occurring within the species, and was rapid, punctuating static episodes. In Sheldon's Ordovician trilobites, there was a constant rate of change within the lineages studied. Determination of the nature of the variation helped demonstrate the presence of periodic reversals in trends.
- Understanding the **nature of the data compilation** is extremely important in examining broad-scale patterns. In the case of the observed periodicity of extinctions, the nature of the original data source was of variable quality, including some 'families' of dubious biological value. Rigorous reassessment of some data sources suggests that the use of strictly monophyletic families creates a non-periodic pattern.

22
Studies in Palaeoenvironmental Analysis

In this chapter the application of fossils in palaeoenvironmental analysis and palaeobiogeography is examined.

22.1 GENERAL CONSIDERATIONS OF PALAEOECOLOGY AND PALAEOENVIRONMENTS

In seeking to determine the nature of ancient ecologies and interpret the factors which control them, five elements are of importance: determination of auto-chthony; recurrence of association; taxonomic uniformitarianism; population structure; and comparison with other data sources.

1. **Determination of autochthony**. Fossil assemblages are entities created by vir-tue of an interplay of two factors: the nature of the original community and the nature of the sedimentary environment. The original community structure, often referred to as the **life assemblage**, may be complex and composed of a number of biological entities, with both hard- and soft-bodied organisms. The fossil record is such that soft-bodied organisms are rarely preserved, other than under the mostly exceptional circumstances of low oxygen and high sedimen-tation rate (Chapter 2). As the soft-bodied components are usually lost to diagenesis and biochemical break-down, most fossil assemblages do not closely resemble the living community. This is because the remainder of the assemblage will be represented mostly by the shelly components or other hard body parts of a range of organisms, which upon their death are available for incorporation into the sedimentary record, either directly after death or even-tually after a period of transport. To approximate to the living community,

assemblages should consist of largely autochthonous species. In general, auto-chthonous fossils are those which, through direct observation, can be proven to be in life position. This is most applicable to cementing or otherwise sessile organisms on the sediment surface, or to burrowing organisms clearly pre-served in a life attitude in the sediment. Most other fossils, such as mobile benthonic, nektonic or planktonic organisms, or sessile benthonic organisms since removed from their point of attachment or washed from their burrows, are open to transport by a variety of wave and current activities, especially in the shallow marine environment. It is the determination of the extent of such transport that is critical in any consideration of the ecological significance of the assemblage.

Several criteria may be used to determine the extent of transport and re-working (Table 22.1). These mainly reflect the interpretation of the original life position of the organism, and the extent of sorting and/or damage to the skeletal materials, and as such they are necessarily an imperfect measure, but serve as a none the less valuable guide.

2. **Recurrence of association**. Assemblages may be found to recur at intervals through the geological record, and as such may be considered as chance accumulations of specific skeletal components, or as approximations to the original community structure, with a recurrent set of organisms reflective of the prevailing environmental parameters. The most convincing argument in favour of the latter is a consistent association with a particular facies type in the case of benthonic associations.

Table 22.1 *Criteria for determination of autochthony*

Criterion	Comments
Normal life position	Through comparison with living organisms it is possible to determine the nature of the normal life position. In many cases, the attitude of shells and other skeletal components may give an indication of their stability under high-energy conditions.
Clustering	Natural clusters of benthonic organisms may be detected through their interaction with each other. For example, valves in close contact will often be irregular.
Articulation	Dependent on the nature of the organism, an estimate of transport can be given, based on the articulation of its skeletal components. As such, brachiopods may be expected to be intact more often than echinoderms.
Breakage and abrasion	Breakage and other damage may be caused by biological factors, such as age and predation prior to incorporation in the sedimentary record. However, physical damage such as shell faceting, breakage and abrasion are most likely to be a function of transport before burial.
Sorting	Dependent on the wave and current energy, fossils may be sorted into assemblages which show current alignment and distinct size classes demonstrating the nature and direction of flow.

3. **Taxonomic uniformitarianism**. Taxonomic uniformitarianism is the key to any palaeoecological or palaeoenvironmental interpretation. It is an approach which assumes that the mode of life of fossil species is similar to that of living forms (Chapter 3). In general terms, the accuracy of the taxonomic uniform-itarian approach decreases with advancing age, so that in the later Cenozoic there is a greater likelihood that the fossil species being studied will have a living relative which can be directly compared. This allows for the determina-tion of a set of environmental factors which are known to control the abund-ance and diversity of the living relative, and the extrapolation by inference that the same factors will have controlled the abundance and diversity of the fossil. This is flawed by the absence of direct descendants in many forms, and by the potential for a shift in the ecological tolerance of organisms through time, so that the fossil organisms lived under very different environmental conditions than do the living representatives.

4. **Determination of population structure**. Limiting factors commonly control the density (abundance) and diversity of particular assemblages (Figure 3.8). As discussed in Chapter 3, the interpretation of relative abundance and diversity in fossil assemblages and associations can provide an important yardstick with which to assess the nature of the palaeoenvironment. In general, species diver-sity can often be taken as an important indicator of the nature of the palaeoen-vironment (Figure 3.8). Factors controlling diversity patterns are given in Table 22.2. In general, high-stress environments associated with increased salinity or decreased oxygen levels, for example, produce low-diversity body and trace fossil assemblages, although density may be high. Stable environments tend to have diverse communities, although often with relatively low abundance (Figure 3.8). Such assemblages commonly have a low dominance rating, each species making up no more than a few per cent of the assemblage.

Populations can also be analysed from the point of view of age and size frequency. Some assemblages may represent mass mortalities, with young,

Table 22.2 *Faunal diversity and palaeoenvironment*

Diversity	Controlling factors
Reduced	High stress, such as low oxygen levels, increased or reduced salinities, increased turbulence, and so on.
Reduced	Pioneer or opportunistic species associated with the colonisation of a new habitat. Often opportunistic species are representative of periodic colonisation of high-stress environments.
Maintained or increased	Environmental stability; opportunists are increasingly replaced by specialists able to subdivide resources.
Maintained or increased	Ecological maturity; mature ecosystems are more stable, and can often survive periodic die-offs, for example.
Maintained or increased	Ecological resource partitioning is high.

Source: Goldring, R. (1991) *Fossils in the field*. Longman, Harlow.

juveniles and adults present in the same assemblage, as would be the case in a normal, living population. In such cases, it is possible to get a clearer idea about the nature of the population and its success in its environment through analyses of the age and size distributions of individuals in the population. This can also be achieved without mass mortality in trilobite and ostracod assemblages because of the presence of the moult stages.

5. **Comparison with facies and other data sources.** Fossils are just part of the story, as the sediments which contain them provide as many clues to the nature of the environment as the fossils themselves. It is good practice to consider fossils and sediments together in any palaeoenvironmental study. Clearly, this is most appropriate with benthonic organisms associated with particular substrates, and it should be expected that fossil communities would be associated with specific substrates. A good example is the association of rock-boring bivalves, cementing bivalves and barnacles with the hard substrate rocky shoreline – a repetitive association for much of the Mesozoic and Cenozoic.

In addition, isotope analyses of shell chemistry are appropriate in determining the ratio of stable isotopes of carbon and oxygen in the skeletal carbonates. As these will have been precipitated in equilibrium with the water column, it is possible to determine enrichments in particular isotopes which are clear indicators of temperature and salinity variations.

The following case studies demonstrate how palaeoenvironments can be determined from the fossil record.

22.2 INTERPRETING ANCIENT SALINITY LEVELS
(Hudson, 1963)

1. Introduction

Most marine and freshwater organisms are limited in their abundance and distribution by salinity. Measured in parts per thousand ($^o/_{oo}$), normal marine salinities are around $35^o/_{oo}$, while fresh waters are between 0 and 0.5 $^o/_{oo}$ (Table 22.3). Surprisingly, although environments in which levels of salinity fluctuated in the geological past must have been common, relatively little is known about the nature of their fauna.

Table 22.3   *Typical water salinities*

Salinity ($^o/_{oo}$)	Term
> 40	Hypersaline
30–40	Euhaline
18–30	Brachyhaline
5–18	Mesohaline
0.5–5	Oligohaline
0–0.5	Freshwater

Source: Fürsich (1994).

Salinity levels are prone to fluctuation, and sedimentary facies associations suggest that there have been at least two settings where this has been especially the case in the geological past: in largely land-locked marine basins separated from the main ocean circulation through tectonic or other events; and in the boundary between marine and terrestrial environments, at the coast. Although recognition of the former is possible through the association of sedimentary bodies such as evaporites, the more subtle salinity fluctuations of the coastal region are difficult to assess directly from the composition of the sedimentary facies, and their recognition is based largely upon the interpretation of the ecological tolerances of the contained fossils. The recognition of salinity-controlled benthonic assemblages is therefore of great value in the interpretation of the nature of the ancient sedimentary environment. An excellent review of the palaeoecology and evolution of salinity-controlled fossil assemblages is given in Fürsich (1994), but one of the most important preliminary studies in this field remains that of Hudson (1963).

2. The Middle Jurassic Great Estuarine Group

In 1963 John Hudson completed a study of the palaeoecology and sedimentology of the Great Estuarine Group, a succession of Middle Jurassic limestones, sandstones and shales which crop out in the Isle of Skye in northwest Scotland. As illustrated by its name, the Great Estuarine Group had long been considered to have been deposited under non-marine or brackish-water conditions. The limestone and shale formations which characterise the group have lithologies which are laterally persistent, but which vary rapidly from bed to bed up the succession; their contained fauna demonstrates the same characteristics (Figure 22.1). These formations also show evidence of shallow-water conditions, with mud-cracks demonstrating periodic desiccation of the sediments, and the most likely interpretation of the environment is that of a series of lagoons partially separated by a bar from the open-sea environment. Sandstones represent the periodic growth of deltas into the lagoons. Hudson compared the Middle Jurassic environment of the Inner Hebrides with the present-day Texas coast, where a series of lagoons with brackish-water conditions are developed.

3. General Characteristics of the Fauna

The Great Estuarine Group is dominated largely by molluscan fossils. For the most part, Hudson found that these fossils occur in assemblages of semi-autochthonous shells. They were rarely found in life position, and the valves were mostly disarticulated and a little sorted by wave action. However, Hudson considered that these shells were not fully allochthonous, and that they are broadly representative of the local environment, because many were found in recurring associations, there was little evidence of strong currrent activity in the surrounding shale beds, and many of the assemblages were completely different even though separated by a few centimetres of sediment.

4. Characteristics of Recent Brackish and Great Estuarine Group Faunas

The most striking characteristics of modern brackish faunas, such as those of the Texas lagoons, are that their diversity is reduced, although individuals may occur in great numbers (i.e with a high density), and that they are composed

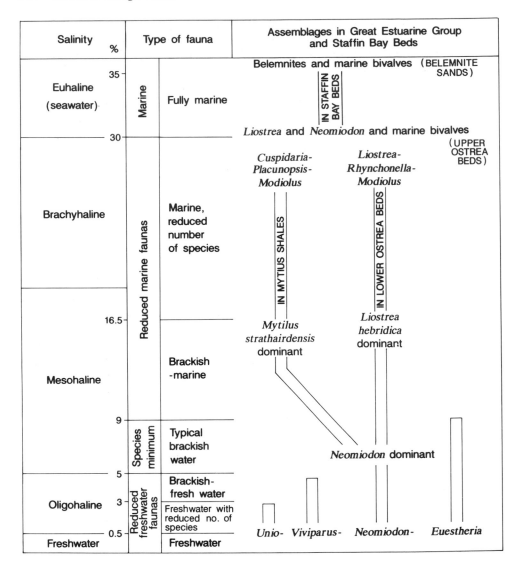

Figure 22.1 *Salinity-controlled molluscan assemblages from the Jurassic Great Eustarine Group of northwest Scotland [Modified from: Hudson (1963)* Palaeontology, **6**, *Fig. 1, p. 325]*

mostly of marine species. A series of criteria for the recognition of salinity-controlled assemblages, based upon the observation of modern brackish-water faunas, was reviewed by Hudson (1963), and more recently by Fursich (1994). Hudson recognised that salinity-controlled assemblages would be:

1. low-diversity faunas, often forming dense shell beds;
2. lacking in organisms which have a narrow salinity tolerance range, such as corals, cephalopods, echinoderms, most bryozoans (such organisms are known as **stenohaline**);

3. dominated by organisms with a broad salinity range, such as bivalves, gastropods and ostracods (such organisms are known as **euryhaline**);
4. associated with marine and freshwater sediments demonstrating the facies relationships.

Hudson found that the Great Estuarine Group fauna fitted these criteria:

1. The total number of fossil species, of all types, was 50. This was extremely poor in comparison with contemporaneous faunas from fully marine limestones in England, which have over 400 molluscan species alone.
2. Corals and cephalopods are unknown, and other stenohaline forms (echinoid and bryozoan fragments) are limited to one small part of the Great Estuarine Group.
3. Bivalves, gastropods and ostracods dominate the fauna.
4. Marine beds occur above and below the Great Estuarine Group; one or two freshwater beds occur within it, and drifted plant remains are common. No evaporites, indicative of hypersaline conditions, are recorded.

Hudson was able to recognise a range of salinity-controlled assemblages within the Great Estuarine Group, based on the known tolerance levels of living organisms in similar environments, such as the coastal lagoons of Texas. These assemblages are composed of molluscan groups, as illustrated by Figure 22.1 and described below.

1. *Unio, Viviparus, Neomiodon* and *Euestheria*. *Unio, Viviparus* and *Euestheria* live in fresh waters today, although the first two can tolerate low salinities in modern estuarine settings. *Neomiodon* is extinct, and may have been euryhaline, as it occurs with both freshwater and marine fossils. These were considered to be typical of fresh to brackish–freshwater (oligohaline) conditions in the range of 0–$5^{\circ}/_{oo}$.
2. *Liostrea* and *Mytilus* commonly occur in monotypic shell beds, resembling living oyster and mussel beds. These were considered by Hudson to be representative of brackish marine, mesohaline faunas with a salinity range of 9–$16.5^{\circ}/_{oo}$.
3. *Liostrea* and *Mytilus* also occur with fully marine organisms such as rhynchonellid brachiopods. Hudson considered this assemblage to be representative of reduced-marine salinities, brachyhaline faunas with a salinity range of 16.5–$30^{\circ}/_{oo}$.
4. Cephalopods occur in the sandstones above the Great Estuarine Group, and are demonstrative of fully marine, euhaline conditions in the range of 30–$35^{\circ}/_{oo}$.

These results were later substantiated through carbon and oxygen stable isotope analyses of the skeletal carbonates (Tan and Hudson, 1974).

5. **Comment**

This example is clearly demonstrative of the principles of palaeoenvironmental analysis. The assemblages recognised by Hudson were considered in terms of their autochthony and occurrence. The environmental parameters limiting the diversity and abundance of the molluscs were deduced through taxonomic uniformitarian comparison with living relatives. Sedimentary associations and isotopic data provided corroborating evidence.

6. References

Fürsich, F.T. 1994. Palaeoecology and evolution of Mesozoic salinity-controlled benthic macroinvertebrate associations. *Lethaia*, **26**, 327–346.

Hudson, J.D. 1963. The recognition of salinity-controlled mollusc assembalges in the Great Estuarine Series (Middle Jurassic) of the Inner Hebrides. *Palaeontology*, **6**, 318–326.

Tan, F.C. & Hudson, J.D. 1974. Isotopic studies on the palaeoecology and diagenesis of the Great Estuarine Series (Jurassic) of Scotland. *Scottish Journal of Geology*, **10**, 91–128.

22.3 PALAEOXYGENATION STUDIES
(Rhoads and Morse, 1971; Savrda and Bottjer 1986)

1. Introduction

Black shales are relatively common in the geological record, and consist of finely laminated shales commonly containing 1–20% organic carbon by weight. As such, these shales are economically important, and it has been estimated that around 70% of the world's mineral oil resources are derived from Mesozoic black shales. Black shales develop in oxygen-deficient basins, where the water column becomes stratified, commonly with surface waters having near-normal oxygen saturation levels of 6–8.5 ml O_2/l (millilitres of oxygen per litre of water), and bottom waters which may be oxygen deficient with levels of 0–1 ml/l of dissolved oxygen. It is generally agreed that stratification occurs because of differences in temperature or salinity between the lower and upper levels of the water column, generally producing high-density bottom waters and low-density surface waters. Mixing may occur periodically. A recent review of the formation of black shales has been published by Wignall (1994).

Understanding the levels of oxygenation in ancient sedimentary basins is important for many reasons. Firstly, the economic importance of black shales is such that a clearer understanding of the conditions which formed them is important. Secondly, we now know that the early development of life on Earth took place in low-oxygen conditions, and therefore a study of the interaction of organisms with their environment through geological time is clearly of the greatest value to our appreciation of the evolution of life.

2. Palaeoxygenation Models

One of the most important contributions to our understanding of the level of palaeoxygenation in ancient sedimentary basins was made by Donald Rhoads and John Morse in 1971. Rhoads and Morse (1971) used taxonomic uniformitarian models to interpret the level of oxygen saturation in bottom waters of the early Cambrian and determine its bearing on the early diversification of the fossil metazoans. Rhoads and Morse set out to study the relationship of organism diversity with oxygen levels in two basins known to have low levels of dissolved oxygen, the Black Sea and the continental borderland basins of southern California. Both basins are enclosed, with little connection with well-oxygenated oceanic waters. A third basin, the Gulf of California, was also examined, and here, although there is open connection with oxygenated surface waters, bottom waters were found to have low oxygen levels. In all three examples, a clear diversity decline was noted, with increasing depth and decreasing levels of dissolved oxygen. The greatest diversities were found to be associated with oxygen levels in excess of 1.0 ml O_2/l, and water depths of less than 150 m. In general, organisms with heavily calcified shells were not found in abundance in oxygen levels less than 1.0 ml O_2/l, with poorly calcified organisms and soft-bodied taxa occuring at much lower oxygen levels.

From their studies in these Recent environments, Rhoads and Morse concluded that: diversity declines sharply as oxygen levels fall below 0.5–1.0 ml/l; soft-bodied organisms are the commonest benthonic organisms below 1.0 ml O_2/l; and heavily calcified taxa are largely restricted to oxygen levels greater than 1.0 ml/l. They recognised three biofacies, broad assemblages of taxa which can be used to interpret the nature of the ancient environment: the aerobic biofacies, comprising a diverse, heavily calcified fauna in well-bioturbated sediments; the dysaerobic biofacies, comprising soft-bodied, burrowing species in bioturbated sediments; and the anaerobic biofacies, comprising well-laminated sediments apparently devoid of life (Figure 22.2). The disappearance of heavily calcified taxa in bottom waters with less than 1.0 ml/l of dissolved oxygen was interpreted as a result of the stress in the production and retention of a shell in such low-oxygen, high-CO_2 and lowered-pH conditions. Rhoads and Morse were able to demonstrate that the three biofacies recognisable in modern environments are commonly represented in the fossil record.

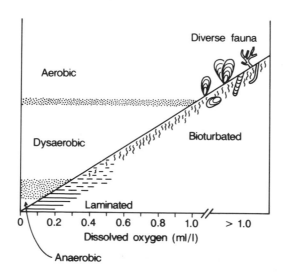

Figure 22.2 *The Rhoads and Morse model of oxygen-related biofacies [Reproduced with permission from Doyle et al., (1994)* Key to Earth History, *Wiley, Box 5.6, p. 95]*

3. Trace Fossils and Palaeoxygenation

The Rhoads and Morse model relied on the recognition of the disappearance of shelly fossils and well-bioturbated sediments (aerobic to dysaerobic facies), and the transition from bioturbated to laminated sediments (dysaerobic to anaerobic facies). Savrda and Bottjer (1986) confirmed these broad conclusions, but were able to take the level of precision in the recognition of oxygen-controlled biofacies still further through the study of the diversity of trace fossil assemblages in black shale successions.

Savrda and Bottjer used three indices of oxygenation based on trace fossils: diversity of the trace assemblage; maximum burrow diameter; and tiering of the trace fauna – the relationship of trace fossils with the sedimentary succession and each other. In general, low-oxygen conditions are associated with low-diversity trace fossil assemblages, and it has been demonstrated that the feeding burrow *Chondrites* is usually the first to colonise laminated black shale sequences. Burrow diameter is taken as an indicator of oxygen levels primarily because, as recognised from recent successions, as the concentration of dissolved oxygen in bottom water decreases, so does the relative size of benthonic organisms. Clearly, large burrows are indicative of larger organisms and therefore increased oxygen levels. Tiering – the vertical stacking of traces within the sediment – is reflective of the successive colonisation of a substratum by a group of organisms. It is represented by the cross-cutting relationships of traces as organisms burrow deeper into the sediment in search of food or dwelling space. Put simply, in low-oxygen conditions, there will be few tiers, or levels of colonisation, while in increased-oxygen conditions, the number of tiers will increase, with organisms mining successively lower levels and cross-cutting the traces already created. In general, as the oxygen level decreases, so ichnogenera feeding at successively deeper levels in the sediment progressively disappear: shallow, large burrow diameter *Planolites* or *Thalassinoides* go first, followed by complex feeding burrows such as *Zoophycos* and, finally, by the deeper-burrowing, feeding trace *Chondrites* (Figure 22.3).

Taken together, these lines of evidence can be used to interpret not only the ancient levels of oxygen, but also the colonisation history of the basin with respect to increased or decreased oxygen levels, in the creation of relative oxygenation curves.

4. Relative Oxygenation Curves

Using trace fossil assemblages, Savrda and Bottjer were able to reconstruct the pattern of oxygenation in two basins: the Miocene Monterey Formation in California, and the Cretaceous Niobrara Formation in Colorado. Successive levels of oxygenation were demonstrated graphically using first appearances of three taxa – *Planolites*, *Thalassinoides*, and *Zoophycos* – and the presence or absence of laminated facies. *Chondrites* was found to occur in all facies except the laminated beds. These lines represent the threshold of oxygen above which each of these traces could be produced within the fabric of the sediment. This was correlated with burrow diameter, and a curve of oxygenation created to demonstrate the oxygenation history of the basins (Figure 22.3).

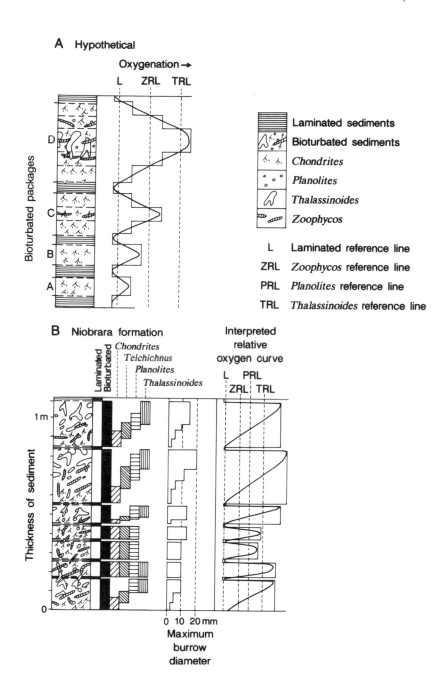

Figure 22.3 *Palaeoxygenation curves based on trace fossil colonisation. The curves are drawn relative to increasing trace fossil diversity. **A:** Hypothetical example to demonstrate the technique. **B:** The worked example of Savrda and Bottjer for the Cretaceous Niobrara Formation of California [Modified from Savrda and Bottjer (1986)* Geology **14**, *Fig. 3, p. 5]*

5. Comment

This case study demonstrates the application of the uniformitarian principle in palaeoenvironmental studies, and the particular value of trace fossils. Trace fossils are rarely anything other than autochthonous. Rhoads and Morse's original study identified the critical threshold of oxygen with biofacies, or assemblages directly related to levels of oxygen. Savrda and Bottjer have demonstrated that these assemblages are recurrent throughout the geological record. Detailed study of modern analogues has shown that the number of stacked tiers, burrow diameter and diversity are directly related with oxygen levels, and therefore has led to the acceptance that it is possible to determine oxygenation events based upon the nature of the colonisation history of the successive traces.

6. References

Rhoads, D.C. & Morse, J.W. 1971. Evolutionary and ecologic significance of oxygen-deficient marine basins. *Lethaia*, **4**, 413–428.

Savrda, C.E. & Bottjer, D.J. 1986. Trace fossil model for the reconstruction of paleoxygenation in bottom waters. *Geology*, **14**, 1–6.

Wignall, P.B. 1994. *Black Shales*. Clarendon Press, Oxford.

22.4 GENERAL CONSIDERATIONS OF PALAEOBIOGEOGRAPHY

Biogeography is the determination of the patterns of geographical distribution of living animals and plants, and the study of their underlying causes. Palaeobiogeography is therefore the determination of the distribution patterns of ancient plants and animals, and the analysis of their underlying causes, as deduced from the fossil record. Palaeobiogeography is in effect an extension of palaeoecology and palaeoenvironmental analysis; like these subjects, it seeks to interpret the patterns of diversity and density of groups of organisms, but unlike them, the patterns investigated in palaeobiogeography are on a much wider, sometimes global, scale. The study of palaeobiogeography involves several processes:

1. **Determination of pattern**. The determination of the original distribution patterns of fossil organisms is the prime objective of palaeobiogeography. This is carried out through three processes: primary data collection; secondary data collection; and compilation of results for given time intervals on appropriate maps.

   Primary data collection is most appropriate when the aim of the study is to determine the distribution patterns on a local scale, and it involves the detailed collection of fossils from given stratigraphical intervals from a range of stratigraphical sections over the area studied. Accurate biostratigraphical control is needed in order that a proper comparison of the distribution of fossil organisms in time and space can be made. Secondary data collection involves the compilation of all published records on the occurrence of given fossil groups for given time intervals. As with all secondary data sources, the quality of the data varies according to the level of accuracy of the original study. Common problems include the imperfect or inaccurate dating of the sampled sequences, and incorrect identification of the fossil taxa. The repository for the data collected is a set of palaeogeographical maps of appropriate scale. However, in some cases, in particular for the early Palaeozoic interval, such maps are difficult to use for this purpose, as they are themselves partially created through interpretation of the fossil occurrences. For late Palaeozoic to Recent, accurate maps are available through interpretation of palaeomagnetism and other geological and geophysical data, and these form the basis for accurate distribution plots.

2. **Interpretation of pattern.** The determination of pattern is the first component in any palaeobiogeographical study, but the interpretation of the underlying causes is one of its fundamental aims. The recognition of **endemism**, the restriction of organisms to particular parts of the globe, is an important part of the process. Groups of organisms can show increasing levels of endemism, so that **realms** and **provinces** define areas of the globe characterised by the distributions of clusters of families or other higher taxonomic groupings; while **endemic centres** reflect the distribution of small clusters of taxa, usually at generic or specific levels. The recognition of levels of endemism is carried out through detailed analysis of similarity, using statistical clustering and other analytical techniques.

The recognition of the pattern of endemism forms the basis for the interpretation of the pattern in terms of factors which limit the global or local distribution of organisms. Typical causes invoked are ecological, physiological, climatological and oceanographic. In general, recognition of absolute causes is difficult, and is open to a greater degree of speculation than the distribution patterns themselves.

3. **Applied palaeobiogeography.** Applied palaeobiogeography involves the use of palaeobiogeographical patterns to infer geological events or evolutionary dispersal. Palaeobiogeography has been widely used in the determination of palaeogeography (the distribution of continents and oceans) through the reassembly of areas which possess similar faunal groups, for example.

The following case study provides an example of the application of palaeobiogeography in geological studies.

22.5 LOWER PALAEOZOIC FAUNAS AROUND GONDWANA
(Cocks and Fortey, 1988)

1. Introduction

For the later Mesozoic and Cenozoic intervals, it is often possible to determine an accurate picture of continental reconstructions through purely geophysical means, such as palaeomagnetism. In older rocks, however, continental configurations are less easily constructed because of the complexities of later tectonic episodes deforming the sedimentary basins, and because of the destruction of pre-Mesozoic ocean crust through subduction. In such rocks, therefore, there is less reliance on palaeomagnetism, and a greater consideration of the value of fossil distributions. This is particularly important in benthonic organisms which are restricted to the shelf seas, and which may have been physically or ecologically limited to specific geographical areas. For the Lower Palaeozoic, several schemes use combinations of brachiopods, trilobites and graptolites in the development of global palaeogeographical maps. One such study is the reconstruction and interpretation of the early geological history of the continent of Gondwana by Cocks and Fortey (1988).

2. The Continent of Gondwana

Gondwana was one of the original supercontinents reconstructed by Alfred Wegener in the development of his original ideas of continental drift. It was first reconstructed through comparison of the coastlines of South America and Africa. Other geological and palaeontological evidence – in particular, the occurrence of the tree fern *Glossopteris* – led to the addition of the continents of Antarctica, Australasia and India to this supercontinent. Since the confirmation of Wegener's studies in the late 1960s, Gondwana's core of South America, Africa, India, Antarctica and Australia has not been in doubt. However, the peripheral areas which may have formed small microcontinents around the continental margins are still under active debate. For example, the southern margins of Britain and Newfoundland may well have formed a microcontinental mass ('Avalonia') which drifted northwards from Gondwana during the Ordovician. The distribution of fossils in the sedimentary rocks of these continental areas therefore provides an important key in determining the early relationship of continental masses, and in the interpretation of their geological history.

3. Early Palaeozoic Biofacies and Faunas

The distribution of biofacies around a continent is associated with a range of physical and biological parameters. Typical physical parameters operating over a geological time scale are plate movements, water depth and climatic variation. Typical biological parameters are the availability of species suitable to colonise a particular habitat; the ecological tolerances of individual groups; and the local availability of food. Study of the faunas of Lower Palaeozoic successions shows that these parameters operated in restricting certain fossil groups throughout early Palaeozoic times. In such cases, it is important to determine whether physical or biological factors played the major part in delimiting species, and the nature of their relationship. For example, the northward drift of Avalonia from Gondwana (by plate-tectonic processes) would have physically limited shallow-water species, but individual species may be limited along a shelf by variation in food supply or other ecological considerations.

In their study, Cocks and Fortey reviewed all the available literature and determined that there was a set of **biofacies** determined by the nature of their contained faunas and associated with the continental margins which appeared to be recurrent at appropriate times through the early Palaeozoic. These biofacies were found to be associated primarily with ecological parameters; limited by water depth, the benthonic, nektonic or planktonic nature of their constituents or the availability of niches. These were considered to have the greatest potential in continental reconstructions. Three biofacies were recognised:

- **Inner-shelf faunas**, adapted to living in the wide expanse of shallow sea, commonly affected by local environmental conditions, and dominated by brachiopods. Inner-shelf faunas were generally bound to Gondwana and were found at the leading edge of transgressions which flooded the continental masses. These faunas represent a suite of endemic faunas adapted to specific parameters (palaeoclimate, etc.) associated with the supercontinent itself.

- **Outer-shelf faunas**, adapted to the deeper-water, rather quieter conditions of the outer shelf, and commonly composed of trilobite taxa. Outer-shelf faunas are most valuable in recognising and mapping-in the outer margin of the supercontinent, as they represent the outermost fringe of the continental mass. However, the fauna inhabiting this biofacies was not necessarily bound to Gondwana itself, as it may be used to determine the outer limits of other continents.

- **Oceanic faunas**, living in the open waters and not necessarily affected by continental position. Typical faunas are dominated by graptolites, and they provide the greatest service in determining the presence of the oceanic margins to a continental mass such as Gondwana.

4. Biofacies around Gondwana

Cocks and Fortey plotted the distribution of these biofacies through time on a palaeogeographic reconstruction for Gondwana (Figure 22.4). Data was derived from the published records of the distributions of appropriate taxa in the component parts of what was the continent of Gondwana. They were able to recognise a series of brachiopod, trilobite and graptolite faunas associated with these biofacies throughout the early Palaeozoic and, in particular, observed changes in the brachiopod and trilobite genera associated within inner- and outer-shelf faunas. This was of great value in the determination of palaeogeography, because it determined the coastline of Gondwana for Ordovician to Silurian times; helped confirm the spread of Avalonia from Gondwana during the same interval, marked by differences in faunal composition with time; and demonstrated a hitherto unsuspected pattern of continental flooding and regressions determined from the distribution patterns of the inner-shelf fauna of brachiopods and trilobites.

5. Comment

Although relying primarily on secondary data, Cocks and Fortey were able to determine the nature of the ancient palaeogeography of Gondwana through the plotting of brachiopod and trilobite distributions around the supercontinent. This provided important new information about the regressive and transgressive episodes and the flooding of the continent through the early Palaeozoic, while demonstrating the nature of the continental construction of Gondwana. This example demonstrates the value of biogeography in geological studies. The pattern of three biofacies was demonstrated through the recognition of the recurrent association of inner-shelf, outer-shelf and oceanic

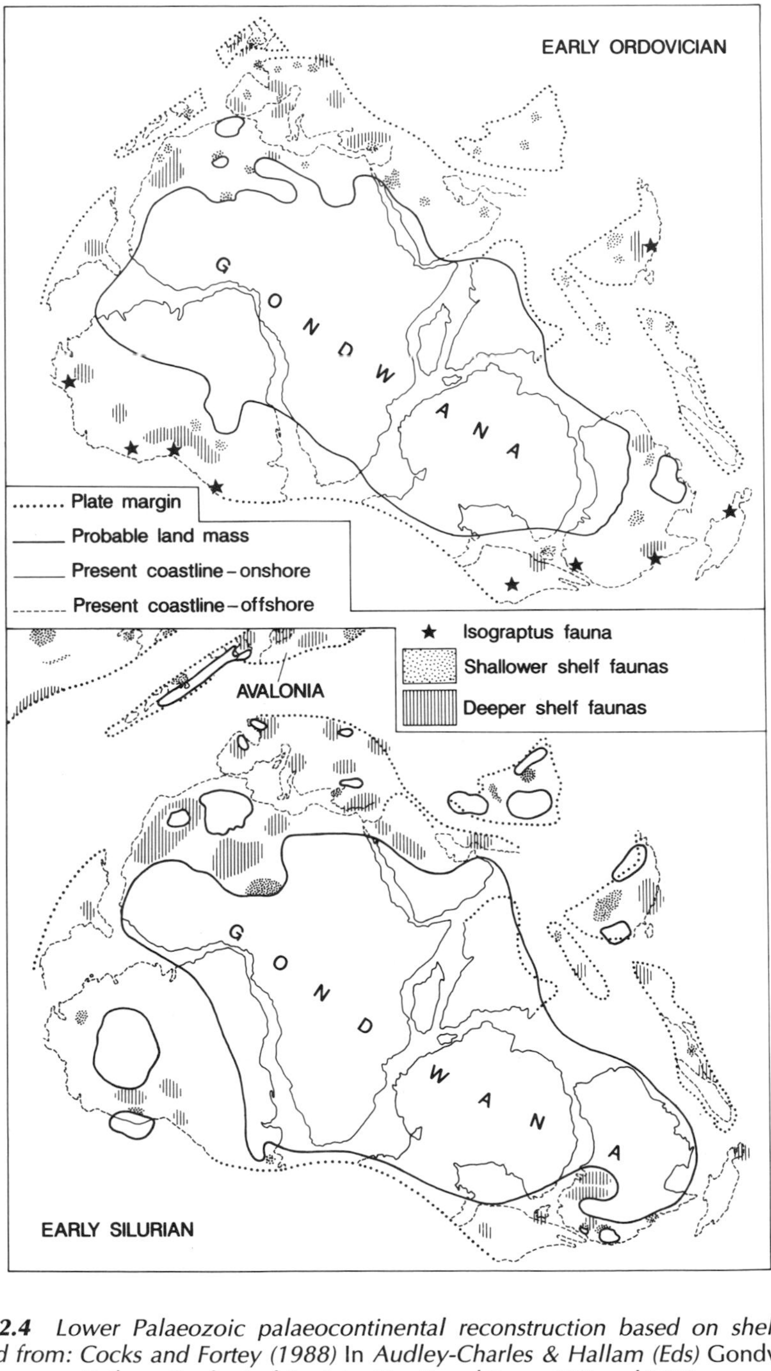

Figure 22.4   *Lower Palaeozoic palaeocontinental reconstruction based on shelly faunas [Modified from: Cocks and Fortey (1988)* In *Audley-Charles & Hallam (Eds)* Gondwana and Tethys, *Geological Society, Figs 2 and 8, pp. 187 and 195]*

faunas. These were interpreted in the light of physical and environmental parameters, and applied in the determination of the continental boundary of Gondwana, and in the recognition of transgressive–regressive episodes.

6. **Reference**

Cocks, L.R.M. & Fortey, R.A. 1988. Lower Palaeozoic facies and faunas around Gondwana. *In* Audley-Charles, M.G. & Hallam, A. (eds) *Gondwana and Tethys*. Geological Society Special Publication 37, London, 183–200.

22.6 SUMMARY OF KEY POINTS

- Fossils represent arguably the most important indicators of the nature of the palaeoenvironment, because as living creatures they were limited in occurrence and diversity by a range of environmental parameters which can be directly deduced from the fossil record.
- In determining ancient ecologies, it is important to take into consideration the following factors which control the degree of confidence which can be attached to any interpretation: the determination of autochthony; the recurrence of association; the application of taxonomic uniformitarianism; the determination of the nature of the population structure; and corroboration with sedimentary facies.
- In the case studies examined, each of these factors was important in determining the relative values of salinity and oxygenation. Hudson's molluscan assemblages were largely semi-autochthonous and recurrent; they had living relatives to serve as analogues; they had high density and low diversity; and the brackish-water faunal signal was corroborated by the sedimentary facies. Oxygen-related biofacies may be recognised because trace fossils are by nature autochthonous; recurrent oxygen-related trace fossil assemblages may be recognised for the present day as well as the geological past; diversity is related to oxygen levels, and low-oxygen trace fossil assemblages are associated with otherwise barren, black shales.
- Fossils are important in palaeobiogeographical studies. There are three processes in any palaeobiogeographical study: determination of pattern; interpretation of the pattern; and application.
- In Cocks and Fortey's case study, the pattern of three biofacies was demonstrated: inner-shelf, outer-shelf and oceanic early Palaeozoic faunas. These were interpreted in the light of physical and environmental parameters, and applied in the determination of the continental boundary of Gondwana and in the recognition of transgressive–regressive episodes.

23
Studies in Stratigraphy

One of the most widely considered uses of fossils in geology is in biostratigraphy. This chapter explores the practical application of fossils in biostratigraphy.

23.1 GENERAL CONSIDERATIONS

Biostratigraphy is the subdivision and correlation of the rock record on the basis of fossils. This has been discussed in Chapter 5. In the determination of the biostratigraphical and ultimately chronostratigraphical application of fossils, there are three phases: data collection; data analysis; and correlation. These are discussed below.

1. **Data collection**. Biostratigraphy relies upon two sources of data: primary data based on the stratigraphical distribution of fossils through the rock record, and examination of secondary data collected by other workers and available in a variety of published and unpublished sources.

   Undoubtedly, the most important source of information for the development of any biostratigraphy is the primary data source. Primary data collection will largely be through a combination of search and systematic sampling of given stratigraphical sections. In each case, the section in question is systematically sampled bed by bed, but a deliberate bias towards a specific group considered to be of value in biostratigraphy is introduced. However, this is mostly appropriate only for macrofossils; with microfossils, sampling is done 'blind' through the collection of bulk samples for laboratory analysis, and therefore a sufficient level of resolution is needed to compensate. Primary data collection has as its aim the compilation of **range charts** for the fossil groups (Figure 23.1), from their first to their last appearance in the rock record, with the assumption that both events will occur at the same time everywhere. In biostratigraphy,

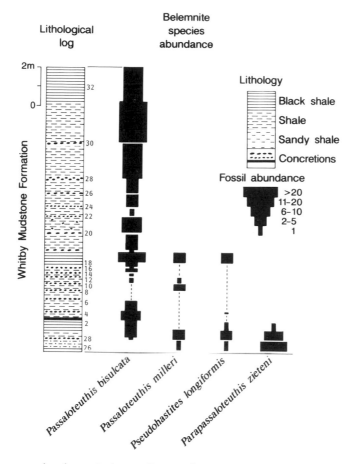

Figure 23.1 *An example of a typical compilation of species ranges relative to stratigraphical thickness based on data collection in the field. The thickness of each bar represents the abundance of a particular species through time [Modified from: Doyle (1990) Monograph of the Palaeontographical Society, The British Toarcian (Lower Jurassic) belemnites, **584**, Fig. 3, p. 4]*

secondary data collection mostly involves the compilation of published range charts for each fossil group under investigation in other sections in other parts of the region or country, in order to put together a correlation chart. Biostratigraphy above the biozone level is effectively beyond the capability of a single palaeontologist (at least in a single lifetime) and so secondary data are of the greatest importance in the recognition of stages and above.

2. **Data analysis**. Data analysis in biostratigraphy is based upon the suitability of the fossil group for correlation, the compilation of stratigraphical ranges, and the development of a biostratigraphical scheme.

The suitability of a fossil group for correlation is primarily a function of the resolution needed. At biozone level, a high degree of resolution and accuracy is needed. Therefore, the suitability of a given fossil needs to be assessed, and this is most effectively achieved against the six guide fossil criteria already described (Figure 5.3). However, it can be seen that three criteria are the most important. In effect, the best guide fossils are those which are widespread, fast to evolve and readily preserved. At coarser levels of resolution, suitability of a given fossil group is primarily a function of recognisable intervals of appearance (evolution) or disappearance (extinction) from the stratigraphical record. Adaptive radiations (e.g. the Cambrian explosion) or mass extinctions (e.g. the Permian extinction) are examples of this process.

The compilation of stratigraphical ranges for a given fossil group is the most important part of the data analysis. Ranges should be plotted accurately, as secondary use of the data may lead to errors being compounded and multiplied. There are several factors which may lead to a particular fossil group being present or absent in the fossil record. These are given in Table 23.1. The most important factors are the actual evolution and extinction of a given group or species. However, these may be difficult to evaluate where there is an imperfect fossil record or poor sampling. Once ranges are compiled, a biostratigraphical scheme can be developed. At biozonal level, this involves the creation of a biozonal scheme based upon the ranges of individual taxa. Range biozones are recognised to be of the greatest value, and are based on the total stratigraphical range of a species from its first to its last appearance (total range biozones) (Figure 5.4). In the case of microfossils, which are often abundant, and where great accuracy in sampling is achievable, it is often possible to develop a biozonation based upon evolving lineages, with the biozones reflecting the consecutive ranges of the evolving species (Figure 5.4). Fossils with longer ranges may also be employed, as it is possible to develop schemes based on the overlap of ranges to define partial range biozones, and this is taken to its greatest extent with assemblage biozones, composed of the ranges of a great number of taxa (Figure 5.4).

3. **Correlation**. Correlation is possible through the comparison of the accumulated range data from a given area with those from another region. The possibility of correlation is affected by three factors: errors in the initial data collection; the dispersal of the fossil groups to be used in correlation; and diachronous extinction/appearance of fossil groups.

The question of error in the initial data collection phase has been discussed above, but it is clear that this will be compounded where collection necessarily involves the compilation of numerous local data sets in the development of the biostratigraphical schemes. Some error is inevitable, and the possibility of its existence should therefore be flagged in every published scheme, so that its implications can be assessed by the compiler. The dispersal of individual fossil groups has the most obvious effect on the applicability of a biostratigraphical scheme. At the crudest level, it is relatively uncommon to find fossils which can be used in the correlation of both terrestrial and marine sequences. In fact, only wind-blown pollen and spores are widely used for this purpose, as birds and other flying organisms are rarely represerved.

On land or in the sea, organisms will also be geographically limited by a range of environmental factors. In some cases, the value of certain fossil groups may change as geographical limitation, or provincialism, develops with time.

Table 23.1 *Controls on the stratigraphical ranges of fossils*

Control	Interpretation and potential effect on stratigraphical range
Evolution	Ideally, the first appearance of a fossil group in the record is coincident with its evolution.
Extinction	Ideally, the last appearance of a fossil group in the stratigraphical record is coincident with its extinction.
Ecology	Fossils may be present or absent from a given stratigraphical section because of a change in local environmental conditions or ecology. This may lead to the recognition of both false 'extinctions' and false first appearances.
Migration	Organisms may be subject to restrictions due to broader environmental factors such as climate, water masses, physical barriers, environmental stability, food sources, and so on, which lead to their migration in and out of the region, and an interruption of their ranges in the record.
Preservation	Fossils may be absent from the stratigraphical record simply because they have not been preserved. Equally, fossils may be present in great abundance because of favourable conditions or through hydraulic accumulation from waves or currents, for example.
Reworking	Fossils may be eroded from older rocks and reworked into overlying sediments. These will produce an anomalous biostratigraphical signal.
Stratigraphical completeness	Incomplete stratigraphical sections will have the greatest effect in creating error at the top and bottom of a group's stratigraphical range.
Sampling	The sampling procedure for a given section may be flawed. For example, the resolution may be insufficient to pin-point extinction or evolutionary events with sufficient accuracy.

As an example, this particularly applies to Jurassic ammonites. At the beginning of the Jurassic, ammonite species were more or less cosmopolitan, and hence global correlation of marine sequences is possible. By the end of the Jurassic, however, correlation between southern and northern regions is limited by the development of strongly provincial ammonite groups. Finally, correlation using biostratigraphical schemes which employ what are effectively facies fossils, limited by substrates or other environmental factors, can only really be effected within relatively small geographical areas.

The following case histories demonstrate the principles of fossil applications in stratigraphy.

23.2 THE CAMBRIAN–PRECAMBRIAN BOUNDARY
(Brasier *et al.*, 1994)

1. Introduction

The boundary at the base of the Cambrian System has great chronostratigraphical significance, because it is not only a system boundary but also the lower boundary of both the Palaeozoic Erathem (the interval of 'ancient life') and the Phanerozoic Eonothem (the interval of 'evident life'). In effect, the base of the Cambrian System can be considered to be coincident with the lowermost boundary beyond which biostratigraphy is mostly impractical.

The Cambrian System was first erected by Adam Sedgwick in 1835 on the basis of the sedimentary rocks of North Wales. From Sedgwick's day until the late 1940s the base of the Cambrian was taken to coincide with the first appearance of trilobites in the stratigraphical record. Beneath this level, and into the Precambrian, geologists had long encountered successions which clearly lacked highly organised metazoan life. In Britain, for example, geologists were content that the base of the Cambrian System could be defined on the presence of trilobite remains and a widespread regional unconformity. However, discoveries from the late 1940s were to change the face of early Palaeozoic stratigraphy.

2. **Precambrian Metazoans, Trace Fossils and Early Cambrian 'Small Shelly Fossils'**

By the late 1940s the existence of a diverse and widespread metazoan biota had been discovered in what had traditionally been considered as Precambrian rocks. This biota, the Ediacaran Biota, was first discovered in the Ediacara Hills of South Australia and was identified in many other localities across the globe, including Britain, Russia, North America and Africa (Figures 2.10 and 7.4). At no locality were trilobites found associated with representatives of the biota, and for the most part there was a considerable thickness of strata between the Ediacaran organisms and the first trilobites. In the 1960s Russian scientists working in Siberia discovered a surprisingly diverse range of what were called 'small shelly fossils' (SSFs) (Figure 23.2). The use of this rather ambiguous term for this collection of fossils demonstrates that many are difficult to assign to living phyla, although some appear to resemble primitive molluscs or sponges, for example. These minute shells were all found in rocks barren of trilobites, between the Ediacaran Biotas and the trilobites. Further studies demonstrated that the SSF fauna was widespread and relatively common (e.g. Brasier, 1985). The final piece in the jigsaw puzzle was the discovery of abundant trace fossils in the Precambrian–Cambrian transition. Trace fossils below the first occurrence of SSFs consist mostly of a low-diversity, horizontal feeder trace assemblage characterised by the ichnogenus *Harlaniella*. Trace fossils comtemporary with the SSFs include ichnotaxa typical of the Cambrian and even the late Phanerozoic, with penetrative feeding and dwelling burrows typified by the ichnogenus *Phycodes* (Crimes, 1987; Landing, 1994) (Figure 23.3).

3. **The Precambrian–Cambrian Boundary Stratotype**

In order that detailed correlations can be made with the global chronostratigraphic scale, each system must be characterised by a lower and upper boundary which is fixed at a reference rock sequence, and which contains fossil and other evidence enabling the correlations to take place. These boundary stratotypes are decided by international agreement; on ratification by committee, a symbolic 'golden spike' is driven into the succession to denote the decision made. A golden spike was needed for accurate consideration of the boundary of the Cambrian with the Precambrian.

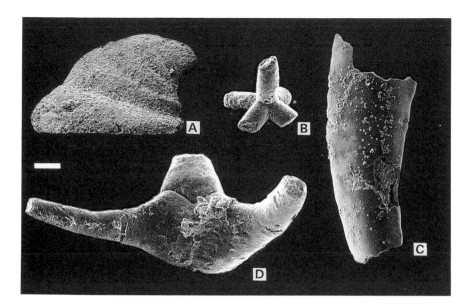

Figure 23.2 *Small shelly fossils (SSF) typical of the Precambrian–Cambrian boundary.* **A:** *Bemella, a probable early mollusc with a calcareous shell.* **B:** *A fragment (spicule) of a siliceous sponge.* **C:** Torellella, *a curved phosphatic tube of unknown affinity.* **D:** Chancelloria, *a star-like, calcareous fossil of unknown affinity. Scale bar approximately 200 μm [Photographs: M. Brasier]*

The Precambrian–Cambrian working committee had three alternative localities to consider as boundary stratotype sections: two in carbonate rock sequences in Russia containing SSFs; and one in Newfoundland, in a clastic sedimentary sequence with SSFs and abundant trace fossils (Figure 23.3). The committee had already decided several points: that the boundary was to be marked by a biostratigraphical tool; that the first appearance of trilobites was in the Cambrian; that the Ediacaran Biota was Pecambrian; and that the boundary was to be drawn at some point between these two biological markers. The committee therefore had two potential sets of guide fossils: the so-called small shelly fossils and a set of trace fossils.

Detailed study of the SSF faunas showed that they were most diverse in carbonates, and that they were long-ranging, restricted in geographical distribution and highly variable in form. The occurrence of deep-burrowing trace fossils appeared to be remarkably constant and in a range of facies. Therefore, the decision was made to designate the section at Fortune Head, on the Burrin peninsula in Newfoundland, the Global Stratotype for the Cambrian–Precambrian boundary, and that the boundary be drawn at the first appearance of both the trace fossil *Phycodes* and the SSF fauna (Figure 23.3). The basal Cambrian was taken to include the pre-trilobite sequence of shelly fossils, and was determined world-wide by the appearance of infaunal traces for the first time.

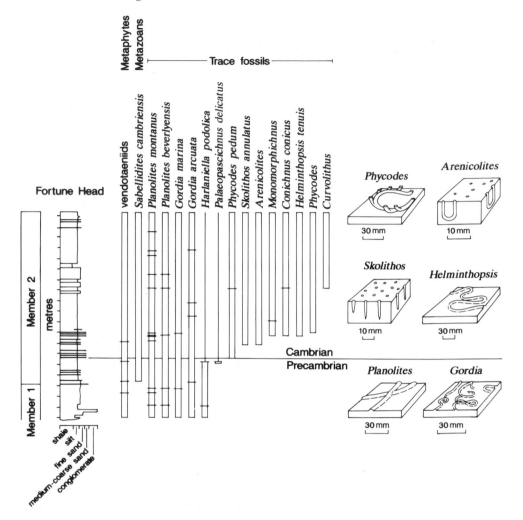

Figure 23.3   *The Precambrian–Cambrian Global Stratotype Section and Point (GSSP) at Fortune Head in Newfoundland. The ranges of the important fossil groups are illustrated. The boundary is defined on the appearance of typical Cambrian trace fossils, particularly* Phycodes *[Modified from Brasier et al. (1994) Fig. 3, p. 6]*

4. Comment

This example demonstrates the importance of biostratigraphy to the development of the Chronostratigraphical Scale, and illustrates the validity of using the first appearance of a wide variety of taxa, in this case, relatively poorly understood 'small shelly fossils' and trace fossil taxa. The example also clearly demonstrates the three phases of any biostratigraphical study: the initial data collection of the various fossil groups from the candidate stratotypes; the data analysis phase in the determination of the validity of the SSF and trace fossil faunas as guide fossils; and finally, the ultimate correlation of the boundary using these tools.

5. References

Brasier, M. 1985. Evolutionary and geological events across the Precambrian–Cambrian boundary. *Geology Today*, **1**, 141–146.

Brasier, M., Cowie, J. & Taylor, M. 1994. Decision on the Precambrian–Cambrian boundary stratotype. *Episodes*, **17**, 3–8.

Crimes, T.P. 1987. Trace fossils and correlation of late Precambrian and early Cambrian strata. *Geological Magazine*, **124**, 97–119.

Landing, E. 1994. Precambrian–Cambrian boundary global stratotype ratified and a new perspective of Cambrian time. *Geology*, **22**, 179–182.

23.3 GRAPTOLITES AND INFRAZONAL BIOSTRATIGRAPHY
(Cooper and Lindholm, 1990)

1. Introduction

Graptolites have often been held up as examples of the perfect guide fossils, and a great many biozonal schemes have been developed for local, regional and global correlation. As discussed above, the global stratotype for the Ordovician–Silurian boundary is taken at the base of the *acuminatus* biozone in Dobs Linn, in the Southern Uplands of Scotland, for example (Box 5.5). Graptolites are well suited as guide fossils because they were planktonic and able to disperse widely; they were not restricted to latitudinal belts controlled by temperature; most species lived in the surface waters and are distributed in both deep- and shallow-water sediments; and many species have relatively short stratigraphical ranges. As a consequence, graptolites have been used to erect numerous biozonal schemes for Lower Palaeozoic rocks. However, graptolites have considerable potential in the precise correlation of sequences across the world at a finer, infrazonal scale.

2. Infrazonal Correlation Using the Graphic Method

The potential exists to use the graphic correlation technique developed by A.B. Shaw (Box 5.4) in the biostratigraphical correlation of global sequences using the first and last appearances of many graptolite taxa, rather than the few guide fossil taxa selected for use in biozonation schemes. This provides the potential for fine-scale subdivision and correlation to a high degree of accuracy.

In using this technique in the correlation of Ordovician sections from around the world, Cooper and Lindholm (1990) selected a standard sequence rich in graptolites to which 14 other sections could be correlated. Other sections were selected from the published literature, and were used only if they were accurately measured. Some difficulty was apparent because many authors were not precise in their determination of zonal boundaries and first appearances. Comparison and correlation were achieved by plotting the section to be compared against the standard section on a two-axis graph (Figure 23.4). The first and last appearances of numerous graptolite taxa for each of the sections were plotted on the graph, and a line of correlation, the 'best fit' through the array, plotted (Figure 23.4). The most important taxa involved in the comparison were those that were distinctive, abundant and short-ranging.

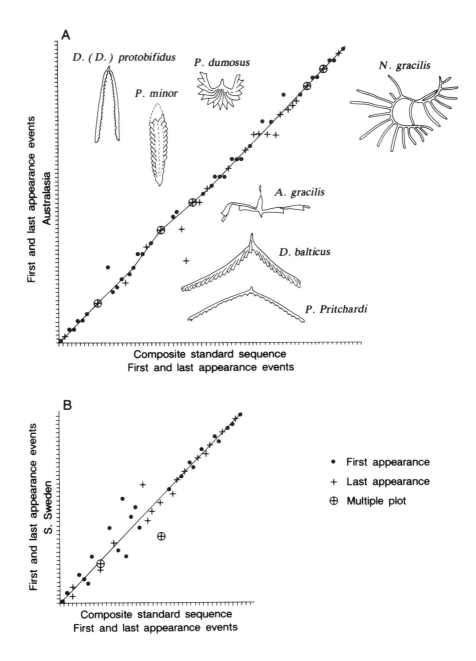

Figure 23.4 *Graphic correlation of graptolite events for the Ordovician, comparing Sweden and Australasia with the composite standard sequence. Abbreviations:* D. (D.) protobifidus, Didymograptus (Didymograptellus) protobifidus; D. balticus; Didymograptus balticus; P. dumosus, Pseudisograptus dumosus; P. minor, Pseudotrigonograptus minor; P. Pritchardi, *should be* Paradelograptuspritchardi. *[Modified from: Cooper and Lindholm (1990)* Geological Magazine, *127, Fig. 3, p. 504]*

3. Correlation of Global Ordovician Sequences

A Composite Standard Sequence of Ordovician graptolites was created from the correlation exercise, based on the first appearance of 103 graptolite taxa, and the first and last appearances of a further 45 taxa. This standard sequence illustrates the presence of between 66 and 73 successive appearance and extinction events which can be used in global correlation. Spacing between events is estimated at 0.7–0.8 million years, giving a high resolution of correlation.

4. Comment

This example demonstrates that the data compiled from numerous sources can provide the basis for a high degree of accuracy in correlation. The data in this case were the primary data from an expanded sequence in Australia, and its comparison with secondary sources from other parts of the world. Data analysis involved the consideration of the validity of the results when compared against a standard sequence composed of an accurately measured section and plotted ranges. Correlation was achieved through the semi-quantitative graphic method. This example also demonstrates the validity of biostratigraphy outside the strictures of the standard biozonation schemes.

5. Reference

Cooper, R.A. & Lindholm, K. 1990. A precise worldwide correlation of early Ordovician graptolite sequences. *Geological Magazine*, **127**, 497–525.

23.4 HIGH-RESOLUTION STRATIGRAPHY AND AMMONITES
(Buckman, 1893, 1910; Callomon and Chandler, 1990)

1. Introduction

The early Middle Jurassic is a time now known to heve been of exceptional importance in the evolution of the ammonites. Three major groups which dominated the world's ammonite fauna into the Cretaceous – the Haplocerataceae, Stephanocerataceae and Perisphinctaceae – appeared and radiated, although their exact origins are obscure. It is also of importance because no clear Boreal and Tethyan marine realms can be distinguished for this brief interval of Jurassic time, so that early Bajocian ammonites from Alaska and Oregon are almost identical to those from Dorset, for example. This similarity is remarkable given the absence of any similarity in under- and overlying successions at these localities, of Aalenian and late Bajocian age. Clearly, understanding the nature of this faunal interchange relies upon accurate global correlation of these ammonite faunas so that the patterns of their evolution and migration can be established, and so that the wider implications of global correlation can be determined.

2. S.S. Buckman and the Inferior Oolite of Southern England

The Jurassic chronology and palaeontology of southern England were the life's work of one remarkable man, S.S. Buckman (1860–1930). An eminent Victorian, Buckman was a prolific writer, and history has left a legacy of two contradictory pen-portraits of the man: as a careful observational scientist, and as an obsessive 'splitter' – author of countless ammonite 'species' based on minute differences in shell morphology. Among many other works, Buckman is largely remembered for his palaeontological work on ammonites and brachiopods from the Inferior Oolite, an oolitic limestone facies which formed in the rich, shallow water of southwest England in the early Middle Jurassic. The Inferior Oolite is largely incomplete and condensed – it was Buckman who once remarked: 'a schoolboy once defined a net as a series of holes strung together, and the Dorset Inferior Oolite might be defined as a series of gaps united by thin bands of deposit' (Buckman, 1910, p. 90).

The Inferior Oolite contains a remarkably rich fauna of ammonites, brachiopods and other shelly fossils, and Buckman's early work led him to realise three important conclusions: that the five biozones so far recognised for the interval could be further subdivided; that there were distinct horizons on a centimetre scale which could be identified by their ammonites; and that not all horizons were present in other parts of England. Buckman determined the name *hemera* for these horizons, which were thought to represent the rock record deposited during extremely limited periods of geological time, and as such were thought to represent fractions of the biozones already devised for the Jurassic.

Buckman's early, detailed, field observations and collecting from the thin (1–10 m) succession of the Inferior Oolite of Dorset and southwest England led to the development of the hemeral system. His later work was marred by its reliance on theoretical evolutionary ideas to develop a stratigraphical scheme without recourse to field work of any kind. This involved the placement of ammonites in 'evolutionary order' based on the ideas of Alphaeus Hyatt, and on the assumption that each ammonite species would denote a separate hemera. As such, Buckman went on to subdivide the whole of the Jurassic into 370 hemerae, a tenfold increase on the 33 biozones originally defined (Arkell, 1933). Once the evolutionary basis for Buckman's scheme had been discredited, and the reliability of his data questioned, the hemeral system fell into disrepute, despite its original basis in sound scientific observation.

3. The Ammonite Horizons of the Inferior Oolite

Recently, the ammonite successions of the Inferior Oolite have been subject to reinvestigation. Callomon and Chandler (1990) have carried out a detailed bed-by-bed investigation of all of the most important sections exposing these beds. The Inferior Oolite contains abundant ammonites and clearly definable horizons deposited within just a few million years. In their study, Callomon and Chandler were able to measure and collect with great accuracy from the sections now exposed, some of which were originally visited by Buckman; and to determine the range in variation of each ammonite species (because of the great number of specimens) at each level and to identify almost true 'populations' living within an extremely short space of time, perhaps measurable in tens of years.

Callomon and Chandler were able to determine a system of 33 ammonite horizons identifiable on the basis of successive populations of ammonites, each horizon denoted by a separate guide fossil (Figure 23.5). Each one of these was originally identified by Buckman. This represents a considerable refinement of the ten biozones currently recognised for the Aalenian–Bajocian, and forms the basis for high-resolution correlation. The detailed collecting and observation of the successive populations of what were fast-evolving Jurassic nekton provides the basis for considerable precision in intercontinental correlation, as the next step is the identification of the same series of horizons – hemerae in Buckman's parlance – which will allow for the accurate interpretation and correlation of events in two widely disparate areas.

4. Comment

This example shows the importance of the data collection phase. Buckman's orginal work involved a high degree of precision in collecting and measure-ment of stratigraphical sections which demonstrated the potential for the high-resolution correlation scheme he later constructed. Although Buckman's later excesses cast doubt on the accuracy of this work, detailed observations have shown it to be broadly correct and of great importance in long-distance correla-tion with North America, for example. Clearly, the excesses of Buckman's later theorising have long held back an important contribution to detailed, high-resolution ammonite biostratigraphy.

5. References

Arkell, W.J. 1933. *The Jurassic System in Great Britain*. Clarendon Press, Oxford.

Buckman, S.S. 1893. The Bajocian of the Sherborne District: its relation to sub-jacent and superjacent strata. *Quarterly Journal of the Geological Society of London*, **49**, 479–522.

Buckman, S.S. 1910. Certain Jurassic (Lias–Oolite) strata of south Dorset; and their correlation. *Quarterly Journal of the Geological Society of London*, **66**, 52–89.

Callomon, J.H. & Chandler, R.B. 1990. A review of the ammonite horizons of the Aalenian–Lower Bajocian stages in the Middle Jurassic of southern England. *Memorie Descrittive della Carta Geologica d'Italia*, **40**, 85–112.

23.5 SUMMARY OF KEY POINTS

- Biostratigraphy is the subdivision and correlation of rock sequences on the basis of fossils, and most fossils can be of some use in stratigraphy, if only in the broad recognition of Phanerozoic or Precambrian eonothems, for example.
- In any biostratigraphical study (or chronostratigraphical study for that matter, if based on fossil data) there are three phases: data collection, involving primary and secondary sources; data analysis, involving determination of the suitability of a particular group for the job, and compilation of range data; and correlation, which may be affected by errors of data collection or original fossil dispersals.
- The examples chosen each demonstrate these three stages. The Precambrian–Cambrian boundary stratotype was based on detailed compilation of world-wide range data and their comparison. Surprisingly, it was a trace fossil, *Phycodes*, which demonstrated the greatest potential, after months of analysis. The world-wide graptolite correlation demonstrates that there is more to the fossil record than its biozonal sequences, and this, together with the ammonite

Ammonite horizons			Ammonite biozones	
	Aa-16	*Euhoploceras acanthodes*	Concavum	Formosum
	Aa-15	*Graphoceras formosum*		Formosum
	Aa-14	*Graphoceras concavum*		Concavum
	Aa-13	*Graphoceras cavatum*		Concavum
	Aa-12	*Brasilia decipiens*	Bradfordensis	Gigantea
	Aa-11	*Brasilia gigantea*		Gigantea
	Aa-10	*Brasilia bradfordensis, similis*		Bradfordensis
	Aa-9	*Brasilia bradfordensis, baylii*		Bradfordensis
	Aa-8	*Brasilia bradfordensis, subcornuta*		Bradfordensis
LOWER BAJOCIAN	Aa-7	*Ludwigia murchisonae*	Murchisonae	Murchisonae
	Aa-6	*Ludwigia patellaria*		Murchisonae
	Aa-5	*Ludwigia obtusiformis*		Obtusiformis
	Aa-4	*Ancolioceras opalinoides*		Haugi
	Aa-3	*Leioceras bifidatum*	Scissum	
	Aa-2	*Leioceras lineatum*	Scissum	
	Aa-1	*Leioceras opalinum*	Opalinum	
	Bj-19	*Teloceras bladgeni / banksi*	Humphriensianum	Bladgeni
	Bj-18	*Teloceras bladgeni*		Bladgeni
	Bj-17	*Stephanoceras blagdeniforme*		Humphriesianum
	Bj-16	*Stephanoceras gibbosum*		Humphriesianum
	Bj-15	*Stephanoceras humphriesianum*		Humphriesianum
	Bj-14	*Poecilomorphus cycloides*		Cycloides
	Bj-13	*Witchellia pinguis*	Sauzei	
	Bj-12	*Stephanoceras rhytum*	Sauzei	
AALENIAN	Bj-11	*Otoites sauzei*	Sauzei	
	Bj-10	*Witchellia laeviuscula*	Laeviuscula	Laeviuscula
	Bj-9	*Witchellia ruber*		Laeviuscula
	Bj-8	*Shirbuirnia trigonalis*		Trigonalis
	Bj-7	*Witchellia connata*		Trigonalis
	Bj-6	*Sonninia 'ovalis'*	Ovalis	
	Bj-5	*Witchellia romanoides*	Ovalis	
	Bj-4	*Bradfordia inclusa*	Ovalis	
	Bj-3	*Hyperlioceras walkeri* β	Discites	
	Bj-2	*Hyperlioceras walkeri* α	Discites	
	Bj-1	*Hyperlioceras rudidiscites*	Discites	

Figure 23.5   *Ammonite horizons in the Aalenian and Bajocian of southern England [Modified from: Callomon and Chandler (1990)* Memorie Descrittive Della Carta Geologica D'Italia, **40**, *Figs 5 and 6, pp. 101 and 102]*

horizons, shows how the detailed analysis of both primary and secondary data sources can lead to a greater degree of precision than was first appreciated.

24
Summary of Part III

This chapter summarises the most important concepts from Part III, in which the application of fossils in evolutionary studies, palaeoenvironmental analysis and stratigraphy was examined through the use of worked case studies. These case studies demonstrate the methodology of applied palaeontology.

24.1 DATA FROM THE FOSSIL RECORD

The vast majority of sedimentary rocks contain some type of fossil. Deposits of marine origin contain the most fossils, particularly those formed in shelf environments, but many other fossiliferous deposits exist, each with the potential to supply information on the nature of the palaeoenvironment. Traditionally, fossils were collected without due regard to details of stratigraphical horizon or geographical location, and museums are full of beautifully preserved but poorly located specimens. It is good practice, therefore, not to remove a fossil from its containing sedimentary rock before detailed observations are made. This may entail the creation of a geological map and suitable graphic log of the sedimentary succession. In general, there are three principles which govern field data collection: firstly, every fossil-bearing succession should be logged prior to collection; secondly, collecting should be carried out according to a set strategy; and thirdly, loose specimens should be avoided unless of use in determining morphological variation.

24.2 FOSSILS IN EVOLUTIONARY STUDIES

The fossil record is of great value in illustrating evolutionary pattern and rate, at both microevolutionary and macroevolutionary scales. Four factors are of importance in the determination of evolutionary patterns. Firstly, the completeness of the stratigraphical succession is of great importance as it determines the level of confidence in the accuracy of any interpretation. Estimates of stratigraphical completeness can be calculated with reference to present-day accumulation rates in environments equivalent to those existing in the geological past. Secondly, the nature of the sampling procedure is determined by the completeness of the stratigraphical succession. For example, the finest possible sampling has determined that in the Neogene bryozoan *Metrarabdotos* and in the Ordovician trilobites of Builth Wells, central Wales, the respective modes of punctuated equilibrium and phyletic gradualism can be identified. Fine-scale sampling has also teased out a complex story of stepped extinctions in the foraminifera before and after the global iridium event which is taken to mark the termination of the Cretaceous. Thirdly, establishing the range in variation of morphology within a species for a given time interval is also important as it allows a clearer understanding of any of the lineage changes, rapid or gradual, which might occur through time. Finally, for macroevolutionary patterns it is important to be aware of the imperfect standard of the data collection, which may give rise to false extinctions and/or appearances in the fossil record. For example, the 26 million year periodicity of mass extinctions has been challenged as an artefact of an imperfect data set.

24.3 FOSSILS IN PALAEOENVIRONMENTAL ANALYSIS

Fossils are arguably the most reliable indicators of the nature of ancient environments. As living organisms they were limited in distribution and diversity by a range of environmental parameters. Through the application of uniformitarian principles it is possible to compare living and fossil assemblages in order to determine the nature of the ancient palaeoenvironment. This is limited by the age of the assemblage, as there may be no living analogues, and by the degree to which a fossil assemblage approximates to a once living community. A number of factors need to be considered in determining ancient ecologies. Firstly, it is important to determine the level of autochthony of the assemblage. Fossil benthonic organisms should be largely autochthonous to qualify as approximating to a fossil community. Secondly, it is important to consider the recurrence of association. In many cases, recurrence of a particular assemblage as an association adds additional weight to its determination as a once living community. Thirdly, taxonomic uniformitarianism, the comparison of living and fossil organisms, is the key to interpreting ancient environments, on the premise that the fossil organism would have been limited by the same factors as the living organism. Fourthly, analyses of the population structure of the fossil assemblage, particularly diversity/density and age studies, are important tools. Finally, it is not good practice to study fossils in isolation, as the nature of the enclosing sediments can help with the palaeoenvironmental interpretation. Autochthonous benthonics, such as molluscs and other shelly fossils preserved in life attitude, and trace fossils, are the most important indicators of palaeoenvironment, in some cases, as with the worked examples, allowing determination of relative salinity and oxygenation levels within the water column.

On a broad scale, fossils are of great value in palaeobiogeographical studies. These rely on the compilation of published data sources, and on three processes: the determination of geographical distributions for fossil organisms; the interpretation of such patterns in the light of limiting factors; and the geological application of such patterns. The most important geological application is in palaeocontinental reconstructions, particularly in displaced terranes and in early Palaeozoic studies where there is little reliable evidence.

24.4 FOSSILS AND STRATIGRAPHY

Traditionally, the greatest application for fossils has been in the correlation and relative ordering of rock successions on the basis of fossil content. This continues to be of great value to the geologist and is the basis for most correlation exercises. Stratigraphical studies rely simply on the collection of suitable data, in this case, the vertical ranges of taxa from detailed field collecting, or the compilation of such ranges from published literature, with a corresponding decrease in reliability; the analysis of the data, particularly in the consideration of the suitability of particular groups in correlating rock successions; and the actual correlation exercise itself. At the finest level, the resolution of the stratigraphical record is determined by the rate at which species are replaced, and in the case of the ammonites this can be surprisingly rapid, with a corresponding increase in value in detailed correlation. World-wide correlation can also be surprisingly accurate, and the use of semi-quantitative methods such as the graphic correlation technique provides a reasonably rigorous test. Finally, even trace fossils may be considered of value in stratigraphy, particularly where they are effectively picking out a global event – the first burrowing activity within the sediment by the metazoans of the earliest Cambrian. Because of this, the first appearance of traces such as *Phycodes* has the greatest significance in determining the lower boundary of the Cambrian, and correspondingly, of the whole of the Phanerozoic.

Subject Index

Formal taxonomic names are given in the systematic index. Page numbers given in italics refer to illustrations.

Abundance (density) 59–62, *62*
Actualism (uniformitarianism) 49, 65
Adaptive radiations 85, 87, 89
  association with mass extinctions 89
  of bivalves 149–50
  of brachiopods 192–3
  Cambrian explosion *90*, 88, *123*, 124
  of foraminifera 284–5
  of gastropods 150
  of plants 124, 134
Adductor muscles (bivalves) *138*, 142
Adductor muscles (brachiopods) *183*, 184
Ahermatypic corals 247
Alar septa 244
Allochthonous fossils 19–22, *23*, 56, 328
Allopatric speciation 77, 79, 153
Alps (Italian and Austrian) 21
Amber 15
  as a conservation trap *37*, 41
Ambulacra *203*, 205
Amino acids 70, 72
  in brachiopod shells 195–6
Ammonites *164*, 165, *167*
Ammonoids 164–6, *164*, *165*, 172, *172*, *173*
  coiling and shape 164
  heteromorphs 165, *166*
  suture lines 163, *164*, 165
  swimming speed 164, *165*
Ammonoid groups 164–6, *167*
  ammonites *164*, 165, *167*
  ceratites *164*, 165, *167*
  goniatites *164*, 165, *167*
Amphibians *90*, 128, 134

crossopterygian ancestry of 128
  labyrinthodonts 128
Anaerobic bacteria 22
Anagenesis 77, 80, 85
Ancestrula *269*, 270
Aniosgraptid fauna 259, *264*
Angiosperms (flowering plants) 35, *90*, 124, *125*, 126, 133
Antarctica 18, *19*, 170
Antennules *291*, 292
Apical system 204
Aptychi 165–6
Archaean life 116–19
  cell fillaments 116–17, 131
  stromatolites 116, *117*, *118*, 119, 131
Arenaceous foraminifera 281–2, *282*
  textularines 281–2, *282*, *283*
Arthropods 19, 220–2, 292
  Ostracods 129, 278, 290–301
  Trilobites 129, 220–37, 290
Arizona fossil forest 27, *28*
Assemblages 55–6, 65
  allochthonous 56
  autochthonous 65
  death 55
  life 55–6
Associations 55
  recurrent 356
Asteroids 201, 212
Astogeny 261
Astrophic articulate brachiopods 190–1
  pentamerids 185, 190–1, *193*
  rhynchonellids 185, 190–1, 193, *193*, 194

Astrophic articulate brachiopods (*cont.*)
  terebratulids 35, 185, 190–1, 193, *193*, 194
Astrophic hinge margin 185
Autochthonous fossils 19–22, *23*, 65, 328
Autochthony 355–6
Autothecae 255, *256*
Autotrophy 120
Avalonia 61, 368
Avon Gorge (England) 99
Axial complex 241, *243*, 244–5
Axis (in trilobites) 221

Bactritids 172
Baltica 61
Barnacles *98*, 99
Bases 71, *71*
Base pairs 71, *71*
Bathgate (Scotland) 128
Belemnites 166–8, *168*, *169*, 173
Benthonic foraminifera 279–80, 281–4, *283*,
  285, *286*
Benthonic organisms 60
Bernissart (Belgium) 37, *38*
Biofacies 64
  use in reconstruction of Gondwana 369,
  370
Biogeography 59
Biomeres 234, *235*, 236
Biometry 45–6, *46*
  bivariate analysis 46, *46*
  multivariate analysis 46
Biosphere 85, 117, 134
Biostratigraphy 97–105, 108–9, 372–84
Biostratinomy 18–22
Bioturbation 31, 63
Biozonations
  ammonite 179, 381–3, *384*
  coral-brachiopod 99, 250, *251*
  graptolite 106, 379–81
  mammal-like reptile 130–1, *130*
  trilobite 234, *235*
Biozones 101–5, *103*, 108, 374
  acme 101
  assemblage 101, 131, 156
  consecutive range 101
  Oppel 101–2
  partial range 101
  total range 101, 156, 179
Biramous appendages 221, *221*
Birds *98*, 100, 128, 134
Bithecae 255, *256*
Bitter Springs (Australia) 119
Bivalves (lamellibranchs, pelecypods)
  136–58
  classification of 140

  dentition of 142, *143*
  distinguished from brachiopods 137, *138*,
  141
  distinguished from ostracods 137
  evolution of 149–50, *149*
  general characteristics of 136–9, *138*
  limiting factors of 154
  mode of life 137–9, *138*, 154–6, *155*
  shell morphology of 141–7
Bivalve applications 150–6
  in evolutionary studies 152–3
  in functional morphology studies 150–1
  in stratigraphy 156, *157*
Bivalve groups 142–7
  epifaunal 144–6, *147*, 155
  deep infaunal 143–4, *145*, 155
  shallow infaunal 142–3, *144*, 155
Black shales 362
Body fossils 11–12, 41, 110, 301
Bottjer, David 364–6
Brachidium 184, *186*, *187*
Brachiopods 129, 141, 150, 182–200
  biomolecules in 195–6, 199
  classification of 183–4, 185
  distinguished from bivalves *138*, 141, 182
  evolution of 192–4, *194*
  general characteristics of 182–3, *183*
  homeomorphy in 186, *188*, 189
  limiting factors of 197
  mode of life 182–3
Brachiopod applications
  in evolutionary studies 195–6, 199
  in functional morphology studies 194–5,
  196
  in palaeobiogeography 197–8, *198*, 199,
  367–371
  in palaeoenvironmental studies 196–8
  in stratigraphy 198–9
Brachiopod groups
  articulates 184–91, 192
  inarticulates 184, 191, 192, *192*
'Brain corals' 240
Brinkman, Ronald 176, 179
Brood chambers (bryozoan) 270
Brood pouch/chambers (ostracod) 291,
  292, *294*
Bryozoans (polyzoans, ectoprocts) 129,
  267–77
  colony form in 268, *269*, 270, 275–6
  contributing to reefs 273, 276
  distinguished from corals 268–9
  evolution of 273, *274*
  general characteristics of 267–9, *268*
  limiting factors of 275–6, *276*
  mode of life 268–70

morphology of 270–3
Bryozoan applications 273–7
   in evolutionary studies 274, 341–4
   in functional morphology studies 273, 277
   in palaeoenvironmental analysis 275–6, 276, 277
   in stratigraphy 277
Bryozoan groups 270–3
   gymnolaemates 270, 272, 272, 273
   phylactolaemates 270
   stenolaemates 270–2, 271, 273
Buckman, S.S. 381–2
Build-ups 328–30
Builth (Wales) 344
Burial rate 17, 18, 33
Burgess Shale (Canada) 24, 37–41, 54
'Button corals' 240
Byssus 137

Calcareous foraminifera 282–4, 282, 283
   fusulinids 282, 282
   globigerinids 282, 283, 284
   miliolids 282–4, 282
   rotalines 282, 283, 284
Calice 239, 243
Calyx 211
Cambrian explosion 88, 90, 124
Cambrian fauna 35, 90, 115, 121–2, 122, 133, 220, 318–19
Cambrian-Precambrian boundary 375–9, 378
Cambrian System 375
Camerae (chambers) 160, 161, 162
Cameral deposits 164, 171
Carapace 291, 291
Carboniferous Coal Forests 124
Cardinal fossula 244
Cardinal process 185
Cardinal proseptum 244
Cardinal teeth 142
Casts (pseudomorphs) 26, 27
Cementers 137
Cephalon 221, 221
Cephalopods 148, 160–81
   buoyancy of 159–60, 168, 169–71, 171, 173
   classification of 161–2
   distinguished from gastropods 160–1, 161
   evolution of 169–73
   general characteristics of 159–61
   limiting factors of 177
   mode of life 159–61
   sexual dimorphism in 174
   shell implosion in 173–4, 174, 177–8, 180

   shell morphology of 162–9
Cephalopod applications
   in evolutionary studies 175–6, 175, 176, 179
   in functional morphology studies 173–4
   in palaeobiogeography 178–9
   in palaeoenvironmental analysis 177–9
   in stratigraphy 179, 180
Cephalopod groups 162–9
   ectocochleates 162–6
   endocochleates 166–9
Ceratites 164, 165, 167
Chambers, Robert 68
Characters in cladistics 50–51
   apomorphic 50
   homology of 50–51
   plesiomorphic 50
   polarity of 50
Charnian Biota (Ediacaran Biota) 25, 120
Cheetham, Alan 342
China 54, 173
Chitin 221
Chordates 127, 131
Chromosomes 69
   composition of 70
   of fruit-fly 69–70
   of humans 69–70
Chronostratigraphical Scale (Geological Time Scale) 105–7
Chronostratigraphical units 4, 5
Chronostratigraphy 105–8
Clades 50, 89
Cladistics (phylogenetic systematics) 47, 50–1, 87
Cladogenesis 7
Cnidarians 238–40, 245, 267, 269
   characteristics of 238–9
   classification of 239–40
   corals 56, 71, 129, 238–52, 267
Cnidarian groups 238–52
   hydrozoans 238–9, 245
   jellyfish 238–9, 245
   sea anemones 238, 240, 245, 267
Coaptative structures 227, 229
Coccoliths 98
Cocks, Robin 368
Coleoids (endocochleate cephalopods) 166–9, 173
Columella (coral) 241, 244
Columella (gastropod) 138, 147
Communities 55–6
Comparative anatomy 44, 52, 111
Compound corals 240
Conodonts 127, 127, 131, 134

Concentration Lagerstätten 36–7, *37*
Concentration Lagerstätten, examples
  Bernissart Mine 37, *38*
  Ludlow Bone Bed 37
  Rancho La Brea 15, 37
Conservation Lagerstätten 37–41
  obrution *37*, 38–41
  stagnation *37*, 38–9
Conservation Lagerstätten, examples
  Arizona fossil forest 27, *28*
  Bathgate 128
  Burgess Shale, *24*, 39–41, 221
  Lebanon 173
  Mazon Creek 39, 41
  Messel 38, *40*
  Posidonienschiefer 38
  Rhynie Chert 124
  Santana Formation 20–1, *292*
  Solnhofen Limestone 15, *17*, 38, *39*
Conway Morris, Simon 54
Coprolites 12, 14
  preservation of 31
Corals 56, 71, 129, 238–52, 269
  classification of 239–40
  distinguished from bryozoans 268
  evolution of 245–6, *246*
  general characteristics of 238–9, *239*
  limiting factors of 239, 247–8, *248*
  morphology of 240–5
  septal insertion in 241, 244, *244*, 245
Coral applications 246–50
  in evolutionary studies 246–7, 250
  in determining length of Devonian year
    250–1
  in palaeoenvironmental analysis 247–50
  in stratigraphy, *98*, 99, 250, *251*
  in terrane analysis 249–50
Coral groups 240–5
  rugosa *35*, *239*, 240–4, *243*, 245, 247–9
  scleractinians (hexacorals) *35*, 240, *243*,
    244–8
  tabulates 240–1, *242*, 245, 247–8
Corallite 240
Corallum 240
Counter proseptum 244
Counterlateral septa 244
Cranidium 223, *224*
Cretaceous-Tertiary boundary 345–50, *349*
Crick, Francis 71
Crinoids 12, 19, 201, *202*, 203, *203*, 209–11,
    211, 212, 216, *217*
Crinoidal limestone 201, *202*, 211
Crura 186
Cruralium 190
Crustaceans 290, 292–3

  ostracods 278, 290–301
Cuttlefish 166, 168, *170*, 173
Cuvier, Georges 44, 97
Cyanobacteria 116, 133
Cytoplasm 69, 72, 278, *279*

Darwin, Charles 34, 68–9, 75, 79, 97, 231
Darwinian theory 67–9, 72, 91
  heredity 68, 69–73
  natural selection 68, 72–4
Death assemblage 55
Deltidial plates 185
Delthyrium 185
Density (abundance) 59–62, *63*
Detorsion 140–1
Diachronism 95, *96*
Diagenesis 26–30, *26*, *33*, 41
  compaction and deformation 27, *30*, *32*,
    41
  encrustation, *26*, 27, 41
  impregnation, *26*, 27, *28*, 41
  preservation of original shell 26, *26*, *28*,
    41
  recrystallisation and replacement 26–7,
    26, 41
  solution *26*, 27, *29*, *30*, 41
Dibranchiate cephalopods 161–2
Dichograptid fauna 259, *264*
Diductor muscles *183*, 184
Dinosaurs 2, 7, 12, *13*, 37, *38*, 52, *52*, 128
  concentration Lagerstätten at Bernissart
    37, *38*
  evolution of 128
  extinction of 87
  footprints and trackways *303*, 314
  mania 7
  reconstructions at Crystal Palace *52*
  skin impressions of 18
Diplograptid fauna 259, *264*
Dissepimentarium 241, 242, *243*, 244, 245
Dissepiments (coral) *239*, 241
Dissepiments (dendroid graptolite) *256*,
    257, 259
Diversity 59–62, *63* , 357, 360
DNA 70, 71, *71*, 72, 74, 91
  from fossils 70
Dobs Linn (Scotland) 106, 376
Dodo 75
Dentition (bivalve) 142, *143*
  desmodont *143*
  dysodont *143*
  heterodont 142, *143*
  taxodont 142, *143*

Echinoderms 129, 201–19

classification of 203–4
evolution of *205*, 212, *213*
general characteristics of 201–3, *203*
limiting factors of 215
mode of life 203
morphology 204–11
preservational states of 215–16
Echinoderm applications
in evolutionary studies 214–15, 218
in functional morphology studies 212–14,
214, 218
in palaeoenvironmental analysis 215–18
in stratigraphy 98, 217–18
Echinoderm groups
asteroids 201, 212
crinoids 12, 19, 201, *202*, 203, *203*, 209–11,
211, 212, 216, *217*
echinoids 201, 203, *203*, 204–9, *205*, *206*,
208, *210*, 212, 215–16
holothurians 203, 212
Echinoids 201, 203, *203*, 204–9, *205*, *206*,
208, *210*, 212, 215–16
Ecophenotypes 72
Ecospace 88
Ectocochleate cephalopods 162–6
ammonoids 164–6, *164*, *165*, 172–3, *172*,
173
nautiloids 162–4, *163*, 171–2, *172*
Ectoprocts *see bryozoans*
Ecuador 73, 75
Ediacara Hills (Australia) 120, 376
Ediacaran Biota 25, 120, *120*, 133–4, 212,
231, 238, 240, 245, 376–7
Eldredge, Niles 79–80, 233, 341
El Kef (Tunisia) 348–9
El Haria Formation (Tunisia) 348
Endemic centre 367
Endemism 367
Endocochleate cephalopods (coleoids)
166–9
belemnites 166–8, *168*, *169*, 173
cuttlefish 166, 168, *170*, 173
squid 166, 168, *170*
Endoderm 238
Endogenic traces 31, *31*, 305
Enteron 238, *239*
Epirelief *31*
Epitheca 240
Epithelium 141, 162
Equilibrium species 62, *63*
Erathems 107, *108*
Ethology 53, 303
Eukaryotes 69, 91, 115, 117, *118*, 119–20,
133
Euryhaline organisms 361

Event horizons 107, 316
Evolution 67–92
biological theory 67–74, 89
macroevolution 74–85
microevolution 74–85
role of palaeontology in 67–8, 74–89
Evolutionary faunas, *90*, 121–4
Cambrian 35, *90*, 121–2, *122*, 133, 220,
318–19
Modern or Mesozoic/Cenozoic *90*,
123–4, 133, 267, 279, 296, 318–19
Palaeozoic, *90*, 123–4, 133, 201, 238, 253,
267, 279, 296, 318–19
Evolutionary lineages
in *Globorotalia* 86–7, 287
in *Gryphaea* 80, 153
in horses 78
in *Infulaster-Hagenowa* 215, 218
in *Kosmoceras* 176, *176*
in *Micraster* 215, 218
in *Metrarabdotos* 274, 341–4, *343*
in *Monograptus* 262
in *Orbulina* 84, *84*
in *Phacops rana* 233, 235
in *Poecilizonites* 153
in Welsh Ordovician trilobites 233, 235,
344–5, *346*
in *Zaphrentis* 247
Exceptional preservation
of hard parts 28, 36–7
of soft parts 18, 20–1, 37–41
Exogenic traces 31, *31*, 305

Facies 64–5, 93–5
Facies fossils 99, 277
Fascioles 209, *210*
Feeding strategy in bivalves and
gastropods 154
Fig Tree Group (Africa) 117
Fish, evolutionary history of *90*, 126–8, 134
agnathans 126–7
arthrodires 126–7
bony-fish 127
'lung-fish' 127–8
sharks 127
Fixed cheeks 221, 223, *224*
Flowering plants (angiosperms) 115
Foramen (foraminiferal) 281
Foraminifera 84, 86–7, 129, 278–90
classification of 280
coiling in *279*, 281
evolution of 284–5, *285*
general characteristics of 278–80, *279*
limiting factors of 287–8
mode of life 279–80

Foraminifera (*cont.*)
  morphology *279*, 281–4, *282, 283*
  test wall structure in 281–4, *282*
Foraminifera applications 285–8
  in evolutionary studies 84, *84*, 86–7,
    285–9, 345–50, *349*
  in palaeoenvironmental analysis *286,*
    287–8
  in palaeotemperature analysis 287–8
  in stratigraphy, *98*, 101, 288
Foraminifera groups 281–4
  allogromines 280, 284
  arenaceous 281–2, *282*
  calcareous 281–4, *282*
Formation (lithostratigraphy) 93
Fortey, Richard 368
Fossiliferous deposits 328–30
Fossil record 33–6, 41, 67, 91, 115–19
  adequacy and completeness of 33–6, 41,
    75, 115
  data retrieval from 330–6, 385
  definition of 33
  and evolution 75–9, 80, 84–5, 91
  major features of 115–29, 318–19
Fossilisation (taphonomy) 12–42, 110
Fossils 11–12
  collection of 334–6
  controls on stratigraphical ranges of
    374–5
  early concepts of 43–4, 111
  and evolution 67–92, 319–21, 338–54,
    385–6
  in folklore and society 6, 43
  functional morphology studies 54–5,
    319–20
  as living organisms 43–66
  in palaeobiology 318–21
  in palaeoenvironmental analysis 321–2,
    355–71, 386–7
  as scientific tools 7, 318–23
  and sediments 327–30
  in stratigraphy 93–109, 323, 372–84, 387
Fossulae *243*, 244
Free cheeks *221*, 223, *224*
Fringe pits *227*, 230
Full relief 305
Funiculus 268, *268*

Galapagos Islands 73, 75
Gametes 69
Gametophyte stage 124, *125*
Gape 137, 146
Gastropods 136–58
  coiling in 147, *148*
  classification of 140–1

evolution of 150–1
general characteristics of *138*, 139–40
limiting factors of 154
mode of life 140, 154
shell morphology of 147, *148*
Gastropod applications 150–6
  in evolutionary studies 153
  in functional morphology studies 151–2,
    152
  in palaeoenvironmental analysis 153–6
  in stratigraphy 156
Genal angle 223
Genal spines 223
Gene pool 77
Genes 69, 72
  dominant 72
  heterozygous 72
  homozygous 72
  recessive 72
Genetic code 69, 71, 91
Genetics 69–72
Genotype 72
Geological time scale
    (Chronostratigraphical time scale) 4–5,
    5
Gesner, Conrad 43
'Golden spike' 107, 376
Gondwana 59, 367–71
  reconstruction from faunal assemblages
    367–71
Gould, Stephen 79–80, 341
Glabella, *221*, 223
Global Stratotype Section and Point (GSSP)
    377, *378*
Globigerinid ooze 280
Glossopetrae ('tongue stones'), 44
Goniatites *164, 165, 167*
Grain growth 27
Grant family 73
Graphic correlation 104–5, *104*, 379–81,
    380
  of graptolite-bearing sequences 379–81,
    380
Graphic log 331–2, *333*
Graptolites 129, 253–66
  classification of 255
  depth relationships of 262–3
  evolution of, *232*, 260
  general characteristics of 253–5, *254*
  limiting factors of 262–3
  mode of life 254, 257, 261, *262*
  morphology of, *254*, 255–60, *256*
  structure of periderm in 254, 264
Graptolite applications 261–4
  in evolutionary studies 261–2, 264

in functional morphology studies 261, *262*, 264
in palaeobiogeography 367–71
in palaeoenvironmental analysis 262–3, 265
in stratigraphy *98*, 100, 253, 263–4, *264*, 265, 379–81
Graptolite groups 255–60, *256*
  dendroids 255, *256*, 257–9, *258*, 260
  graptoloids 255, *256*, *258*, 259–60
Graptoloids 255, *256*, *258*, 259–60
  anisograptids 259–60
  dichograptids, *256*, 257, *258*, 259–60
  diplograptids, *256*, 259–60
  monograptids, *256*, *258*, 259–60
'Grave-wax' 21
Great Barrier Reef (Australia) 238
Great Estuarine Group (Scotland) 359–62
Guide fossils (index or zone fossils) 97–101, *98*, 108
  ammonites, *98*, 100, 179
  belemnites 179
  bivalves 156
  bryozoans 277
  coccoliths *98*
  corals *98*, 99, 250, *251*
  foraminifera *98*, 278–88
  gastropods 156
  graptolites *98*, 100, 253, 263–4, *264*, 265
  ostracods 299–300
  trilobites 234
  criteria for good examples 97–100, *98*, 108
Gun Flint Chert (Canada) 119
Gymnolaemate bryozoans 270, 272–3, *272*, 273
  cheilostomes 272–3, *272*, 273
Gymnosperms, evolutionary history of *90*, 124, *125*, 126, 133
  conifers 126
  cycads 126
  ginkgos 126

Hardgrounds 328–9
Heart-urchins (echinoids) *205*, 207, 209, *210*
Hemera 382
Hemichordates 253–4, *254*, 255, 260, 267
Herculaneum (Italy) 15
Heredity 68, 69–73, 91
Hermatypic corals 245–7, *248*
Heterochrony 74, 76–7
  in ammonites 175–6
  in graptolites 261–2
  paedomorphosis 76–7, 232
  peramorphosis 76–7

in trilobites 232
Heterodont dentition 142, *143*
Heteromorph ammonites 165, *166*
Heterotrophy 120–1
Hexacorals (scleractinians) 240, *243*, 244–5
Holaspid stage 232
Holochroal eyes 223, *224*, *230*
Holothurians 205, 212
Holzmaden (Germany) 13, *15*
Homeomorphy, in brachiopods 186, *188*, 189
Horizons 382–3, *384*
'Horn corals' 240
Horses, evolution of 78
Hudson, John 359
Humans 67–9, 129
  evolution of 67–8
Huxley, Julian 69
Huxley, Thomas Henry 78
Hyponome 160, *160*
Hyporelief 31, 305
Hypostome 223

Iapetus Ocean 61, 234
'Ice man' 21
Ichnofacies 63–4, 315
Ichnofossils (trace fossils) 301–17
Ichnology 62–3
Ichnotaxa 304
Ichthyosaurs 38, 128
Index fossils *see guide fossils*
Ink sac 168, *170*
'Impact winter' 89
Implosion of cephalopod shells 173, *174*, 177
Inarticulate brachiopods 191, *192*
  craniaceans 191
  inarticulates 191–2, *192*
  lingulates 192, *192*
Inferior Oolite (England) 381–3, *384*
Instars 292
Intraspecific variation 47
Iridium 89, 345
Irregular echinoids 204, *205*, 206–9
  early irregular echinoids 206, *208*
  heart-urchins (deep burrowing) *205*, 207, 209, *210*
  sand-dollars (shallow burrowing) *205*, 207–9, *210*

Jellyfish 238
Jet-propulsion in cephalopods 159–60

Karroo Basin (South Africa) 130–1
Keller, G. 348–50

Kingdoms 47, *49*, 65

Labrum 207
Lagerstätten 36–42, 56
Lagerstätten, types of 36–41
    concentration 37–41, *37*, *42*
    conservation 36–7, *37*, *42*
Lamarck, Jean-Baptiste 68
Lamellibranchs *see* bivalves
La Plata (Argentina) *331*
Lateral teeth 142
Laurasia 61
Lazarus taxa 35, *35*
Life assemblage 55–6, 355
Limiting factors 57–63
Limpets 139
Linnaeus, Carolus 48
Lithostratigraphy 93–6, 108
'Living fossils' 319
'Lizzie the lizard' 128
Logging 330–1, *332*, *333*
Lophophore (brachiopod) 183, *184*, 186,
    186, *187*, 197
Lophophore (bryozoan) 267
Ludlow Bone Bed (England) 37
Lunules 209, *210*
Lycopods *90*, 124
Lyell, Charles 34

Macroevolution 74, 85–9, *90*, 91, 111
Madreporite 204
Mammal-like reptiles 129, 130–1, *130*, 134
Mammals *90*, 128–9
Mammoths 13, 14
Mandibles, *291*, 292
Mantel, Gideon 52
Marine environments, classification of 60
Marginal pores 293
Marsh, O.C. 78
Mass extinctions 85, 87–9
Mass extinctions, causes of 88–9
Mass extinction events *88*
    end-Cambrian 231
    late Devonian 88, 123, 212, 231, 245
    end-Ordovician 88, 122–3, 172, 193, 212,
        231, 273
    end-Permian 87, 122, 173, 193, 212, 231,
        241, 245, 273, 284, 298
    end-Triassic 193, 212
    end Cretaceous (K-T) 87, 89, 124, 285,
        287, 298, 345–50, *349*
    late Pleistocene 88
Mass extinctions, periodicity of 89, 350–3,
    351, *353*
Mass mortality 15

of belemnites 172, *178*
of elephants 13–14
of fishes 20
of mammoths 13–14
Mauritius, *75*
Maxillae, *291*, 292
Mazon Creek (USA), 39, 41
Medusae 239
Meiosis 69
Mendel, Gregor 69–70, 72
Mendelian ratio 72
Meraspid stage 232
Mesentaries 239, *239*
Messel (Germany) 38, *40*
Metasomatism 27
Metazoans 120, 238, 302
Microevolution 74–85, 91, 111
    definition of 74–5
    fossil record and 75–9
    lineages 75, 78, *80*, 81, *83*
Microfossils 2, 101, 278–301
    coccoliths *98*, 278
    conodonts 127, *127*, 131, 134
    diatoms 278
    foraminifera, *98*, 278–89
    ostracods 278, 290–301
    radiolaria 278
'Missing links' 77
Mitosis 69
Modern or Mesozoic/Cenozoic fauna *90*,
    123–4, 133, 267, 279, 296, 318, 319
Molluscs 100, 124, 129, 136–81
    bivalves and gastropods 136–58
    cephalopods 159–81
Molluscan archetype 147–8
Molluscan assemblages and salinity 359–62
Monograptid fauna 259, *264*
Monophyletic groups 50, 87
Montana (USA) 18
Monterey Formation (USA) 364
Morphological resemblance 45
Morphological variation 339, *341*, 354
Morse, John 362
Moulds *26*, 27, *29*
    external 27, *29*
    internal 27, *29*, 30
Multilocular tests 281
Mummies 11, 18, *19*, 21
Mussels 142, 144, 146
Mutations 69, 73–4, 91
Myodocopid ostracods *291*, 296
Myxinoids 127

Natural selection 68, 72–4
Nautiloids 162–4, *163*, 171–2

actinoceratids 162, 172
  endoceratids 162, 171–2
  orthoceratids 162, 171–2
Nektonic organisms 60
Nema 254
Neo-Darwinian synthesis 69, 72
Neolithic man (ice man) 18, 21
Niobrara Formation (USA) 364, 365
Norman, David 38
Nucleid acid 70
  deoxyribonucleic acid (DNA) 70–2
  ribonucleic acid (RNA) 71–2
Nucleus 69

Obrution 37–41
Ontogeny 175
Operculum (bryozoan) 270
Operculum (gastropod) 139
Oppel, Albert 101–2
Opportunistic species 62, 63
Orthids 185–8, 189, 192–3, 193
Orthocones 163, 163
Ossicles 203, 211, 211
Ostracods 129, 278, 290–301
  classification of 292–3
  distinguished from bivalves 137, 290
  distinguished from brachiopods 290
  evolution of 297–8, 297
  general characteristics of 290–2, 291, 292
  limiting factors of, 298, 298–9
  morphology of 293–6
  moulting and ontogeny 292
  sexual dimorphism in 291, 292–4, 294
Ostracod applications 298–300
  in palaeobiology 298, 300
  in palaeoenvironmental analysis 298,
    298–9, 300
  in stratigraphy 299–300
Ostracod groups 293–6
  archaeocopids 297
  leperditicopids 297
  myodocopids 293
  palaeocopids 293–4, 294, 297–8
  podocopids 293, 297–8
Oysters 142, 144–5, 153
Oxygen levels and fossilisation 17–18, 22–5, 33
Oxygen-related biofacies 22, 363, 363
  aerobic biofacies 22, 363, 363
  anaerobic biofacies 22, 363, 363
  dysaerobic biofacies 22, 363, 363

Palaeoautecology 57–62, 65
  definition of 57, 65
  limiting factors 57–63
Palaeobiogeography 59, 61, 366–71

applied studies 367–71
  endemism 367
  pattern 366–7
Palaeobiology 2, 3, 110, 129, 338–54
Palaeocopid ostracods, 291, 293–4, 294
Palaeoecology 52–63, 65–6, 111
  definition of 53, 65
  palaeoautecology 57–62, 65
  palaeosynecology 55–7, 65
Palaeoenvironmental analysis 2, 3, 52, 55,
    64–6, 110–11, 129, 355–71
Palaeontology 1–3, 12, 43–4, 66, 68, 110
  definition of 1–2, 110
  early history of 1, 12, 43–4, 66
  scope of 2, 3
Palaeosynecology 55–7, 65
  communities 55–6
  definition of 55, 65
  symbiosis 56–8
Palaeoxygenation 362–6
Palaeozoic fauna, 90, 123–4, 133, 159, 192,
    201, 238, 253, 267, 279, 296, 318–19
Pallial line 142, 145–6
Pallial sinus 142–3
Paraphyletic groups 50
Patagonia 62
Patterson, Colin 351–2
Pectinids 144
Pedicle 183, 183
Pedicle foramen 185
Pelecypods *see* bivalves
Pentamerids 185, 190–1, 193
Periderm 254
Periostracum 141
Periproct 204
Peristome 205
Petrification 27
Phanerozoic life 90, 115–16, 121–9
  evolutionary faunas 90, 121–4, 122
  terrestrial flora 90, 124–6
  vertebrates 90, 126–9
Phenotype 72
Phillips, John 107–8, 116
Photosynthesis, development in
    Precambrian 117–19
Phragmocone 162, 166
Phyla 47, 49, 65
Phyletic gradualism 77–9, 79, 80, 82, 85, 91
  in *Globorotalis* 86–7
  in *Gryphaea* 80, 83, 153
  in *Infulaster-Hagenowa* 215, 218
  in *Kosmoceras* 176, 176
  in *Micraster* 83, 83
  in Welsh Ordovician trilobites 233, 235,
    344–5, 346

Phyletic gradualism (*cont.*)
  in *Zaphrentis*, 247
Phylogenetic systematics (cladistics) 47,
  50–1, 87
Phylogeny 51
Planktonic foraminifera 278, 280, *283,
  284–8, 286*
Planktonic organisms 60
Plastron 209
Pleurae *221*, 223
Posidonienschiefer (Germany) 38, *39*
Podocopid ostracods *291, 293–6, 295, 296*
  bairdaceans 294–5, *295*
  cytheraceans *295, 296, 296, 298*
  cypridaceans 295–296, *295, 296, 298*
  darwinulaceans *298*
Pollen *98*, 100, 126
Polyp 239, *239*
Polyphyletic groups 50, 192
Polyzoans *see bryozoans*
Pompeii (Italy) 15
Population structure 357
Pore canals 293
Pore pairs 205
Precambrian atmosphere 117–19
Precambrian life *90*, 115–20
  in the Archaean *90*, 116–19, *119*
  in the Proterozoic *90*, 119–20, *119*
Predation 16, 57
Principle of faunal and floral succession
  96–7
Principle of priority 48
Principle of superposition 96
Prokaryotes 117, *118*, 133
Proloculus 281
Pro-ostracum 167, *168, 169*
Proparian facial suture 223, *224*
Prosepta 244
Protaspid stage 232
Proteins 70
Proterozoic glaciation 121
Proterozoic life 119–20
Protozoans 278, 280
  foraminifera 84, 86–7, 129, 278–89
Province 367
Pseudomorphs (casts) *26*, 27
Pseudopodia *279*, 280
Pteropods 156
Punctuated anagenesis (punctuated
  gradualism) 84, *85*
  in *Gryphaea* 84
  in *Orbulina* 84, *84*
Punctuated equilibrium 79–84, *80, 85*, 91,
  103, 262, 274
  in *Globorotalis* 86–7

in *Gryphaea* 80, *83*, 153
in *Metrarabdotos* 274, 341–4, *343*
in *Micraster* 83, *83*
in *Phacops rana* 233, 235
in Pliocene bivalves 81
in *Poecilizonites* 153
Punctuated equilibrium, observational bias
  towards 82
Purbeck-Wealden facies 299
Pygidium 221, *221*

Radula 139, 148
Rancho La Brea (USA) 15, 37
Range charts 373
Raup, David 350
Realms 178, 367
Recliners 137
Recrystalisation 26–7
  by francolite 20–1
  through grain growth 27
  through metasomatism 27
  by pyrite 26
  by silica 26
Reefs 238, 245–6, 248, 273, 276
  latitudinal and longitudinal restriction of
    248–9, *249*
Regular echinoids 203, 204–5, *205, 206, 207,
  208*
Relative chronology 93, 96
Reptiles *90*, 128, 134
  cotylosaurs 128
  crocodiles 128
  dinosaurs 2, 7, 12, *13*, 37, *38*, 52, *52*, 128
  mammal-like reptiles 129, 130–1, *130*, 134
  marine reptiles (ichthyosaurs and
    plesiosaurs) 38, 128
  pterosaurs 128
  thecodonts 128, 134
Resolution analysis 340
Reworking, *23*, 27
Rhabdosome 255, *257*
Rhoads, Donald 362
Rhynchonellids 185, 190–1, 193–4, *193*
Rhynie Chert (Scotland) 124
Ribosomes 72
RNA 71–2, 74
Rostrum 167, *168, 169*
Rowe, Arther 214
Rudist bivalves 140, 150–1, *152*, 156
  clingers or encrusters 150, *152*
  elevators 150, *152*
  recumbents 151, *152*
Rugose corals *35, 239*, 240–5, *243*, 247–9

Salinity levels from fossils 358–62

Sampling strategy 331, 334, 339
  search 334
  systematic 334, 339
  random 334
Sand-dollars (echinoids) *205, 207–9, 210*
Santana Formation (Brazil), 20–1
Savrda, Charles 364–6
Scavenging 18–19
Scheuchzer, Johann 44
Schizochroal eyes *224, 224,* 229
Scleractinian corals (hexacorals) 35, 240,
  243, 244–8
Sea anemones 238
Sedgwick, Adam 376
Sedimentary environments 94
Seilacher, Adolf 64
Semi-autochthonous fossils 22, 328
Semirelief 305
Sepkoski, John 350
Septa (cephalopod) *160, 161,* 162
Septa (coral) *239,* 240
Serial sectioning *186, 187*
Setae 293
Sexual dimorphism 45
  in ammonites 174
  in belemnites 45
  in ostracods *291, 292–4, 294*
Shape analysis 47
Shark Bay (Australia) 116
Shaw, A.B. 379
Sheldon, Peter 233, 344–5
Sicula *254,* 255
Sieve plate 293
Siphons (bivalve) *138,* 139
Siphons (gastropod) *138*
Siphuncle *160, 161,* 163, *163*
Slugs 141
Small shelly fossils (SSF) 376–8, *377*
Smith, Andrew 351–2
Smith, William 97, 101, 107
Soft part preservation
  mineral coating *24, 25*
  mineral replacement 20–1, *20*
  physical impression 25, *25*
Solitary corals 240
Solnhofen (Germany) 15, *17,* 38–9
Solution *26, 27*
  moulds *26, 27, 29, 30*
  pseudomorphs (casts) *26, 27*
Speciation 74
  allopatric 77, 79, 153
  sympatric 77
Species, definition of 44, 65
  in biology 44, 65
  in palaeontology 44–7, 65

Species, methods of determining 45–7
  biometry 45–6, *46*
  morphological resemblance 45
  shape analysis 47
Sphenopsids 124
Spiralia 186
Spiriferids 185–90, 193, *193*
Spondylium 160
Sponges 121, 129
Spores 101, 124, *125*
Sporophyte 124, *125*
Spreite, *306,* 314
Squid 166, 168, *170*
Stagnation, *37,* 38–9
Stasis 79, 274
  in Pliocene bivalves 81
Stenohaline organisms 360
Stenolaemate bryozoans 270–3, *271*
  cyclostomes 270, *271,* 273
  fenestrates, *271,* 272–3
  trepostomes, *271,* 272
Stensen, Niels (Steno) 1, 43
Stereom system 202
Stipes 255
Stolon 253, *254*
'Stony' bryozoans 272
Stratigraphical completeness 338–40, 353
Stratigraphy 2, *3, 4,* 93–110, 129
  biostratigraphy 97–105, 108–9, 372–84
  chronostratigraphy 105–8, 375–9
  lithostratigraphy 93–6, 108
Stratotype 4, 106–7
  Ordovician-Silurian boundary, Dobs
    Linn (Scotland) 106, 379
  Precambrian-Cambrian boundary,
    Fortune Head (Newfoundland) 376,
    378
Stromatolites 116, *117, 118,* 119, *119,* 131,
  314
Strophic brachiopods 186–90
  orthids 185–8, *189,* 192, 193, *193*
  spiriferids 185–90, 193, *193*
  strophomenids 185–6, 188, *189,* 193, *193*
Strophic hinge margin 185
Strophomenids 185–6, 188, *189,* 193, *193*
Substrate preference in bivalves and
  gastropods 154, *155*
Suture lines in cephalopods 163, 165, *167*
  agoniatitic 165, *167*
  ammonitic *164,* 165, *167*
  ceratitic *164,* 165, *167*
  goniatitic *164,* 165, *167*
  nautiloid (simple) 163, *167*
Sutures in trilobites 221, 223, 224
  gonatoparian 223, 224

Sutures in trilobites (*cont.*)
  marginal 223
  opisthoparian 223 224
  proparian 223 224
Symbiosis 56–9, *56*
  commensalism 56–7, *56*
  epibiosis 56–8, *56*
  mutualism 56–7, *56*
  parasitism 56–8, *56*
Symbiosis, examples
  of hermit crabs and hydractinians 58–9
  of hermit crabs and sea anemones 58
  of zooxanthellae in hermatypic corals
    246–8
Sympatric speciation 77
Systematics (taxonomy) 2, 3, 47, 85
Systems (Chronostratigraphy) 106

Tabulae *239*, 240
Tabulate corals 240–1, *242*, 245, 247–8
Taphonomy 12–33, 41–2
  death 12–17, *16, 17,* 41
  preburial processes (biostratinomy)
    12–22, 41
  post burial processes (diagenesis) 22–30, 41
Taxodont dentition 142, *143*
Taxonomic heirarchy 47–9, 65
Taxonomic uniformitarianism 49–53, 57, 65,
    111, 298, 357
Taxonomy (systematics) 2, 3, 47, 85
  procedure in 48
Tectonic deformation of fossils 27, *30,* 32–3
Terraces 234
Terebratulids, *35,* 185, 190–1, 193–4, *193*
Terrestrial flora
  applications of 132–3
  colonisation of the land 124, 133–4
  evolution of *90,* 124–6, 133–4
  reproductive system of 124, *125*
Test (echinoid), 202
Test (foraminiferal) 278, *279*
Tethys Ocean 150, 156
Tetrabranchiate cephalopods 161–2
Thecae 254–5, *254*
Thecideaceans 194
Thorax (ostracod) 290, *291*
Thorax (trilobite) 221, *221*
Torsion 140–1
Trace fossils (ichnofossils) 12, 41, 30–1, 66,
    110, 302–17
  ethological classification of 53, *53,* 304,
    306
  general concepts of their application
    62–3, 313–14
  Linnaean classification of 303–4

morphologies of 305–12
preservational classification of 30–1, *31,*
    304–5
tiering of 315, *315,* 364
Trace fossil applications 313–16
  in evolutionary studies 314, 316
  in functional morphology studies 314,
    316
  depth-related ichnofacies 63–4, 315–16
  in palaeoecology 62–3
  in palaeoenvironmental studies 314–16
  in palaeoxygenation studies 362–6, *365*
  in stratigraphy, *313,* 315–16, 375–9, *378*
Trace fossil groups 304–12
  dwelling traces (domichnia) 304, *306,*
    307, *308, 309*
  feeding burrows (fodinichnia) 304, *306,*
    309, *311, 312*
  grazing traces (pascichnia) 304, *306,*
    307–9, *310*
  locomotion traces (repichnia) *303,* 304–7,
    306, 307
  resting traces (cubichnia) 304–5, *306*
Transport of fossils 19–22
Traps, types of
  concentration 37, *37,* 41
  conservation *37,* 41
Trilobites 129, 220–37, 290
  classification of 222
  enrolment in, *221,* 227–8, *227, 229,* 233
  evolution of 230–1, *232*
  eyes of *221,* 223–5, *224,* 229–30, *230, 232*
  fringes of *227,* 230
  facial sutures 223, *224*
  general characteristics of 220–2
  limiting factors of 233–4
  mode of life 221–2
  morphology of *221,* 223–30
  moulting and ontogeny in 220–1, *222,*
    232, 235
  trace fossils associated with *221,* 233, 235,
    314
Trilobite applications 231–4
  in evolutionary studies 233
  in functional morphology studies 231–3,
    235
  in palaeobiogeography 61, 233–5, 367–71
  in palaeoenvironmental analysis 233–4
  in stratigraphy 234, 235, 236
Trilobite groups 225–30
  Cambrian trilobites 225–6, *225, 226*
  post-Cambrian trilobites *210,* 226–30, *227,*
    228, 229
Tube feet 202
Type specimen 48

Uniformitarianism (actualism), 59, 65
Umbo (bivalve) *138*, 141
Unilocular tests 281

Valves (bivalve) *138*, 141
Valves (brachiopod) *138*, 184
Vertebrate evolution *90*, 126–9, 134
Virgella *254*
Virgula *254*
'Volcanic winter' 88–9

Wall structure in foraminifera
   agglutinated 281, *282*
   hyaline 281, *282*
   membranous 281, *282*
   microgranular 281, 282

   porcellaneous 281, *282*
Warrawoona Group (Australia) 116
Water-vascular system 202
Watson, James 71
Worms (annelids) 129
Wilson, J.T. 61

Zigzag commissure in brachiopods 195,
   196
Zoarium 267, 270
Zoecium, *268*, 270
Zone fossils *see guide fossils*
Zooid (bryozoan) 267, *268*
Zooid (graptolite) 253, *254*
Zooxanthellae 56, 246–7
Zygotes 70

Systematic Index

This index lists all formal taxonomic names used in this book; informal groups are included within the subject index. In this index, genera and species are given in italics, with the informal groups to which they belong in brackets. Taxa with a rank greater than genus are given in upright script, with taxonomic hierarchy demonstrated by cross-referencing. Numbers in italics refer to illustrations.

Acrotretida *194*, *see also* Inarticulata
Actinoceras (nautiloid) *163*
Agnostida 222, *see also* Trilobita
Agnostus (trilobite) *225*
Agriopleura (bivalve) 152
Allanopora (bryozoan) *269*
Allogromiina 280, *285*, *see also* Foraminiferida
Allogromina (foraminiferan) *279*, *280*, *285*
Alveolina (foramininferan) *288*
Ammonia (foraminiferan) *283*
Ammonoidea 162, *172*, *see also* Cephalopoda
  Ammonitina *174*
Amphicorna (foraminiferan) *283*
Amplexizaphrentis (coral) *251*
Anaklinoceras (ammonite) *166*
'*Anakosmoceras*' (ammonite) *176*
Angelina sedgwickii (trilobite) 27, 32–3, *32*
Animalia *49*, 117, *see also* Eukaryota
Anisograptus (graptolite) *264*
Anisotrypa (bryozoan) *269*
Anthracomya (bivalve) 156, *157*
  A. modiolaris 157
  A. phillipsii 157
  A. tenuis 157
Annelida 123
Anomalodesmata 140, *149*, *see also* Bivalvia
Anthozoa 240, *see also* Cnidaria
  Zoantharia 240
Aphelaspis (trilobite) *235*

Archaeocopida 293, 297, *see also* Ostracoda
Archaeocyatha 123
Archeohippus (horse) 78
Archaeopteryx (bird) 6, 38, 100, 128
Archimedes (bryozoan) 271, *272*
Arctica (bivalve) 144
Arenicolites (trace) *378*
Articulata 184, *193*, *194*, *see also* Brachiopoda
  Atrypida 185
  Orthida 184–6, 192, *193*, *194*
  Pentamerida 184–5, 190, *193*, *194*
  Rhynchonellida 184–5, 190–1, *193*, *194*
  Spiriferida 184–6, 188, *193*, *194*
  Strophomenida 184–6, 188, *193*, *194*
  Terebratulida *35*, 184–5, 190–1, *193*, *194*
Arthropoda, 123, 220, 222, 292
  Crustacea 137, 292–3
  Trilobita 220, 222, 232
Asaphida 222, *see also* Trilobita
Astarte (bivalve) 155
Asteriacites (trace) 305, *306*, 313
Asteroidea 204, *213*, *see also* Eleutherozoa
Athleta (gastropod) 148
Athyridina 189, *see also* Spiriferida
Atrypa (brachiopod) 189, *189*
Atrypida 185, *see also* Articulata
Atrypidina 189, *see also* Spiriferida
Aulocephalodon (reptile) 130
Aulophylum (coral) 243, 244
Australopithecus (early human) 67

Baculites (ammonite) 165
Bairdacea 294, *see also Podocopida*
Bairdoppilata (ostracod) 295
Belemnitina 178, *see also Coleoidea*
Belemnopseina 178, *see also Coleoidea*
Belemnopsis (belemnite) 168
Belonechitina (alga) 46
   B. latifrons 46
   B. lauensis 46
   B. mortimerensis 46
Bemella (SSF – small shelly fossil), 377
Bergamia (trilobite) 346
Beyrichia (ostracod) 291
Bivalvia 136, 140, 182, *see also Mollusca*
   Anomalodesmata 140, *149*
   Isofilibranchia 140, *149*
   Heteroconcha 140, *149*
   Palaeotaxodonta 140, *149*
Blastoidea 204, *213, see also Pelmatozoa*
Brachiopoda 33, *49, 123,* 137, 182, 184
   Articulata 184, *193, 194*
   Calciata 183
   Inarticulata 184, *192, 193, 194*
   Lingulata 183–4, *192, 193*
Brisaster (echinoid) *214*
Bryozoa 266, 270
   Gymnolaemata 270, 272–3, *274*
   Phylactolaemata 270, *274*
   Stenolaemata 270, 273, *274*
Buchia (bivalve) 156
Bulminia (foraminiferan) *283*
Burgessochaeta (annelid) 24

Calciata 183, *see also Brachiopoda*
Calcirhynchia (brachiopod) *190*
Calippus (horse) 78
Callistocythere (ostracod) 296
Calymene (trilobite) 221, 227
Canadaspis (crustacean) 24
Canidae 49
Caninia (coral) 99, *251*
Canis (dog) 49
   C. dingo 49
   C. familiaris 47,49
Carbonicola (bivalve) 156, *157*
   C. communis 157
   C. similis 157
Carinocythereis (ostracod) 296
Castanipora (bryozoan) 272
Cenoceras (nautiloid) 163
Cephalopoda 159, 162, *see also Mollusca*
   Ammonoidea 162, *172*
   Coleoidea 162, *172*
   Nautiloidea 162, *172*
Ceratites (nautiloid) *164*

Chancelloria (SSF – small shelly fossil) 377
Charnia (Ediacaran organism) 25, 240
   C. masoni 25
Cheilostomata 272, *see also Gymnolaemata*
Cheirothyris (brachiopod) *188*
Chondrites (trace) *306,* 309, *313, 315,* 364,
   365
Chordata 49, 126
Cidaris (echinoid) *208*
Cirroceras (ammonite) *166*
Cleistopora (coral) 99
Climacograptus (graptolite) *264*
Clorinda (brachiopod) *198*
Clypeaster (echinoid) *210*
Cnemidopyge (trilobite) 344–5, *346, 347*
Cnidaria 123, 237, 239–40, 266, 269
   Anthozoa 240
   Petalonamae 240
Coleoidea 162, *172, see also Cephalopoda*
   Belemnitina 178
   Belemnopseina 178
Composita (brachiopod) 189, *189*
Compsognathus (dinosaur) 128
Conichnus conicus (trace) *378*
Crinoidea 203–4, *213, see also Pelmatozoa*
Crustacea 137, 292–3, *see also Arthropoda*
   Ostracoda 290, *293*
Cruziana (trace) *64, 64, 233,* 305, *306, 314,*
   315
Cryptosula (bryozoan) 269
Curvolithus (trace) *378*
Cuspidaria (bivalve) 360
Cyclomedusa (Ediacaran organism) 120
Cyclopyge (trilobite) 230, *230*
Cylindroteuthis (belemnite) *169*
Cyclostomata 270, 273, *274, see also*
   Stenolaemata
Cypridacea 295, *298, see also Podocopida*
Cyprideis (ostracod) 296
Cytheracea 296, *298, see also Podocopida*
Cythereis (ostracod) 295

Dalmanites (trilobite) 224, *227, 228*
Darwinulacea *298, see also Podocopida*
Dawsonoceras (nautiloid) 163
Dendroidea 232, 255, 257, *see also*
   Graptolithina
Diaperoecia (bryozoan) 269
Dibunophylum (coral) 99, *125, 243, 251*
Dicanthopyge (trilobite) 235
Diceras (bivalve) 152
Dichograptida 259, *see also Graptoloidea*
Dickinsonia (Ediacaran organism) 120
Dictyonema (graptolite) 256, *258, 264*
Dicynodon (mammal-like reptile) 128, *130*

D. laterticeps 130
Didymogruptus (graptolite) *256, 259, 260, 264*
Didus ineptus (bird) *75*
Digonella (brachiopod) *190*
Dimorphichnites (trace) *233, 314*
Diplocraterion (trace) *304, 306, 309, 311*
Diplograptida *259, see also Graptoloidea*
Discammina (foraminiferan) *283*
Drosophila (insect) *69, 70*
Dunderbergia (trilobite) *235*

Echinocardium (echinoid) *214*
Echinodermata *49, 123, 201, 203–4*
  Eleutherozoa *204, 213*
  Pelmatozoa *204, 213*
Echinoidea *203–4, 213, see also Eleutherozoa*
Echinus (echinoid) *208*
'Ectoprocta' *270, see Bryozoa*
Eleutherozoa *204, 213*
  Asteroidea *204, 213*
  Echinoidea *203–4, 213*
  Holothuroidea *204, 213*
Ellipsocephaloides (trilobite) *235*
Elrathia (trilobite) *225*
Elvinia major (trilobite) *235*
Encrinurus (trilobite) *229*
Eocelia (brachiopod) *198*
Eohippus (horse) *78*
Epidiceras (bivalve) *152*
Epihippus (horse) *78*
Equidae *78, 78*
Equus (horse) *78*
Euciphoceras (nautiloid) *177*
Euestheria (crustacean) *360, 361*
Eukaryota *117*
  Animalia *49, 117*
  Fungi *117*
  Plantae *117*
  Protista *117*
Eulimulus (crustacean) *15, 17*
Euomphalopteris (gastropod) *151–152, 152*

Favosites (coral) *243*
Felidae *49*
Felis (cat) *49*
  F. domesticus 49
  F. leo 49
Fenestrata *272, see also Stenolaemata*
Fenestella (bryozoan) *271, 272*
Foraminiferida *278, 280, see also Protozoa*
  Allogromiina *280, 285*
  Fusulinina *280, 282, 285*
  Globigerinina *280, 284, 285*
  Miliolina *280, 282, 285, 286*

  Rotaliina *280, 284, 285, 286*
  Textulariina *280–1, 285, 286*
Fordilla (bivalve) *149*
Fungi *117, see also Eukaryota*
Fungia (coral) *243*
Fusulinina *280, 282, 285, see also Foraminiferida*

Gastrochaenolites (trace) *304, 307, 309*
Gastropoda *136, 141, see also Mollusca*
  Opisthobranchiata *141*
  Prosobrachiata *141*
  Pulmonata *141*
Geospiza fortis (bird) *73*
Glenobotryodion (eukaryotic cell) *119*
Globigerinacea *286, see also Globigerinina*
Globigerinina *280, 284, 285, see also Foraminiferida*
  Globigerinacea *286*
Globigerinoides (foraminiferan) *283*
  G. sicanus 84
Globoconella (foraminiferan) *287*
Globorotalia (foraminiferan) *86, 86, 287*
  G. conomiozea 86–7, 86
  G. inflata 287
  G. pliozea 86, 87
  G. puncticulata 86
  G. spericomiozea 86, 86
Glossopteris (seed fern) *132, 132, 368*
Glycimeris (bivalve) *143*
Glyptograptus (graptolite) *256*
Goniastrea (coral) *243*
Gordia (trace) *378*
Graptolithina *253, 255, see also Hemichordata*
  Dendroidea *232, 255, 257*
  Graptoloidea *232, 255, 257, 259*
Graptoloidea *232, 255, 257, 259, see also Graptolithina*
  Dichograptida *259*
  Diplograptida *259*
  Monograptida *260*
Gryphaea (bivalve) *6, 77, 80, 83, 84, 153, 321*
  G. arcuata 77, 83, 153
  G. arcuata incurva 83
  G. arcuata obliquata 83
  G. gigantea 77, 83, 153
  G. mccullochi 83, 153
Gymnolaemata *270, 272–3, 274, see also Bryozoa*
  Cheilostomata *272*
Gypidula (brachiopod) *190*
Gyrochorte (trace) *305, 306*

Hagenowa (echinoid) *215, 218, 321*
  H. blackmorei 215

Hantkenina (foraminiferan) *283*
Hallucigenia (uncertain) 54–5, *54*
Halysites (coral) 242
Harlaniella (trace) *376, 378*
Hemichordata 253, 255, 266
    Graptolithina 253, 255
    Rhabdopleura 253–5, *254, 257,* 261
Heteroconcha 140, *149, see also* Bivalvia
Hiatella (bivalve) *155*
Hipparion (horse) *78*
Hippuritidae 150–1, 156
Holectypus (echinoid) 206
Holothuroidea 204, *213, see also* Eleutherozoa
Homo (human) 67
    '*H. diluvii testis*' 44
    H. sapiens 69
Homeorhynchia (brachiopod) *194*
Hustedia (brachiopod) 190
Hybodus (shark) *15*
Hypohippus (horse) *78*

Iguana (reptile) 52
Iguanodon (dinosaur) 37, *38, 52, 52*
    I. bernissartensis 38
Illaenurus (trilobite) 235
Illaenus (trilobite) 227
Imitoceras (ammonite) *164*
Immanitas (bivalve) 152
Inarticulata 184, *192, 193, 194, see also*
    Brachiopoda
    Acrotretida *194*
Infulaster (echinoid) 215, 218, 321
    I. excentricus 215
Isofilibranchia 140, *149, see also* Bivalvia
Isograptus (graptolite) *256, 258*

Jeletzkyteuthis (squid) *170*

Kannemeyeria (mammal-like reptile) *130*
Kosmoceras (ammonite) 176, *176, 179,* 321

'Lamellibranchiata' 140, *see* Bivalvia
Latimeria (fish) 128
Leonaspis (trilobite) 228
Leptaena (brachiopod) *189*
Leperditicopida 293, 297, *297, see also*
    Ostracoda
Leptoceras (ammonite) *166*
Lima (bivalve) 154
Limnocythere (ostracod) *298*
Limulus (crustacean) 220
Lingula (brachiopod) 100, 191–2, 197, *198,*
    319
Lingulata 183–4, 192, *193, see also*
    Inarticulata

Linguloidea *192*
Linguloidea *192*
Liostrea (bivalve) 360, 361
    L. hebridica 360
    L. liassica 153
Lithophaga (bivalve) 304
Loganograptus (graptolite) 262
Loligo (squid) 177
Lonsdaleia (coral) 242, 243, *251*
Lovenia (echinoid) 214
Loxoconcha (ostracod) 291
Lutraria (bivalve) 145
Lystrosaurus (reptile) 128, *130*
Lytoceras (ammonite) *174*

Macrosaria (ostracod) 295
Macrypsilon (ostracod) 294
Mammalia 49
Marrella (arthropod) 24
Marsupites (crinoid) 217
Meandrina (coral) 243
Melita (echinoid) 210
Merychippus (horse) *78*
Mesohippus (horse) *78*
Mercenaria (bivalve) 155
Metrarabdotos (bryozoan) 274, 321, 342–3,
    343, 353–4, 386
Micraster (echinoid) 83, *83, 210,* 214–15,
    217–18, 321
    M. coranguinum 83 214–15
    M. decipiens 83 214–15
    M. leskei 83, 214
Microporina (bryozoan) *269*
Missiquoia (trilobite) 235
Miliolina 280, *282, 285, 286, see also*
    Foraminiferida
Mimella (brachiopod) 188, *189*
Modiolus (bivalve) 146, *360*
Mollusca 49, *123,* 136, 140, 147, 159, 161,
    162
    Bivalvia 136, 140, 182
    Cephalopoda 159, 162
    Gastropoda 136, 141
Monera 117, *see also* Prokaryota
Monmorphichnus (trace) *378*
Monograptida 260, *see also*
    Graptoloidea
Monograptus (graptolite) *254,* 321
    M. flemingi 262
    M. hercynicus 262
    M. priodon 262
    M. revolutus 262
    M. vomerinus 262
Montlivaltia (coral) 235

Myodocopida *291, 293, 296, 297, see also*
 Ostracoda
Mytilus (bivalve) *142, 143,* 146, *147,* 155,
 360, 361
 M. strathairdensis 360
Mya (bivalve) *143, 155*

Nannippus (horse) *78*
Natica (gastropod) 139, *148*
Nautiloidea 162, *172, see also Cephalopoda*
Nautilus (nautiloid) 16, 100, 159, 160, *160,*
 162, 164, 173, 319
Nellia (bryozoan) 276
Neohipparion (horse) *78*
Neomiodon (bivalve) *360,* 361
Neptunea (gastropod) *148*
Nereites (trace) 64, *64,* 307, *310,* 315
Nipponites (ammonite) 165
Nobiliasaphus (trilobite) *346*
Nostoceras (ammonite) *166*
Nothofagus (angiosperm tree) 59, *62*
Nucleolites (echinoid) *208*
Nucula (bivalve) *155*

Ogygiocarella (trilobite) 344, *346*
 O. angustissima 344, *346*
 O. debuchii 344, *346*
Ogyginus (trilobite) *346*
Olenellus (trilobite) 225, *225*
Olenus (trilobite) 225
Onnia (trilobite) 230
Onniella (brachiopod) 189
Ophiomorpha (trace) *306,* 307
Opisthobranchiata 141, *see also Gastropoda*
Orbiculoidea (brachiopod) 192
Orbulina (foraminiferan) 84, *84,* 283
 O.suturalis 84
 O. universa 84
Orohippus (horse) *78*
Orthida 184–6, 192, *193, 194, see also*
 Articulata
Ostracoda 290, *293, see also Crustacea*
 Archaeocopida *293, 297*
 Leperditicopida *293, 297, 297*
 Myodocopida *291, 293, 296, 297*
 Palaeocopida *291, 293, 294, 297, 297*
 Podocopida *291, 293, 294, 297, 298*
Ostrea (bivalve) 142, *146, 155*
Oxynoticeras (ammonite) *164*

Pachytraga (bivalve) *152*
Paguristes (hermit crab) 58
Palaeocopida *291, 293*–4, *297, 297, see also*
 Ostracoda
Palaeopascichnus (trace) *378*

Palaeosmilia (coral) *243, 251*
Palaeotaxodonta 140, *149, see also Bivalvia*
Paleodictyon (trace) 307, 309, *310,* 313
Paludina (gastropod) 156
Paradoxides (trilobite) 224, 225, *225*
Parahippus (horse) *78*
Parapassaloteuthis zieteni (belemnite) *373*
Passaloteuthis (belemnite) *373*
 P. bisulcata 373
 P. milleri 373
Patella (gastropod) *148*
Pecten (bivalve) 146, 154, *155*
'Pelecypoda' 140, *see Bivalvia*
Pelmatozoa 204, *213, see also Echinodermata*
 Blastoidea 204, *213*
 Crinoidea 203, 204, *213*
Pentamerida 184–5, 190, *193, 194, see also*
 Articulata
Pentameroides (brachiopod) 190
Pentamerus (brachiopod) 198
Phacopida 222, *see also Trilobita*
Phacops (trilobite) 224, 227, 229
 P. rana 233, 235
Pholas (bivalve) *155*
Phycodes (trace) 314, *376*–7, *378,* 387
Phylactolacmata 270, *274, see also Bryozoa*
Phylloceras (ammonite) *174*
Phyllograptus (graptolite) 255, 259, 260
Pinna (bivalve) *155*
Placenticeras (ammonite) 16, *16*
Placoparia (trilobite) 229
Placunopsis (bivalve) *360*
Planolites (trace) 364, *365, 378*
Planorbis (gastropod) *148*
Plantae 117, *see also Eukaryota*
Platycalymene (trilobite) 222, 344, *346*
Plectothyris (brachiopod) 190
Plesiodiceras (bivalve) *152*
Pleuroceras (ammonite) *164*
Pleurotomaria (gastropod) *148*
Pliohippus (horse) *78*
Podocopida *291, 293*–4, *297, 298, see also*
 Ostracoda
 Bairdacea 294
 Cypridacea 295, *298*
 Cytheracea 296, *298*
 Darwinulacea *298*
 Podocopina 294
Poecilizonites (gastropod) 153
Pojetaia (bivalve) 149
'Polyzoa' 270, *see Bryozoa*
Praeorbulina (foraminiferan) 84
 P. glomerosa circularis 84
 P. glomerosa curva 84
 P. glomerosa glomerosa 84

Prehousia (trilobite) 235
Pristiograptus (graptolite) 264
Productus (brachiopod) *189*
Prokaryota 117
  Monera 117
Prosobrachiata 141, *see also Gastropoda*
Protichnites (trace) 314
Protista 117, *see also Eukaryota*
  Protozoa *34*, 278, 280
Protozoa *34*, 278, 280, *see also Protista*
  Foraminiferida 278, 280
Psammoactinia (hydractinian) 58
Pseudohastites longiformis (belemnite) 373
Pugnax (brachiopod) 190, *194*
Pulmonata 141, *see also Gastropoda*
Pygaster (echinoid) 206, *208*

Rangea (Ediacaran organism) 120
Redlichiida 222, *see also Trilobita*
Reptilia *49*, 240
Retziidina 189, *see also Spiriferida*
Rhabdopleura (hemichordate) 253, 254, *254*,
  255, 257, 261
Rhizocorallium (trace) 309, *313*
Rhynchonella (brachiopod) *360*
  R. subvariabilis 187
Rhynchonellida 184–5, 190–1, *193*, *194*, *see
  also Articulata*
Rotaliina 280, 284, *285*, *286*, *see also
  Foraminiferida*
Rotalipora (foraminiferan) *286*
Rouillieria ovoides (brachiopod) *187*
Rugosa *35*, 240–1, 245, *246*, 248, *see also
  Zoantharia*
Rusophycos (trace) 233, 305, *306*, 314

Sabellidites (SSF – small shelly fossil) *378*
Saccocoma (crinoid) 216, *217*
Saetograptus (graptolite) 256
Saukia (trilobite) 235
Scaphites (ammonite) 166
Scleractinia *35*, 240, 244, *246*, *see also
  Zoantharia*
Seirocrinus (crinoid) *39*, 216
Seminula (brachiopod) 99, *251*
Sepia (coleoid) 160
Simplicioceras (nautiloid) 177
Siphonodendron (coral) 243, *244*, 251
Skolithos (trace) 64, *64*, *306*, 307, *308*, 315,
  378
Spirifer (brachiopod) *186*, 189
Spiriferida 184–6, 188, *193*, *194*, *see also
  Articulata*
  Athyridina 189
  Atrypidina 189

  Retziidina 189
  Spiriferidina 189
Spiriferidina 189, *see also Spiriferida*
Spiroraphe (trace) 307
Spirula (squid) 162
Spriggina (Ediacaran organism) 231, 240
Stenolaemata 270, 273, 274, *see also Bryozoa*
  Cyclostomata 270
  Fenestrata 272
  Trepostomata 272
Stigmaria (lycopod tree root) 23
Stricklandia (brachiopod) *198*
Stomatopora (bryozoan) 271
Strophomenida 184–6, 188, *193*, 194, *see also
  Articulata*
Symphysurina (trilobite) 235
Syringopora (coral) 242

Tabulata 240–1, *246*, *see also Zoantharia*
Tabulipora (bryozoan) 271
Teichichnus (trace) 365
Terebratella (brachiopod) *186*
Terebratulida *35*, 184–5, 190–1, *193*, *194*, *see
  also Articulata*
Teredolites (trace) 307
Tetractinella (brachiopod) *188*
Tetragraptus (graptolite) 258, 259, *264*
Textulariina 280, 281, *285*, *286*, *see also
  Foraminiferida*
Thalassinoides (trace) *306*, 309, *312*, 315, 364,
  365
Thecosmilia (coral) 243
Ticinella (foraminiferan) *286*
Torellella (SSF – small shelly fossil) 377
Trachyteuthis (squid) 170
Trepostomata 272, *see also Stenolaemata*
Tribrachidium (Ediacaran organism) 120,
  212
Tribulus (angiosperm plant) 73
Trigonia (bivalve) *30*
Trilobita 220, 222, 232, *see also Arthropoda*
  Agnostida 222
  Asaphida 222
  Phacopida 222
  Redlichiida 222
Trimerus (trilobite) 224, 227
Trinucleus (trilobite) 227, 230
Tropidostoma (mammal-like reptile) *130*
Turrilites (ammonite) 165, *166*
Turritella (gastropod) 148

Uncinulus (brachiopod) 196
Unio (bivalve) *360*, 361

Valletia (bivalve) 152

Venus (bivalve) *143*
Viviparus (gastropod) *148, 360,* 361

Westlothiana lizziae (reptile) 128
Whittardolithus (trilobite) *346*

Xenophora (gastropod) 151–2

Youngibelus (belemnite) *45*

Zaphrentis (coral) 99, *239,* 244, 247, 250, *251,* 321
Zoantharia 238, 240, *see also Anthozoa*
   Rugosa *35,* 240–1, 245, *246,* 248
   Scleractinia *35,* 240, 244, *246*
   Tabulata 240–1, *246*
Zoophycos (trace) 64, *64, 306,* 309, *311,* 314, 315, *315,* 316, 320, 364, *365*
'*Zugokosmoceras*' (ammonite) *176*